Changing State Feminism

Also by Joyce Outshoorn
THE POLITICS OF PROSTITUTION: Women's Movements, Democratic States and the Globalization of Sex Commerce (*editor*)

Also by Johanna Kantola
FEMINISTS THEORIZE THE STATE

Changing State Feminism

Edited by

Joyce Outshoorn
Professor of Women's Studies
University of Leiden, The Netherlands

and

Johanna Kantola
Senior Lecturer in Politics
University of Helsinki, Finland

First published 2007 by
PALGRAVE MACMILLAN
Houndmills, Basingstoke, Hampshire RG21 6XS and
175 Fifth Avenue, New York, N.Y. 10010
Companies and representatives throughout the world

PALGRAVE MACMILLAN is the global academic imprint of the Palgrave
Macmillan division of St. Martin's Press, LLC and of Palgrave Macmillan Ltd.
Macmillan® is a registered trademark in the United States, United Kingdom
and other countries. Palgrave is a registered trademark in the European
Union and other countries.

ISBN–13: 978-0-230-51661-8   hardback
ISBN–10: 0-230-51661-0   hardback

This book is printed on paper suitable for recycling and made from fully
managed and sustained forest sources. Logging, pulping and manufacturing
processes are expected to conform to the environmental regulations of
the country of origin.

A catalogue record for this book is available from the British Library.

A catalog record for this book is available from the Library of Congress.

10   9   8   7   6   5   4   3   2   1
16   15   14   13   12   11   10   09   08   07

Printed and bound in Great Britain by
Antony Rowe Ltd, Chippenham and Eastbourne

Contents

List of Tables

Preface

Most post-industrial states developed institutions to deal with women's issues over the last decades to meet the challenge of second-wave feminism. It is by now well established that these institutions, generally known as women's policy agencies, have been important in realizing women's movements' demands in policy-making and in gaining access for women in decision-making arenas, making the case for state feminism. Research on this theme took off with the seminal book edited by Dorothy McBride Stetson and Amy Mazur, *Comparative State Feminism* (1995); subsequent research by the many members of the Research Network of Gender Politics and the State (RNGS) has established a solid empirical base, showing how women's policy agencies dealt with demands from women's movement groups and were able to insert their framing of the issues into policy-making, as well as analysing under what conditions alliances between agencies and movements arose and their efforts met with success.

Since 1995, however, there have been dramatic changes in the political context, such as globalization, regionalization, welfare state restructuring, privatization and the rise of multilevel governance, leading us to ask how the institutions to improve women's status have coped: have they been able to strengthen their position and continue to further women's demands or have they been forced to downscale their activities and lose their original mission? The research in this book is designed to find answers to these questions, in a comparative and systematic way, based on original research on twelve post-industrial states: Australia, Austria, Belgium, Finland, France, Germany, Great Britain, Italy, the Netherlands, Spain, Sweden and the United States. The book is based on qualitative research in these countries and the overall aim of the book is to offer elaborate and detailed analyses of changing state feminism.

Stimulated by our many friends and colleagues, we developed the original design for this study in 2004. Many of our authors attended the workshop we organized for the Joint Sessions of Workshops of the European Consortium for Political Research (ECPR) at Granada, entitled *State Feminism and women's movements: assessing change of the last decade in Europe* in April 2005. In April 2006, we were able to come together again for a special conference organized by Amy Mazur at the University of Washington, Seattle. Draft chapters were also presented at the panel on

Equality, Diversity and Gender Politics in Europe at the ECPR Third Pan-European Conference on EU politics in Istanbul in September 2006.

Many people have made this book possible. In particular, we would like to thank our authors: Christina Bergqvist, María Bustelo, Karen Celis, Alessia Donà, Maria Guadagnini, Anne Maria Holli, Sabine Lang, Joni Lovenduski, Amy Mazur, Dorothy McBride, Petra Meier, Jantine Oldersma, Tanja Olsson Blandy, Candice Ortbals, Diane Sainsbury, Birgit Sauer and Marian Sawer. We are also grateful to all the participants of the 2005 Granada workshop for their suggestions and lively debates, and those attending the Istanbul panel. We thank specially Amy Mazur for organizing the Seattle conference and the Centre for West European Studies, the European Union Centre, the Jackson School, the Centre for Comparative Law and Society, Politics, the Society Colloquium Series and the Departments of Scandinavian Studies and Women's Studies at the University of Washington, for their very generous sponsoring of the meeting and the warm hospitality we received. John Keeler, the Director of the Centre for West European Studies and the European Union Centre, deserves special mention for his help with the funding. We would also like to express our thanks to the discussers at this conference: Rachel Cichowski, Annicka Kronsell and Angelika von Wahl. Furthermore, our thanks go to Remco van der Laan and Vincent Post, research assistants at the Department of Political Science of Leiden University, for their substantial help in preparing the manuscript. Finally, we are grateful for the critical and helpful comments from the anonymous reviewer(s) of Palgrave Macmillan. Thanks, too, go to Alison Howson, Gemma d'Arcy Hughes and Amy Lankester-Owen at Palgrave Macmillan for their editorial assistance.

Joyce Outshoorn and Johanna Kantola

Notes on the Contributors

Christina Bergqvist has been Associate Professor of Political Science at the Department of Government, Uppsala University since 2002. She received her Ph.D. in 1994 on women's representation in Swedish political institutions and the corporatist sector. Her research fields include gender and political representation, gender and public policy and feminist comparative policy. Recent publications in English include: 'The Debate about Childcare Allowances in the Light of Welfare State Reconfiguration: the Swedish Case' in Melissa Haussman and Birgit Sauer (eds) *Gendering the State in the Age of Globalization: Women's Movements and State Feminism in Post-Industrial Democracies* (2007); 'Gender (In)Equality, European Integration and the Transition of Swedish Corporatism', *Economic and Industrial Democracy* (2004); 'Alive and Fairly Well: Welfare State Restructuring and Child Care in Sweden' (with Anita Nyberg), in Rianne Mahon and Sonya Michel (eds) *Child Care at the Crossroads: Gender and Welfare State Restructuring* (2002); 'Adaptation or Diffusion of the Swedish Gender Model?' (with Ann-Cathrine Jungar), in Linda Hantrais (ed.) *Gendered Policies in Europe: Reconciling Employment and Family Life* (2000). She was the editor-in-chief of *Equal Democracies? Gender and Politics in the Nordic Countries* (1999).

María Bustelo has a Ph.D. in Political Science, and is Associate Professor in the Department of Political Science and Public Administration at the Compultense University, Madrid (UCM), Spain, where she has been teaching undergraduate and Ph.d. courses in public policies and gender policies analysis and evaluation since 1994. She is team leader of the QUING and MAGEEQ EU-funded projects in Spain. She has written articles on gender equality policies and the analysis and evaluation of public policies, for *Evaluation*, *The Greek Review of Social Research*, *Revista Española de Ciencia Política*, and *Revista Española de Desarrollo y Cooperación*. She has also written several chapters in edited volumes around the topic of evaluation theory and methodology. She has published a book on the evaluation of gender policies in Spain (2004), and has co-edited a book with Emanuela Lombardo on gender equality policies in Spain that won the 2006 Ángeles Durán Prize for scientific innovation in the study of gender equality.

Karen Celis has taught at the Department of Management Science of the Hogeschool Gent since 2004. She studied Contemporary History at the Catholic University of Louvain before specializing in Women's Studies at the University of Antwerp. Her Ph.D. in Political Sciences was on the political representation of women in the Belgian Lower house (*Vrouwen vertegenwoordigen. Substantiële en descriptieve vertegenwoordiging van vrouwen in de Kamer tijdens de begrotingsdebatten (1900–1979)*. She has published on the political representation of women, abortion, gender and socialism and women and war. Her most recent publications in English include: 'Substantive Representation of Women and the Impact of Descriptive Representation. Case: the Belgian Lower House 1900–1979', *Journal of Women, Politics and Policy* (2006); 'Flanders: Do It Yourself and Do It Better? Regional Parliaments as Sites for Democratic Renewal and Gendered Representation' (with Alison Woodward), in J. Magone (ed.) *Regional Institutions and Governance in the European Union. Subnational Actors in the New Millenium* (2001), 'The Abortion Debates in Belgium (1974–1990)', in Dorothy McBride Stetson (ed.) *Abortion Politics, Women's Movements and the Democratic State. A Comparative Study of State Feminism* (2001).

Alessia Donà is a Lecturer in Public Policy Analysis and Comparative Politics and a member of the teaching staff of the Master in 'Gender Policies' at the Faculty of Sociology, University of Trento. She received her Ph.D. degree in Comparative and European Politics in 2004 from the University of Siena. Her research area includes comparative social policy, European Union social dimension and gender equality policies. She has published articles in Italian: 'La nascita della politica per le pari opportunità in Italia e Regno Unito tra pressioni europee e vincoli interni', *Rivista Italiana di Politiche Pubbliche* (2004); 'Il Metodo di Coordinamento Aperto e l'Italia: il caso della politica per le pari opportunità', *Giornale di diritto del lavoro e delle relazioni industriali* (2005) and in English 'Italy as Negotiator in the EU Equal Opportunities Policy', *Modern Italy* (2004) (Special Issue on 'Italy in the EU'). Her most recent published work includes a book on the condition of Italian women, *Le pari opportunità. Condizione femminile in Italia e integrazione europea* (2006).

Marila Guadagnini is Associate Professor of Political Science at the University of Turin, Faculty of Political Science. Her research and teaching interests focus on comparative politics, Italian politics and gender studies. Her books include: *Il sistema politico italiano. Temi per una discussione* (1997); *Un soffitto di cristallo? Le donne nelle posizioni decisionali in Europa* (1999) (ed. with Graziella Fornengo); *La stagione del disincanto? Cittadini,* *cittadine e politica alle soglie del 2000* (2001), and she was editor of *Da elettrici a elette. Riforme istituzionali e rappresentanza delle donne in Italia, in Europa e negli Stati Uniti* (2003). She has published numerous chapters and articles on gender and politics in English, and wrote the chapters on Italy in Dorothy McBride Stetson and Amy Mazur (eds) *Comparative State Feminism* (1995); Amy Mazur (ed.), *State Feminism, Women's Movements and Job Training: Making Democracies work in the Global Economy* (2001); Joni Lovenduski, Petra Meier, Diane Sainsbury, Marila Guadagnini and Claudie Baudino (eds) *State Feminism and Political Representation* (2005); and Melissa Haussman and Birgit Sauer (eds) *Gendering the State in the Age of Globalization* (2007).

Anne Maria Holli obtained her Ph.D. in political science at the University of Helsinki, and is Research Fellow (Academy of Finland) at the Department of Political Science, University of Helsinki. Her major areas of research are in the fields of public equality policies, Nordic gender equality discourses and gender and politics. Her most recent publications include: *Discourse and Politics for Gender Equality in Late Twentieth Century Finland* (2003) and chapters on Finland in Amy Mazur (ed.) *State Feminism, Women's Movements and Job Training: Making Democracies Work in the Global Economy* (2001); Joyce Outshoorn (ed.) *The Politics of Prostitution. Women's Movements, Democratic States and the Globalisation of Sex Commerce* (2004); Joni Lovenduski, Petra Meier, Diane Sainsbury, Marila Guadagnini and Claudie Baudino (eds) *Feminism and Political Representation of Women in Europe and North America* (2005); Melissa Haussman and Birgit Sauer (eds) *Gendering the State in the Age of Globalization* (2007). She is also co-editor of *Women's Citizenship and Political Rights* (with S.K. Hellsten and K. Daskalova) (2005).

Johanna Kantola obtained her Ph.D. from the University of Bristol; currently she is Senior Lecturer at the Department of Political Science at the University of Helsinki. Her most recent publication is *Feminists Theorize the State* (2006). She has published articles about gender and the state in the *International Feminist Journal of Politics*, *European Journal of Women's Studies* and *European Political Science* and contributed chapters to various edited volumes. These include chapters on Britain and Finland in two volumes coming out of the work of the Research Network on Gender, Governance and the State (RNGS) in Joyce Outshoorn (ed.) *The Politics of Prostitution* (2004); and Joni Lovenduski, Claudie Baudino, Marila Guadagnini, Petra Meier and Diane Sainsbury (eds) *State Feminism and Political Representation* (2005). She has also published a monograph *The*

Mute, the Deaf and the Lost: Gender Equality at the University of Helsinki Political Science Department (2005). She is the co-editor of the *Finnish Women's Studies Journal*.

Sabine Lang is Assistant Professor of European Studies at the H.M. Jackson School of International Studies of the University of Washington. She received her Ph.D. in political science at the Free University in Berlin and has held previous teaching positions at the University of Leipzig and at the J.F. Kennedy-Institute of the Free University Berlin. From 1990 to 1994 she was Director of the Public Affairs Department and the Executive Office of the State Secretary for Labour and Women's Issues in Berlin. Her areas of research are gender politics, the civic sector and political communication. Her publications include 'The NGOization of Feminism: Institutionalization and Institution Building within the German Women's Movements', in Bonnie G. Smith (ed.) *Global Feminisms since 1945* (2000); and 'Unifying a Gendered State: Women in Post 1989 Germany', in Stuart Taberner and Frank Finlay (eds) *Recasting German Identity. Culture, Politics, and Literature in the Berlin Republic* (2002).

Joni Lovenduski is Anniversary Professor of Politics at Birkbeck College, University of London. Her published work on gender and politics includes *Feminizing Politics* (2005); *State Feminism and Political Representation* (edited with Claudie Baudino, Marila Guadagnini, Petra Meier and Diane Sainsbury) (2005); *The Hansard Report on Women at the Top* (with Sarah Childs and Rosie Campbell) (2005); *Gender and Political Participation* (with Pippa Norris and Rosie Campbell) (2004); *Women and European Politics* (1986); *Contemporary Feminist Politics* (1993) (with Vicky Randall); *Political Recruitment: Gender, Race and Class in the British Parliament* (1995) (with Pippa Norris); and *High Tide or High Time for Labour Women* (1998) (with Maria Eagle MP). She was co-editor of *The Politics of the Second Electorate* (1981), *The New Politics of Abortion* (1986), *Gender and Party Politics* (1993), and editor of *Feminism and Politics* (2000), as well as many articles and essays in edited collections on issues of gender and politics. Her current research is on gender and the state, including political representation and public policy debates.

Amy G. Mazur is Professor in the Department of Political Science at Washington State University. Her research and teaching interests focus on comparative feminist policy issues with a particular emphasis on France. Her books include: *Comparative State Feminism* (1995) (editor, with Dorothy McBride Stetson); *Gender Bias and the State: Symbolic Reform at Work in*

Fifth Republic France (1995); *State Feminism, Women's Movements, and Job Training: Making Democracies Work in the Global Economy* (2001) (editor); and *Theorizing Feminist Policy* (2002). She has published articles in *Political Research Quarterly, French Politics and Society, Policy Studies Journal, West European Politics, European Journal of Political Research, European Political Science, Review of Policy Research, Contemporary French Civilization,* and *Travail Genre et Société* and *Espace-Temps*. She is co-convenor of the Research Network on Gender Politics and the State, and convener of the French Politics Group of the APSA. She is co-editor of *Political Research Quarterly*. In Fall, 2001, she was the Marie Jahoda Professor of International Feminist Studies at Ruhr University, Bochum and a Havens Center Visiting Scholar at the University of Wisconsin in Spring, 2003. Through 2005–06 she was an expert for the United Nations for the Expert Group Meeting on Equal Participation of Women and Men in Decision-making Processes and rapporteur of the final meeting report. She has received over $500.000 in research grants from the National Science Foundation, the European Science Foundation, and the French Ministry of Social Affairs.

Dorothy E. McBride is Professor Emeritus of Political Science at Florida Atlantic University and co-convenor of the Research Network on Gender Politics and the State (RNGS). She is author of *Women's Rights in the USA: Policy Debates and Gender Roles*, 3rd edn (2004). Her RNGS publications include *Abortion Politics, Women's Movements and the Democratic State* (2001) (editor); 'The Invisible Issue: Prostitution and Trafficking of Women and Girls in the United States', in Joyce Outshoorn (ed.) *The Politics of Prostitution: Women's Movements, Democratic States, and the Globalisation of Sex Commerce* (2004); 'The Women's Movement Agenda and the Record of the Clinton Administration', in Todd G. Shields, Jeannie M. Whayne and Donald R. Kelley (eds) *The Clinton Riddle: Perspectives on the Forty-second President* (2004) and 'Measuring Feminist Mobilization: Cross-National Convergence and Transnational Networks in Western Europe', in Myra Marx Ferree and Aili Tripp (eds) *Global Feminism: Transnational Women's Activism, Organizing and Human Rights* (2006). She was co-editor (with Amy Mazur) of *Comparative State Feminism* (1995).

Petra Meier is Lecturer at the Politics Department at Antwerp University. Her major research interests are feminist theories on representation, the conceptualization of measures to promote social groups in decision-making and their interaction with electoral systems, feminist approaches to public policies, the political opportunity structures of the Belgian women's movement and state feminism. She recently published *De macht van het geslacht. Gender, politiek en beleid* (2005) (with Karen Celis), and edited *Genre et science politique en Belgique et en Francophonie* (2005) (with Bérengère Marques-Pereira) as well as *Vrouwen vertegenwoordigd, Wetstraat gekraakt? Representativiteit feministisch bekeken* (2004) (with Karen Celis). She has also published in *European Journal of Women's Studies, Party Politics, European Political Science, Acta Politica, Res Publica, Greek Review of Social Research, Tijdschrift voor Sociologie, Ethiek en Maatschappij* and in edited volumes.

Jantine Oldersma studied political science, social history and communication at the University of Amsterdam and received her Ph.D. from Leiden University. She is an Assistant Professor at the Department of Public Administration and a fellow of the Joke Smit Institute, Research Centre for Women's Studies, both at Leiden University. Her dissertation was on women and corporatism in the Netherlands: *De vrouw die vanzelf spreekt, gender en representatie in het Nederlandse adviesradenstelsel* (1996). She was co-editor of a volume on gender and theories of power, *The Gender of Power* (1991) (with Kathy Davis and Monique Leijenaar) and has published on gender and politics, public policy and (political) culture. Recent publications include 'More Women or more Feminists in Politics? Advocacy Coalitions and the Representation of Women in the Netherlands 1967–1992', *Acta Politica, International Journal of Political Science* (2002); and *'High Tides in a Low Country'*, in Joni Lovenduski, Claudie Baudino, Marila Guadagnini, Petra Meier and Diane Sainsbury (eds) *State Feminism and Political Representation of Women* (2005), and (with Joyce Outshoorn) the chapter on the Netherlands in Melissa Haussman and Birgit Sauer, (eds) *Gendering the State in the Age of Globalization: Women's Movements and State Feminism in Post-Industrial Democracies* (2007).

Tanja Olsson Blandy is a Ph.D. Candidate at the Department of Government at Uppsala University, Sweden. Her main field of interest is gender equality in general and in the face of European Integration in particular. Her current research focuses on the repercussions of the European Equal Pay policy at the domestic level. Her publications include 'Equal Pay and the Impact of the European Union', in P.O. Öberg and T. Svensson (eds) *Power and Institutions in Industrial Relations Regimes: Political Science Perspectives on the Transition of the Swedish Model* (2005).

Candice D. Ortbals studied political science at Indiana University, where she received her Ph.D. for her dissertation *Embedded Institutions,*

Activisms, and Discourses: Untangling the Intersections of Women's Civil Society and Women's Policy Agencies in Spain. Currently she is an Assistant Professor at Pepperdine University, Malibu, California, and has a grant from the Ministry of Education in Spain to conduct research on women's policy agencies in the Canary Islands. The Canary Islands research will complete her investigation into regional women's policy agencies in Spain, which also includes analyses of Galicia and Andalusia. She is a research member of the Research Network on Gender, Politics, and the State (RNGS) and has authored forthcoming journal articles in *International Feminist Journal of Politics, PS: Political Science and Politics*, and *Politics and Gender.*

Joyce Outshoorn studied political science and contemporary history at the University of Amsterdam. Since 1987 she has been Professor of Women's Studies at the Joke Smit Centre for Research in Women's Studies at Leiden University, Leiden, where she is also affiliated to the Department of Political Science. She is co-convenor of the Research Network on Gender Politics and the State. Her Ph.D. was on abortion politics in the Netherlands, *De politieke strijd rondom de abortuswetgeving in Nederland, 1964–1984* (1986). She edited *The Politics of Prostitution. Women's Movements, Democratic States and the Globalisation of Sex Commerce* (2004); *The New Politics of Abortion* (1986) (with Joni Lovenduski) and co-edited *A Creative Tension. Essays in Socialist Feminism* (1984). She contributed the chapter on the Netherlands in: *Abortion Politics, Women's Movements, and the Democratic State*, edited by Dorothy McBride Stetson (2001) and (with Jantine Oldersma) in Melissa Haussman and Birgit Sauer (eds) *Gendering the State in the Age of Globalization: Women's Movements and State Feminism in Post-Industrial Democracies* (2007). She has published articles in *Public Administration Review, Acta Politica, Social Politics, European Journal of Women's Studies, European Journal of Political Research, Journal of Contemporary European Studies* and *Journal of Comparative Policy Analysis* (forthcoming 2008).

Diane Sainsbury is Professor Emerita, formerly Lars Hierta Professor of Political Science, at Stockholm University. She is author of *Gender, Equality and Welfare States* (1996), editor of *Gendering Welfare States* (1994), and *Gender and Welfare State Regimes* (1999), and a contributing editor of *State Feminism and Political Representation* (2005). Among her recent publications are 'Rights without Seats: the Puzzle of Australian Women's Legislative Recruitment', in Marian Sawer (ed.) *Elections: Full, Free & Fair* (2001), 'US Women's Suffrage through a Multicultural Lens: Intersecting Struggles of Recognition', in Barbara Hobson (ed.) *Recognition Struggles* *and Social Movements* (2003), 'Women's Political Representation in Sweden: Discursive Politics and Institutional Presence', *Scandinavian Political Studies* (2004), and 'Party Feminism, State Feminism and Women's Representation in Sweden' in Joni Lovenduski, Claudie Baudino, Marila Guadagnini, Petra Meier and Diane Sainsbury (eds) *State Feminism and Political Representation* (2005).

Birgit Sauer is Professor of Political Science at the Department of Political Science, University of Vienna. She studied political science and German literature at the University of Tübingen and at the Free University of Berlin. Her Ph.D. was on political rituals in the GDR (1993 at the Free University of Berlin); her *Habilitation* on state and democratic theory in gender perspective (University of Vienna, 2000). Her research fields include gender and political culture, gender in political institution, state theory, gender and governance. Recent publications include: 'Taxes, Rights and Regimentation. Discourses on Prostitution in Austria', in Joyce Outshoorn (ed.) *The Politics of Prostitution. Women's Movements, Democratic States and the Globalisation of Sex Commerce* (2004); 'Conceptualizing the German State. Putting Women's Politics in its Place', in S.S. Nagel and A. Robb (eds) *Handbook of Global Social Policy* (2000); *Die Asche des Souveräns. Staat und Demokratie in der Geschlechterdebatte* (2001); Geschlechterdemokratie und Arbeitsteilung. Aktuelle feministische Debatten, in *Österreichische Zeitschrift für Soziologie* (2006).

Marian Sawer is a Professor of Political Science and heads the Democratic Audit of Australia at the Australian National University. She was made an Officer of the Order of Australia in 2004 for her contributions to women and to political science and is a Fellow of the Academy of Social Sciences in Australia. She has worked inside and outside government on gender policy issues, has been *rapporteur* for two UN Expert Group Meetings on gender policy mechanisms and has chaired the International Political Science Association Research Committee on Gender, Politics and Public Policy. Her books in this area include *Sisters in Suits* (1990), *Working from Inside* (1994) (with Abigail Groves) and *The Ethical State?* (2003). She has also published widely on issues of democracy and representation and has a new co-edited book *Representing Women in Parliament* (2006).

List of Abbreviations

ACT	Australian Capital Territory
AIRC	Australian Industrial Relations Commission
APEC	Asia Pacific Economic Community
AUD	Australian dollar
BAG	*Bundesarbeitsgemeinschaft lokaler Frauenbüro* – the Federal Association of Local-Government Women's Offices
BZÖ	*Bündnis Zukunft Österreich* – Alliance for the Future of Austria
CAPOW!	Coalition of Participating Organizations of Women! (USA)
CCWI	Congressional Caucus for Women's Issues (USA)
CDC	Center for Disease Control and Prevention (USA)
CDU	*Christlich Demokratische Union* – Christian Democratic Union (Germany)
CEDAW	Convention on the Elimination of All Forms of Discrimination against Women
CEHR	Commission for Equality and Human Rights (Great Britain)
CELEM	*Coordinadora Española para el Lobby Europeo de Mujeres* – Spanish Coordinator for the European Women's Lobby
CNPPO	*Commissione Nazionale per la parità e le pari opportunità* – National Commission for Equality and Equal Opportunities (Italy)
CRE	Commission for Racial Equality (Great Britain)
CSU	*Christlich Soziale Union* – Christian Social Union (Germany)
DACOWITS	Defense Department Advisory Committee on Women in the Services (USA)
DCE	*Directie Coordinatie Emancipatiebeleid* – Department for the Coordination of Equality Policy (Netherlands)
DHHS	Department of Health and Human Services (USA)
DRC	Disability Rights Commission (USA)
DTI	Department for Trade and Industry (USA)
DWF	*Donna Woman Femme* (Italy)
ECJ	European Court of Justice

EEOC	Equal Employment Opportunity Commission (USA)
EMU	European Monetary Union
EOC	Equal Opportunities Commission (Great Britain)
ER	*Emancipatieraad* – Emancipation Council (Netherlands)
EU	European Union
EWL	European Women's Lobby
FDA	Food and Drugs Administration (USA)
FDP	*Freie Demokratische Partei* – Free Democratic Party (Germany)
FETD	Employment or Framework Equal Treatment Directive
FI	*Feministiskt initiativ* – Feminist Initiative (Sweden)
FOI	Freedom of Information
FPÖ	*Freiheitliche Partei Österrreichs* – Freedom Party of Austria
GFMK	*Gemeinsame Frauenministerinnenkonferenz* – Conference of the Women's and Equality State Ministers (Germany)
HREOC	Human Rights and Equal Opportunities Commission (USA)
IAM	*Instituto Andaluz de la Mujer* – Andalusian Women's Institute
ICE	*Interdepartementale Coördinatiecommissie Emancipatie* – Interdepartmental Committee for Women's public policy (Netherlands)
IIAV	*Internationaal Informatiecentrum en Archief voor de Vrouwenbeweging* – International Institute and Archives for the Women's Movement (Netherlands)
IMAG	*Interministerielle Arbeitsgruppe Gender Mainstreaming* – Interministerial Working Group Gender Mainstreaming (Austria)
JämO	*Jämställdhetsombudsman* – Equal Opportunities Ombudsman (Sweden)
LEFÖ	*Lateinamerikanische emigrierte Frauen in Österreich* – Latin American Emigrant Women in Austria
LO	*Landsorganisationen* – Swedish Trade Union Confederation
LOCE	*Ley Orgánica de Calidad de la Enseñanza* – Organic Law on the Quality of Education (Spain)
LOGSE	*Ley de Ordenación General del Sistema Educativo* – Law on the General Organization of the Education System (Spain)
LPF	*Lijst Pim Fortuyn* – List Pim Fortuyn (Netherlands)
MAIZ	*Autonomes Integrationszentrum von und für Migrantinnen* – Autonomous Integration Centre of and for Migrant Women (Austria)
MEP	Member of European Parliament

NGO	Non-governmental organization
NIH	National Institute of Health (USA)
NPM	New Public Management
NSW	New South Wales
NVR	*Nederlandse Vrouwenraad* – The Dutch Women's Council
NWHIC	National Women's Health Information Center (USA)
NYTKIS	Naisjärjetöt Yhteisyössä – Coalition of Finnish Women's Associations
OIWI	Office for International Women's Issues (USA)
ORWM	Office of Research on Women's Health (USA)
OVAW	Office on Violence Against Women (USA)
ÖVP	*Österreichische Volkspartei* – Austrian People's Party
OWH	Office on Women's Health (USA)
PAC	Political Action Committee (USA)
PACA	Provence-Alpes-Côte d'Azur
PDS	*Partei des Demokratischen Sozialismus* – Party of Democratic Socialism (Germany)
PICW	President's Interagency Council on Women (USA)
PP	*Partido Popular* – People's Party (Spain)
PRWORA	Personal Responsibility and Work Opportunity Reconciliation Act (USA)
PSOE	*Partido Socialista Obrero Español* – Spanish Socialist Workers' Party
PvdA	*Partij van de Arbeid* – Party of Labour (Netherlands)
SDA	Sex Discrimination Act (Great Britain)
SETA	*Seksuaalinen Tasavertaisuus* – Sexual Equality (Finland)
SGI	*Servizo Galego de Igualdade* – Galician Equality Service
SPD	*Sozialdemokratische Partei Deutschlands* – Social Democratic Party of Germany
SPÖ	*Sozialdemokratische Partei Österreichs* – Social Democratic Party of Austria
STV	*Stichting tegen Vrouwenhandel* – Foundation against Trafficking of Women (Netherlands)
TCO	*Tjänstemännens Centralorganisation* – Confederation for Professional Employees (Sweden)
UFF	*Unabhängiges Frauenforum* – Independent Women's Forum (Austria)
UFV	*Unabhängiger Frauenverband* – Independent Women's Association (Germany)
UK	United Kingdom
UN	United Nations

UNAR	*Ufficio Nazionale Antidiscriminazioni Razziali* – National Office Against Racial Discrimination (Italy)
UNIFEM	United Nations Development Fund for Women
VAWA	Violence Against Women Act
VCE	*Visitatiecommissie Emancipatiebeleid* – Commission for the Assessment of Women's Public Policy (Netherlands)
WEL	Women's Electoral Lobby (Australia)
WEP-I	Women's Exchange Programme International (Netherlands)
WESNET	Women's Emergency Services Network (Australia)
WEU	Women and Equality Unit (Great Britain)
WI	Women's Institute – *Instituto de la Mujer* (Spain)
WNC	Women's National Commission (Great Britain)
WU	Women's Unit (USA)

1
Changing State Feminism
Johanna Kantola and Joyce Outshoorn

The second wave of feminism challenged the state in post-industrial democracies with its demands; in response, states set up women's policy agencies to improve women's status. Studies from the 1980s and 1990s have shown that 'state feminism' exists: many agencies are important in realizing women's movements' demands in policy-making and in gaining access for women to decision-making arenas. The starting point for this book is the restructuring of the political context, where state feminism is situated, over the last decade. As a result, both 'the state' and 'feminism' have changed in significant ways. On the one hand, there have been major developments, such as globalization, regionalization, welfare state restructuring, privatization and the rise of multilevel governance. On the other hand, state feminists have to deal with new gender equality policies that include a focus on diversity and gender mainstreaming. Both developments demand rethinking state feminism and new empirical research and comparative analysis on the topic.

This volume will systematically analyse the effects of these changes on the institutionalization of women's public policy in twelve Western democracies since the mid-1990s. The countries examined include Australia, Austria, Belgium, Finland, France, Germany, Italy, the Netherlands, Spain, Sweden, the United Kingdom and the USA. All these countries have an array of well-established women's policy agencies and a wide range of women's movement organizations, which makes it interesting to explore how the current changes have affected their position and power.

The central question raised in this book is whether women's policy agencies have been able to develop, maintain or enhance their roles in transformed political contexts. How have the processes of state reconfiguration affected women's policy agencies and how have the agencies responded to these changes? This key question can be broken down into a number of sub-questions.

- What ties have the women's policy agencies established with various institutions of the EU and what are the effects of EU policy and, in the case of the two non-EU countries researched here, Australia and the US, the UN?
- Is regionalization resulting in an emergence of substate feminism?
- How is welfare state reform impacting on the work of the agencies?
- To what extent has their original mandate been affected by gender mainstreaming?
- Have changes within the women's movements affected women's policy agencies and have they established links with new women's movement groups of migrant women?

In this introductory chapter we shall, first, discuss the key concepts used in this volume to analyse the country-cases. We define terms such as state feminism, women's policy agencies and the women's movement. Second, we discuss the previous research and findings on state feminism and the conditions for its success. This provides a background for a discussion on the significance of the changing context for the success of state feminism. Third, we examine this changing context of state feminism both in relation to the state – supra and subnational influence, welfare state reform, neoliberal ideologies – and feminism – gender mainstreaming and gender diversity.

Defining the concepts

State feminism can simply be defined as the advocacy of women's movement demands inside the state (Lovenduski et al., 2005, p. 4). But as with many political concepts, the issue of defining state feminism is more complex and the meaning of the term varies according to the context. For example, in the Nordic countries, state feminism signifies the achievement of gender equality through the state. The combined pressure that feminists exert on the state from below (women's movements) and from above (feminists in the state) are theorized to result in women-friendly welfare policies in the Nordic countries (Hernes, 1987; Siim, 1988). Alternatively, state feminism has more pejorative connotations in the former communist countries, the so-called Soviet bloc, where it signifies the policies directed at women but imposed from above by male elites (Temkina and Zdravomyslova, 2003). Most commonly, however, 'state feminism' is used to denote the efforts by women's policy machineries to pursue social and economic policies beneficial to women. This work is carried out in special units charged with promoting women's rights including offices, commissions, agencies, ministries, committees, secretaries, or advisers for the status of women (Chappell, 2002; Goetz, 2003; Rai, 2003a; McBride Stetson and Mazur, 1995; Weldon, 2002a). State feminism is, thus, an overarching term. Scholars studying state feminism in this third sense, use more specific notions to capture the meaning of the term. Here the concepts of 'institutional mechanisms for the advancement of women' (Rai, 2003a; Staudt, 2003; Goetz, 2003) or 'women's policy agencies' (McBride Stetson, 2001a; Mazur, 2001a; Outshoorn, 2004a; Lovenduski et al., 2005) are used. This terminology follows the example set by the United Nations (UN), which uses the language of 'national machineries in promoting women-specific issues'. The UN defines these as bodies recognized by the government as the institutions dealing with the promotion of the status of women (UN, 1993). Women's policy machinery, thus, describes any structure established by government with its main purpose being the betterment of women's social status. This specific use of the term distinguishes this type of machinery from other ways of looking at women's role in government (McBride Stetson and Mazur, 1995, p. 3, p. 5).

Women's policy agencies take different forms. For example, they might be (i) advocacy or *advisory units* located in a central political unit responsible for promoting attention to gender issues and giving advice to various government units, (ii) *policy monitoring units* that have the right to review projects before approval, (iii) *units with implementation responsibilities* that create programmes, respond to policy needs that are not well catered for elsewhere (for example violence against women), or (iv) *commissions with investigation powers*, that is women-dedicated public ombudspersons or public protectors, equipped to receive and investigate complaints by the public regarding gender-based rights violations (Goetz, 2004, pp. 2–4).

The concepts of state feminism and women's policy agencies have generated heated debates. A first set of criticisms asks how feminist are these bodies: are they really to be called state *feminist*? This viewpoint reflects the disjuncture between feminist theory and praxis. Feminist theory emanating from the Anglo-American countries has long been characterized by anti-statism and feminists have felt ambivalent about the possibilities about engaging the patriarchal state (Kantola, 2006a, pp. 5–7; Rai, 2003b, pp. 18–19; McBride Stetson and Mazur, 1995, p. 2). Such engagements are thought to compromise a more critical feminist stance. In practice feminists have engaged with the state for example, through the work done in the women's policy agencies. In Western Europe and Australia the debate about the state was settled in the 1980s in favour of using the state. The groups from the autonomous women's movement most opposed to the state disappeared, became professionalized or remained small remnants on the fringes.

Nevertheless, this suspicious attitude towards the state prevails in feminist literature and has led many feminist scholars to question the motives of governments that set up these offices in response to international pressure especially in the developing countries. Here it is pointed out that governments can make important political gains at the international and domestic levels by espousing gender equality, without serious risk of being held accountable and having to operationalize the promises made in top-level rhetoric (Goetz, 2003, p. 91). Half-hearted support is also evidenced in the under-resourcing of the agencies. Many have expressed concerns that their creation may 'co-opt' women's demands – or worse, promote non-feminist ends – at the same time that they reduce the mobilization power of women's movements (e.g. in recent years Franceschet, 2003; Weldon, 2002a). In short, the feminist credentials of these bodies have been under debate.

Here two issues become central: the usage of the term women's policy agencies as opposed to state feminism and women's policy agencies' relationship to the women's movements. First, in relation to some of the controversies surrounding the concept of state feminism, we see that the term women's policy agency is more specific than state feminism. There is no a priori assumption that women's policy agencies are feminist. Rather the extent to which they are feminist is an empirical question where feminism itself can be defined and operationalized in a number of different ways, including, for example, 'the broad goal of challenging and changing gender relations that subordinate women to men and that thereby also differentially advantage some women and men in relation to others' (Ferree and Tripp, 2006, p. vii). Notably, feminism can be practised in a variety of institutional contexts and there are many different strategies and practices that are consistent with this goal (Ferree and Tripp, 2006, p. vii). This signifies that feminism itself is contested both as a concept, a theory, and a form of practice.

The notion of women's policy agency, however, eclipses another issue relating the to concept of state feminism – the *state*. Below we discuss the tendencies towards multilevel governance in a 'reconfigured' state (Banaszak, Beckwith, and Rucht, 2003). This discussion below and in the chapters of the book indicates that there is a new diversity of mechanisms and partnerships that may be involved in the promotion of gender equality in the reconfigured state. *State* feminist bodies may thus be located at the regional and supranational levels as well as the national state level. In this context, we make some reference to work on substate and suprastate feminism (Celis and Meier, in this volume; UN, 2005; Woodward and Hubert, 2006). The significance of these changes in the state is indeed one of the key issues studied in this book.

Second, despite the difficulties of defining *women's movements* it has been suggested that they are characterized by political mobilization aimed at improving women's lives or the primacy placed on women's issues, leadership and decision-making (Beckwith, 2000; Molyneux, 1998). The relationship between the state and the movement is an important one in the scholarly literature on social movements. In studies on state feminism, women's policy agencies are theorized as the links between the state and the women's movement and their effectiveness in doing this job becomes an empirical question. In this literature, there is a tendency to make a representative claim: women's policy agencies are feminist in a sense that they claim to help the actors that speak for women and gender equality (Mazur, 2005, p. 3; for a discussion see Squires, forthcoming 2007a, pp. 159–160). The relationship between the women's policy agencies and women's movements turns into a question of women's policy agencies' accountability to their imagined constituency, women's movements. Laurel Weldon suggests that women's policy agencies in consultation with women's movements better represent women's concerns and claims for justice than unorganized groups of women in the legislature (Weldon, 2002b, p. 1161). Yet there are no formal mechanisms of accountability by which the women's movement might hold the women's policy agencies to account (Squires, 2007a) and indeed, the women's policy agencies are formally accountable only to the government (Goetz, 2004, p. 6). One can therefore inquire whether the women's policy agencies perhaps represent only certain parts of the women's movement and not others (Squires, forthcoming a).

The second set of criticisms deals with the use of women instead of gender in naming the policy machineries *women's* policy agencies. In the 1970s and 1980s, the latter term pointed to the mandate of the then existing agencies. Recently, it has been argued that the focus on women rather than gender does not reflect the remit of the agencies that are charged with issues relating to gender equality. This recent development can also be seen at the UN level with the new definition of the main task of the national machinery in the Beijing Platform for Action 1995: 'to support government-wide *mainstreaming* of a *gender*-equality policy perspective in all policy areas' (Rai, 2003a, p. 2, our emphasis). Many scholars now write about gender equality agencies rather than women's policy agencies (Bergqvist et al., 1999; Olsson Blandy, 2004). The strength of this concept is that it also encompasses men's role in achieving gender equality. It does, however, raise interesting questions about the agencies' account-ability to the women's movements – should this now encompass men's movements? (see Holli and Kantola, this volume). The term gender equal-ity machineries furthermore assumes that *equality* is the goal of women's movements and women's public policy, which is not necessarily the case with those movements pursuing identity politics. Nevertheless, the ques-tion of naming equality machineries is becoming a burning one as some countries in Europe are moving towards 'single equalities bodies' that bring together different bases of discrimination and do not deal only with gender-based inequalities (see Lovenduski, Bergqvist, Olsson Blandy and Sainsbury, in this volume).

State feminism before

Previous research on state feminism has explored two questions in par-ticular. First, whether the women's policy agencies have been successful in advancing women's concerns both substantively and descriptively? Second, what the specific conditions for their success or failure have been? This research has made a strong argument for the important role played by state feminism in aiding women's demands in public policy-making. It has been established that women's policy agencies constitute effective links between women's movements and the state, and facilitate women's access into decision-making processes. The role of the women's policy agencies has been explored in relation to different policy debates from abortion, domestic violence and prostitution to job training and political representation (Lovenduski et al., 2005; Mazur, 2001a; Outshoorn, 2004b; McBride Stetson, 2001a; Weldon, 2002a).

The measures for and evaluations of success differ however. For instance, success can be evaluated in terms of whether advocates have been able to achieve an institutionalized position within the bureaucracy, and the extent to which these activists have been able to apply a gender analysis to pub-lic policy-making (Chappell, 2002). Alternatively, the Research Network on Gender, Politics and the State (RNGS) studied the role of the women's policy agencies in terms of two dimensions: is the women's policy office an advocate of women's movement goals or not in the policy-making process? Is it effective in gendering and changing the terms of the policy-making process to coincide with those of the women's movements? Has it enabled women to enter the decision-making arena, by promoting their participation and offering access into the corridors of power? (McBride Stetson, 2001a; Mazur 2001a; Outshoorn, 2004b; Lovenduski et al., 2005).[1]

Shirin Rai (2003b), in turn, distinguishes location, resources and strong democratic movements holding these bodies accountable as important conditions for success of the agencies. Women's policy agencies need to be located at a high level within the decision-making hierarchy to influence government policy. They need to have a clear mandate and functional responsibility, and human and financial resources. Links with civil society groups supportive of the advancement of women's rights and enhancement of women's status are important to assure accountability of the national machinery itself (Rai, 2003b, p. 26).

Other studies, namely those coming out of the RNGS, have shown that the probability of women's policy success is higher when the policy sub-system in question is moderately closed or open in character (the character of the subsystem ranges from amorphous networks and wide participation of actors to more clearly defined organization and several actors trying to dominate), the left is in power, and the women's movement which is mobilized by the debate is close to the left, the issue is of high priority to the movement, and the various strands of women's movements are unified on the issue (Mazur, 2001a; McBride Stetson, 2001a; cf. Outshoorn 2004a, p. 291). Another factor is the compatibility of the framing of women's movement demands with the dominant discourse in the policy arena (Outshoorn, 2004a). Furthermore, different policy sectors seem to offer very different political opportunity structures from women's point of view (Mazur, 2002, pp. 184–5; Holli, 2006). Women's movements have tended to be more successful where women's policy agencies have gendered policy debates in ways that have coincided with women's movement goals. By contrast, the movements have been less successful when women's policy agencies have played some other role, whether it be marginal, non-feminist or symbolic (Holli, 2006).

These conditions for success or failure have sometimes proved to be contradictory. For example, location at high level may be a problem rather than a source of influence: proximity to high office can work against women's machineries making them overly-associated with the chief executive and subject to its control, making them unattractive to the women's movement (Goetz, 2004, p. 4). Laurel Weldon (2002a, p. 156) makes a strong argument for the interaction between autonomous women's organizations and effective women's policy machinery. Anne Marie Goetz, in turn, finds this useful because it brings two key issues of relevance to the impact of national women's machineries to the fore: the overall quality of governance and the capacity of women's movements to make power-holders accountable (Goetz, 2004, p. 4).

Thus previous research has established that women's policy agencies' success is shaped by and varies according to the political context, the agencies' resources, general framing of policy debates, their links to the women's movement, and questions about accountability among other things. These factors affect the activities of women's policy agencies in different ways. In this volume, we are interested in the changes in the political context where state feminism is situated more broadly. We do not focus on the specific factors of success, as they are being debated, but intend to explore the effects of the changes in the state and feminism that we find pertinent and empirically interesting in relation to state feminism.

The new context of state feminism

Multi-level governance

The starting point for this book is that the states, where women's policy agencies are located, have undergone significant structural changes in the last decade. These represent some fundamental challenges to the women's policy agencies (see also UN, 2005). States are now situated in a multi-level governance framework, where the national level is influenced by supranational and subnational developments. Arguably, the state has 'reshaped, relocated, and rearticulated its formal powers and policy responsibilities' throughout the 1980s and 1990s (Banaszak, Beckwith and Rucht, 2003, p. 3). As a result, women's movements and women's policy agencies face a 'reconfigured' state that offers opportunities for advancing women's concerns but also threatens their successes. Lee Ann Banaszak, Karen Beckwith and Dieter Rucht (2003) conceptualize these changes through the notions of uploading, downloading, lateral loading and offloading. State authority has been *uploaded* to supranational organizations and *downloaded* to substate, provincial or regional governments. A weakening of the power of elected state spheres and a growing reliance on other and partly non-elected state bodies represent *lateral loading* (Banaszak, Beckwith and Rucht, 2003, pp. 4–5). *Offloading*, in turn, signals delegating state powers and responsibility to actors in civil society. As governments have increasingly engaged in lateral loading and offloading, women's movements have been presented with a depoliticized and more remote set of state policy-making agencies at the national level (Banaszak, Beckwith and Rucht, 2003, pp. 6, 7).

We find the framework useful in researching changing state feminism because it draws attention to some of the key processes. We aim to be specific when analysing the different phenomena that relate to this state restructuring and thus refer to supranationalization, Europeanization, regionalization, welfare state reform, the rise of neoliberalism and the rise in right-wing parties as specific processes. The chapters approach these as context specific processes, the extent of which is a matter of empirical research.

A radical understanding of the tendencies towards uploading is represented by those scholars who argue that as a result of globalization, the state has lost its powers to markets and transnational corporations (Strange, 1996). The claims have been contested as inaccurate and dangerous, and many now argue that the states retain important powers (Hayward and Menon, 2003; Weiss, 2003) and that the state needs to be reclaimed as a political space (Youngs, 2000). Yet, most scholars recognize that states cannot be studied in isolation from international developments including international human rights regime, policies emanating from the UN, transnational organizing as well as the international economy. Instead, there is a need to deal with the complexity that multilevel governance generates by looking at the mobility of discourses and institutional changes beyond the state (Kantola, 2006, p. 129). This allows for the linkages between, and the mutually constitutive character of local, national and supranational levels to come to the fore.

Studies on women's policy agencies have focused on the positive impact of supranational governance and transnational networks on women's organizing in nation-states. To start with, the UN was pivotal in the creation and establishment of national machineries in many countries. Studies show that actors in transnational networks also have a significant impact on domestic politics and policy after the establishment of women's policy agencies (True and Mintrom, 2001, p. 28; Keck and Sikkink 1998). Transnational networks serve as conduits of information about differing policy models and of knowledge concerning alternative political strategies and how they may be applied to further promote gender policy change (True, 2003, p. 377). Furthermore, international bodies are an important source of leverage for women's policy agencies in a number of countries.

Europeanization represents a different understanding of uploading. The term captures the way in which a European dimension becomes an embedded feature framing politics within European states through the impact of the EU (Liebert, 2003, p. 16; Radaelli, 2006, p. 69). Europeanization is a process of convergence towards shared policy frameworks which does not, however, require uniformity, or imply an erosion of the domestic or overriding of member states' internal processes (Liebert 2003, p. 15, p. 16). The study of Europeanization has often been located within a broadly institutionalist discourse, and domestic institutions are viewed as filtering the impact of EU-level innovations (Cram, 2001, p. 606). Yet, the EU often operates within the boundaries of 'soft law' – guidelines, recommenda-tions and action plans, and not with legally binding directives ('hard law'). This indicates the need to broaden the study of Europeanization to processes, discourses and actors. The EU itself forms a part of a more com-plex institutional architecture of multilevel governance that has been built in Europe. For instance, the Council of Europe has exerted important influence in terms of gender mainstreaming (Lovecy, 2002, p. 272).

More specifically, the EU can have a binding, top down effect on member-states' gender equality policy for example when equality legislation needs to comply with the EU law, although member-states can have some leeway in the implementation of directives (Van der Vleuten, 2005). Women's policy agencies increasingly develop national strategies in order to profit from the opportunity structures provided by the EU (Olsson Blandy, 2004, p. 2). They are not only mediating factors in the process of Europeanization but rather they adopt new strategies to legitimate norms emanating from the EU, they propose special policies, and actively frame the discussions (Olsson Blandy, 2004, p. 27; see also Lombardo, 2004). The EU is an import-ant source of funding that has both maintained and established women's policy agencies, as for example in Spain under the Conservative govern-ments. Alessia Donà (2004) has shown, however, that the women's policy agencies and women's movements can have very different capacities when lobbying the EU. Whilst the Italian women policy agencies have become influential in the EU arena, the Italian women's associations are only start-ing to learn how to lobby in a context of complex EU governance (Donà, 2004; 2006). The EU can also be theorized as another location of state feminism, perhaps to be termed as 'suprastate feminism'. Alison Woodward and Agnes Hubert (2006) show that there is indeed a wide array of women's policy agencies in the EU. These represent new actors in both the EU and member states' policies on gender equality.

The research questions addressed in this book thus focus upon the opportunities and challenges that the supranational level, and especially Europeanization, provides for the women's policy agencies. How does this influence the work done by women's policy agencies? How do the women's policy agencies and women's movements view and use the EU level of governance? The extent and the limits of uploading of state powers in relation to women's policy agencies are thus explored.

Similarly, tendencies towards state powers and responsibilities shifting to the local level are scrutinized in this book. One aspect of this is region-alization. The states are passing responsibilities to local level municipalities and regional bodies. Again this represents another location of state femi-nism, namely substate feminism. Notably, 'substate' can mean different things in different countries and range from the federal to the municipal levels of governance. The local level is identified as the more accessible political arena for women in some countries (e.g. Basu, 1995; Chappell, 2002b), but more difficult than the national level in others (Holli, Luhtakallio and Raevaara, 2006).

Regionalization in Spain and France and devolution in the UK have opened new windows of opportunity for women's policy agencies and for women's movement organizations. A positive reading of substate feminism holds that it allows for adaptation to the surrounding context, results in better usage of windows of opportunities and has a contagious effect, where regional and municipal bodies learn from one another (Celis and Meier, in this volume). The negative effects, in turn, include questions about certain regions having no women's policy agencies, some regions lacking behind, and lack of continuity and fragmentation. Furthermore, national women's policy agencies can lose power vis-à-vis the regional bodies, which may result in more piecemeal equalities policies and potential for regional inequalities as there are no common standards (Celis and Meier, in this volume).

A significant aspect of multilevel governance is the shift of responsibility from state to non-state actors. This can take the form of welfare state reform, privatization, outsourcing and New Public Management, all manifestations of the trend towards neoliberalism. Whereas under Keynesian welfarism the state provision of goods and services was understood as a means of ensuring social well-being, neoliberalism is associated with the preference for a minimalist state. Markets are understood to be a better way of organizing economic activity because they are associated with competition, economic efficiency and choice. In conjunction with the general shift towards the neoliberal tenet of 'more market', deregulation and privatization have become central themes in debates over welfare state restructuring (Larner, 2000, p. 5). Deregulation and privatization transfer power away from democratically elected governments with a mandate to ensure universal service provision, towards private capital.

Wendy Larner (2000) argues that the way in which neoliberalism is understood shapes the readings of the scope and content of possible political intervention. Analyses that characterize neoliberalism as either a policy response to the exigencies of the global economy (policy), or the capturing of the policy agenda by the 'New Right' (ideology) run the risk of underestimating the significance of contemporary transformations in *governance* (Larner, 2000, p. 6). Neoliberalism, thus, is a form of governance that encourages both institutions and individuals to conform to the norms of the market. Welfare agencies are now to be governed not directly from above, but through technologies such as budget disciplines, accountancy and audit, competition and the consumer, and have become the norms of public service (Larner, 2000, pp. 5–17).

Whilst it is important to understand these changes in the governance structures, it is crucial to comprehend that even where neoliberalism is vigorously pursued and is firmly embedded in political discourse and policy decisions, it is neither monolithic nor uncontested (Teghtsoonian 2004, p. 270). Rather, it exists in relationships of coexistence and challenge with a range of alternative political impulses which both shape, and are themselves shaped by local particulars of neoliberal policy and discourse (Fraser, 1993; Larner, 2000; Teghtsoonian, 2004). Studying the context-specific particularities of neoliberalism is one of the contributions of a comparative book like this one.

Despite feminist anxieties about welfare state reform, the feminist relationship to the welfare state was never a straightforward positive one. Rather, feminist scholars have been critical of welfare states in different locations (Wilson 1977; McIntosh 1978; Lewis, 1993; Sainsbury, 1994; Ostner and Lewis, 1995). For example, critiques of the Nordic welfare states include women's move from private dependency on fathers and husbands to public dependency on the state, the sameness route to equality based on the norm of the male worker, oversight of rights other than social ones, and the inability to cope with diversity (Dahlerup, 1987; Siim, 1988; Lindvert, 2002; Sainsbury, 1996; 1999; Borchorst and Siim, 2002). The patriarchal welfare state has been contrasted with the work done in the women's policy agencies which are seen to promote women's concerns more actively than welfare states: 'Whereas the welfare state has tended to lock women into roles as clients of services rather than as participants in determining outcomes, women's policy machineries have used resources to help nongovernmental feminist and women's advocacy organizations fight their own policy agendas' (McBride Stetson and Mazur, 1995, p. 273).

Welfare state reform represents special challenges to women's policy agencies. First, its impact can be gendered, which raises a number of issues for women's policy agencies representing women's concerns at the state level. Second, the state's diminishing role in welfare provision has an impact on women's lives as service providers and workers in the public sector and as clients of welfare state services (UN, 2005, p. 13). For example, in relation to the first, one might ask, how can women's policy agencies influence recruitment policies and pay policies in the private sector? In relation to the second, the question for the women's policy agency becomes how to campaign for ending discrimination within the private sphere in terms of women's access to privatized provision of services (Rai, 2003b, p. 36).

Welfare state reform has an impact not only on the issues that need to be tackled but also on the resources of women's policy agencies. The tendency is towards diminishing resources and contracting out. Ultimately, this may result in dismantling women's policy agencies, like in Australia and the US (Sawer; McBride, this volume). This highlights that whilst standard forms of representation, such as the right to vote, have proved to be irreversible, the gains in state feminism and women's policy agencies may well be reversible. The ethos of neoliberalism can be antithetical to that of women's policy agencies. For example, social justice goals can become undermined by a corporate management style that privileges efficiency, cost-effectiveness, and other values central to neoliberalism (Eisenstein, 1996, pp. 189–94).

The issue is complicated by the fact that as state bodies women's policy agencies are embedded in the changing modes of governance. Here location becomes interesting: the closer the women's policy agency is to the neoliberal government, the more co-opted it might be to the neoliberal discourse. Ultimately, its work may provide legitimacy to neoliberal measures. In particular, concentrating narrowly on gender mainstreaming, discussed in more detail below, entails some dangers in the context of neoliberal reform. For example, gender mainstreaming budgets might not alter in any significant way the government's commitment to fiscal restraint and economic restructuring (Teghtsoonian, 2004, p. 268).

Whilst both left- and right-wing parties in many countries have embraced the need to make cuts to the welfare state, closely related to the welfare state reform is the rise of the political right and sometimes also what Marian Sawer (in this volume) calls 'backlash politics': the rise of the men's rights movements and anti-feminist women's groups (see also UN, 2005, p. 14). As indicated above, women's policy agencies tend to have been more successful under left-wing than right-wing governments. Previous research has also shown that left-wing parties tend to have more women as candidates and elected representatives than the right-wing ones and they have also been more willing to include gender-related rules, such as internal or electoral quotas, in their structures (Caul, 1999; Holli, 2006; Leijenaar, 2004; Dahlerup, 2006). Pippa Norris (1987) found that left-wing power had contributed to the decrease of the horizontal and vertical segregation of the labour market, whereas right-wing power tended to increase it.

One of the issues researched in this book is whether a combination of welfare state reform and right-wing party power are detrimental to women's policy agencies and whether this can actually have mobilizing effects on the women's movement. We are interested in the context-specific nature of these changes. Key questions addressed in this book include: how do the changes in the welfare state have an impact on women's policy agencies? How are women's policy agencies affecting the changes? What has been the significance of the rise in the right-wing parties for women's policy agencies?

New equality policies

This book looks not only at changes in the state, but also changes in 'feminism'. This means studying the ways in which gender equality is pursued in states. Two developments are especially relevant: gender mainstreaming and gender diversity, which have been actively adopted and disseminated by the UN and the EU. A key question for this book is: how do the women's policy agencies interact with these developments?

Gender mainstreaming

Like women's policy agencies, gender mainstreaming emerges from the international level, namely the UN. The Beijing Platform for Action states: 'a national machinery for the advancement of women is the central policy coordinating unit inside government. Its main task is to support government-wide mainstreaming of a gender-equality perspective in all policy areas' (quoted in True and Mintrom, 2001, p. 33). Currently, the EU also exerts pressure on its member states to adopt gender-mainstreaming, which was endorsed as the official policy approach to gender equality in the EU and its member states in the Amsterdam Treaty (1997). New member states have been obliged to adopt a gender mainstreaming approach as a condition of joining the EU (Rees, 2005). Gender mainstreaming can be defined as:

> the process of assessing the implications for women and men of any planned action, including legislation, policies or programmes, in all areas and at all levels. It is a strategy of making women's as well as men's concerns and experiences an integral dimension of the design, implementation, monitoring and evaluation of policies and programs in all political, economic and societal spheres, so that women and men benefit equally and inequality is not perpetuated. The ultimate goal is to achieve gender equality. (Rai, 2003b, p. 16)

Feminist research shows that gender mainstreaming can take the form of an integrationist, agenda-setting, or transformative policy (Jahan, 1995; Lombardo, 2005; Squires, 2005; Verloo, 2005). In its *integrationist* form, it focuses on experts and the bureaucratic creation of evidence-based knowledge in policy-making. Here gender mainstreaming addresses gender issues within existing policy paradigms. In its second, *agenda-setting* form, it entails a focus on the participation, presence, and empowerment of disadvantaged groups via consultation with civil society organizations. This, in turn, involves a reorientation of the agenda rather than merely integrating a gender perspective into an existing agenda (Squires, 2005, p. 371). Yet, some scholars argue that mainstreaming can only adequately address inequality when it pursues a *transformative* agenda by focusing on the structural reproduction of gender inequality and aiming to transform the policy process such that gender bias is eliminated (Beveridge and Nott, 2002, p. 300; Squires, 2005, p. 370).

Theresa Rees suggests that there appear to be very few examples of a gender mainstreaming approach where promoting gender equality is the main policy goal (agenda-setting) in Europe. More often, gender mainstreaming is used as a means of delivering on or is subsumed under another policy (integration) (Rees, 2005). Yet, gender mainstreaming has transformative potential, and its meaning can go beyond the two first forms. Mainstreaming is not simply a neutral tool, a strategy to promote a predetermined end state of 'equality', but a governance concept which addresses the methods and principles which govern the social interaction of political actors (Beveridge and Nott, 2002, p. 302; Shaw, 2002). Thus it has important implications *beyond* the specific policy areas that might be mainstreamed. That is why it also is so important in relation to women's policy agencies.

According to some scholars, women's policy agencies and gender mainstreaming have been tied together from the beginning. Some scholars call women's policy agencies the 'institutional mechanisms for gender mainstreaming' (True and Mintrom, 2001) and the 'key facilitators of the mainstreaming process within and across states' (True, 2003, p. 380). Others use women's policy agencies and gender mainstreaming interchangeably (see Teghtsoonian, 2004), but in this volume we treat the relationship between the two as an empirical issue.

Gender mainstreaming is potentially an important tool for achieving gender equality for the women's policy agencies. It has provided women's policy agencies with further development of such policy instruments as gender-monitoring, checklists, guidelines, interministerial committees, gender awareness training, and integrating gender to national plans (Goetz, 2003, p. 77). Furthermore, the thinking that underpins gender mainstreaming is that gender equality outcomes cannot occur in sideline, peripheral units, but must be addressed in the budget and institutional core of mainstream policies and agencies (Staudt, 2003, p. 41). At best, this results in governmental actors dedicating resources to gender mainstreaming, which in turn frees up women's policy agencies resources for other issues.

Yet, in the worst cases gender mainstreaming can be interpreted as a replacement for specific gender policies and structures (Lombardo, 2005, p. 414; Stratigaki, 2005). When gender equality becomes everybody's responsibility, there appears to be no need for specific structures, such as women's policy agencies. Gender mainstreaming can, indeed, be an excuse for dismantling well-established women's policy machinery. Others point out that it also threatens other gender equality policies, such as legislation, mechanisms, actions to address specific women's interests, research and training (Stratigaki, 2005, p. 168). Some have suggested that even if this does not happen, mainstreaming places new demands upon the limited resources of women's policy agencies (Mazey, 2002, p. 228).

This book aims to provide some empirical findings on the relationship between women's policy agencies and gender mainstreaming. It asks: how is gender mainstreaming interpreted in relation to women's policy agencies in certain political contexts? How does gender mainstreaming affect the position of women's policy agencies? What kind of gender mainstreaming do women's policy agencies in different countries promote? How do the institutional settings of women's policy agencies, including location, budget, expertise, political context, impact on this?

Diversity

Women's policy agencies have to deal increasingly with the second tendency in equality politics – a move towards theorizing equality and diversity. The concern with diversity is closely associated with developments in both feminist theory and practice. The concern with multiple equality 'strands' resonates with the theoretical work on 'intersectionality' that highlights the mutual constitution of the inequalities, such as gender, race and class (Crenshaw, 1998). Notably, diversity itself is nothing new – what is new is that it is increasingly on the political agenda, either as a result of lobbying by gay and lesbian, migrant and disability rights movements (Squires, 2005; Cooper, 2004) or the increasing tensions surrounding multiculturalism, anti-racism, and migration (Yuval-Davis, Anthias and Kofman, 2005). The increasingly fragmented women's movement also exerts pressure on the women's policy agencies to account for gender diversity. Women's policy agencies tend to represent particular voices from within the women's movement, while failing to represent others. Which voices prevail will vary according to the institutional and cultural context (Squires, 2007a, pp. 169–70).

This concern with diversity has made its way both to the corporate sector and to the UN and EU. In the corporate sector, it takes the form of diversity management, which emerged as a central equality strategy at more or less the same time as gender mainstreaming (Squires, 2006). In the UN human rights discourse, intersectionality is increasingly used to account for the intersections of gender and race (Yuval-Davis 2006, p. 196). The EU's equality politics, in turn, has come to entail three strands: ensuring formal anti-discrimination, working towards substantive equality, and managing diversity (Bell, 2003). The EU now recognizes, in Article 13 EC, six key characteristics as requiring measures to combat discrimination: sex, racial and ethnic origin, disability, age, religion and sexual orientation. Class is treated more implicitly, and is embedded in conceptions of poverty (Walby, 2005, p. 462, p. 463).

Judith Squires argues that at a time when EU directives require member states to promote equality in relation to sexual orientation, age, and religion, in addition to race, gender and disability, it simply does not make sense to look at gender equality in isolation from other forms of equality (Squires, 2005, p. 367). The intersecting hierarchies of gender, race, economic class, sexuality, religion, disability and age represent a significant challenge for contemporary equality theorists. Feminist concerns about diversity include the worry that the greater emphasis on for example race and disabilities will be at the expense of gender issues (Mazey, 2002, p. 229). Yet, other contexts provide examples of levelling up gender equality legislation as a result of bringing the six strands together (see Lovenduski, this volume).

Institutionally the focus on diversity can entail a creation of more equality commissions, one for each of the strands, or merging existing equalities bodies into a new body that addresses them all (Walby, 2005, p. 462). The integration of the relevant governmental agencies may entail the dispersal of expertise, loss of contact with the specific constituencies, and a diluted approach, or it might be an opportunity for more efficient deployment of resources and a stronger approach (Walby, 2005, p. 462). In terms of policies feminist scholars have paid attention to the intersections of gender mainstreaming and diversity (Squires, 2005; Beveridge and Nott, 2002, p. 311; Verloo, 2006) and mainstreaming has been related to anti-racism and disability policies (Shaw, 2004). Yet, feminists have inquired whether the equality tools needed by diverse disadvantaged groups are sufficiently similar so that they can share institutional spaces and policies rather than each needing their own (Walby, 2005, p. 462). Mieke Verloo (2006, p. 222) argues in relation to gender, race, class and sexuality that these bases for inequality are so dissimilar that the tools to tackle one form of inequality (for example gender mainstreaming) cannot simply be adapted for other forms.

It is evident that the move towards emphasizing diversity gives rise to a number of questions in relation to women's policy agencies. The following are tackled in this book: How do women's policy agencies in different countries deal with the diversity? Do women's policy agencies give voice to minority women and represent their concerns? What is the relationship between the women's policy agencies and these parts of the women's movement?

This book

The changes discussed above have the potential to produce significant institutional and discursive shifts in the opportunities and structures that women's policy agencies and women's movement actors face. These can provide new opportunities for mobilization or erect new obstacles for their continuation and power. It is highly likely that they have an impact on the institutional arrangements set up to improve women's status, putting women's policy agencies under pressure or providing them with new leverage. They are changing the basic policy discourses about women's status and give rise to new policy instruments, such as gender mainstreaming. Supra-national institutions are encroaching on state capacity, while in many polities national level power and responsibilities have been decentralized, delegated or privatized. Many studies, especially in the gender and welfare state tradition, have already shown how these have impinged on women's social policy (Sainsbury, 1996; 1999; Daly, 2000; Daly and Rake, 2003) and on the capacity of the women's movement to gender public debate and influence the most controversial issues on the political agenda (Haussman and Sauer, forthcoming; Liebert, 2003). However, there has been little work on how these processes are affecting the institutionalized structures of states to develop and implement women's public policy, the mobilization of women's movement actors (see however Banaszak, Beckwith and Rucht, 2003; Sawer, 2003; Haussman and Sauer, forthcoming) and in how far these have already led to significant discursive shifts.

This volume discusses these issues and aims to provide some answers to the questions outlined above through country-specific case studies. The chapters address the issues in the following order. First, they situate the country in the context of wider comparative research on state feminism, welfare state typologies, and social movement research, and identify the most prominent problems in the context that need explaining. Second, they discuss the political context and map some of the most important changes that have taken place in the given country. Third, they address the most significant institutional changes in relation to women's policy agencies and discuss the potential changing policy priorities of these agencies. Finally, the chapters discuss the women's policy agencies' relationship to the women's movement. We have given the authors the liberty to discuss Europeanization, regionalization, the reform of the welfare state, gender diversity and gender mainstreaming within these sections in the order that best fits the chapter in question. The final chapter of the book will draw some comparative conclusions on the findings in the chapters.

Note

1. RNGS is a long-term research project on women's movements and the state, that focuses on the links among women's movements and states through women's policy agencies. For the project's website see http://libarts.wsu.edu/polisci/rngs/ (accessed 21 October 2006).

2
Australia: the Fall of the Femocrat

Marian Sawer

Introduction

During the 1970s there was a conjuncture in Australia of women's move-ment mobilization, a political tradition of 'looking to the state' to promote social justice and the election of reforming governments. Women's move-ment activists promoted the need for government machinery to ensure the needs of women as well as of men were recognized and addressed in all areas of policy. Quite sophisticated policy responses were developed to the new ways in which the women's movement was framing policy prob-lems. The United Nations (UN) drew on the Australian model as an example of good practice and international researchers drew attention to the distinctive ways in which the Australian women's movement had operated through the state to achieve gender-sensitive policy and the funding of feminist services (e.g. Eisenstein, 1996; McBride Stetson and Mazur, 1995).

This chapter will examine the changed political context brought about by the rise of neoliberal discourse and the elevation of market choices over social justice policy objectives. The relationship between the women's movement and state agencies was affected by neoliberal framing of non-government organizations as 'special interests' rather than as legitimate community representatives. Significant changes had also taken place in the women's movement by the 1990s, reducing its visibility. It will be sug-gested that these changes contributed to the perception by governments that they could downgrade and dismantle women's policy machinery with relatively little backlash from the community. The chapter will show how, having been a leader in developing women's policy agencies in the 1970s, Australia led the way in the 1990s in the dismantling of policy machinery and gender analysis within government (Sawer, 2003).

Developing government machinery

Australia took an early lead in the development of women's policy agencies. The first Women's Adviser to the Prime Minister, Elizabeth Reid, appointed in 1973, clearly articulated the need to monitor Cabinet submissions from across government for their impact on women. Then Prime Minister Gough Whitlam concurred with the need for the monitoring of all Cabinet documents for gender implications and for machinery in the Department of Prime Minister and Cabinet to do this 'on a continuing and official basis.' (Whitlam, 1975, p. 1926). Reid helped institutionalize the feminist insight that policy was unlikely to be gender-neutral in its effect, given the different location of men and women in the social and economic division of labour. It could not be assumed that any proposals, whether to do with tax, tariffs or transport would be gender-neutral. Previously public servants had assumed that policies directed at goals such as economic development would benefit women equally with men – a presumption most blatantly displayed in overseas aid policies where development policies targeted at men notoriously increased the workloads of women left behind in the subsistence farming sector.

Reid took her ideas about the need for women to have a presence in the heart of government with her to the UN, where she led the Australian delegation to the First World Conference on Women in Mexico City and chaired the drafting group at the preparatory meeting in New York. Out of these meetings came the World Plan of Action agreed to by UN member states. It aimed to eliminate discrimination and promote the status of women, to integrate women in development and to increase the involvement of women in political life and international peace-making. For these things to happen, it was agreed, there needed to be national machinery to advance the status of women, as well as an international convention on discrimination against women.

The sharing of these ideas at international meetings and at three subsequent UN World Conferences on Women resulted in a global diffusion of policy innovation that was unprecedented in its rapidity (True and Mintrom, 2001, pp. 27–57). During the UN Decade for Women (1976–85), many UN member states established some form of government machinery to advance the status of women – 127 countries had done so by 1985. Australia continued to contribute to international good practice in the 1980s and its invention of women's budget statements became influential internationally under the rubric of gender budgets or gender-responsive budgets. Such mechanisms embody the insight that budgetary measures routinely have gender-differentiated effects, whether in areas such as tariff, tax or industry policy. The Fourth World Conference on Women (the Beijing Conference) in 1995 provided further impetus for the development of machinery to implement 'gender mainstreaming'. By 2004, 165 countries had established government machinery for the advancement of women and early initiatives by countries such as Australia and Canada were being emulated in many parts of the world.

While Australia had been a pioneer in terms of formal machinery for women's policy advice and in areas of government-funded women's services, in terms of social policy it was generally categorized along with Canada, the United Kingdom and the United States as a liberal welfare state regime as contrasted with a more generous social democratic welfare state regime. Nonetheless on employment issues Australia was more like the Scandinavian welfare states, due to a strong centralized industrial relations system based on compulsory arbitration of wages and conditions (O'Connor et al., 1999; Sainsbury, 1994).

In terms of its women's movements, Australia had a strong tradition of non-party women's political advocacy directed primarily towards the state and utilizing repertoires such as the election candidate questionnaire. The national and international role played by the Australian Federation of Women Voters and its affiliates in the earlier part of the twentieth century was later formally handed on to Women's Electoral Lobby (WEL), a 'second-wave' organization. WEL played an important role in the development of Australia's wheel model of policy machinery (hub in the chief policy co-ordinating agency of government, spokes in line departments) and its dissemination to other levels of government. It provided pressure from outside while femocrats, who were often WEL members, set up the new policy co-ordination agencies inside. It helped ensure that the model adopted at the federal level was replicated eventually in all States and Territories.

Some services, originally delivered by WEL and women's liberation groups, such as women's information services, became innovative forms of government service delivery, while others such as refuges, rape crisis and women's health and women's legal centres became government-funded services run by collectives or, increasingly, semi-collective organizations. In the area of violence against women, for example, a study of 36 democracies found that Australia and Canada had the most comprehensive policy responses due to the conjuncture of strong women's movements and effective women's policy machinery within government (Weldon, 2002a, Ch. 6).

Australia's federal system meant when political opportunities contracted at one level of government they might expand at another and regular inter-governmental meetings of women's advisers were able to maintain some momentum and pressure on their respective governments. In this way, the device of requiring gender analysis of all Budgetary allocations (Women's Budget Statements) was spread to all jurisdictions after being pioneered at the federal level in 1984. Similarly women's movement activists attempted to 'make use of the political leverage afforded by multi-layered government, switching their focus between state and federal arenas', as opportunities arose (Chappell, 2002, p. 159). By the 1990s, however, political opportunities were shrinking in most jurisdictions due to major discursive shifts; neoliberalism had increased its influence, even over Labor governments. The changed political context made the pursuit of collective goals through social action seem increasingly elusive.

By the 1990s the women's movement was also becoming less visible and less effective as a political base for feminist initiatives in government (RSSS, 1998). The reduced level of public protest and media coverage led in turn to loss of interest by governments in courting the women's movement and less influence for women's advocacy organizations. Women's movement interventions did continue, but had little impact in stemming the tide of labour-market deregulation, social security 'reform' and inadequate funding of human services.

Discursive shifts

In the early 1970s Australia enjoyed an unusually favourable political opportunity structure for new social movements and their policy engagement with the state. Governments responded to new discourses naming new policy problems and also recruited social movement actors with expertise in these new policy areas. At the same time, the seeds of a less favourable discursive environment were being sown. A speaking tour by free market economist Milton Friedman in 1975 was to inspire new free-market think tanks and to radicalize older ones. They had ready access to the Murdoch press (News Corporation), which was to achieve a dominant position in the Australian metropolitan newspaper market. The Murdoch press played a central role in the dissemination of neoliberal discourses and the leaders of political parties feared its scorn for those who held up market reforms. The Murdoch press also led the way in engaging anti-feminist columnists who reproduced American frames about feminists being out-of-touch elitists who ignored the preferences of the majority of women.

By the 1990s, ruling concepts had become those of 'competition' (reducing the role of the public sector, putting services out to competitive tender and marketizing public utilities) and 'micro-economic reform' (reducing the role of unions and of the centralized wage-fixing system). The welfare state was framed as discouraging competitiveness and encouraging welfare dependency, particularly among groups such as sole parents. In 1995 the Liberal Leader and future Prime Minister, John Howard, summarized the programme he would bring to government the following year as 'governing for the mainstream' (Howard, 1995). There would be an end to the attempts to ensure equal opportunity by accommodating difference, now regarded as 'special treatment of special interests' at the expense of the mainstream (see below). Over the next decade governing for the mainstream was to mean demoting the Office for Multicultural Affairs from the Department of Prime Minister and Cabinet, abolishing the Aboriginal and Torres Strait Islander Commission and finally demoting the Office for the Status of Women.

In general, those who promoted and defended the welfare state and its gender equality initiatives were now framed as 'new class elites' or university-educated radicals with a vested interest in the expansion of the public sector. Feminists who campaigned for equal opportunity were depicted as interested in well-paid jobs administering equal opportunity legislation and programmes. They had pursued an expansion of publicly provided community services and labour market programmes, at the expense of ordinary taxpayers and business. Feminists were seeking to do better out of the state than they could out of marriage or the market. But not only were they self-interested, it was also claimed that they had contempt for ordinary women (Sawer, 2007).

Such populist framing of those who believed in the role of the public sector to address gendered and market inequalities was reinforced by public choice analysis of the motivation of public interest groups. Public choice theory, developed by American economists in the 1950s and 60s, promoted the idea that all institutions were driven by the same utility maximizing motives as market individuals (Buchanan and Tullock, 1962; Niskanen, 1971; Shaw, 2002). Hence public-interest groups were really 'special interests' – a discourse that was adopted by influential elements in the Labor Party in the 1990s, as well as by the conservative parties.

One of the most dramatic impacts of public choice discourse has been to delegitimize the advocacy work of public interest groups. Whereas operational funding was previously made available to strengthen 'weak voices' in policy debate and to balance the influence of powerful business and professional interests, this is now framed as privileging various 'industries' that have a vested interest in expanding the welfare state – whether the poverty industry, the multicultural industry, the Aboriginal industry or the feminist industry.

Operational funding for non-government organizations (NGOs) representing disadvantaged sections of the community has been increasingly replaced by project-funding, tied to competitive tendering for service provision with no scope for representational or advocacy work. Moreover, funding contracts now contain clauses requiring advance notice to government of media activity and NGOs seen to be representing constituencies outside the mainstream and/or critical of government have been defunded (Maddison et al., 2004).

Changes in the international opportunity structure

While Australia does not belong to a regional body with strong human rights norms, such as the European Union, it has historically played an active role within the UN human rights system. Australian governments have put considerable investment into multilateral diplomacy, seeing this as a significant way to augment what would otherwise be a very modest place in world affairs. Reputation is an important resource in multilateral work and Australian initiatives on the status of women were seen as contributing to this reputation. The desire of Australian governments to be regarded as a significant player in international human rights arenas and to maintain a reputation as a good international citizen created the potential for a 'politics of embarrassment' on the part of social movements. Indigenous NGOs, in particular, effectively used such politics of embarrassment to advance domestic claims.

For its part, the Australian women's movement had always seen itself as part of an international movement using international forums to advance the claims of women. Through international affiliates, such the International Alliance of Women, the International Council of Women or the Women's International League of Peace and Freedom, Australian women's organizations engaged with the League of Nations and the UN. Such multilateral organizations were seen as playing a vital standard-setting role on status of women issues and as a way to push forward the agenda as well as to provide domestic leverage (Sawer, 1999, pp. 217–28).

For example, feminist Jessie Street, a member of the Australian delegation to the founding conference of the UN, played an important role in ensuring the UN Charter included equality provisions and was also a moving force in the establishment of the UN Commission on the Status of Women. Later, the work of the Commission in preparing the UN Women's Convention (CEDAW) provided a Constitutional basis for the Australian government to enact sex discrimination legislation. Although the Australian federal government did not have a human rights power, it did have an external affairs power and could sign up to international treaties, such as the UN Women's Convention, which then gave it the capacity to enact domestic legislation.

As we have seen, some 30 years later Elizabeth Reid played an equally significant role in the preparation of the World Plan of Action adopted by the first UN Women's Conference. Such international instruments and the reporting processes associated with them helped provide impetus for the preparation of domestic plans of action and also to legitimize the kind of women's policy machinery Australia had been developing. Justice Elizabeth Evatt, as chair of CEDAW, was also important in extending the jurisprudence of the Women's Convention to cover violence against women, and in encouraging the participation of women's NGOs in the reporting process.

The opportunities presented in the past to promote the status of women via official, expert or NGO activity in UN forums has shrunk dramatically over the past decade. The Australian government has prioritized its alliance with the United States and followed the latter rather than the UN in a range of areas, including support for the Iraq War (2003–). The Australian government has distanced itself from the UN human rights system, so the latter no longer provides effective leverage domestically. In particular, the Howard government (1996–) has reacted sharply to criticisms by UN human rights committees of its treatment of asylum seekers and of Indigenous Australians. In September 2000, the Australian Foreign Minster told the UN General Assembly that treaty committees were losing credibility because they paid too much attention to NGO submissions and insufficient to the views of democratically elected governments.[1] (As part of the distancing of itself from the UN human rights system, Australia has refused to sign or ratify the Optional Protocol to CEDAW, which establishes an individual complaints procedure, despite having taken a prominent role in its drafting. The Australian government ignored the sustained protests from a broad spectrum of women's organizations over this.

Changes in public sector philosophy: the new public management

The discursive shifts over the decade since 1996 have made policy influence increasingly difficult for a women's movement oriented to looking to the state to achieve social justice. Moreover the importation of private sector models of governance into the public sector (the new public management) created structural problems for the kind of institutional mechanisms that had been developed to promote gender equity.

The consequences have included the devaluation of 'in-house' policy expertise of all kinds, including gender expertise, in favour of management skills and contracting out. Without gender expertise, it is difficult to evaluate policy at source for gender impact or to audit the gender outcomes of government activity. Accountability through performance agreements between chief executive officers and ministers, without independent and expert scrutiny, is unlikely to be effective.

Along with contracting out has come increased volatility of bureaucratic structures and a continuous change environment. Within this environment, and with the associated loss of corporate memory, it is difficult to sustain the structures needed for long-term projects, such as advancing gender equality. Moreover, within the commercial product format and outcomes focus associated with NPM there is a devaluing of process, including the kind of consultative policy processes required for the empowerment of women. This outcomes focus reinforces the public choice distrust of non-government organizations and consultative processes as leading to policy capture by sectoral interests (Teghtsoonian, 2004, pp. 267–84).

Another problem arising from NPM is the introduction of compulsory competitive tendering processes in all areas of service provision. The tendering process makes little room for policy advocacy and community education functions associated with second-wave women's services, let alone the kind of democratic structures intended to achieve women's empowerment. NPM is also at odds with the organizational philosophy of services provided from within government, such as the women's information services that exist in all Australian jurisdictions. The women's information services allow women to talk until they reach the real question that is of concern to them, rather than trying to reach preset quantitative targets.

Contesting women's gains: the men's rights movement

Another change in the political context in the decade since 1995 has been the rise of a very vocal men's rights movement seeking to roll back the changes in gender relations that flowed from second-wave feminism. The rise of this movement in the 1990s may have been in part an unanticipated consequence of femocrat compromises within government. There had been extensive concern by femocrats over the poverty of sole parents and the unwillingness of politicians to act on this issue. Politicians perceived sole parents as an electorally unpopular group and rejected suggestions of community education campaigns to turn such attitudes around.

In the face of reluctance to use public money to address the poverty of sole parents, one senior femocrat devised a new child support system, deriving from a scheme in Wisconsin. It involved the Tax Office collecting child support from non-custodial parents, the amount being determined by a formula based on capacity to pay. This scheme was controversial within the women's movement because it maintained a financial relationship with former partners but it did increase the level of payments to many sole parents. What was not anticipated was the level of resentment over this scheme, which helped fuel a new men's rights movement. The arrival of the Internet meant instant access by activists to the discourses found on US men's rights websites.

Groups appeared such as 'Dads Against Discrimination' (also found in Canada and the USA), the Men's Rights Agency, Equality for Fathers and Men's Rights Confraternity. The older Lone Fathers Association Australia achieved a new prominence. These groups shared the belief that feminists had captured state power and were responsible for policies and legislation victimizing men (Kaye and Tolmie, 1998, pp. 162–94). The child support formula was a central concern, but there was also resentment over access and other aspects of family law and over domestic violence programmes that focused on men as perpetrators. The men's rights movement positions men as the new victims of feminist elites and of gender bias in the state.

The men's rights movement has been much more successful over the past decade in mobilizing letter-writing campaigns and lobbying on issues such as child support and family law than today's women's movement. Men's groups and non-custodial parents generated around two-thirds of submissions to an Australian parliamentary inquiry into family law and child support (Keebaugh, 2003, p. 175). Moreover, the men's rights movement encountered a newly favourable political opportunity structure with the election of the conservative Howard government in 1996. The newly-elected government gave considerable access to men's rights groups and acted on many of their demands.

Dismantling the national machinery

At the federal level in Australia the Howard government's commitment to 'governing for the mainstream' meant a commitment to eliminate feminist influence and gender analysis within government. At first the Prime Minister moved relatively cautiously, waiting to see the extent of community reaction to the dismantling of state feminism. In his first year in government, he cut the budget of the Human Rights and Equal Opportunity Commission by 40 per cent and the budget of the Office of the Status of Women by a similar amount. He left the position of Sex Discrimination Commissioner unfilled for 14 months, eventually making an appointment after considerable pressure from women in his own party. At the same time his government began quietly abolishing women's units across all portfolios.

The venerable Women's Bureau in the employment portfolio, in existence since 1963, disappeared in 1997 (Russell and Sawer, 1999, pp. 362–75). Policy units across government, established in the 1970s and 1980s, soon suffered the same fate. Units that disappeared in the latter half of the 1990s included the Office of Indigenous Women, the Migrant Women's Advisor, the Gender and Curriculum Unit, the Equal Pay Unit, the Work and Family Unit, the Women's Health Unit, the Women's Sport Unit and the Women's Policy Unit in Social Security. As one researcher trying to investigate gender mainstreaming in Australia commented: 'Femocrat tools have been confiscated and any survivors are left to hide "Anne Frank like" within mainstream departmental units' (Donaghy, 2006, p. 1).

Corresponding inter-governmental bodies, such as the Women's Subcommittee of the Australian Health Ministers Advisory Committee, were also disposed of. Women's health activists did, however, have a win in 2005 with the achievement of women-specific indicators in Commonwealth/State funding agreements, which helped protect State-based women's health services. The two federal rural women's units established in the 1990s, which briefly flourished under the protection of the Nationals, the rural-based partner in the Coalition Government, had been mainstreamed by 2004, although a Regional Women's Advisory Council continued. Targeted programmes also disappeared, such as the Women's Programme of the Australian Film Commission (1976–99) and the weekly Women Out Loud Programme on Radio National (1975–98).

In the Australian context of 'governing for the mainstream', the new international language of gender mainstreaming, promoted by the Beijing Platform for Action, was seized upon to legitimate the dismantling of units with expertise in promoting equal opportunity for women and designated groups (Bacchi and Eveline, 2003, pp. 98–118). This was the opposite of the intent of this language and, ironically, while this dismantling was taking place at home, overseas the Office of the Status of Women was taking a leading role in the setting up of a gender integration framework in the Asia Pacific Economic Community (APEC). Some other minor gains occurred in the international area: Australia's development assistance agency (AusAID) recreated a Health, Population and Gender section in 2005 and the following year gender equality was reinstated as a core principle of the aid programme, along with renewed emphasis on health and education.

'Gender mainstreaming', as promoted by the UN, was meant to foster a structural approach comparable to the wheel model and gender budgeting exercises pioneered in Australia. In the second half of the 1990s, however, it became the rationale for eliminating such structures and processes and dropping whole-of-government co-ordinating functions such as the preparation of women's budget statements. Gender mainstreaming became the reason to undo mainstreaming mechanisms and to focus on a few 'special initiatives', particularly in the area of violence against women. Although responsibility for gender mainstreaming was now supposed to inhere in all officers, little capacity building or training was provided for the purpose of fostering gender expertise among those with these new responsibilities (Donaghy, 2006, p. 1).

In 2004, the Office of the Status of Women, in existence since 1974 and the hub of Australia's national machinery, was demoted from the Department of Prime Minister and Cabinet and relocated as 'The Office for Women' in the Department of Family and Community Services. This move, from the main co-ordinating arm of government, into a line department where women could be subsumed under family policy and programmes, was a repudiation of Australia's historic model of women's policy. It followed the abolition of the Department of Women by the New South Wales State (Labor) government earlier in the year. It is thought that the lack of any significant community protest at State level encouraged the federal government to make its move. While in 2006 there was still a staff of about 50 in the Office, many were involved with programme delivery in areas such as women's safety (domestic violence and sexual assault) rather than with cross-sectoral policy monitoring. The femocrat who headed the federal Office at the height of its powers, Dr Anne Summers, published a book with the eloquent title, *The End of Equality*, charting the dismantling of feminist initiatives within the federal government and the retreat from equality objectives (Summers, 2003).

The demotion of the Office of the Status of Women came immediately after a federal election where the government failed to press release its women's policy, which instead crept quietly onto the party website in the last week of the campaign. Labor did launch a women's policy, but without any commitment to the Office.[2] Gender-disaggregated data on government performance has become much more difficult to obtain and gender expertise has become increasingly rare in government. In 2006 CEDAW regretted the lack of sufficient statistical data disaggregated by sex and ethnicity in the combined fourth and fifth periodic report of Australia and requested that the next periodic report include adequate statistical data and analysis disaggregated by sex, ethnicity and disability (CEDAW,

2006, paras 12 and 16). Analysis of the distributive outcomes of government policy is generally unwelcome. Changes have been made to child support formulae without any prior modelling of the effects on sole parent poverty. More and more contradictions emerge in the realm of social policy. 'Dependency' is seen as a major social problem, yet the dependency of married women is actively encouraged through tax and transfer policies and can lead overnight to the wrong kind of dependency. Increased dependency on the whims of employers is encouraged through labour market deregulation and removal of unfair dismissal protections but is never named as such.

Government attempts to weaken the Sex Discrimination Act, including an exemption to allow the advertising of men-only teachers' scholarships (2004), were at first defeated because it lacked control over the Australian Senate. When the government gained control of both Houses in 2005 it foreshadowed renewed amendments to the Act. The bleak picture at national level should be qualified by considering some important initiatives still occurring at the sub-national level. For example, in late 2005 the South Australian government announced an upgrade of its women's policy machinery and the creation of new Inter-Ministerial Council on Women's Issues. The achievement of equality between South Australian women and men was described as a fourth plank of the Labor government's agenda, along with economic development, social inclusion and environmental sustainability (Key, 2005). The Australian Capital Territory is another jurisdiction where women's policy machinery was upgraded under the Stanhope government elected in 2001 and a Select Committee on the Status of Women established.

Moreover some inter-governmental mechanisms continue, such as the quarterly meetings of women's advisers from the nine Australian jurisdictions and from New Zealand. These women's advisers meetings, held since the 1970s, have been an important forum for sharing of best practice. Annual Ministerial Conferences also continue, bringing together ministers with responsibility for the status of women in the same ten jurisdictions. Nonetheless, some of the opportunities previously afforded by 'multilevel games' have been constrained by increased centralization of power in the hands of the federal government.

Policy and policy contestation

The changes in the political context described above, and particularly the new dominance of neoliberal discourse greatly constrained the possibilities for effective feminist policy interventions. I shall take only two of many possible examples here, those of industrial relations and domestic violence. The dismantling of Australia's historic system of centralized wage fixing was finalized with the federal government's Work Choices legislation of 2005. It has brought an end to further progress towards equal pay and arbitrated work/family provisions, at least for the time being. Historically wages and conditions in Australia have been determined by tribunals handing down legally enforceable awards. Decisions by such tribunals on issues such as equal pay or maternity leave have flowed on fairly rapidly through Federal and State awards. This has been of significant benefit to women workers, who characteristically have had less negotiating muscle than male workers because of the nature of their employment and the kind of industries in which they have been located.

Moves to create a more 'flexible' labour market were initiated under a federal labour government with the adoption of the 'enterprise bargaining principle' in 1991. This was strongly contested by feminists inside and outside government but feminist interventions before the Industrial Relations Commission resulted only in delay on grounds of concern over gender impact, and did not prevent its introduction some months later. From 1996 the Howard conservative government was intent on much more radical deregulation of the labour market and some resistance did come from State Labor governments. Women's policy units within State governments produced analysis showing the serious implications for women, including vulnerable groups such as migrant women, of individualized wage bargaining and deregulation of conditions of employment. These concerns were taken up by ministers attending the 2005 Commonwealth, State, Territory and New Zealand Ministers' Conference on the Status of Women but the Conference Communiqué simply noted 'there would not be agreement between the Australian Government and the State and Territory Ministers on this issue' (MINCO, 2005, p. 2).

At the federal level women's units dealing with labour market and industrial relations issues were abolished by the Howard government and there was no possibility of policy resistance from within government. Furthermore, the national secretariats through which women's NGOs were now funded (see below) were informed by the Office of Women in 2005 that if they used their government grant money to commission modelling of the consequences for women of the intersection of labour market deregulation and changes to sole parent and disability pensions they would forfeit the money. It was made clear to them that women's NGOs were being funded to undertake consultations with women but not to undertake research. Previously gender analysis of policy would have been commissioned by women's units within government, but now even the commissioning of such analysis by NGOs was being impeded (in the event it was funded by other means).

Ironically, a final test case on parental leave provisions was decided by the Australian Industrial Relations Commission (AIRC) in 2005 only months before the AIRC was stripped of its powers. There were very substantial submissions by WEL and by the Human Rights and Equal Opportunity Commission (HREOC) to the test case and the AIRC granted new rights relating to the length of unpaid parental leave and return on a part-time basis, based on UK provisions. The significance of the HREOC intervention underlined how significant the statutory independence of human rights bodies had become when internal women's policy agencies were powerless to advocate on behalf of women. In 2006 HREOC undertook joint work with two women's NGOs, the National Foundation for Australian Women and WEL on equal pay (WISER, 2006), an issue it was no longer possible to research or pursue within the federal government.

The advantages of statutory bodies such as human rights agencies is their relative independence from government and their public voice, creating the potential to bring pressure on government from outside. A recent example of this in Australia was the high-profile campaign (2002–04) for paid maternity leave by the Commonwealth Sex Discrimination Commissioner, in the context of an extremely conservative Commonwealth government. While mechanisms within government were unable to promote this issue, the statutory independence of the Sex Discrimination Commissioner (and her media skills) and the creation of alliances with bodies such as the Australian Council of Trade Unions helped build momentum. The outcome was not paid maternity leave in a form meeting International Labour Organization (ILO) Convention 183 standards but a compromise in the form of a universal maternity payment. Thanks to the rise of populist discourse paid maternity leave for women in the workforce was framed by government as discriminating against women who were full-time homemakers.

While it might be expected that conservative governments would attempt to deregulate the labour market and dismantle requirements for equal pay and family-friendly workplaces, another development over the past decade could not have been so easily anticipated. Generally during the past three decades the election of conservative governments has seen the displacement of policies requiring intervention in the labour market (equal pay) or public expenditure on community services (such as childcare) and a prioritizing of themes such as 'small government' and law and order. Femocrats were nonetheless able to tailor the issue of domestic violence to fit conservative themes by emphasizing its cost to the economy and its lawless character.

The Howard government began in the way that might have been anti-cipated, dismantling women's labour market programmes but announc-ing, in 1997, a large new programme called 'Partnerships against Domestic Violence'. While the federal government does not have juris-diction in the area of the criminal law and domestic violence, it does fund refuges and other services in conjunction with the States and Territories and has played a role in national community education campaigns since 1986. The Partnerships programme was to fund pilot projects relating to the prevention of domestic violence, including work with perpetrators, and to facilitate the dissemination of best practice information. From 2001 another fairly large programme was funded – the National Initiative to Combat Sexual Assault. In 2005 new funding of AUD 75 million was announced for the 'Women's Safety Agenda', building on the previous domestic violence and sexual assault programmes.

While these new programmes funded some worthwhile projects, they were not immune to the increasingly conservative drift of the government. For example, in 2003 the federal government 'borrowed' AUD 10 million from its domestic violence and sexual assault programmes to pay for a con-troversial anti-terrorism campaign involving the mailing out of fridge mag-nets urging Australians to be 'alert but not alarmed'.

Men's rights groups were also exercising increased influence over the nature of the federal government's domestic violence education pro-grammes. Groups such as the Men's Rights Agency vociferously opposed the portrayal of men as the perpetrators of domestic violence and refused to acknowledge the legitimacy of any campaigns that did not start from the premise that women were equally as violent as men. They claimed vic-tory when a 'No respect, no relationship' government advertising campaign was cancelled just before Christmas 2003 but still complained when a modified 'Australia Says No' campaign was launched the following year.

The influence of the men's rights movement was such that only the government's 'preferred service providers' and no women's services were permitted to tender for the helpline and referral service associated with the 'Australia Says No' campaign. Existing domestic violence referral services around Australia were bypassed. This is indicative of the current freezing out from policy access of women's services and their peak bodies such as the Women's Emergency Services Network (WESNET). Despite the fears of men's rights groups, feminist peak bodies were not consulted in the development of federal domestic violence awareness programmes such as 'Australia Says No'.

Another indication of men's rights influence over policy came with the attempted suppression by government of a 2004 report detailing the cost of domestic violence to the economy. Although commissioned by the Office of the Status of Women from one of the government's preferred economic consultants, the report did not conform to the men's rights movement's insistence (see above) that women were just as violent as men. It found that the cost to the economy of domestic violence was AUD 8.1 billion and that 98 per cent of perpetrators were male. It was only eventually released as a result of a successful Freedom of Information (FOI) application from the *Australian* newspaper.

In 2006 the federal government's 1996 Women's Safety Survey was repeated, but this time as the 'Personal Safety Survey'. The executive summary accompanying it included misleading figures that appeared to endorse the views of the men's rights movement that similar proportions of men and women were assaulted by opposite-sex partners. It claimed that '38 per cent of women were physically assaulted by their male current or previous partner compared to 27 per cent of men who were physically assaulted by their female current or previous partner'. These figures were immediately seized upon by men's rights activists as killing off feminist myths about violence. In fact the figures referred only to the proportion of assaults by an opposite-sex perpetrator that were by a partner, and relatively few assaults on men are by an opposite-sex perpetrator. The more general findings were that 31 per cent of women who had been physically assaulted in the previous 12 months had been assaulted by a current or previous male partner while 4.4 per cent of men who had been physically assaulted had been assaulted by a female partner (Flood, 2006).

Despite the facts of domestic violence, the men's rights movement, with the support of the federal government in particular, has had a significant effect on community opinion. A survey commissioned by the Labor government of Victoria showed that between the Women's Safety Survey of 1996 and the Personal Safety Survey of 2006, the proportion of those believing that women were equally likely as men to violently assault their partner had risen from 9 to 20 per cent (AAP, 2006). So even in a policy area where conservative governments might have been expected to do well, the policy access provided by politicians to the men's right's movement has impeded the efforts of remaining feminists within government.

Women's policy agencies and the women's movement: changing directions

While policy agencies were set up as a result of women's movement demands, they also became an important source of funding programmes to sustain women's advocacy organizations. Australia has often provided operational funding to strengthen weak voices in policy debate and to ensure representation of groups whose lives are significantly impacted by government policy. This encouraged increased diversity in the organized women's movement as funding programmes initiated by femocrats enabled new groups of women to achieve their own national peak organizations, including immigrant women[3] and women with disabilities. These groups had suffered from lack of focus on their issues by 'mainstream' ethnic community organizations or disability organizations and the lack of understanding they experienced in women's movement organizations. Women's grants programmes under federal Labor governments from the 1980s helped foster peak bodies for new groups of women, from women with disabilities to Muslim women, from sex workers to immigrant women and lesbians. Increased organizational diversity in the women's movement enriched debates over subjects ranging from prostitution and trafficking to Islamic dress codes. By 2003 the Office of the Status of Women was recording the presence of 92 national women's organizations in Australia. There was less success in achieving a national body to represent Indigenous women due to localized loyalties within Indigenous communities. A number of efforts eventually ran into the ground, despite increased policy engagement of Indigenous women with health and violence issues.

There was also increased specialization of advocacy organizations as bodies such as women's legal services, women's emergency services, sexual assault services and women's health services all developed their own peak advocacy bodies supported by government. Some of these represented very large numbers of services, for example the Women's Emergency Services Network represented 350 government-funded women's services in 1999. This diverse constellation of movement organizations had varying levels of access to government, often depending on its political complexion. Labor governments characteristically provided more access for community (non-business) groups, but both Labor and Conservative governments had funded a broad spectrum of advocacy organizations.

The Howard government, however, was committed to diminishing the influence of 'special interests' on policy or at least of some 'special interests'. It proceeded cautiously at first, given the well-accepted role of such bodies in providing 'consumer input' into the policy process. Increasing control was exercised, however, over government/NGO relations. Operational funding for women's advocacy organizations was continued at first, along with ministerial round-tables for consultation purposes. The Howard Government even encouraged the creation of some new advocacy bodies, such the Australasian Council of Women and Policing.

A significant change, however, occurred in relations between women's advocacy organizations and the Office of the Status of Women in 1999, after the Howard government had been successfully returned to office. The programme that had provided operational funding for organizations representing diverse communities of women was abolished. In its place, three 'national secretariats' were funded, to convey women's views to government. Loosely, these were to represent young women, older women and businesswomen. National women's organizations objected that this corporatization of women's representation to government meant: 'a loss of pluralism and diversity in the voices being heard by government. In particular the most disadvantaged groups have the right to autonomy of voice, for example women from non-English Speaking Backgrounds, Indigenous women and women with special needs' (Australian Women's Organisations Conference, 2001). This view was reiterated in the 2005 NGO Shadow Report on CEDAW implementation. This Report, endorsed by over 100 organizations, called for the addition of national women's secretariats specifically representing Indigenous women and women from migrant and refugee backgrounds (Women's Rights Action Network Australia, 2005, p. 7).

One constituency that mobilized later than city-based women was the women in agriculture movement, achieving a belated presence within the federal government, with the establishment of a Rural Women's Unit in 1995 (Pini et al., 2007). The election of a coalition government including a rural-based party saw the addition of a 'Women in Rural Industries' unit, as well as the creation of a Regional Women's Advisory Council. Moreover, when the new corporatized structure for women's movement interface with the federal government was created in 1999, rural women were the only group who were successful in their lobbying over lack of representation, thanks to their political clout. A fourth national secretariat serving a National Rural Women's Coalition was funded in 2002 and 2005.

But while farmwomen had made a successful claim on the state, success was very much on the government's terms as with the other sectors. The operational funding for women's secretariats was not intended to give them public voice – there was to be no public comment without prior notice to government and, as was made clear from 2005, neither was any of the money to be spent on researching the gender impact of government policy. So while women's units in government were being closed down, together with their capacity to commission research into gender impact of policy, so there was a tightening of control over non-government women's groups and their capacity to take over such research.

Indigenous women continued to lack a national organization and, for example, an individual Indigenous woman was included along with organizational representatives of farm women and others in the Rural Women's Coalition. Although the annual Ministerial Conferences of Ministers responsible for the status of women was preceded by an Indigenous Women's Gathering, different Indigenous women attended each year and did not represent Indigenous organizations.

The changing relationship between women's movement actors and government policy agencies was reflected in the nature of the latter's websites. While there is international interest in using information technology more effectively to facilitate the interface between government and the community, this is very much a one-way process for government gender units. While NGO websites include links to government gender units, this is rarely reciprocated. The latter are also notable for the absence of interactive components whereby women in the community can convey their views to government – apart from 'customer' surveys on the actual design of the website!

The year 1999 not only signalled a shift to a corporatized relationship between surviving women's policy agencies and the women's movement, but also another new departure. The federal government announced two years operational funding for the Lone Fathers Association Australia, on the basis that it was needed to address the gender imbalance in policy development. Supposedly feminists had enjoyed too much influence over policy. The concurrent defunding of the National Council for Single Mothers and their Children was only reversed after extensive public outcry. In the same year the Lone Fathers Association received funding from the ACT government for a men's refuge for men who were the victims of relationship break-up. Despite the restored funding of the National Council for Single Mothers, lone fathers gained much more access to government than single mothers and obtained substantial changes to the Child Support Scheme, the Family Law Act and family tax benefits, favouring non-custodial parents. These changes reflect the beliefs of the men's right movement that the pendulum had swung too far in favour of women.

The number of national women's organizations recorded by the Office of the Status of Women continued to increase, rising from 50 in 1998 to 92 in 2003. Increased diversity and specialization did not necessarily weaken the movement and NGOs undertook new coalition-building activities, assisted by the availability of new information and communication technologies. The Coalition of Participating Organizations of Women (CAPOW!), created in 1992, used a fortnightly fax-stream to disseminate information about threats and opportunities and to share policy submissions. It lost its government funding, however, as punishment for co-ordinating a critical NGO CEDAW shadow report in 1997. It was replaced by the cheaper Pamelas-List, which networked national women's organizations by email and which still continues. Another electronic initiative, designed to link activists, academic policy experts and feminists in government, was Ausfem-Polnet, a moderated electronic list created in 1996. By 2003 it had some 900 subscribers. Vigorous debates were conducted on Ausfem-Polnet on issues such as prostitution and trafficking, on which there very different positions among women's movement actors (Sullivan, 2004). Such virtual feminist policy communities were no substitute, however for the kind of media visibility and electoral pressure provided by the women's movement in the 1970s.

Conclusion

The fall of the Australian femocrat is a telling example of the vulnerability of feminist gains within reconfiguring states. The policy impact created by the combination of a visible women's movement, receptive political parties and effective women's policy agencies within government had largely dissipated by the mid-1990s. Multiple institutional and discursive shifts created a hostile environment for feminist advocacy either outside or inside government. Changes in the political opportunity structure explored in this chapter have included the shift in the dominant discourse away from an equal opportunity discourse legitimizing the welfare state towards discourses of choice prioritizing market freedoms. This discursive shift helped demobilize gender identity, replacing collective identities with the construct of the individual as author of their own choices, unconstrained by inequalities of power or expectations. This shift to neoliberal discourses also brought in its wake the framing of feminists as members of a self-interested elite, seeking to perpetuate an interventionist welfare state at the expense of ordinary taxpayers. A newly visible men's rights movement was able to position men as victims of state feminism – denied their rights as fathers but made to pay nonetheless.

These discursive shifts were accompanied by major institutional changes, reinforced by the election of a federal government dedicated to 'governing for the mainstream' and eliminating the influence of special interests such as the feminist, multicultural, Indigenous or poverty industries. 'Mainstreaming' carried away almost all women's policy agencies or programmes at the federal level. Other significant changes in the opportunity structure included the decreased domestic influence of the UN human rights regime as the Australian government became more resistant to the politics of embarrassment and more oriented to the international positions adopted by the United States.

At the sub-national level of the federal system, however, some Labor governments provided a less hostile environment for the survival of gender equity initiatives, due in part to feminist pressure within the Labor Party. This was not uniform and, as we have seen, 2004 was marked not only by the demotion of the federal Office of the Status of Women but also by the abolition of the Department for Women in NSW. While discursive and institutional changes have created a difficult context for women's policy agencies, it is changes in the women's movement that have contributed most directly to the fall of the femocrat. Governments have found they can abolish agencies without widespread community protest and the fear of electoral backlash. As an early femocrat once said, 'Give me first my political base and I shall give you the keys to the kingdom of heaven'. Without that base, even the best thought-out feminist strategies for identifying opportunities within the changing architecture of politics are unlikely to be successful.

Acknowledgements

My thanks to Gwen Gray for her extremely insightful and helpful comments on this chapter and to the editors.

Notes

1. Foreshadowed by a Joint Media Release of the Minister for Foreign Affairs and Trade and the Attorney-General FA97, 29 August 2000.
2. Contrary to the party platform, which included a commitment to strengthen the Office.
3. Since the 1970s Australia has had policies directed to ensuring access and equity for immigrants from non-English speaking backgrounds (NESB) but more recently the term 'from culturally and linguistically diverse backgrounds' (CALD) has become the official term for this equity target group.

3
What Happened to the Model Student? Austrian State Feminism since the 1990s[1]

Birgit Sauer

Austria is characterized by a conservative welfare regime (Esping Andersen, 1990) with a dominant male breadwinner model (Sainsbury, 1996). Although social democratic governments since the early 1970s tried to 'individualize' women by integrating them in the labour market, the gendered division of labour did not change significantly. Until now, women have higher unemployment rates, the gender-hierarchical work segregation is strong, female part-time employment is high and the gender wage gap is still huge. Also, the number of public child-care facilities is rather low. In the ranking of the World Economic Forum of 2005, for instance, Austria attained place 28 out of 58 countries, showing a rather poor performance in educational attainment and economic participation and opportunities of women (Lopez-Claros/Zahidi, 2005, p. 8).

The causes for the slow transformation of the conservative gender regime are located in the structure of the political system. Austrian corporatism with its particularly intensive cooperation of social partnership, parties and the bureaucracy is a fortified structure of 'male-bonding' (Appelt, 1995). This setting makes the substantive representation of women in policy processes concerning the labour market and social security especially difficult, even though the quantitative political representation of women in elected bodies increased. From 1994 to 2005 the share of female ministers in government has been raised from 22.7 per cent to 50 per cent and the percentage of women in parliament from 21.9 per cent to 32.8 per cent (Steininger, 2006, pp. 254–6).

This rather women-unfriendly picture is in contrast to other research, which showed that since the 1970s the Austrian women's movement has been successful in bringing in women and movement goals into women's policy processes and to gender policy debates (Köpl, 2001; 2005; Sauer, 2004). Women's policy agencies have been established on the national,

on federal and community levels which cooperated with women's movement groups and which mediated between movement demands and state
apparatus.

The 1990s especially were characterized by successes of the women's
movement. In 1993 an equal opportunity law for the public service with
a 40 per cent quota system came into force and the major parties in the
Austrian parliament adopted quotas for election lists. Moreover, Austria
has a rather liberal abortion law and laws on prostitution and trafficking
in women have been amended in order to protect women. And in 1996
Austria was the first European country to pass a law against domestic
violence, which allows the police to expel the perpetrator from the common apartment or house and requires him to submit to anti-violence
counselling (Dearing and Haller, 2000). Finally, in 1998 the Austrian
constitution was amended with a paragraph on affirmative action due to
EU requirements.

These successes are to a large part due to the stabilization, upgrading
and expansion of the federal women's ministry and the expansion of
women's policy agencies to the provincial and community levels since
the beginning of the 1990s. The social democratic ministers for women
put women's issues on the political agenda and cooperated with women's
movement actors. In the second half of the 1990s Austria became a 'model
student' in a European comparison (Falkner, 1995) – it had a fully-fledged
women's ministry on the national level, and women-friendly legislation
in several policy fields.

Previous research has also shown that Austria has developed a path-
dependency in state feminism (Köpl, 2001, 2005; Sauer, 2005a): In issues
which have been traditionally on the social democratic agenda – like
abortion and political representation of women – women's policy agencies
from the social democratic party helped women's movement actors to
bring in their views and demands in policy processes since the 1970s. In
issues which were contested inside the ruling social democratic party
SPÖ (*Sozialdemokratische Partei Österreichs* (Austrian Social Democratic
Party) (in government coalitions from 1971 to 2000) and which were
neither on the social democratic women's organization's agenda nor on
the agenda of the autonomous women's movement – like prostitution – the
Austrian state did not respond to women's movement demands until
the mid-1990s. On labour issues the movement was not successful – due
to the male-dominated network of social partnership (Buchinger and
Rosenberger, 2001).

Also, the two branches of the Austrian women's movement – women's
organizations in and around parties and trade unions and the autonomous

movement – became consolidated at the beginning of the 1990s. While the party and union movement gained political visibility and representation in state institutions, the autonomous branch diversified, professionalized and arranged cooperation with state institutions. In the second half of the 1990s, the Austrian movement was even re-emerging in the public sphere: in 1997 the women's movement association UFF (*Unabhängiges Frauenforum* – Independent Women's Forum) launched a 'Women's Referendum', a people's initiative for the amendment of the Austrian constitution in favour of affirmative action. It attained much public attention and turned out to be one of the most successful people's initiatives after the Second World War.

However, since the mid-1990s Austria's women's policy had to confront several challenges and contradictory influences, which resulted from the transformation of the state and policy-making in the process of multilevel governance. Through 'uploading' of state power to supranational levels, by 'downloading' and devolution to regional levels and through 'offloading' of state responsibilities to society (Banaszak, Beckwith and Rucht, 2003, p. 7) new arenas of power, new actors and new forms of women's representation emerged.

The *first challenge* came from Austria's accession to the European Union in 1995. Since then the European level gained more and more importance for women's policy issues and various obligations under European law regarding gender equality had to be incorporated into national law. The first question this article wants to answer therefore is: How do international multilevel governance regimes and shifts of power affect Austrian state feminism and equal opportunity politics?

Second, since the beginning of the new century, the European Union strategy of gender mainstreaming has been implemented in the Austrian administration. This poses the question if gender mainstreaming is an opportunity or a challenge for Austrian state feminist institutions and equal opportunity policy-making.

A *third* influence comes from CEDAW, which was ratified by Austria in 1982.[2] Again, this chapter asks for the effects of the CEDAW reporting on women's politics and opportunities for women's movement actors to influence policy processes in Austria. A *fourth* challenge has been regionalization of equal opportunity politics. Is devolution and regionalization of women's policy agencies an opportunity for deepening equal opportunity processes or does this development run the risk of delegating responsibility and accountability with the effect of a non-decision?

Another, *fifth*, challenge has been the restructuring of the welfare state since the mid-1990s. Re-privatization of care-work, the work going to families and women characterizes the Austrian welfare regime. Also, budget cuts do affect public funding of women's projects. These last processes have been accelerated since a new right-wing government came to power in 2000 – the *sixth* challenge to women's politics. This has led to a reorganization of the national women's policy agency and to a shift in women's issues ranging on the policy agenda. The main question here is: do parties and governments matter for the case of state feminism? One last challenge (*seventh*) might be added – the implementation of diversity policies since the beginning of the new century: How do gender and diversity politics interact? Are they competing or cooperative strategies? – These challenges and influences build a puzzling picture, which this chapter sets out to explain.

Conservatives attacking the social partnership: the political context

Since the end of the Second World War the institutional framework of the Austrian political system was characterized by a polar party system and a high degree of centralization and privilege of the monopoly-like interest organizations in policy making (Appelt, 1995, p. 612). The representatives of organized interests took part in the pre-parliamentary policy process through developing drafts for laws, assessments in law making processes and partially in the implementation of policies (Tálos, 1997, pp. 443–4). These mechanisms strengthened the male-bonding structure of Austrian corporatism. Only in 1966 did the first woman enter an Austrian government. Yet not only the 'manned-ness' of the tripartite negotiation network excluded women and women's issues. The organized interests in the social partnership were 'fraternal male interests', mainly interests of waged labour (Neyer, 1997, p. 185). Only in the 1980s the gradual erosion of the social partnership and the cooperation of women from the Social-Democratic Party with the autonomous women's movement built the opportunity structure for equal opportunity policies.

One major change since the 1990s was a new style of policy making in the 'grand coalition' between social democrats (SPÖ) and the Christian conservative Austrian People's Party (*Österreichische Volkspartei*, ÖVP). 'Package solutions' tried to balance the different ideological strands of the government, mainly in budget policy. While the ÖVP sought a restrictive budget policy through cuts in social provisions, the SPÖ tried to satisfy its voters who were afraid of loss of jobs and a drop in the standard of living in the case of budget restrictions. In 1996 the first law on budget restriction (*Strukturanpassungsgesetz*) – the first 'economy package' – was accepted by the Austrian parliament. Reduction of social provisions, for instance for single parents and pensioners, were the main components of this package.

The ensuing debate over the 'crisis' of the Austrian welfare state and the discourse on alleged *misuse* of welfare state benefits legitimized further cuts in welfare state spending. Due to these cut-backs, the Austrian gender regime was gradually retreating to a more patriarchal and family oriented regime with rising gender inequality in waged labour. However, the SPÖ tried to balance neoliberal restructuring and the privatization of care work to families by strengthening, for instance, public child care provisions.

One of the major debates and changes in the 1990s was Austria's EU integration. The governing parties were pro-European; the Green Party and the right-wing *Freiheitliche Partei Österreichs* (Austrian Freedom Party, FPÖ) were against the accession. While the Greens changed their opinion, the FPÖ initiated a people's initiative against the common currency Euro in 1997. Also, the people's initiative 'Veto against Temelin' (a nuclear power plant in the Czech Republic) in 2002 was a symbolic instrument of the FPÖ to mobilize against the EU membership of former state-socialist countries.

In 2000 the new coalition government between the right-wing FPÖ and the conservative ÖVP came to power. The EU 'banned' Austria because the FPÖ under the leadership of populist Jörg Haider became part of the government. When Haider did not take over a ministry because of the intervention of the Austrian president, a group of seniors sent by the European Union lifted the ban. The new government announced a 'new politics' for Austria, which aimed at breaking the long tradition of social democratic politics; it especially tried to weaken the social partnership in the Austrian neocorporatist institutional setting. The Austrian 'consensus democracy' was to be transformed into a 'conflict democracy'.

Immediately after the new government took power, civil society mobilized against the government and organized weekly 'Thursday demonstrations', mainly in Vienna, but also in other cities. This was new for the Austrian democracy, used to consensus solutions and not to street protest. Moreover, Austrian consensus democracy has been known after the Second World War for the absence of strikes; the country therefore was shocked by the first strikes of public railway workers in 2004.

Other major policy debates in the late 1990s and at the beginning of the 2000s were, *first*, migration and a new law on citizenship, the adjustment to the Schengen border regime, racism within the Austrian police, leading to the death of two African immigrants, and police raids against African communities justified with the argument of drug dealing. A *second* topic was the privatization of state owned industries and public services, for instance the 'autonomization' of universities. Thus, the ÖVP, which represents the interests of industry, craft professions and farmers, had the opportunity to go forward with the deregulation of the economy and the dismantling of the welfare state, dissolving the social democratic welfare compromise. The *third* emerging debate was family policy in the context of demographic decline. Family policy issues moved to the centre of politics around the quest for a complete reconfiguration of the welfare state. The Law on Child-care Allowance of 2001 (*Kinderbetreuungsgeldgesetz*), like the unsuccessful attempt to include the protection of the family in the constitution, illustrates this shift towards family orientation and new state–society relations (Sauer, 2007).

After the BZÖ (*Bündnis Zukunft Österreich*, Alliance for the Future of Austria) under the leadership of Jörg Haider separated from the FPÖ in spring 2005, and because of growing unemployment rates and cuts in welfare benefits, the conservative party ÖVP has been replaced by social democratic governments in two provincial elections. At the national elections of 1 October 2006, the ÖVP lost dramatically (8 per cent) and the SPÖ lost only 1.2 per cent. The latter now have the most seats in the parliament (68), the ÖVP 66. The Greens and FPÖ both have 21 seats. There is thus no clear majority. A majority government was only possible either as a grand coalition of SPÖ and ÖVP or as a threeparty government – with the right-wing FPÖ or right-wing BZÖ. In January 2007 the grand coalition took office.

From women's policy to gender mainstreaming: institutional changes in the women's policy machinery

The Austrian women's policy machinery has been characterized by a history of institutionalization and de-institutionalization since 1979 (Rosenberger, 2006, p. 746), when the first women's policy agency on the federal level, the State Secretary's office for 'general women's issues' was installed in the Federal Chancellery.[3] Johanna Dohnal, a well-known SPÖ feminist with strong backing from the party's women's organization and with strong ties to the autonomous women's movement, was appointed to head the office. In 1990 negotiations in forming the new coalition government resulted in a restructuring and upgrading and the state secretary for general women's issues became the Federal Ministry of Women's Affairs. Johanna Dohnal became the first Austrian women's minister.

The minister was politically appointed and had a cross-sectional mandate (Bundesministeriengesetz, 2003). The ministry was able to expand its staff from 17 people in 1992 to 33 in 1999 (Österreichischer Amtskalender, 1992–2000) and to design three new sub-departments. The minister's status also expanded beyond the previously limited advisory function; she had a veto right in the Cabinet of Ministers as well as the power to initiate further political women's initiatives.

In addition to the federal women's ministry an equal opportunity structure has been established in all federal ministries since the end of the 1990s. All ministries had to implement the Act on Equal Treatment in Federal Service (B-GBG) (1998). Meanwhile all ministries have adopted Plans for the Advancement of Women, which give 'preference to female applicants in areas where they are under-represented' (CEDAW, 2004a, p. 27) until a 40 per cent quota of women is achieved. All ministries established women's officers to enforce the law.

Since the mid-1990s the women's policy agency has gone through several institutional changes, caused by new government constellations, the process of regionalization and Europeanization, and the challenges by the strategy of gender mainstreaming and diversity politics.

Government constellations

In 1995, Helga Konrad, a social democrat from the party apparatus, succeeded Dohnal. In December 1996 she started an initiative called 'Fifty-Fifty' (Real guys make fifty-fifty/*Ganze Männer machen Halbe-Halbe*) which demanded that men and women should share the same load of house and care work. This campaign was highly contested in the media, by ÖVP and FPÖ, but also within the SPÖ (Dackweiler, 2003, pp. 142–5). The intensity of the conflict forced Konrad to resign soon after the campaign. In 1997, Barbara Prammer (SPÖ) took over the office. In the course of restructuring the federal government in 1997, the Ministry of Women's Affairs also took on the field of consumer protection, which might be interpreted as first attempts to minimize the visibility of a single ministry for women's issues.

By the turn of the century, the picture of Austrian women's politics changed with the new government coalition of the Christian-conservative ÖVP and right-wing FPÖ: The government dissolved the Federal Ministry of Women's Affairs in 2000 and shifted its agenda to the Ministry of Social Welfare, Family and Generations. The ministry was headed first by a female minister from the FPÖ (Elisabeth Sickl). She was soon replaced by a male appointee of the FPÖ (Herbert Haupt). The Minister of Social Affairs legitimated the dissolution of the women's ministry with the argument that in the era of gender mainstreaming there was no need for a special ministry for women. Despite these institutional cut-backs, the quantitative representation of women in the right-conservative government is remarkable: it had 50 per cent female ministers – and the Minister of Justice gave birth to a baby in July 2006.

Also with the argument of gender mainstreaming the male minister established a 'men's unit' in the ministry in 2000 – equipped with staff and budget. 'Women's emancipation makes the focus on men necessary' – was the unit's leader's argument for the institutionalization (Mayrhofer, 2006). The goals of this unit are to coordinate and initiate research on men's roles and needs and to support those men facing discrimination such as fathers claiming their rights to children in the case of divorce. One success of the men as a 'discriminated group' was the law on joint custody between mother and father, which was highly criticized by women's groups.

This institutionalization was not backed by a strong national or international men's movement. To the contrary, it was promoted by a 'fathers' rights' group close to the right-wing *Lager* (political camp), which opposed women's emancipation and especially the tradition of mothers' custody for children in the case of divorce. The men's unit therefore can be interpreted as an 'anti-institutionalization' to the social-democratic tradition of women's policy agencies. The women's movement did not publicly oppose the institutionalization but does not cooperate with the unit.

In 2000–01 the women's section in the Ministry of Social Welfare and Generations employed 28 people (in five departments) (Österreichischer Amtskalender, 2000–02). The office was led by a bureaucrat with a cross-sectional mandate, but has become powerless and silenced compared to the 1990s. After early elections in 2002, the women's ministry was re-established within the Ministry of Health in May 2003. Head of the ministry became Maria Rauch-Kallat, the leader of the women's section in the ÖVP. The Ministry for Social Welfare, Family and Generations kept the agenda for families.

The women's policy agency was degraded to a section within the Ministry of Health – and the health issue seems to be one of the major tasks of the ministry, which is publicly much more present than women's issues. This section two of the Federal Ministry for Health and Women is responsible for women's issues. In 2006 it had 42 employees in six departments, responsible for instance for gender mainstreaming, violence against women, legal questions, equal treatment of women in the public and private sectors, women's projects, international service and migrant women (Geschäftseinteilung, 2006). A women's ministry was re-established in 2007, led again by a woman Social Democrat, Doris Bures.

Adjunct to the Ministry of Health and Women's Issues is the Commission for Equal Treatment (*Gleichbehandlungskommission*) of men and women in the labour market (established in 1979) and the ombudsman's office for equal treatment of women in the labour market (established in 1990). The commission is an arbitration committee in cases of labour discrimination and has the task to enforce the law on equal treatment from 1979. Since 2001 the position of the chairwomen in the equal treatment commission is a fulltime position. The ombudsman's office gives legal advice in cases of labour discrimination. Since 1999 regional ombudsman's offices for the equal treatment of women in the labour market have been established in six of the nine Austrian provinces.

Regionalization and devolution

During the mid-1990s a sub-state feminism emerged and the women's policy machineries have been regionalized: in all nine Austrian provinces the governments have ministries or departments for women's issues (*Landesrätinnen für Frauen*), some of them responsible for 'women plus', for instance 'minister for women, families and generations' in Lower Austria or 'women and migrant integration' in Vienna. In the province of Salzburg the office is established at the office of the provincial governor, an SPÖ woman, while in Carinthia the women's section is institutionalized at the office of the deputy provincial governor, the SPÖ chairwoman in Carinthia. Moreover, all provinces adopted – step by step – regional laws for equal treatment of men and women in the provincial civil service (CEDAW, 2004a, p. 30). Women's offices in the regional administration (*Landesfrauenreferentin* or *Frauenbeauftragte*) are responsible for the advancement of women in the provincial administration. They organize a regular meeting, the Conference for Women's Officers (www.bmgf.gv.at, accessed 23 January 2006).

Also, some major cities like Linz, Innsbruck, Salzburg, Graz and Vienna, have established women's offices as an interface to a wider public (www.noel.gv.at, accessed 24 January 2006). Some of the regional women's policy agencies and municipal departments for women have their own budgets enabling them to fund women's projects. For instance the Vienna women's office (Municipal Department 57) has a special budget – the 'small project funds' – for women migrants, new technologies and the labour market, from which projects might get maximum three-year subsidies (CEDAW, 2004a, p. 27).

Regionalization of women's policy machineries has been a way to promote gender equality politics and to broaden the network of women's policy agencies. Austria has a weak federal system in which the regions and provinces have to fight for political space and decision-making power. The regionalization of the women's policy agencies made them visible on the provincial and community level and made it easier to promote equal opportunity politics as well as for women and women's groups to dock on these institutions. Moreover, Austrian local politics is rather male-dominated; regionalization of women's policy agencies built an opportunity to crack male-bonding.

Also, the network of women's policy agencies – some of them under social democratic, some of them under Christian conservative governments – builds the opportunity structure for women's movements to bring in their ideas into state policies. The women's policy success of the 1990s is to a large part due to the stabilization, upgrading and expansion of the federal women's ministry but also due to the expansion of women's policy agencies to the provincial and community level. All in all, regional women's policy agencies are forming a favourable political opportunity structure and helped regional and local women's projects to flourish. Moreover, networks of regional women's services strengthened their bargaining positions towards national administration.

Another aspect has changed the women's project landscape in Austria and their funding situation: Austrian provinces actively took part in the EQUAL-projects of the European Structural Funds, supporting women's projects and implementing a gendered perspective in Austrian local and regional politics. This deepened the process of regionalization of women's policy.

Since the beginning of the new century, regionalization under conservative augury took place. The government launched the idea to rewrite the Austrian constitution and to rearrange Austrian federalism, giving the provinces less power. Although the process failed and the constitution was never decided, the struggle over centralized and regionalized power is going on. Until now, this discourse does not have a negative impact on regional women's policy agencies.

Gender mainstreaming

The new government adopted the gender mainstreaming strategy in July 2000 – under the leadership of the Minister for Social Welfare – and started to establish a gender mainstreaming infrastructure in the national administration, according to the 'top-down-focus' of the mainstreaming strategy: The national administration should implement gender mainstreaming from above, that is by ordinary bureaucrats at the top of the administration. An inter-ministerial working group for gender main-streaming (IMAG Gender Mainstreaming, *Interministerielle Arbeitsgruppe Gender Mainstreaming*) was formed in order to implement gender main-streaming at the level of national government, chaired by the Minister for Health and Women's Issues. It consists of representatives of all federal ministries, the Constitutional Court, the Appellate Administrative Court, the Court of Audit and the Ombudsman's Office, the Parliamentary Administration and the public service trade union (www.imag-gender mainstreaming.at).

The IMAG's task is to watch, to advise and to coordinate the imple-mentation of the gender mainstreaming strategy in all government departments. The working group organizes workshops, gender trainings and 'best practice' in order to develop criteria and standards for the implementation of gender mainstreaming (CEDAW, 2004a, p. 29).

Due to the initiatives of the IMAG GM all ministries have at least adopted the language of gender mainstreaming and established a sec-tion on gender mainstreaming on their homepages. Most of the min-istries started to implement gender mainstreaming by organizing gender trainings by external gender experts, who are to alert bureaucrats for gender inequalities. Since 2000 all ministries have established gender-mainstreaming officers, encouraged by the women's ministry. In some ministries former equal opportunity officers took over this position and now label their task – to promote women within the bureaucracy – as gender mainstreaming (Frauen sind anders, 2005). Moreover, all ministries have implemented measures against the discrimination of women and support policies and projects in this field (Bericht der Bundesregierung, 2005).

The Federal Ministry of Finance, for instance, set up a working group on gender mainstreaming, which made a report on the gender effects of the tax reform (Arbeitsgruppe Gender Mainstreaming, 2001). Rather active in the field of gender mainstreaming is the section for science within the Ministry of Education, Science and Culture. Several femocrats in the ministerial administration have implemented and gendered the research funds of the ministry (CEDAW, 2004a, p. 37). The same ministry launched an Action Plan 2003 – Gender Mainstreaming and Advancement of Women in Schools and Adult Education and several other programmes and a pilot project for instance to encourage young girls for a technical career (CEDAW, 2004a, p. 38).

Gender budgeting is another issue of the federal women's ministry. In 2004 an IMAG gender budgeting was established, also headed by the women's minister: Its task is to evaluate state budgets in a gender sensitive perspective. In April 2005, the minister organized a conference in Vienna on the issue with national experts to elaborate standards for gender budgeting (www.bmgf.gv.at, accessed 10 January 2006).

Moreover, the provincial governments followed the national administration and slowly integrated gender mainstreaming in the provincial administration (CEDAW, 2004a, p. 30). In 2004, all provincial governments adopted the principle of gender mainstreaming in all areas of provincial policy making (CEDAW, 2004b, p. 24). Some of the social democratic governments – as for instance the province of Vienna – built the vanguard of gender mainstreaming, signallizing a more women-friendly policy environment than the national government (www.IMAG-Gendermainstreaming.at, accessed 21 September 2006).

Gender mainstreaming is viewed rather sceptically by women's movement organizations in Austria – due to the experience of the dissolution of the women's ministry. Gender mainstreaming is seen as bureaucratic, as weak and soft law, which helps to abolish women's policy institutions and helps to erode women's rights especially in the field of labour (Rosenberger, 2003). The national government therefore claims to apply a dual-track approach: it wants to implement gender mainstreaming as a method to reveal the structural obstacles against the active participation of women in all spheres of society and to alert policy makers for gender differences. At the same time existing women's policy machineries within the national administration should not be dissolved.

However, on the level of federal ministries gender mainstreaming remains in its infancy and at the stage of pilot projects. The focus of gender mainstreaming is in the field of labour, although gender equality in the National Action Plans is weakly implemented. Moreover, most of the former measures for women are now labelled as gender mainstreaming, and some femocrats adopt the language of mainstreaming to legitimize their feminist strategy. State feminism and gender mainstreaming therefore are not always competing strategies in Austria, rather gender mainstreaming might build an opportunity to reinforce state feminism. But in the process of state public university restructuring, for instance, the strategy of gender mainstreaming had the effect of weakening the existing institutions and instruments for equal opportunities (Sauer, 2005a). All in all, the gender mainstreaming approach in Austria has not been transformative or agenda setting; it has been implemented as a technocratic tool and as an integrationist approach. One of the major problems is that NGOs and civil societies of women's groups are not integrated in the mainstreaming strategy and it therefore does not contribute to the development of gender democracy in Austria (Verloo, 2005).

EU influence: multilevel governance and institutions of diversity

Austria's accession to the EU also had an impact on the institutional structure of the women's policy agency. The minister and the women's section in the ministry have been traditionally representing Austria on the EU as well as on the UN level. All in all, the Austrian Minister for Women and the women's section within the ministry sees the international level positive. However, international policies are sometimes only reluctantly implemented in the Austria national context.

One of the major impacts on the institutional setting was the implementation of European anti-discrimination legislation: Austria implemented the European Council directive 2000/43/EC on anti-discrimination by establishing two further Commissions for Equal Treatment at the ministry for health and women (amendment of the equal treatment law in 2004): Chamber II of the commission is now monitoring equal treatment in the labour market, irrespective of ethnicity, religion, age and sexual orientation. Chamber III deals with discrimination on the grounds of ethnicity in other social spheres such as social security, housing and education (www.bmgf.gv.at, accessed 10 January 2006). These commissions have a sort of ombudsman's task to consult people who feel discriminated and to support them for instance at court.

To sum up: although dramatic changes took place in the structure of the women's policy machineries, they have not been generally downsized. The changes could be characterized as deregulation through gender mainstreaming and diversity politics on the national level. But it can also be characterized as strengthening the provincial level, especially where the SPÖ, in opposition on the national level, is in government. However, the main changes took place in the tasks of the women's policy machinery on the national level: it took only a weak mandate in issues of labour and reconciliation of job and care work. This is left to the family policy environment, that is the Ministry for Social Welfare and Generations, and in this environment the issue is framed in a conservative hegemonic discourse.

Policy priorities: from equality to difference

Major women's policy issues in the second half of the 1990s were violence against women, including stalking, trafficking in women and prostitution, again abortion, the linking of public party subsidies to the advancement of women in politics, and reconciliation of job and care work. While the women's movement was successfully influencing the policy processes on abortion and violence against women, it failed in gendering the debates on political representation of women, reconciliation and family policies and was only partly successful in the issue of prostitution and trafficking (Köpl, 2001; 2005; Sauer, 2004; Sauer, 2007).

The failures of the movement might be explained by the challenge the issue posed to men's political power – as for instance in the issue of political representation, which was too challenging to the (male) party elite in all parties. This prevented the women's policy agency to act in favour of women's movement demands in the case of political representation.

The success of the women's movement as for instance in the abortion debate can be explained with a sort of path-dependency of the legislation, with the active involvement of the women's ministry in favour of women's movement goals and also with the influence of inter- and supranational norms and organizations.

International agenda setting

The international arena was rather important for some of the Austrian policy successes: In the issue of domestic violence, trafficking and sex work international regulations played an important role. Framing women's issues as human rights issues by international (women's) organizations made it possible to open the policy process for women's movement activists in Austria by referring to international regulations. The women's policy agency in the 1990s – at that time led by social democrats – also referred to international regulations and mediated between state institutions and women's movement aims, especially in the issue of violence against women.

The law against domestic violence (in force 1997) was triggered by the UN 1993 conference in Vienna where violence was defined as women's rights violation. Women's groups against violence against women took the opportunity to bring forward anti-violence legislation in Austria. The 1997 law for the first time made male 'private' violence a public offence. Moreover, 'intervention centres' were created, which support victims against their abusers. These centres also institutionalize the cooperation of women's movement organizations with the police and courts (Dearing and Haller, 2000). Since 1999, each of the nine provinces has established one intervention centre (CEDAW, 2004a, p. 31). Also, since July 2006, stalking became a criminal offence.

The new conservative government also passed several law amendments, which have been triggered by international conventions. In 2004 the penal code redefined pimping, and the paragraph on trafficking in women was changed in 2004, in line with the UN Palermo Protocol to prevent trafficking in persons and to minimize harm of trafficked people. One of the most active women's projects, LEFÖ (*Lateinamerikanische emigrierte Frauen in Österreich*; migrated Latin American women in Austria) has been lobbying for years on the issues of prostitution and trafficking and was able to promote legal change with reference to international norms. The law against marital rape (2004), which abolished the privileged treatment of rape and sexual coercion within marriage or cohabitation, was passed only after urgent recommendations of CEDAW.

Austria's accession to the European Union generated and accelerated gender equality legislation, such as the directives on the right of parents to part-time work and women's work at night (2002) and the amendment of the constitution with the possibility of affirmative action (1998). Moreover, the jurisdiction of the European Court of Justice opened the Austrian military for women and expanded equality at the workplace.

Women's policy versus family policy? Governments do matter

A rather contested issue in the second half of the 1990s was public child-care and the reconciliation of paid labour and care work. The 'kindergarden-billion' (*Kindergartenmilliarde*) of the SPÖ/ÖVP-coalition aimed at funding more public child-care facilities and was a compromise within the government. Another issue was gender injustice in the state pension system, which discriminated women when leaving a job for child-care. In the late 1990s a law recognized years spent on child-care in the state pension system. However, on both issues, which are important for the status of women, the influence of the women's ministry was rather low. The decisions on the issues were made in the Ministries of Labour and Finance and the social partnership and the women's policy agencies had not much say in the policy process.

When the new government came to power reconciliation was – institutionally and discursively – shifted to family policy. In the debate on the law on child-care allowance since 2001 the women's ministry did not intervene in the policy process, although the law had important implications for the reconciliation of waged labour and child care – running the risk of pushing women back to unpaid family work (Sauer, 2007). All in all, the Ministry had no focus on waged labour and reconciliation – this is left to the Ministry of Social Welfare and Generations. In this discourse environment the issue is not framed in terms of gender equality but as family policy. The family orientation is one of the major shifts in the restructuring of the Austrian welfare state – referring to demographic metaphors and revitalizing the family as the nucleus of society.

Shift of frame: 'traditional violence' and diversity

At first glance there has not been much public debate around the issue of diversity and anti-discrimination, nor on diversity and gender. The women's movement did not give the issue of intersectionality much priority and the government implemented the European directive on anti-discrimination (2007/78/EG of the European Council of 2000) half-heartedly. A new anti-discrimination law is in force since 1 July 2004 (BGBl. No. 66/2004), but the enforcement is rather weak.

Only in the field of domestic violence women's movement groups focused on ethnic migrant minorities, pointing out specific forms of violence (as for instance forced marriage) and problems of migrant women in getting help in the case of violence – for instance the problem of residence. The major issue of the conservative federal ministry since 2004 is violence against women, for instance marital rape, domestic violence and trafficking in women. During the Austrian EU-presidency in the first half of 2006, the women's minister exclusively focused on 'traditional violence' against women, for instance genital mutilation, honour killing and forced marriage (www.bmgf.gv.at, accessed 10 January 2006). Genital mutilation (amendment of the Penal Code in 2001) is now illegal in all cases, even in the case of consent it is a public offence). Also forced marriage is a public offence since 2006.

Some of these issues were put on the Austrian agenda by international obligations, for instance the law amendment on trafficking in women and the reform of marital law. Moreover, these issues emerged in the context of a strong anti-violence policy in Austria, due to the successful lobbying of women's groups dealing with violence against women in a multicultural context – as for instance LEFÖ, Orient Express (www.orientexpress-wien.com) and Peregrina (www.peregrina.at). This shift matches the fact that diversity has become an issue of the Austrian women's movement; the movement itself became more diverse, and efforts were made to not only organize as women, but as different women. For instance, LEFÖ and the Autonomous Integration Centre by and for Migrant Women (MAIZ – *Autonomes Integrationszentrum von und für Migrantinnen*) in Linz are women's movement groups organizing female migrants in Austria since the mid-1990s. In Vienna lively African women's and Muslim women's groups are claiming the right for difference and recognition.

However, the politicization of these issues at the intersection of gender, race and ethnicity had an ambivalent outcome in the conservative Austrian context. On one hand, Austrian laws have been change in order to protect migrant women from different forms of violence, but on the other hand, the xenophobic and islamophobic tendencies in the Austrian right-wing parties FPÖ and BZÖ were fostered by these policies of othering migrant men and women – assuming that their traditions make them more violent and different from Austrian dominant society. This shift to intersecting issues of gender, race, culture and religion indicate a tendency of the conservative ministry to downplay women's issues in the labour market such as the deepening wage gap and the re-familizing of care work. A silent shift of funding is moved to these organizations at the cost of other women's projects.

Also, the issue of violence against women seems to be compatible with the conservative gender agenda, to protect women, to see women as victims of men and to focus on policing as policy measure.

Distant cooperation: relationship between the women's policy agency and women's movement actors

The women's movement since the second half of the 1990s has been characterized by organizational and thematic continuity, but also by ruptures, especially after the new government came to power. The Austrian women's movement has a long tradition in the social democratic party and in the bourgeois women's movement of the late nineteenth century. Several of these traditional women's groups still exist – and they are becoming more relevant because they are the Austrian representatives in the European Women's Lobby (EWL).[4]

The most powerful women's organization with an important role in society and in politics is the SPÖ women's caucus, founded in the nineteenth century. It has always been connected to the women's organization in the trade unions. The conservative ÖVP also formed a women's association according to the party's organization principle of associations within the party, such as farmers, pensioners – and women. The ÖVP's women's organization tried to modernize since the end of the 1990s: it was renamed as the 'women's offensive' and tried to mobilize a young female constituency with a campaign labelled Strong-Black-Female,[5] with icons, symbols and wordings of the feminist movement. The FPÖ women's group *(Initiative Freiheitliche Frauen,* Platform of women from the Freedom party) split after the BZÖ separated; the BZÖ has a women's spokesperson but up to now no organization. The Green party also has no special women's section, but a spokesperson for women's issues.

The autonomous branch of the Austrian women's movement is more or less distant from these institutionalized groups. Since the late 1980s, the autonomous movement has consolidated as a 'project movement' organizing to work on specific issues and campaigns and in close cooperation with allies inside state and party institutions, some of them originating in the women's movement (Kogoj, 1998, p. 239). Movement organizations are state-funded, for their work in the fields of violence against women, education and job training, counselling of migrant women, feminist journals and archives, info-centres and art groups, and feminist research (Ruß, 2004).

In the mid-1990s, when the government launched first austerity programmes, movement activists together with Johanna Dohnal, the former Minister for Women, mobilized to form a women's party (Kogoj, 1998, pp. 253–5). Although the party never materialized, the idea stimulated a public debate on women's issues and the role of the women's movement. Thus, at the time of the 'women's referendum', a peoples' initiative on women's issues, movement supporters were mobilizing and activism was re-emerging.

Previous research has shown that the cooperation between the women's movement groups and the women's policy agency was one important condition for women's policy success in Austria (Köpl, 2001; 2005; Sauer, 2004). If the movement was able to connect with women in power they have been successful, if the movement was reluctant to work together with state agencies or if the women's policy agency got more distant to the autonomous movement the movement was not successful.

Since the second half of the 1990s robust ties have been established between the social democratic-led women's ministry at the federal level, women's movement projects and movement activists. Although cuts in budget had negative effects on funding, the long established cooperation worked rather well. The state funding situation for women's projects was worsening with the change to a conservative government. But in addition to cuts in budgets the women's movement faced powerful opposition. It was rather symbolic that in the years 2000 and 2001, the celebrations of the International Women's Day on 8 March took place without the participation of the women's ministry (Rösslhumer and Appelt, 2001, p. 214).

An anti-feminist campaign tried to silence the movement. The campaign started with a redefinition of civil society as a sphere of folk culture. Such groups were now supported in order to marginalize and delegitimize critical groups as separatist, criminal and leftist and to justify the plan to shift support from women's projects to associations close to the conservative milieu. A ÖVP deputy, Helmut Kukacka, in 2000 launched this campaign against women's movement organizations. He persuaded a parliamentary commission to review the funding of civil society organizations by the (at that time social democratic) Social Ministry between 1995 and 1999. The commission examined 250 civil society organizations, more than 40 of which were women's groups. LEFÖ and the association *checkArt*, which is editing the feminist journal *An.Schläge*,[6] were publicly summoned to prove that they did not misuse the funds for illegal activities – like supporting 'secret' prostitutes in the case of LEFÖ. Kukacka proclaimed that the new government would not be willing to fund 'green and leftist social policy, party policy and women's policy' (Stichwort Newsletter, 2002, p. 11). As a result of this frontal assault by the rightist parties, women's movement actors moved closer to the left parties, i.e. the social democratic and the Green party.

This backlash had immediate consequences for women's projects. The government has kept women's projects, which are dependent on state money, in a state of insecurity regarding their future financial support. For instance the shelters for battered women and their umbrella organization, which organizes an anti-violence hotline, receive fewer state funds because the Ministry of Justice claims its victim hotline takes care of the need. For some issues the European Union helps to bridge the money gap, through projects such as support for trafficked women and prostitutes, but this help is limited. In Vienna, the social democratic government also has come forward with some help for women's projects.

Since 2004 the new women's minister started to reconnect with movement organizations and tried to demonstrate cooperation. According to the homepage of the ministry, in 2005 about €4.3 million were spent for prevention of violence against women, for instance for the intervention centres for violence against women, women's shelters, for help-lines and the intervention centre of trafficked women in Vienna (www.bmgf.gv.at, accessed 10 January 2006). While funding of these projects was based on yearly funding contracts they now are funded on a longer term base (www.bmgf.gv.at, accessed 10 January 2006).

From the perspective of movement activists, the international level builds an opportunity structure to lobby within the national government on specific issues. For instance, the CEDAW reports built an opportunity structure for Austrian women's movement actors to force the women's minister to declare her policy aims and strategies and to politicize around still existing discrimination. The shadow reports produced by NGO activists, indicate the fields of women's discrimination and backlash tendencies in Austria. However, no forum for continuous discussion, exchange and cooperation has been established between the ministry and the women's project world. Only sporadically does the minister invite women's projects for discussion – for instance to prepare the Beijing plus 10 meeting in New York. All in all the cooperation is individualized.

Conclusions

How can we conclude the Austrian puzzle of state transformation, women's policy agency restructuring, movement success and backlash? All the women's policy issues of the 1970s and 1980s were still – or are again – on the political agenda in the 1990s – abortion, prostitution, job equality, social security and violence. In the second half of the 1990s, the social democrat-led women's ministry was consolidated and was able to expand its scope of policies and collaborate with the women's movement. This was a favourable structure to successfully bring in women's movement demands into the policy process although the leadership of the agency became distant to the autonomous women's movement from the second half of the 1990s. All in all during the long government of the SPÖ state feminism developed mainly on traditional SPÖ issues. In some issues, Austrian women's policy was characterized by path-dependency – the abortion debates ended with a liberal legislation – while prostitution and political representation of women were blocked by male resistance. This changed in the late 1990s when issues of violence against women and prostitution were actively politicized by the women's policy agency. In both issues the international women's movement and international regulations helped to bring forward national women's movement goals.

In issues which affect the sexual division of labour, the organization of family and reproduction, the Austrian state acted more and more against equal opportunities from the mid-1990s – already under the social-democratic led coalition government (Mairhuber, 1999). Although the social democratic partner in government supported the development of women's policies and women's policy agencies, compromises of the grand coalition of SPÖ and ÖVP, the so-called policy packages had rather ambivalent outcomes for women especially with regard to job security, social security and wages. This might also be seen as an outcome of the strong male dominated social partnership structures.

Another finding is, that governments do matter in a consensus democracy like Austria. Compared to the 1990s the weak women's policy agency of the conservative government did not support women's movement goals and did not mediate between the movement and the state. Moreover, the government shifted the focus to the family and changed women's policy into family policy with the exception of violence against women. This can be seen as a tendency of a weakening and hollowing out of state feminism in Austria.

In 2000 the formation of a new conservative government coalition and the implementation of the gender mainstreaming strategy coincided. While the first led to a backlash in women's policy and the dissolution of the federal women's policy agency, gender mainstreaming did not prevent the weakening of the women's policy agency. To the contrary: gender mainstreaming was used to legitimize the cuts in women's policy, the dissolution and ambivalent re-institutionalization of the women's ministry. However, international regulations of EU and CEDAW still helped the Austrian women's movement in some cases. In issues backed by international regulations and debates (violence, prostitution and sex trafficking), the movement was successful even under a conservative government.

Although some researchers hold the gender mainstreaming strategy responsible for the women's policy backlash in Austria, the analysis shows that Austrian state feminism always has been selective. Important in the consensus democracy is the presence in corporatist organizations – either of femocrats or of women's movement activists. Femocrats therefore are still active to transform gender mainstreaming in a strategy which implements women's movement goals. The most dramatic – discursive – change has been the idea of diversity, which in the Austrian context is transformed in an anti-multicultural approach.

Notes

1. Many thanks to Monika Mayrhofer who did a lot of the research for this article.
2. The country drew up its first report in 1988, in 2004 submitted its sixth report, which describes the period of 1999 to 2003 (CEDAW, 2004a).
3. State Secretaries are junior ministers and subordinated to the head of the ministry.
4. Austrian women's organizations have three seats in the presidency of the EWL – two from the Austrian Women's Association (*Österreichischer Frauenring*), an umbrella organization of party women, women from the unions and the churches, and one by the Association of Austrian Women's Groups (*Bund Österreichischer Frauenvereine*), part of the International Council of Women.
5. Black here refers to the political colours of red as socialist and black as conservative-catholic.
6. The title is a combination of the words 'attack' and 'public announcement'. *Anschläge* means both.

4
State Feminism and Women's Movements in Belgium: Complex Patterns in a Multilevel System

Karen Celis and Petra Meier

Introduction

In the aftermath of the Second World War Belgium developed a welfare system with extensive unemployment allowances, social security, pension rights, accessible health and care infrastructure. Notwithstanding a rather conservative gender regime, fed by the Catholic tradition and its impact on politics, the participation of women in the labour market is higher than in the neighbouring countries like Germany or the Netherlands. A decrease in the number of children per woman, but also extensive child care facilities and a growing number of measures to reconcile work and care make women stay on the labour market.

Women's movements have not only fought for equality of the sexes in the labour market, but also in the intimate and public sphere. While Belgium has long been lagging behind when it comes to the position of women in political decision-making, from the 1990s onwards their number has been steadily increasing. Furthermore, by the mid-1990s the federal state level had a women's policy agency with a fully-fledged Minister, cabinet staff and its own civil servants (Hondeghem and Nelen, 2000). In the aftermath of the Beijing UN world conference on women in 1995, the various Belgian authorities have adopted legislation to monitor progress on the Beijing Platform for Action. This legislation is the most important institutionalization of gender equality policies, if we leave aside the explicit recognition of gender equality in the Constitution in 2002.

Parallel to the development of the women's policy agencies, the women's movements, especially the autonomous branches, became less visible in the 1990s. Partly related to the evolution of the second wave feminism, it also had to do with an evolution of their political priorities and strategies (Wiercx, 2005; Wiercx and Woodward, 2004). As political actors, the movements were not easily admitted, but individual actors and their ideas have found their way to decision-making (Hooghe, 1994; 1997), at least up to where political parties in power were willing to let them participate (Meier, 2005).

From the mid-1990s the Belgian women's policy agency underwent major changes. The various Belgian regions have witnessed the development of their own women's policy agencies (Celis and Meier, 2006; Facon et al., 2004; Woodward and Meier, 1998). This multiplication of women's policy agencies is not so much a reaction to broader trends of regionalization than a consequence of the ongoing federalization of the Belgian state, as we can also find in Spain (see Bustelo and Ortbals in this volume). A feminist engagement with federalism and the political opportunity structures of such multilevel contexts is beginning to be explored (on Australia and Canada see for instance Chappell, 2002; Rankin and Vickers, 1998; Sawer and Vickers, 2001). However, most accounts of women's policy agencies focused on national or regional women's policy agencies, but not on an interaction or interdependence of these levels (Mazur, 2001a; Lovenduski, 2005; Outshoorn, 2004a; McBride Stetson, 2001a; but also former accounts on the Belgian women's policy agencies: Celis, 2001; Meier, 2005; Woodward, 2007).

In the present chapter we will assess the changes the Belgian women's policy agency structure underwent over the last decade, focusing on the changing political opportunity structure arising for women's policy agencies and the women's movements in an increasingly multilevel system. This chapter addresses the question how the shift towards an increased multilevel setting impacts on the Belgian women's policy agencies and their interaction with the women's movement.

More institutions, asymmetric coalitions and a new political agenda

The major changes in the reconstitution of the Belgian state since the mid-1990s have their roots in preceding decades. Beginning in the 1970s, a number of constitutional reforms (1970, 1980, 1988–9, 1993 and 2000–3) moved Belgium from a unitary state to a complex system of asymmetrical federalism. The three regions (Flanders, Wallonia, Brussels Capital Region) have territorial boundaries and socio-economic matters such as employment, housing, mobility or infrastructure fall under their remit. Since the last constitutional reform they are also competent for international trade, agriculture and the administrative control of their communities and provinces. The three communities (Dutch-, French- and

German-speaking) are linked to the ethno-linguistic background of citizens and deal with matters such as education or culture. Competencies such as defence, justice and social security remain federal responsibilities. Other competencies such as economy, environment and transportation are shared between the federal state and the regions.

The capstone of these three decades of constitutional reform was the consolidation of the federalization, involving a fully-fledged intermediary political level. Since the mid-1990s the various constituting entities have their own parliament, government and public administration. On the Flemish side, the institutions of the region and of the community were merged. Next, Belgium also followed the international trend to transfer power to local authorities, as is for instance also the case in Italy (see Guadagnini in this volume). Local authorities gained in competencies, but not necessarily in financial capacity, involving ambiguous relations with the central state authorities. Both trends led to a weakening of the central state level.

Since the Second World War the Christian Democrats have been in power with only small breaks, forming coalitions with a variety of other parties, but occupying the post of Prime Minister for most of the time. The electoral defeat of the Christian Democrats in 1999 was a decisive moment in Belgian post war political history. It led to the formation of the first 'purple' federal government, including not only Liberals and Socialists, but also Greens, who governed for the first time. While the Christian Democrats did not manage to re-enter the federal coalition at the 2003 elections, they won the 2004 regional elections in Flanders. In combination with electoral shifts among the Francophone parties, this led to the first asymmetry in governing coalitions. While the Flemish Socialists and Liberals govern in both Flanders and at the federal level, the Christian Democrats are part of the opposition at the federal level but lead the Flemish government.

The sweeping out of government of the Christian Democrats in 1999 and the change of coalition led to a new political line, on economic but especially on ethical issues. Marriage for homosexual couples, their right to adoption and other political issues, that would have been impossible under a Christian Democrat government coalition, were achieved.

From one to many women's policy agencies

The federal women's policy agency: promotion in the periphery

What is generally considered to be the first real Belgian women's policy agency was set up in the wake of the 1985 Nairobi UN World Conference on Women and the women's movement was the driving force behind it. Miet Smet, a former president of the Flemish Christian Democrats' political women's organization *Vrouw en Maatschappij* (Woman and Society) became State Secretary of Environmental Affairs in 1985 and also negotiated an Equal Opportunities portfolio. Officially, the State Secretary's competence covered everything related to equal opportunities, but throughout her mandates Smet focused on violence against women, their economic position and their participation in political decision-making. She also initiated the development of local equal opportunities policies. In 1986 the government installed an advisory body, the Emancipation Council. It contained delegates of the women's organizations of different ideological and socio-cultural persuasions but had a limited scope of action (Kuhl, 1998; Ministerie van Volksgezondheid en Leefmilieu, 1987).

When Smet became Minister of Labour and Employment in 1991, she retained the Equal Opportunities portfolio. More important is that Smet became a fully-fledged minister and was no longer a State Secretary depending on another minister. In 1992 a Unit of Equal Opportunities was set up in the Ministry of Labour and Employment. Smet did not alter her policy priorities. The 1994 gender quota law is one of her most well-known political victories. Smet also got violence against women out of the taboo sphere. She introduced toolkits for police officials dealing with female victims of violence and in 1997 rape within marriage became punishable. Equal wages and opportunities on the workfloor for women were other political priorities.

In 1993 the Council of Equal Opportunities for Men and Women replaced the Emancipation Council. This new advisory body is composed of representatives from a broad range of organizations, such as the social partners, political parties, women's and family organizations etc., and operates more independently from the Minister of Equal Opportunities. A broad range of institutions and actors can ask for advice and the Council can also advise on its own initiative and does so to a large extent. By the beginning of 2006 it has given more than 100 pieces of advice on matters ranging from income security for senior male and female citizens, to gender quotas for electoral lists, maternity protection for the self-employed, the use of the veil, the position of women in top-class sport or domestic violence. But its advice is not binding, which means it lacks political clout (Plasman and Sissoko, 2003; Raad van Gelijke Kansen voor Mannen en Vrouwen, 1997).

The first purple government coalition after the 1999 elections initially had no Minister of Equal Opportunities. Similar to France (see Mazur in this volume), protest from the women's movements made sure that this 'oblivion' was corrected. The Francophone Socialist Laurette Onkelinx, the new Minister of Labour and Employment, took on Equal Opportunities. Since she was also Vice-Premier gender policies rose to the level of the inner cabinet. Onkelinx presented herself less as a feminist than did Smet and neither did she have such direct links with the women's movement. Nonetheless, in 2002 new gender quota laws were enacted and the constitution was amended with an explicit recognition of the equality of men and women. But the political initiatives that led to the gender quota laws and to the constitutional reform started before Onkelinx became Minister of Equal Opportunities and she was not involved in the realization of other feminist goals such as the fund to support divorced parents, mainly women, with financial problems because their ex-partner does not pay the alimony.

After the 2003 elections Onkelinx moved to the Ministry of Justice. Equal Opportunities were again 'forgotten' but added to the portfolio of Marie Arena after protest by the women's movement. Also a Francophone Socialist, she was in charge of the Civil Service, Social Integration, Metropolitan Issues and Intercultural Dialogue. She left her post to her fellow party member Christian Dupont when the Francophone Socialists won the 2004 regional elections. The first man in charge of Equal Opportunities, he had more affinity with the other issues in his portfolio, but notably none of the successors of Smet after 1999 have defended gender equality the way she did.

Onkelinx restructured the federal women's policy agency similar to ideas circulating at the European level. In 2001 she had launched the Institute for Equality of Women and Men. There was a strong tendency within the government to include it into the existing Centre fighting racism and promoting antidiscrimination. The underlying argument was that both institutes have a similar package of responsibilities and that gender mainstreaming made a separate institute on gender policies superfluous. The women's movement was very much against this merging of institutes. It feared the disappearance of a focus on gender equality. Women would not only become a target group among others but they would do so in an environment traditionally focusing on problems of racism. The women's movement was concerned that questions of gender equality would be pushed aside by concerns about racism. In the end, the women's movement won the plea and, contrary to the United Kingdom (see Lovenduski in this volume), a separate Institute on the equality of women and men was set up in 2003.

The Institute is a federal public service monitoring the compliance of equality of women and men, fighting any form of discrimination or inequality based on sex and developing strategies and instruments for an integrated approach of gender issues. The Institute can advise the government or any other actor on matters of gender equality, it prepares and executes government decisions and follows up European or international policy measures on gender equality, but it can also take action in legal disputes regarding the penal code and other legislation on gender equality.[1] This gives the Institute an ambiguous position. It falls under the authority of the Minister in charge of Equal Opportunities, preparing and executing government decisions and reporting to the Minister on the execution of its function on an annual basis. It replaces the administrative branch of the federal women's policy agency. The federal Unit of Equal Opportunities merged into the Institute and the personnel was simply transferred to the Institute. For instance, the director of the Institute represents the Minister on official missions. But the Institute has a degree of autonomy not characteristic of a public administration, by the fact that it can undertake legal action and develop activities going beyond the traditional function of a public administration. Until now the ambiguous position gave the Institute a rather low profile while this position, when exploited strategically, might enable more autonomous action.

In sum, the last decade has been of major importance for the federal women's policy agency. It witnessed a steady upgrading in autonomy, in scope and to a certain extent in the government hierarchy. In terms of resources such as budget and personnel, however, it has always been marginal compared to other Ministers and State Secretaries. And its administrative branch faces an ambivalent position since its transfer to the Institute for Equality of Women and Men. Last but not least the affinity for gender equality of the State Secretary or Minister in charge of the women's policy agency declined since the 1999 change in coalition.

The regional women's policy agencies: development at different paces

The major changes in the Belgian women's policy agencies' structure over the last decade are related to the federalization process. A clear result of this is the development of women's policy agencies for the regions and communities. Flanders was open to a women's policy agency in the mid-1990s, while the other regions and communities followed but recently. Therefore, after the federal women's policy agency, its Flemish counterpart is the next most important one. Since the first Flemish elections in 1995, a Minister has been in charge of Equal Opportunities, but they never stayed for long.[2] Since the regional elections of 2004, a Socialist, Kathleen Van Brempt, is Minister of Mobility, Social Economy and also Equal Opportunities.

The turnover of Ministers led to multiple priorities in equal opportunities policies, even though the weak but stable administrative branch of the women's policy agency gives some continuity. The reason for this turnover is the strong impact of the Minister and of her cabinet on the policy line to follow. A focus on gender by the first Minister, Van Asbroeck, was quickly diverted to diversity by her successors, broadening the scope to sexuality, age, disability and immigrants. Women become one target group among others. The various Flemish Ministers for Equal Opportunities also differ in the type of policy tools they prefer. Van Brempt is against compelling tools such as gender impact assessment, an instrument that had been developed under Van Asbroeck and refined under her successors and that, by assessing policy initiatives under development, increases the extent to which they foster gender equality. Van Brempt prefers soft measures and initiatives, being very much in favour of the open method of coordination, which leaves the appreciation of goals and measures to a large extent to the various actors. With respect to the content, Flemish equal opportunity policies share the federal interest in women's position in the labour market and in political decision-making. Flemish advisory bodies are for instance subject to similar gender quota rules as the federal ones. Other topics such as the position of senior women or of migrant women vary because they depend on the other policy areas for which the Minister is responsible.

While the budget for equal opportunities increased over time and was already three times the initial amount in 2001, it again is marginal as compared to those of other policy areas. Furthermore, the share set aside for gender equality suffers from the increased number of target groups. The Flemish Minister of Equal Opportunities has roughly the same number of advisors as her colleague at the federal level, but her public administration is smaller. Both have three to four advisors on equal opportunities,[3] but the Flemish public administration for equal opportunities only comprises of four to five staff members and not up to 30 as does the federal one. Also different from the federal public administration is that the Flemish women's policy agency is part of the cross-sectional Department of Coordination. Set up in the wake of the UN World Conference on Women in Beijing, equal opportunities were from the beginning defined as a transversal competence crosscutting all other competencies of the Flemish government. The Minister had a coordinating function, and the same goes for the women's policy agency. Gender mainstreaming did not only influence the organizing principle of the Flemish women's policy agency, it was also high on the policy agenda of the women's policy agency. This explains for instance the early focus on the already mentioned gender impact assessment (1996). The federal women's policy agency only started to adopt a cross-sectional approach from 2000 onwards, when the EU had also picked this up. Notwithstanding the different conceptual position the federal and Flemish gender equality policies do not differ that much. All Belgian women's policy agencies concentrate on providing for equal opportunities rather than substantive equality with a focus on equal outcome.

In the other regions and communities, women's policy agencies are limited in size. Since the 2004 regional elections, the Walloon government has a fully-fledged Minister of Equal Opportunities, the Socialist Christiane Vienne, who combines this competence with Public Health and Social Action. Equal opportunities are actually framed in terms of Social Action, promoting the employment and training of women. The Minister has one advisor working specifically on the issue of equal opportunities. The Ministry of the Walloon Government has no women's policy agency. There is also a Walloon Council of Equal Opportunities for Men and Women, which is composed in a similar way and has the same tasks as the federal Council. Since 2001 a service for equal opportunities exists within the Ministry of Brussels Capital Region. Since the 2004 elections the government of Brussels Capital Region also has a State Secretary for Equal Opportunities. Brigitte Grouwels, former Minister of Equal Opportunities in the Flemish government, combines this competence with the Civil Service Affairs and the Port of Brussels. She has one advisor on equal opportunities but again no real women's policy agency at the level of the public administration.

No Minister of the Francophone Community Government is in charge of equal opportunities. The Minister-President officially ensures that bills submitted to parliament contain a gender dimension (Plasman and Sissoko, 2003). But no advisors on equal opportunities are attached to the government. The Ministry of the Francophone Community counts a unit of equal opportunities ever since it has been established. It includes a similar number of staff members as its Flemish counterpart but has a more limited budget and function. Up to date the German-speaking Community has no women's policy agency.

What federalization processes offer women's policy agencies

The federalization process facilitated the creation of new women's policy agencies, but the far-reaching autonomy of the different constituting entities led to an asymmetric structure of such institutions. Given the central role of the latter in generating laws and/or actions to foster gender equality, the asymmetric structure of women's policy agencies created a vacuum on gender equality policies in certain regions or communities. The asymmetric women's policy agencies' structure at the regional and community level might also refrain the federal women's policy agency from cooperating with the existing women's policy areas in order to avoid preferential treatment, but so far there is no evidence for this.

However, the multitude of women's policy agencies in similar positions can have a competing effect also known from the interplay of parties (Matland and Studlar, 1996; Meier, 2004). The early Flemish focus on gender mainstreaming stemmed from the wish to be more progressive than the federal women's policy agency. The Flemish craving for autonomy, stimulated by the belief that it does better than the rest of the country if it can operate by itself, might be part of the explanation for the early start and relative success of the Flemish women's policy agency. The Flemish women's policy agency wanted to prove that it was more modern and progressive than its federal predecessor. Similar tendencies are considerably less present in the other regions and communities. But once that a Flemish women's policy agency has existed, a certain amount of competition between the regions and communities stimulates the laggards to follow. This contagion effect explains the recent boost of women's policy agencies in the other regions and communities than the Flemish one.

The frequent level hopping of Ministers strengthened the contagion effect, which is itself stimulated by the fact that the Belgian federal system does not distinguish between national and regional parties. The same parties operate at all levels of the political system. Since politicians are not strictly attached to one level but move back and forth, the federalization process stimulated the turnover in Ministers responsible for gender policies from one level to another, causing a diffusion of expertise. The Brussels government introduced a portfolio for equal opportunities once the Flemish Minister of Equal Opportunities joined that government. And the government of the French-speaking Community introduced some – be it formal – sensitivity to gender issues once the federal Minister of Equal Opportunities took over the lead of that government. In both cases, these political actors had not only been in charge of gender policies at another institutional level. They also came from a policy-making environment with a certain tradition in gender equality policies. But the frequent turnover of Ministers also led to a constant reorientation of policies, involving a lack of continuity in gender equality policies, each Minister wanting to leave personal marks. A federal structure might make expertise travel, but it undermines stability.

In a federal system women's policy agencies operate in different contexts, which allows them to adapt to the specific needs of their political environment. Federalism, in this respect, facilitates more efficient gender equality policies. In 1995 Flanders was able to move ahead in a direction for which the other regions and communities were not prepared at that time. However, it is too early to see whether this possibility to adapt to the specific needs of the context will, first, involve a diversity of goals, policies and tools, and, second, a more efficient promotion of gender equality. For the time being, there seems to be an overlap in policy initiatives rather than a differentiation. All women's policy agencies, for instance, pay attention to the position of women in decision-making. Over the last years the federal and the Flemish women's policy agency ordered similar research. The various studies on the sex-balance in decision-making partly overlapped but were also incompatible. For the moment it looks as if the federalization process and the subsequent multiplication of women's policy agencies led to a fragmentation of resources, which, if taken together, could generate more output.

The supranational institutions: not just another level

The United Nations, the European Union and the Council of Europe have an important impact on Belgian gender equality policies. The international community played a decisive role in the creation of women's policy agencies (Tavares da Silva, 2004). The UN and the Council of Europe's arguments that women's policy agencies are important instruments to improve the status of women were stimuli in the Belgian case (Vogel-Polsky, 1982; 1985; 1994). The federal and the Flemish women's policy agencies are to a large extent the result of supranational influence. The federal women's policy agency was set up in the wake of the World Conference on Women in Nairobi in 1985, the Flemish one in the wake of the 1995 Beijing World Conference on Women. The structural orientation of the latter was also strongly inspired by Beijing, as illustrated by the emphasis on gender mainstreaming. Also, the recent federal institute for the equality of women and men has been strongly inspired by the EU plans for a European gender institute. Belgian legislation regarding equal opportunities is also inspired by supranational influences. Nearly all current Belgian legislation on the discrimination against women and on equal opportunities is based on European directives.[4]

The presence of different women's policy agencies in a federal setting enhances the influence of supranational initiatives. Different levels of policy-making are directly involved in the common supranational project. The presence of women's policy agencies at regional or community levels also allows for the adaptation of actions, instruments and discourses to the specific needs, expectations and culture of these political environments. But the far-reaching autonomy of the regions and communities and the asymmetric structure of the Belgian women's policy agencies temporarily excluded some policy areas from supranational input. This increased the cleavage between constituting entities of a federal state in the extent to which they develop gender equality policies. The Belgian case illustrates this last point. Comparing the number and range of actions in the critical areas defined by the Beijing Platform for Action between Flanders, on the one hand, and the Brussels and the Walloon regions, on the other, it becomes clear that the lack of women's policy agencies in the latter had a strong negative effect on the implementation of policies that the UN considers of crucial importance for improving the situation of women (Kingdom of Belgium, 2004).

Trends in Belgian gender equality policies over the last decade

We can define a couple of trends in Belgian gender equality policies over the last decade. A first trend that has already been mentioned is the fact that old and new women's policy agencies to a large extent focus on similar topics. Two further trends underline differences between the different women's policy agencies. These are the trends to define gender equality policies along the lines of gender mainstreaming and in terms of diversity policies.

Gender mainstreaming first appeared in Belgian gender equality policies as the organizing principle of the Flemish women's policy agency. At the beginning it also dominated the policy agenda. The Flemish women's policy agency invested in the development of tools in order to be able to mainstream a gender perspective, relying heavily on the Beijing Platform of Action and the Dutch experience with gender mainstreaming. In its first years, much of the resources earmarked for research went to the gathering of sex-segregated data and of a gender impact assessment tool. This was to be followed by a media-impact assessment tool, measuring the presentation of men and women as well as of male and female images in the media.

Notwithstanding the fact that the federal Minister in charge of Equal Opportunities was more hesitant on gender mainstreaming, seeing the potential pitfalls of an erosion of attention and resources paid to gender equality issues, the federal level was the first to adopt legislation imposing a follow-up of the Beijing Platform of Action in 1996. This act is based on a gender mainstreaming logic, given the fact that it requests a detailed account of the Ministers on the progress made regarding the Platform for Action. The overall impact of the 1996 act was weak, because it only contained an indirect stimulation to mainstream gender equality issues. The government is obliged to report on the progress made, but it does not have to make progress in meeting the targets defined in Beijing. The 1996 act imposes a state of the art, not an evaluation of the progress made. The Flemish government adopted a similar act in 1997, its Walloon and Francophone counterparts did so in 2002. The latter contains some elements of evaluation, but does not impose the obligation to make progress.

Since the creation of the federal Institute for Equality of Women and Men, the federal women's policy agency pushes a gender mainstreaming logic. It prepared a bill on gender budgeting, a precise identification of the strands in the budget earmarked for the fostering of gender equality, and a gender check list for policy initiatives. Also, the federal government is supposed to define a number of strategic objectives with respect to the improvement of gender equality at the beginning of the legislature, objectives that should be monitored and evaluated. The current reporting on the progress made in meeting the Beijing resolutions will be brought down from an annual to a bi-annual one, given the fact that it will play a secondary role once the bill will be adopted. The bill has a more result oriented character than any previous initiative regarding gender mainstreaming but much depends on the precise formulation of the final act. For the moment it looks as if the gender check of the budget will take place once it has been voted; it will not be a prerequisite for its approval. Independent of the final outcome of the bill, the Institute ordered a training module and toolkit for policy actors.

The idea to define a couple of strategic objectives at the beginning of each legislature flows from a pilot project in 2000/2001, the *cel gender mainstreaming* which had been inspired by similar Dutch examples. Up to date it is one of the most concrete initiatives to initiate a gender mainstreaming process in Belgian politics. All federal Ministers decided upon a strategic objective to promote gender equality, and the *cel gender mainstreaming*, a group of academics, was meant to help their cabinet and administration in operationalizing and implementing these objectives. A parallel project focused on gender budgeting. The projects were no overall success for many of the objectives got stuck at the level of implementation, but they generated awareness on the issue of gender equality and knowledge on pitfalls to be avoided when putting gender mainstreaming into practice.

While the federal women's policy agency seems to have overtaken the Flemish one when it comes to gender mainstreaming, the latter is still more active in this field than its counterparts. The Walloon advisory council on equal opportunities pro-actively screens policy initiatives taken by its government, but it does so on its own initiative. The definition of its advisory activity in terms of gender mainstreaming is inspired by and dependent on a very active president and several of its members.

Contrary to the other policy levels, the early Flemish efforts to mainstream a gender perspective were partly inspired by a New Public Management logic. The gender impact assessment tool developed in the second half of the 1990s was to be embedded in the newly designed cycle of policymaking. At the other levels, gender mainstreaming is defined in terms of promoting equality rather than a modern bureaucracy.

The New Public Management discourse nonetheless affected all the women's policy agencies, and through them the women's movement. A more precise definition of strategic objectives, their putting into operation, implementation, monitoring and evaluation, as well as a more rigid allocation of financial resources, forces the women's policy agencies to be more explicit on their policy line. Having to meet their objectives, and also to fulfil on international agreements, women's policy agencies are more tempted to define the scope of interest of women's movements. The agenda of the latter is progressively inspired by that of the women's policy agenda, which is itself partly inspired by that of the supranational level. Women's movements progressively deliver on the objectives of the women's policy agencies. They lose part of their autonomy since the women's policy agencies define their agenda without much input by the women's movement. Their relationship is not characterized by a form of public–private partnership, but rather by one of outsourcing in a vertical hierarchical setting. Another consequence of the quantifying tendency in New Public Management is the fact that the women's movements face an increased and more complicated administrative burden, making them spend part of their resources on these tasks rather than on feminist action.

Women's policy agencies not only differ in the extent to which they embrace gender mainstreaming, but also diversity. The diversity discourse is the strongest in Flanders, and especially promoted under the latest Minister of Equal Opportunities the Socialist Van Brempt, notwithstanding the opposition of (part of her staff and) the women's movement, who seem to have lost the battle. Future awareness-raising campaigns launched prior to elections will for instance focus on diversity and not on a gender balance. While before 2004 women progressively became one target group among others, the Flemish women's policy agency recently refers to intersectionality, the crosscutting of different dimensions of inequality leading up to new dynamics of inequality. Concrete policy initiatives nonetheless reflect a simple sum of different characteristics rather than a real eye for intersectionality. The Flemish women's policy agency mainly focuses on migrant women from Northern Africa and Turkey, underlining the fact that they lag behind on both migrant men and Flemish women. Intersectionality is reduced to ethnicizing gender, a phenomenon which can also be observed in Germany (see Lang in this volume), involving both a stigmatization of the migrant community and a neglect of other gender related problems.

The launching of an independent federal Institute for the Equality of Women and Men rather than its integration in the existing centre fighting racism, involved a clear-cut exclusion of a focus on intersectionality as we can also find in Finland (see Holli and Kantola in this volume). Federal gender equality policies express a concern for diversity. However, women do not become one target group among others as has been the case in Flanders. Rather, within the group of women a number of subgroups are distinguished. Another indicator for the federal focus on gender is the growing interest in the social position of men and the need to invest in them, a tendency not (yet) to be found in Flanders. All other regional women's policy agencies predominantly tend to focus on women or gender, but not on men, diversity or intersectionality.

Changing relations: the women's policy agencies and the movement

The Belgian women's movement: a diverse and changing scenery

The Belgian women's movement regroups numerous organizations. Defining the women's movement as 'organizations that address women and/or strive for equality between men and women', a recent inquiry identified 900 of them (Amazone et al., 2002). The compartmentalization along ideological and religious/secular lines ('pillarization'), a central feature of the Belgian society, influences to a large extent the structure of the movement. Although the cleavages became less salient over the last decades, the organizing of the women's movements still reflects this segmentation. Numerous women's organizations, such as political women's organizations or women's branches of trade unions and socio-cultural organizations, are active within the various ideological political pillars. Many organizations focus on cultural activities and training, but they also act as pressure groups influencing politics and policies. Being part of an ideological pillar of society is a strategy to act from within the existing structures. But these political women's organizations pay a price for their closeness to the centre of power (and for their financial support). They have to invest in integrating to the organizations and their autonomy is limited. But political parties are also interested in the members and mobilizing potential of the women's movement, which enlarge their electoral basis. The price parties pay is to consider the demands of their women's section. It is mainly the three traditional political groups, the Christian Democrats, Socialists and Liberals who have a political women's branch.

Next to the integrated, there is an autonomous branch of the women's movement, which is characterized by the fact that it goes beyond the traditional cleavages. Main players in this field are the overarching Dutch- and French-speaking Councils of Women (*Nederlandstalige Vrouwenraad, Conseil de Femmes Francophones de Belgique*), regrouping a host of smaller organizations. The other two major autonomous women's organizations are the Flemish *Vrouwen Overleg Komitee* (Women's Reflection Group) and the Francophone *Comité de Liaison de Femmes* (Women's Coordinating Group), coordinating the Dutch- and French-speaking activities with respect to the international women's day. The latter is also composed of affiliated women's groups, the first only of individuals (Wiercx and Woodward, 2004).

In terms of composition and structure, no major shifts occurred during the 1990s. An exception is the establishment of the national contact centre for women and women's organizations, *Amazone*, in 1995.[5] It houses the four umbrella organizations just described and five other women's organizations, is a contact point for many other organizations, and has a documentation centre and an archive. It aims at promoting contacts and cooperation among Flemish and Francophone women's organizations. In 2001 a Flemish counterpart was established: the *Gelijke Kansenhuis* (House of Equal Opportunities), which houses a couple of Flemish women's organizations and a documentation centre. There is no Francophone counterpart.

We also need to stress the recent emergence of loose networks of younger feminists, such as *F.C. Poppensnor* (Footballclub Doll's Mustache) and NextGENDERation Network, focusing on the exchange of information. These groups rely heavily on the Internet as a means of communication and diversity is one of their core concerns. During the last couple of years migrant women's organizations have also emerged on to the political scene. The *Steunpunt Allochtone Meisjes en Vrouwen* (Help desk for Migrant Girls and Women) groups several migrant women's organizations and is supported by the Flemish government. It wants to give them a stronger voice in political debates like the one on wearing a headscarf in public.

Notwithstanding the diverse and fragmented character of the women's movements, they share a series of fields of interests (Wiercx, 2005). During the last decade the women's movements focused on family related issues such as the status of the wife assisting in her husband's profession, men's participation in care work and the sharing of work and family, as well as on equal opportunities in the labour market, equal pay and the glass ceiling. Health issues related to sexuality, birth control, sexually trans-ferable diseases, abortion and euthanasia form another group of com-mon issues. Equal participation in political decision-making is central to the political women's movements, but other organizations also paid attention to these themes. Violence against women in the family and sexual harassment at work have been shared concerns. Recently the head-scarf and by extension the position of 'white' feminism and women's organizations vis-à-vis Islamic women and feminism have become a hot topic (Sjegers, 2005).

A recent study on the Flemish women's movements (Wiercx and Woodward, 2004; see also Wiercx, 2005) showed that their activities and strategies have changed considerably over the last thirty years. The activity in which the Flemish women's organizations nowadays invest most is training and sensitizing. The second and the third most important activities concern press contacts and contacts with other organizations, politicians or civil servants. Parallel to this shift in the nature of activ-ities, a change in strategies has occurred. Women's organizations mainly react to political events, evaluating them. A more proactive attitude, such as lobbying or agenda setting, are considered less important by the majority of the women's organizations. Flemish women's movements rarely use strategies that demand an active engagement of its members or that seek confrontation.

This evolution in type of activity and strategy was sustained by a double attitude of policymakers towards the women's movements (Wiercx, 2005; Hooghe, 1997). On the one hand the former financially support the movements, the major ones structurally, some others on a project basis. Women's movements diverge in size, structure, strategies and aims, but their main financial resources are state subsidies (Van Haegendoren et al., 1994). The regional level is the most important financial resource, fol-lowed by the national level and Europe. Revenues from membership fees, sponsoring, or commercial activities are marginal. On the other hand policymakers are selective in responding to the demands of the women's movement (Hooghe, 1997). The large dependence on public financing combined with the closed character of the political system makes women's organizations get partly 'co-opted' by the state. It needs to be stressed that the institutionalization of the women's movement relates only to a segment of the women's movement. Many smaller women's groups with no official structure and financing are not subject to this development in the same way. Nonetheless, the professionalization of the women's movement marginalizes women without the means to interact with institutionalized branches as we can also see in Germany (see Lang in this volume). Most migrant women's organizations are for instance absent in political debates and interaction.

Federalization, Europeanization and the relation between the women's policy agencies and the movement

The establishment of regional women's policy agencies made the policy structures adapt to those of the women's movement. The integrated women's movement had federalized in the 1970s, in the wake of the splitting up of the national parties in the Flemish and Francophone ones. The new and radical feminist women's groups that emerged in the 1970s immediately organized themselves at a regional level. The federalization of the women's movements made also these organizations fit with the structure of Belgian politics, which raised their potential to respond to cultural and political specificities. Their increased autonomy also released them from constraints playing at the central state level. But federalization also weakened the women's movements, because it hampers national mobilization, which can be necessary on policy matters being a competence of the federal state. The absence of a central state level in the women's movements' organizational structure undermines overarching co-operation. Joint action of the Flemish and the Francophone women's movements is further handicapped by the increasingly diverging evolution of Flanders and Wallonia, which also obstructs solidarity between stronger and weaker women's movements of the same political group.

The federalization of the women's policy agencies increased the links with the women's movements. A women's policy agency at the same level constitutes a stimulus in itself, because of the important source of subsidies, which women's policy agencies are, but also for co-operation with policy-makers. But the asymmetric structure of the women's policy institutions and its absence in certain regions or communities is disadvantageous for the movements depending on these agencies. The Flemish women's policy agency became an important partner for Flemish women's organizations, while others had so to speak no women's policy agency to turn to during the second half of the 1990s. The differences in strength and institutionalization between the Flemish and Francophone women's movements are partly due to the different possibilities provided for by the various women's policy agencies.[6] This difference was explicitly recognized in 2000, when the federal Minister of Equal Opportunities financed a couple of Francophone chairs of feminist studies. This initiative broke with the tradition to treat the various regions and communities equally. Federal subsidies filled in the gap created by the fact that the Francophone side of the country did not have its own women's policy agencies. But the federal women's policy agency does not tend to lend itself for this kind of compensation. On the contrary, national initiatives, such as *Sophia*, the Belgian network for gender studies and feminist research, face growing difficulties in finding financial support. They can only rely on the federal level, which is the more difficult because of the erosion of the central state level.

Supranational influences did not fundamentally alter the relation between the women's policy agencies and movements. The earlier mentioned *Amazone* and overarching women's organizations link Flemish and Francophone women's organizations to the international level. For instance, *Amazone* and the Flemish Council for Women participated in the Deuce-project[7] on equal wages. The Councils for Women are members of the International Council of Women and of the European Women's Lobby (EWL); the Francophone Council for Women is also a member of the International Association of French-speaking Women. The *Comité de Liaison de Femmes* is even a founding member of the European Women's Lobby.[8] The EU level is mainly an extra source of financial resources, making the women's movements less dependent on the various Belgian women's policy agencies. The supranational level is also an important source of knowledge and inspiration, and often referred to in order to justify and legitimize claims. And it facilitates cooperation among Belgian partners. The supranational level allows the women's movements to operate at the regional level, while undertaking collective actions within the framework of supranational initiatives. But on the whole, the Belgian women's movements, notwithstanding their vicinity to the EU or the EWL, do not focus on supra- or transnational partners.

State feminism in a multilevel setting: a two-sided coin

In their short life the Belgian women's policy agencies underwent important evolutions. The steady upgrading of the federal women's policy agency mainly in terms of hierarchy (but not backed up by more finances and personnel), the creation of the Institute for the Equality of Women and Men, and of regional women's policy agencies, are surely the most visible changes that took place since 1990. The creation of the latter is to be explained by the federalization of the Belgian state, a contagion effect between the various state levels, the shifts of ministers and their expertise from one level to another and supranational pressure. Regional women's policy agencies not only differ with regard to the moment they were created, but also regarding their size and policy. The Flemish women's policy agency is more active in gender mainstreaming than the federal one, targets other groups (such as ethnic minorities) and deals with intersectionality. The federal women's policy agency distances itself from diversity politics and focuses on (different groups of) women and, more recently, also on men.

The multilevel setting of the Belgian women's policy agencies is a two-sided coin. The positive effects are that it made them correspond to the structure of the women's movements, enhances the adaptation of policies and supranational initiatives to specific needs and contexts and that competition between the levels stimulates evolution. The most important negative implications of the multilevel setting of the women's policy agencies are overlap and fragmentation of scarce resources and a lack of continuity in gender equality policies due to the high turnover of Ministers in charge of gender equality. Furthermore, the Belgian federalization process led – at least up to now – to an asymmetric structure of women's policy agencies, creating a vacuum on gender equality policies, supranational input and resources in regions with no or weak women's policy agencies. This also has implications for the women's movements. It hampered the movements given the increased financial dependency on and cooperation with the women's policy agencies, which is caused by the professionalization of the former, New Public Management reforms and supranational policies promoting collaboration.

The Belgian case shows that the political opportunity structure of women's policy agencies and of women's movements is influenced by the interdependence of different policy-making levels characterizing many of the current political systems. They deserve attention because they put the potential of feminist actors in a multilevel system in perspective and show a need to investigate the precise interaction between different levels of policy-making, the necessary structural conditions for effective governance as well as for effective output. A lesson from the Belgian case might be that such conditions do exist. A symmetric structure enhances interaction and cooperation, whereas asymmetry can cause a deficit in the policy outcome and in clear-cut governance.

Notes

1. http://www.iefh.fgov.be of 30/6/2006.
2. During the first legislature a Socialist, Anne Van Asbroeck (who left it to a Christian-Democrat, Brigitte Grouwels after two years), occupied this post. Both of them combined it with a competence for Brussels' Affairs. After the electoral success of the Greens in 1999, Mieke Vogels became Minister of Equal Opportunities, combining it with Social Welfare and Health. She resigned due to the disastrous results of the Greens at the 2003 federal elections. Her mandate was taken over by her party colleague Adelheid Byttebier.
3. This is an average number of advisors.
4. http://www.iefh.fgov.be (accessed 30 June 2006).
5. http://www.amazone.be of 30/6/2006 (accessed 30 June 2006).
6. Other explanations are the specific political context in the case of the integrated women's movement and the strength of personalities.
7. Deuce aimed to raise the awareness of wage inequality in the government, in management and trade unions, and among women (www.deuceonline.be).
8. The *Vrouwen Overleg Komitee* is not a member of international organizations.

5
State Feminism Finnish Style: Strong Policies clash with Implementation Problems

Anne Maria Holli and Johanna Kantola

In international comparisons, Finland is regarded as one of the Nordic 'women-friendly' welfare states. In gender equality policy, Finland has been a runner-up which has followed the pioneers Norway and Sweden. Although Finland established its first gender equality machinery, the Council for Gender Equality, simultaneously with them in 1972, it was the last Nordic country to introduce a gender equality law in 1986. In a Nordic comparative analysis of the effectiveness of gender equality policy in the mid-1990s, Finland was placed in the third tier after Sweden and Norway, but before Denmark and Iceland. However, it was also observed that Finland deployed the least money per capita on its gender equality machinery and personnel (Borchorst, 1999, pp. 182, 184–5).

Nevertheless, international comparative studies on gender equality machineries reveal the relatively high success of both Finnish women's movements and state feminism between 1969 and 1999. Finnish women's constituencies tended to achieve what they wanted from the state, if they had demands on the issue. Partly, it was because favourable structural conditions exist for women's policy influence in Finland. Partly, it was because women's organizations, women MPs and gender equality machinery successfully co-operated via 'strategic partnerships' (Halsaa, 1991) on pragmatic policy issues. Before the 1990s, gender equality agencies also seemed to be the necessary links between women's movements and the state (Holli, 2006). The mechanisms for women's policy influence were very different from, for example, Sweden as they included women MPs co-operating across parties in parliament and even occasionally voting against their own party line (Holli, 2001, 2003, pp. 156–71, 2004, 2006; Holli and Kantola, 2005; Aalto and Holli, 2007).

This chapter analyses the situation since the mid-1990s when the gender equality machinery and women's movements began to work more independently from each other, but still in tandem. First, we discuss the changing political context of state feminism. Second, we map the institutional changes in the gender equality machinery and the ways in which they have shaped the contents and priorities of policy. Third, we scrutinize the new issues, such as gender mainstreaming, and the remaining challenges, including gender diversity, municipal gender equality work and complacent ideology. Finally, we return to the relationship between the women's movements and the gender equality machinery. We argue that whilst the gender equality machineries and policies have been strengthened in some significant respects, serious challenges remain in the form of the changed political context and implementation problems.

The reconfigured state as the new context of state feminism

The political context of Finnish state feminism has changed significantly since the mid-1990s. Three factors are particularly pertinent: recession and welfare state retrenchment, EU membership, and decentralization. Changes in the political colour of the governing parties, in contrast, have not impacted on state feminism to the same extent – a point that will be elaborated later. A severe recession in the beginning of the 1990s – caused largely by the collapse of the Soviet Union – is perhaps the most significant factor shaping the restructuring of the state in Finland. The depth of the recession is captured by the following figures: in 1991–93, the GDP fell by almost 12 per cent, and the number of unemployed went up from under 4 per cent to over 18 per cent (Hiilamo, 2002, p. 192). The recession created a crisis, where it was easier to push through changes that would have met with stiff resistance otherwise (Heiskala, 2006, p. 30). The resulting 'welfare society' delegated more responsibility for providing welfare upon individuals, families, the municipalities, the market and the third sector, with a much diminished role reserved for the state (Lehtonen, 2000; Julkunen, 2001, 2002). This was accompanied by a discursive shift to neoliberal values: to economic efficiency and innovation, where there was less room for arguments about social justice and equality (Heiskala, 2006, p. 36).

Notably the recession unsettled the women-friendly welfare state orthodoxy and the welfare state cuts affected women disproportionately (Savola, 2000, pp. 75–7; Lehto and Blomster, 2000, pp. 176–82). The recession had a long term impact on women's labour market participation. There was a loss of public sector employment and women's work now involves fixed short term contract work as opposed to permanent jobs. Furthermore, there are tendencies towards feminization of poverty, resulting from the loss of redistributive policies for single parents. Several commentators suggest that the Finnish welfare model has undergone a shift from an egalitarian to neofamilial model with increased women's dependency on individual men and the state and men's dependency on women's poorly paid care work at home (Julkunen, 2002; Haataja, 2004).

The international context of Finnish gender equality policies was traditionally defined by the United Nations (UN). For example, CEDAW was the key in the drafting of the Gender Equality Act in 1986 and in the consequent establishment of the Equality Ombudsman (Räsänen, 2002; Pentikäinen, 2002; Zwingel, 2005). A dramatic change in the multilevel governance framework came about in 1995 when Finland joined the European Union (EU). The membership's impact on the political system, economy, foreign policy, agriculture and social policy has been studied in a number of texts (Raunio and Wiberg, 2000, 2001). Less well researched is the impact of the membership on gender equality policies. For example, the betterment of individual rights and the strengthening of anti-discrimination legislation have been important for advancing gender equality (Nieminen, 2001). Soft law emanating from the EU, in the form of recommendations, guidelines and action plans, is also shaping gender equality policies in Finland.

A more fundamental impact on gender relations is embedded in the neoliberal tendencies of the EU, the changing forms of governance, state–society relations and New Public Management (NPM). This has the potential to create additional pressure on the traditional Nordic type of the welfare state based on citizenship and living in the country. The European integration challenges social rights that are based on residence and rather promotes free movement of people, which, in turn might result in cutting down national, redistributive, taxation funded social policies (Julkunen, 2001, p. 213).

The three strands discussed above, recession, reconfiguration of the welfare state and EU membership, affected the decentralization of powers to the local and regional level in the 1990s. The Finnish type of 'welfare municipality', in addition to being the basic, self-governing unit for democratic politics, is also the central provider of most welfare services, that is, childcare, basic education, social services, and health care. In 1992–95, a series of institutional reforms were enacted that strengthened the autonomy and independent decision-making powers of the municipalities vis-à-vis the state (Valanta, 2000; Majoinen, 2001; Leväsvirta, 1999). However, this took place at the same time as the municipalities were hit with the worst effects of the recession, making the reforms look very much like the state was delegating the difficult economic cutback decisions to the local level. The local solutions to the problems were partly found in privatization and delegation of responsibilities to the third sector, partly in a rationalization of local administration and services according to the framework of NPM ideologies (Möttönen, 1997).

Finland adopts the Swedish/Norwegian institutional model for state feminism . . .

Attempts to reorganize gender equality agencies started in Finland as early as the first half of the 1990s. When the Gender Equality Ombudsman's office had been created in 1987, the staff of the new Ombudsman and the Council for Gender Equality (*Tasa-arvoasiain neuvottelukunta*, TANE, established in 1972) had been put under the same roof, in the *Gender Equality Office*, under the bureaucratic leadership of the Ombudsman despite their different and independent tasks. This ad-hoc arrangement caused a series of practical problems (Tasa-arvoelinten työnjako, 1995). Finally, the problems were resolved by separating the agencies at the same time as a third, governmental body, the Gender Equality Unit (TASY) was established in the Ministry of Social Affairs and Health in 2001. This solution was influenced by a wish to emulate the Swedish and Norwegian examples for stronger and more effective gender equality policy, by adopting their organizational structure.

Consequently, since 2001, Finland follows the Swedish/Norwegian organizational model where the three different tasks of national gender equality policy are administratively separated (see Holli, 1995; Borchorst, 1999). The *law-enforcing* function, that is, supervising compliance with the Act on Equality between Women and Men, giving statements on individual citizens' complaints on gender discrimination as well as providing advice and information on the law and its application, belongs to the *Equality Ombudsman*. The *executive-administrative* function of preparing and developing governmental gender equality policy is the responsibility of the ministerial *Gender Equality Unit*. It also takes care of gender mainstreaming, EU-policies and international gender equality affairs (see below). *The Council for Gender Equality* embraces a *political-advisory* function. It is a parliamentary advisory body consisting of thirteen members, most often MPs, nominated by the Cabinet on the suggestion by political parties. Since the late 1990s, also NYTKIS (*Naisjärjestöt yhteistyössä* – The Coalition of Finnish Women's Associations) the cross-party co-operative organ of Finnish women's political organizations and NGOs, has had a permanent expert representative in the Council. The aim of the Council is to promote gender equality in society by giving initiatives and statements as well as to promote research and co-operation between various societal actors. Its main task today is to channel new ideas to public debate.

The interviewed femocrats were well aware of additional nuances to this division of labour. '(W)e are the Government', a bureaucrat working in the Gender Equality Unit described the institution (Interview A 4 January 2006). The placement within the Ministry gives some power but it also restricts opportunities for more critical opinions or more radical action, as some interviewees pointed out (Interview 1 February 2006). By comparison, both the Equality Ombudsman and the Council for Gender Equality were depicted as more independent. They were seen as able to offer more critical statements and analyses on various policy issues (Interview 27 February 2006). For the Ombudsman, this status is the result of her high formal independence as a law-enforcing authority. Also the Gender Equality Act, the backbone for the Ombudsman's mandate and tasks, has been strengthened over the years (Interviews A and B 3 February 2006). The Council for Gender Equality, in turn, is not only a governmental body but it also includes representatives from the opposition parties, making its starting-point already more critical. The Council was also regarded as possessing 'more degrees of freedom', and a body that 'can and must propose long-term solutions' (Interviews 4 November 2005; 27 February 2006). The three gender equality offices make good use of their resources and different strengths by dividing various international and domestic tasks between themselves, and they often co-operate on practical policy issues.

The institutional separation of 2001 almost doubled the personnel resources for the Finnish gender equality institutions,[1] but they were not divided evenly. Today, the Equality Ombudsman's office and the Gender Equality Unit are the best resourced, with 10–11 staff in both. The Council for Gender Equality has only two full-time staff and some part-time officers for its subcommittees. Moreover, its budget for activities was reduced more than 40 per cent from 2001 onwards. This has shifted the role of the Council from being a doer towards being an organizer which has to find partners willing to take the financial responsibility for the seminars and other events to be arranged (Interview 24 November 2005).

Additionally, there are three institutions linked to the three agencies described above: the *Gender Equality Board* (a judicial organ for supervising the Act on Equality together with the Gender Equality Ombudsman), the *Minister for Gender Equality* and the *Standing Committee of Labour Market and Gender Equality Affairs* in the Parliament. The role of the latter two changed in the reorganization of the agencies, thus inviting closer examination.

The *Minister for Gender Equality* is the political leader of national gender equality policy. A Cabinet Minister has been given a second portfolio in gender equality issues on top of her or his proper portfolio since 1980. From 1995, the gender equality portfolio has been given to either of the two Ministers of Social Affairs and Health, and all of them have been women with one exception. The ministerial Gender Equality Unit works as an aide to the Minister and as her/his tool in drafting policy and implementing gender mainstreaming. The interviewees generally agree that the establishment of this structure has also strengthened the Minister's role (Interview 1 February 2006). According to the interviewed femocrats, political colour does not affect the Minister's effectiveness but rather her/his feminism and knowledge of gender equality issues. It seems that Finland has been quite fortunate in this respect as most of the gender equality ministers during the last ten years have either had a lively interest in gender equality matters or at least been 'willing to learn', as some of the femocrats put it. This is important, since the minister's role is crucial in looking after gender equality issues in Cabinet meetings and in creating a favourable political and administrative context for the promotion of gender equality, for example by assigning resources.

After the establishment of the Gender Equality Unit, the Standing Committee of Labour Market Affairs in the Parliament formally also adopted a role in gender equality issues, to form a parliamentary check and balance mechanism to the new ministerial structure. This occurred in a framework of a work-form reform of the parliament, in which some of the activists of the Women MPs' Network made a proposal to change the committee's formal duties and saw the reform through. The *Standing Committee of Labour Market and Gender Equality Affairs* investigates governmental bills on gender equality as well as EU directives transposed onto national legislation on behalf of the parliament, by hearing experts and writing statements on the proposals to the decision-making plenary sessions. However, despite its specialized mandate the Committee is seldom consulted by other parliamentary standing committees which also deal with various gender equality issues on their own areas of expertise (Interview 27 February 2006).

In conclusion, both the executive-administrative and law-enforcing institutions for gender equality were considerably strengthened in Finland in the early 2000s. New bodies, such as the Gender Equality Unit and the Standing Committee of Labour Market and Gender Equality Affairs, were created. By contrast, the Council for Gender Equality, which had had a more political character than its Nordic counterparts, became very much weaker, although it still commands a surprising amount of respect considering its diminished resources.

. . . and gets more visible and effective national gender equality policies

The reorganizing of gender equality institutions seems to have fulfilled some of the hopes that motivated it. Gender equality policies have become more visible and effective at the central state level, especially since the turn of the 2000s. Here we scrutinize three aspects of gender equality policies – government programmes, action plans for gender equality, and equality legislation – that constitute the key tools for formal gender equality policy.

The Government Programmes and the Government's Action Plans for Gender Equality are two of the major policy documents that testify of the priority placed on gender equality issues. The *Government Programme* is the agreement by the parties forming the Cabinet coalition and it sets the main targets and tasks to be implemented during the term of office. Especially, the gender pay gap and measures for reconciliating family and working-life have figured in government programmes since the early 1990s. However, gender equality policy as a specific policy area has become much more prominent in Cabinet than previously since 1999. Anneli Jäätteenmäki (Centre Party), the first female Prime Minister of Finland, together with other feminist politicians who participated in the negotiations on the Government Programme (2003), made sure that gender equality issues were exceptionally high on the agenda (Interview 1 March 2006; 6 April 2006). When Jäätteenmäki had to resign after two months in office, the very same programme was adopted by the succeeding Centre-Left government.

The last decade has also witnessed two of the three *action plans for gender equality* ever adopted by the Government of Finland, 1997–99 and 2004–07. The 1997–99 Action Plan was a national plan for implementing the objectives of the Beijing Platform for Action. It targeted gender mainstreaming and violence against women in particular, encompassing a total of 13 issue areas and 30 projects. It was a fragmented collection of projects proposed by the Ministries to the coordinating Council for Gender Equality, prepared on a tight time schedule and with little resources and necessary expertise (STM, 1997; Interview 26 June 1996). By contrast, the 2004–07 Action Plan was a much more coordinated endeavour. It was prepared by the Gender Equality Unit and set out the concrete measures to be taken by the Government to implement the objectives of its Programme

(2003), including, for example, equal pay, gender mainstreaming of the whole administration, redistributing the costs incurred by parental leaves between all employers and preventing prostitution and trafficking (Government's Action Plan for Gender Equality, 2004–07).

Although the agencies contributed to several reforms on gender equality from the 1990s, the strengthening of the *Act on Equality* from 1986 is maybe the most important accomplishment. The first more comprehensive reform in 1995 introduced for public authorities the legal obligation to ensure the balanced representation of women and men (numerical gender quotas) in various indirectly elected or nominated bodies (Law 206/1995). Together with a later reform in 2005 (Law 232/2005) the amendments made the obligations of employers to promote equality much more extensive. A gender equality plan must be prepared annually in all workplaces with at least 30 employees. This includes most of the work-places within the public sector, too, a half of which had fulfilled this obligation in 2005 (Melkas and Lehto, 2005). Moreover, the responsibility of public authorities to promote gender equality were made more detailed in the law, for example, by stating that they must create and establish practices that ensure that gender equality is taken into account in all policy preparation and decision-making. This was one of the legal instruments which were used to aid gender mainstreaming.

Femocrats working in the Ombudsman's Office have emphasized that these extensions to the law have changed both their work as law-enforcers and Finnish gender equality policy in general (Interviews A and B 3 February 2006; 24 February 2006). Notably, developing new legal tools and gender equality planning can be interpreted as carrying on in the national/Nordic tradition of gender equality work, that is, these measures were not dictated by the EU or not even learned from there. On the one hand, these national legal instruments for promoting gender equality can be regarded as inefficient and too bureaucratic (Ahtela, 2001) as well as clashing with the more recent demands for gender mainstreaming; on the other hand, as the example above shows and Mustakallio and Saari (2002, pp. 175–8) also point out, they can be profitably combined for more effective mainstreaming.

Despite the national/Nordic solutions adopted, all femocrats interviewed emphasized that the EU had also strengthened and legitimized the work done in the Finnish gender equality machineries: it had 'backed them up', given them 'new tools' and 'prestige'. The EU was thus viewed very positively: 'The EU is an easy area as far as gender equality is concerned; usually there is nothing there that we'd resist' (Interview 9 February 2006). The Gender Equality Unit officially represents Finland at the EU level and, for example, the director of the unit participates in the meetings of the High Level Group for Gender Mainstreaming, an advisory body that meets twice a year at the beginning of a new European Union Presidency in order to support the implementation of the Gender Mainstreaming Strategy in the framework of the Presidential programme.

The positive impact of the EU is seen directly in the legislative changes that have taken place in the last decade. For example, the amendments of the Gender Equality Act in 2002 and 2005 incorporated EU directives into Finnish legislation. The femocrats emphasized that whilst the EU sets the minimum standard, usually Finland is above it, and there are no pressures to lower the national standards. Specifically, Finnish anti-discrimination legislation has been strengthened in the relation to equal pay, discrimination against pregnant women, indirect discrimination, sexual harassment and compensation for discrimination as a result of EU directives (Interview 3 February 2006).

The interviewees identified the use of different indicators in the EU and the UN as another important dimension of the impact of the trans-national gender equality policies on Finland. These indicators enable the gender equality machineries to draw attention to the fields where Finland is lagging behind (Interview 24 November 2006). The EU-level co-operation has also given better insights to the femocrats where this might take place, such as innovative policies on reconciliation of family and work and women's participation in economic decision-making, when compared to other member states (Interview 9 February 2006). This contrasts to public opinion in Finland that tends to hold that Finland is a model country of gender equality.

Yet, the femocrats did not discern any direct policy impact of the EU in the area of gender equality apart from the legislative amendments. Nevertheless, it is notable that the EU is having indirect impact in relation to a number of fields in terms of soft law rather than hard law. Different soft law measures can, on the one hand, provide legitimacy to many issues that were previously not part of the gender equality agenda in Finland, such as violence against women in its many forms including prostitution and sexual harassment (Kantola, 2006a). On the other hand, this impact can also be negative. For example, the use of soft law in relation to violence against women draws attention away from the criminal law (Nousiainen, 2005). One femocrat argued that the constant pressure emanating from the EU to cut down the public sector and make it more efficient is directly making Finnish women worse off: 'It is clear that substantive equality is not progressing to the same extent as formal gender equality' (Interview 27 February 2006).

Lack of resources was an often mentioned problem in the work of the gender equality machineries in relation to the EU. First, the consultation demands by the EU required a lot of work in a short time span by a small group of civil servants in the agencies (Interviews 4 November 2006; 27 February 2006). Second, personnel shortage impacted on the chances of the Finnish gender equality agencies to influence EU level gender equality policies. According to the femocrats, the EU actors are keen to learn about the Finnish experiences on women's labour market participation and women in political decision-making (Interviews 3 February 2006; 9 February 2006; 6 April 2006). Yet, a major challenge for this policy influence was too few staff which makes it impossible for the agencies to prepare for the EU level meetings as they would wish (Interview 9 February 2006). Finally, the gender equality machineries have not been able to fully use EU level funding because they do not have the sufficient resources and personnel to run the bureaucratically demanding projects (Interviews 24 November 2006; 9 February 2006).

New policy areas: violence, men and gender mainstreaming

The strengthened institutional structures have resulted in the workload of the gender equality machineries to increase disproportionately. The femocrats have thus to prioritize policy issues where they can. Women's participation in the labour market has traditionally been and has remained important in the work done by the machineries. Currently there is a focus on the gender pay gap and indirect discrimination against women, for example, in relation to pregnancy. A new emerging theme, as mentioned above, is the emphasis on gender equality planning in the workplaces. A traditional gender equality issue, municipal childcare, is no longer prominent in the work done by the femocrats (Aalto, 2003; Kantola, 2006a). Rather, there is a new focus on reconciliation of work and family.

Two new themes have become prominent in the 1990s and 2000s. First, *violence against women* was recognized as a serious gender equality problem in Finland in the beginning of the 1990s. The issue gained prominence, not least due to the fact that Finland tops the European domestic violence figures (Kantola, 2006a). The issue was taken up by the Council for Gender Equality and its subcommittee on violence against women. Significant progress has been made. Yet one of the most significant problems is that no other state body has taken up the responsibility to deal with the issue but it remains the responsibility of the equality machineries which do not have the sufficient resources or mandate to deal with it properly. Other forms of violence have entered the agenda as well, including trafficking in women and forced prostitution. Both the women's movement actors and the gender equality machineries lobbied for criminalizing buying sex in line with the Swedish model.

Second, the theme of *men and gender equality* has gained prominence in Finland. A subcommittee on men and gender equality was established under the Council for Gender Equality in 1988, but lately, also as a result of the Nordic influence, the issue has become ever more prominent (Interview B 24 January 2006). The femocrats evaluated that it is being enthusiastically embraced at the EU level, and during its EU presidency in 2006, Finland hosted a conference on the topic. Two competing perspectives can be discerned. On the one hand, there is a focus on men's situation as opposed to women's rights. In the public discussion, men's situation in relation to such themes as divorce, child custody, violence, health, alcoholism and marginalization have gained attention. On the other hand, an alternative perspective focuses upon men's role in gender equality work and women's empowerment. Here the challenge is to make men participate in debates about gender equality, to integrate a 'men's perspective' in gender equality policies, and finally, make clear that gender does not signify women only (Interview B 24 January 2006). In practice, this has meant drawing the men's movement actors, such as 'Fellowship of Men's Associations', *Miessakit*, into the work done by the national gender equality machineries. This poses challenges in itself, because the men's organizations often have limited expertise on mainstream gender equality issues and the overall context of gender equality work and the femocrats have to consider carefully which concerns to integrate into their work and which not (Interview B 24 January 2006).

It is notable that the welfare state retrenchment is not directly an issue for the gender equality machineries. However, indirectly it brings up certain issues, such as fixed short term contract work – as opposed to permanent contracts – that is increasingly common for young women. Furthermore, the gender equality machineries have had to adapt to a new neoliberal discourse. One femocrat noted that gender equality is no longer a value in itself but has to be promoted with the language of NPM, where gender equality is argued to increase productivity or competitiveness (Interview 9 February 2006; cf. Skjeie, 2006).

Gender mainstreaming and gender equality machineries now constitute the two dimensions of the so-called dual strategy for gender equality in Finland. On the one hand, gender mainstreaming is to ensure that gender equality is addressed across public administration and all public policies. On the other hand, gender equality agencies represent the continuation of gender-specific equality policies. The two are not competing but rather complementary and, in practice, the relationship between them is close. One agency – the Gender Equality Unit – is charged with the responsibility of overseeing the implementation of gender mainstreaming in state administration. The Unit has been allocated one project worker for this task. Gender mainstreaming is applied in five areas in particular: (i) preparation of legislation, (ii) projects and programmes, (iii) staff policy, (iv) performance management (*tulosohjaus*), and (iv) budgeting (Onwen, 2004). The areas cover both personnel in and policies emanating from the ministries and they include new forms of management as well as decisions on finances.

Whilst gender mainstreaming has benefited from international pressure, current practices are firmly embedded in the history of gender equality politics in Finland. Since the 1980 governmental gender equality plan, it has been known as 'equality permeation principle' (*tasa-arvon läpäisyperiaate*) (Holli, 1991). Gender mainstreaming has been slowly institutionalized in the governmental gender equality plans and finally in the Government Programme (2003). Indeed, femocrats feel that they are still doing the same thing – only the name has changed to denote a more modern mode of governance (Interview 24 January 2006; cf. Verloo, 2001, pp. 4–6).

The gender equality machineries have had some success in implementing gender mainstreaming. Nevertheless, a number of significant problems remain. First, the gender equality agencies have completely insufficient resources for the scope of gender mainstreaming outlined in the Government Programme. The project worker's time goes into training and consultation; there is little space for co-ordination or in-depth analysis. No integrated knowledge of what has been done in different ministries exists (Interview 24 January 2006). Statistics also point to significant challenges. In 1994, only 1 per cent of all government bills addressed gender equality, in 1998 2 per cent, and in 2004 6 per cent (Jauhola, 2005, p. 8). The government goal to gender mainstream all legislative preparations by 2006 seems unrealistic in the light of these statistics. The femocrats describe the process of implementing gender mainstreaming as 'hitting your head against the wall' and 'taking very small steps at a time' (Interviews 24 January 2006; 9 February 2006).

Second, the lack of resources impacts on the forms of gender mainstreaming that can be promoted. Here the lack of tools that the gender equality agencies have at their hands becomes evident. One civil servant described the tools as to 'inspire, monitor and remind' and no sanctioning mechanisms exist except for the 'shame factor' (Interview 24 January 2006).

In such a process, gender mainstreaming becomes associated with individual actors and their capabilities. It is not embedded in the structures or the workings of the state administration. The know-how and the training are lost when personnel changes (Interview 9 February 2006). This becomes an example of a problematic tendency to adopt some of the components of gender mainstreaming only, especially tools or techniques, in the absence of an overall framework (Daly, 2005, p. 436). Here, gender mainstreaming places an overarching focus on policy-makers acquiring skills and implementing a set of methods and procedures, which in turn, signifies the 'technocratization' of gender mainstreaming. Gender mainstreaming resembles more a mode of delivery than a policy agenda or programme in its own right (Daly, 2005, p. 436; cf. Interview 1 February 2006).

Finally, due to these reasons, the form that gender mainstreaming takes in Finland is integrationist rather than agenda-setting (see Chapter 1 for definitions). Thus, it involves an attempt to try to intervene into existing government policies rather than to reshape or question them. Gender mainstreaming renders legitimacy to the often neoliberal policies of the government. One example is the aim to gender mainstream one of its main strategies, that is, performance management (*tulosohjaus*). There is no critical questioning of the overall goals of performance management, but rather an acceptance of the government policy and values of efficiency, productivity, and result-based pay.

Diversity: dissociated from gender equality

It is as interesting to explore the directions that Finnish gender equality policy *is* taking, as to focus upon the paths that it is *not* following. It is notable that diversity approach has had much less influence on the workings of the gender equality machineries in Finland than gender mainstreaming. Whilst for example in Britain, it is now impossible to talk about equality without diversity (Squires, forthcoming 2007b), in Finland, the two remain largely separate.

This separation is rooted in law and law enforcement. The Act on Equality between Women and Men deals only with gender equality and dates back to 1986. When implementing the EU directives on non-discrimination,[2] new legislation was created and the existing Act on Equality was not opened. The Non-Discrimination Act, which came into force in 2004,[3] was enacted to cover other bases of discrimination: age, ethnic or national origin, citizenship, language, religion, belief, opinion, health, disability, sexual orientation or any other ground in connection to the person. It widened the concept of discrimination and provided new tools including the obligation of authorities to draw up non-discrimination plans promoting ethnic equality, the opportunity for those exposed to discrimination to claim compensation, and the shared burden of proof (Interview 9 March 2006).

The fact that law enforcement is delegated to different authorities further promotes separation and inhibits an integrated approach to equality and discrimination. The Equality Ombudsman's mandate covers only gender based discrimination. Occupational safety and health authorities oversee discrimination in working life. The Ombudsman for Minorities deals with discrimination on the basis of ethnic origin[4] outside employment. One femocrat suggested that the separation resulted from the fact that Finland was satisfied with merely implementing EU directives in a minimal manner and the drafting of the anti-discrimination legislation was not a response to national issues or problems (Interview 27 February 2006).

As a result, significant differences in provision for different strands remain. These discrepancies are important in several respects. First, the patchy legislation is difficult to understand for individual citizens seeking for remedy: some interviewees described the state of affairs as a 'jungle' (Interviews 9 March 2006; 3 February 2006). Second, because the anti-discrimination and gender equality legislation deal with different issues and provide different tools, the Ombudsmen have to sometimes evaluate what is the most effective and successful way to proceed: whether to go for gender or racial discrimination (Interviews 9 March 2006; 24 February 2006). The two cannot be pursued at the same time or in any one case. Third, some strands of equality, such as sexuality, are left completely outside of effective enforcement, as they are covered neither by the Ombudsman for Equality nor the Ombudsman for Minorities, only by the occupational safety and health authorities in employment. Finally, some crimes are not covered by the legislation, including hate crimes or harassment crimes committed by groups against individual persons (Interview 9 March 2006). In sum, the separation of gender equality and diversity is firmly embedded in the legislative structures with palpable effects for both individuals and for the work done by the equality agencies.

Some femocrats expressed concern for and acknowledgement of diversity. They mentioned a training course by the association for sexual rights, SETA (*Seksuaalinen tasavertaisuus* – Sexual Equality in Finland) as important, and the Council for Gender Equality has done some publications on immigrant women and men. Furthermore, the Act on Equality applies also for discrimination faced by trans-people, who thus come under the mandate of the Ombudsman for Gender Equality.

Yet, the femocrats confirmed that diversity is not central to the work done in these agencies. One civil servant suggested that 'there is little space for anything else but the "norm" woman . . . and the man . . . ' (Interview 9 February 2006). In other words, different identities of women are not accounted for in the work done by the femocrats which address the gender equality problems faced by the norm woman and man. Several scholars have noted that Finnish gender equality discourse and policies close off diversity (Kantola, 2002; Raevaara, 2005; Vuori, 2006). There is a fear that gender is bypassed if too much attention is given to the other strands. The same tendency towards separation can be seen in the work of the Ombudsman for Minorities. Gender is not a key category for analysis although the office of the Ombudsman does deal with some gender-specific crimes such as honour killings and residence permits of immigrant women who face domestic violence (Interview 9 March 2006). In sum, the current state of affairs results in lack of tools in dealing with inter-sectionality and multiple bases of discrimination. The civil servants follow the developments in Europe, especially in Sweden, towards bringing different equality agencies and ombudsmen together into one unit, but do not think that it will happen in Finland very soon. Whilst noticing the problems, many are fairly satisfied with the state of affairs. Nevertheless, some femocrats think that bringing the different strands institutionally together might make the case for equality and anti-discrimination stronger, develop the tools to deal with them and enhance the power and influence of the agencies (Interview 1 February 2006).

Gender quotas and municipal equality work

The reorganization of the gender equality agencies, EU membership and new instruments and issues have transformed and partly strengthened Finnish state feminism during the last decade, although many problems, especially in regard to implementation at the municipal level remain. Ironically, perhaps the greatest success of Finnish gender equality policy during the last decade, the introduction of gender quotas for public bodies, may have brought mixed blessings in this respect.

Municipal equality work started in Finland as early as the 1980s, but only less than 10 per cent of Finnish municipalities ever established a gender equality committee. In a context of a restructuring of local democracy and deep economic difficulties, most of the existing equality committees were dismantled in the first half of the 1990s (Holli, 1992; Pincus and van der Ros, 1999, p. 210). In the early 2000s, only ten municipalities (out of 446) still had a gender equality committee. Only some of the most affluent big cities seemed to be able to 'afford' active gender equality work (Holli, Luhtakallio and Raevaara, 2003, p. 40).

From 1995, the amended Act on Equality decreed that all (indirectly elected) public bodies (government inquiry commissions, other similar bodies, municipal executive boards and other municipal boards and committees; the indirectly elected inter-municipal and regional decision-making structures) must be composed of at least 40 per cent of women and men, unless there were special reasons to the contrary (Law 206/1995, Law 232/2005). The gender quotas were very successfully implemented in Finland. Between 1993 and 1997, the proportion of women members in municipal executive boards (local government) increased from 25 per cent to 45 per cent; in municipal boards from 35 per cent to 47 per cent. Also the former strong horizontal gender segregation in local government underwent a period of rapid and vigorous change (Pikkala, 1999; Holli, Luhtakallio and Raevaara, 2003).

Holli, Luhtakallio and Raevaara (2003, 2006) point out that, although the quotas had many positive impacts for the quality and contents of local democracy, they also had negative side-effects. Contrary to hopeful expectations, gender equality work was not energized in Finnish municipalities. The local actors rather tended to interpret the proper implementation of gender quotas as the sole task demanded of them. Most of them were ignorant about gender equality planning and their obligation to promote gender equality or did not consider them of importance (Gustafsson, 2006; Holli, Luhtakallio and Raevaara, 2003, pp. 40–1). As a result, only 31 per cent of the municipalities had prepared a gender equality plan in 2005, making the municipal sector the weakest part of the public sector in this regard (Melkas and Lehto, 2005, p. 16). Quotas have deepened the differences in attitudes towards gender equality between women and men. Recent survey results show that 78 per cent of women but only 36 per cent of men support quotas in local politics (Parviainen, 2006, p. 282).

The gender quotas have thus entailed problematic side-effects for state feminism at the municipal level. Firstly, the strong focus on women's descriptive representation has drawn attention away from other aspects of gender equality work and women's substantive representation, and in many occasions, replaced them. For most politicians and bureaucrats, ensuring gender balance in various public bodies has become synonymous with gender equality, gender equality policy and gender mainstreaming (cf. Holli, Luhtakallio and Raevaara, 2003, p. 41; Nousiainen et al., 2004). Secondly, the achieved gender parity has strengthened the 'gender equality illusion', the idea of Finland having already achieved an extremely high level or even perfect gender equality (Raevaara, 2005; Holli, Luhtakallio and Raevaara, 2006; cf. Skjeie, 2006). The strong presence of women in political and preparatory bodies is seen as a testimony of attained equality. It also functions as a barrier to recognizing gender injustice, strengthening the idea that 'Finnish people need not any more do anything about gender equality' (Holli, 2003, pp. 17–18). Paradoxically, Finnish membership in the EU may have contributed to this tendency as it shifted the framework of national comparison from the other Nordic countries (which were seen as 'better' than Finland as far as gender equality was concerned) firmly on the larger – and 'less' gender equal – Europe. As a result, gender quotas and state feminism function as competing, rather than complementary strategies for gender equality at the municipal level (see Krook and Squires, 2006).

Women's movements and state agencies: institutionalized and independent

Finnish women's movements can be characterized as integrationist and consolidated. The most important women's organizations since the rise of second wave feminism until today have been fourfold. First, there are the women's party sections, one for each political party. Second, the National Council of Women of Finland (*Naisjärjestöjen Keskusliitto*) is an umbrella organization consisting today of 59 women's organizations, with a membership of about half a million women. Third, the League of Finnish Feminists (*Naisasialiitto Unioni*) is a nation-wide independent feminist organization. Finally, long- or short-term women's informal networks have appeared on various themes, projects and issues, especially during the 1980s and 1990s. Notably, all parts of the movement have to some degree adopted feminist demands and actively promote gender equality and women's rights. Typically, they work 'from within the state', through established political channels and structures. Radical feminist grass root activism and protests are rare (Bergman, 1999, 2002).

Research has shown that Finnish women's movements worked very closely together with gender equality agencies to achieve their policy objectives until the 1990s. The involvement of the gender equality agencies seemed crucial for women's political success as they provided both the bureaucratic resources as well as a forum for women's organizations to formulate their joint interests (Holli, 2006, 2003, pp. 156–71). From the early 1990s onwards, there were however signs of a division of labour taking place and an increased autonomy for all sides involved in the 'strategic partnerships'.

There were several reasons for this. First, the severe recession at the beginning of the 1990s mobilized women for mostly defensive action.

It has been suggested that the forced reactive politics took energy from new initiatives, which were more carefully chosen (Aalto and Holli, forthcoming). The situation may also have put pressure for initiating a better division of labour between the actors. Second, in the 1990s the gender equality machinery was hard pressed as far as the workload and the resources were concerned and, moreover, under constant reorganization, which diminished the 'supply-side' it could provide for the movement. Third, the women's organizations and women MPs established new cross-party co-operative mechanisms (NYTKIS, Women MPs' Network in Parliament) by the early 1990s that partly took up the role formerly played by gender equality agencies in women's co-operation (Holli, 2006). Moreover, they also received higher and more permanent financial subsidies from the state, enabling their own permanent staff. And, last but not least, women's position and influence in Finnish politics became stronger, as testified by the election of first female President, first female Prime Minister, 40–50 per cent of the Cabinet Ministers women since 1991, and an increasing number of women as party leaders.

Both the new institutionalized structures for co-operation and women politicians have actively and independently defended gender equality and what they see as women's joint interests. An interviewee described women's co-operation as an extension of the consensus politics typical to Finland: 'we have learnt to discuss over boundaries. And women have been tagging along there inside the parties, but they have not been actors themselves. But here (in women's issues) women have realised that: "Damn, we can make our own consensus if . . . we find an issue where we have a common interest, we will put it through". . .' (Interview 31 March 2006). Another interviewee reported that informal meetings 'for finding common issues' even occurred between women Ministers in the government (Interview 6 April 2006). The results of new forms of women's co-operation were evident on their influence on some important legislation during the 1990s, such as introducing the subjective right to public daycare for children and numerical gender quotas (Aalto, 2003; Aalto and Holli, 2007; Holli, 2006; Holli and Kantola, 2005; Raevaara, 2006; Lejonqvist-Jurvanen, 2004; Ramstedt-Silén, 1999). In both pieces of legislation, women MPs moreover allied over party lines with each other to form a winning coalition in parliament, which can be regarded as extremely rare internationally. Also many femocrats interviewed in this study evaluated that women politicians' feminist work was the foundation for the work done in the gender equality machineries and Finnish women-friendly policies more generally.

The femocrats also saw their relationship with women's organizations as cordial and productive, but there were variations. The Gender Equality Ombudsman and the Gender Equality Unit regularly consult with women's organizations on policy proposals. However, as an interviewee noted, the women's organizations themselves had perhaps not noticed that the Gender Equality Unit is the one that they should lobby now (Interview 9 February 2006). Instead, the organizations still seem to have the closest – also institutionalized – relationships to the Council for Gender Equality.

Conclusion

In this chapter, we have analysed the state of gender equality machineries in Finland in the early 2000s. As a result of institutional restructuring, the Gender Equality Unit was created in the Ministry of Social Affairs and Health. This clarified the mandates between different agencies and resulted in an increase in resources but also in tasks and responsibilities. The context, where the gender equality machineries operate, was shaped by state reconfiguration in relation to both direct and indirect impacts of the welfare state retrenchment and Europeanization. The role of new tools for achieving gender equality – gender equality planning, gender mainstreaming and gender quotas – proved mixed: they had the potential to be transformative but suffered from implementation problems (gender mainstreaming and gender planning) and unintended consequences (quotas). Significant challenges also remained at the municipal level, where gender equality work has virtually disappeared, and in relation to dealing with intersectionality and gender diversity, which remain absent from the political agenda.

The developments are thus somewhat paradoxical. On the one hand, the gender equality machinery seems to have strengthened during the past decade at the state level. The interviewed femocrats seemed very optimistic on many accounts. On the other hand, the analysis pointed to the gap between existing policy objectives and the implementation. One can therefore inquire whether this strengthening of the gender equality machinery has led anywhere, and conclude that on many occasions the answer is still no. The work done for gender equality policy continues to be hampered in particular by the pervasive idea that gender equality has been achieved in Finland.

Furthermore, an internal challenge, pointing to the pitfalls of state feminism as a feminist strategy, can be discerned. The most co-opted agency – the one closest to the government – has the most resources. The most independent actor, the Council, has lost resources and staff. As a result, there is less space for innovative analysis of the gender power order in Finland, for looking at the bigger pictures, for structural analysis of the patriarchy or the direction of gender equality policy.

Notably, the women's movement actors and gender equality machineries have become more independent from one another over the past decade. They join their forces at times and on certain issues, but as a result of the institutional restructuring especially the relatively powerful Gender Equality Unit acts fairly independently in its role in implementing government policy. Female politicians also act independently and in their own networks. This creates a potentially volatile situation, where a great deal of the success of gender equality policy depends on the outcome of elections and the nomination of the Minister for Equality. This, in turn, points to the challenges and the potential for reversal of gains on gender equality, and gives rise to important questions: How much do the Finnish gender equality policies depend on the leadership of a feminist or at least relatively women-friendly Minister, and what will happen in the absence of one? What happens when influential women politicians disagree about the priorities of gender equality policy? How much influence do the gender equality machineries exert in the end?

Interviews

Eleven interviews were conducted from November 2005 to March 2006 with top civil servants and politicians from the Council for Gender Equality, Gender Equality Unit, Office of the Ombudsman for Equality, Standing Committee of Labour Market and Gender Equality Affairs, Office of the Ombudsman for Minorities, and two persons who have worked as Ministers for Gender Equality. For reasons of anonymity, we provide only the dates of the interviews. Three interviews were conducted with the personnel of the Gender Equality Office in the summer of 1996.

Notes

1. According to Borchorst (1999, p. 182), the number of staff of the old Gender Equality Office in 1996 was 13 persons.
2. Race Equality Directive (2000/43/EC) and Employment Equality Directive (2000/78/EC).
3. The Non-Discrimination Act (*Yhdenvertaisuuslaki 21/2004*) is also referred to as the Equality Act, but for the sake of clarity we use the term Non-Discrimination Act.
4. The term 'ethnic origin' refers both to immigrants and Finland's 'old' ethnic minorities such as the Roma, Sámi, Tatars, Jews and representatives of the old Russian community.

6
Women's Policy Agencies, Women's Movements and a Shifting Political Context: Towards a Gendered Republic in France?

Amy G. Mazur

Since the government established the first study group on women's work in the mid-1960s, France has been known for its institutionalized women's policy machinery.[1] At times portrayed as a friend of women's movements and groups; at others, criticized for co-opting women's movement demands, a comparatively well-developed and resourced set of ministerial and administrative structures has been and continues to be a constant on the French political landscape under both governments of the Right and the Left. Since they were mapped out in *Comparative State Feminism* (McBride Stetson and Mazur, 1995), the women's policy offices have become an even more permanent fixture in the fabric of the French state, playing a crucial role, with recently revitalized women's movement groups, in introducing a more gender-sensitive approach to policy and politics.

These important changes have been occurring in the context of a fundamental shift in the French state. Globalization, decentralization, and Europeanization has put into question the *dirigiste*, or strong centralized state tradition, that has dominated French politics. As the chapter argues, for gender politics this means that women's movement groups have more access to state arenas and more influence in policy-making, in large part through the women's policy agencies, and decision-makers outside of state feminist circles are less resistant to feminist policy issues and gender-mainstreaming.

The chapter traces the dynamics and determinants of the emergence of a more gendered Republic and the role of the women's policy agencies and women's movement actors in that process. First, research on French state feminism is examined in a comparative light. Second, the most important changes for state feminism in the French political landscape are presented. Third, the structure, operation and policy approach of the women's policy machineries since 1995 are discussed. Finally, the chapter examines the degree to which women's policy offices and women's movements have taken the opportunities of the new political context to contribute to the formulation and implementation of authoritative policies in some key areas of government action; in other words, to what degree have women's policy agencies, in collaboration with women's movements, contributed to gendering the Fifth Republic.

Situating French state feminism in a comparative context

French women's policy agencies are identified with a high level of institutionalization and variety, similar to Australia's network of national and territorial administrations. Many femocrats and women's movement actors close to the French agencies over the years assert that the heyday of French state feminism was under the tenure of socialist feminist Yvette Roudy as Minister of Women's Rights from 1981 to 1986. However, as comparative research shows, in relation to women's policy offices in other countries, the Roudy Ministry was politicized and marginalized and women's policy offices under subsequent governments have been much more successful in effectively promoting a women's rights agenda.[2] Still, the Socialist Ministry had a significant role in institutionalizing the machineries at all levels of government.

Research also shows that women's rights policies, particularly equal employment policy, often display a symbolic dynamic where the government, typically through the women's ministries, formulates relatively weak policies with little implementation and an absence of interest group mobilization around implementation (Mazur, 1995b; Mazur, 2004). This symbolic dynamic has been an important theme in the work of the women's rights offices; trying to break that imperative has been a major challenge for the agencies.

The symbolic trend in women's rights policies and the limited role of the women's policy machineries in promoting authoritative policy has been identified as a by-product of 'gender-biased universalism',[3] with two contradictory aspects, a dynamic that is not found in other countries to the same degree. First, the 'equality principle' articulated in the Jacobin state since the Revolution of 1789, has emphasized pure equality between individuals and not groups, unless class interests are concerned, where equal treatment is accentuated over equal opportunity. From this deeply embedded standpoint in political culture and the operating principles of political actors both inside and outside of the state, the identification of citizens in terms of specific group affiliation, e.g., race, ethnicity, religion, sex, or sexuality, is seen to undermine the core principle of equality. Second, in contrast to the sacrosanct principle of universal equality, social policy has tended to promote gender-biased notions of women's and men's roles that define women as primary family caretakers who combine part-time work with family obligations, and hence need to be protected, and men as full-time workers with few family obligations. In this view, women are seen as potential mothers and often as a reserve pool of labour and men as full professional and public participants, with no real family duties. Employment and family policies have been built on these traditional notions of gender difference. Efforts to push for authoritative policies that challenge gender-biased assumptions, therefore, have been undermined by a double standard of, on one hand, holding up the value of pure equality without difference, and on the other, of promoting policies that are constructed on and perpetuate traditional differences in men's and women's roles. As the next section shows, this long-established gender-biased model is in flux in the context of larger shifts in the French state.

The 'rudderless state' provides opportunities for state feminism

The French state is undergoing significant change. Today, while the old republican model is in deep crisis, there is no new modus operandi to replace it. As a result, French policy and politics appears to be 'rudder-less' (Levy, Cole and Le Galès, 2005, p. 3). Entrenched bureaucratic elites in Paris continue to cling to the old Jacobin ways and the new government reform efforts, often 'messy and incoherent' (Levy, Cole and Le Galès, 2005, p. 123), occur in a piecemeal and incremental fashion, usually with little public attention or support. At the same time, the French state is opening up in an unprecedented manner to new interests and appears to be 'more pluralist, less State-led, and less hierarchical' (Levy, Cole and Le Galès, 2005, p. 3). Overall, as the analysis shows in the next section, the 'rudderless state' has created new opportunities for the women's policy offices to become a more institutionalized presence in the French state.

Decentralization of Paris-based governing power to elected councils in the regions and municipalities is one of the major aspects of the end of *dirigisme*, a 'silent revolution' (ibid.). Like much of the ongoing reforms, decentralization has been driven by elites at the sub-national levels of government, e.g., presidents of the regional councils and mayors, rather than a shift in public opinion.

Budget reforms first adopted in 1998 by the left-wing parliament have been slowly introduced, often in a confusing and incoherent manner, to make ministers more accountable for their spending through audits and responsibility-based budgeting. New Public Management (NPM) has been introduced, but without any significant 'neoliberal turn' in the overall approach to public administration. Instead, the reforms have consisted of 'ongoing experimentation and the diffusion of incremental reform that bears some features from the NPM toolkit' (Levy, Cole and Le Galès, 2005, p. 123). The 'sectorization' of the French state, where top-level function-based ministries have their power bases and the institutions that house the different corps of the French administrative elite, also based on sectors with deeply entrenched interests, also present formidable obstacles to significant change (Smith, 2005, pp. 106–7).

Despite decades of elite level support and leadership for the European project, the French public dealt a devastating blow to Europeanization in its rejection of the EU constitution in the 2005 referendum. While this rejection also represented a plebiscite against the policies of the right-wing Raffarin government and the leadership of President Chirac, it was indicative of the extent to which Europeanization in France has been the affair of upper level civil servants in their ministerial bastions, rather than a matter for public opinion, the media or a top item on campaign platforms. Smith identifies a 'remarkable level of schizophrenia' in the approach of French policy makers to Europeanization (2005, p. 121). On one hand officials do not hesitate to support putting French policy in line with EU standards and norms, on the other, the general policy process has not been Europeanized. Elected officials and ministers rarely go to Brussels. High level civil servants who do go tend to maintain their loyalties to their ministries, often defending French sovereignty rather than pursuing collaboration in European decision-making (ibid.).

The rudderless nature of French politics can also be attributed to the changes in electoral politics. Since 1995, the stable quadri-bipolar party system with the Socialist and Communist Parties on the Left and the Gaullist and Centrist parties on the Right has become much more fragmented. The right lost its control over the governing majority in 1997 to a left-wing coalition under Socialist Lionel Jospin with the Communists and the Greens. Jospin reversed the failed policies of his right-wing predecessors, pursuing a more socially active agenda. This approach was rejected after five years by the electorate in the shocking presidential election of 2002. Jean-Marie Le Pen, the candidate of the extreme right National Front, won enough votes to be in the second round run-off against incumbent Jacques Chirac. Since 2002, the right-wing government has pursued a slightly more tentative neoliberal agenda, for fear of reproducing the general strikes of 1995, but also aware of the large number of votes for

Le Pen. Regional elections in 2004 placed Socialists in control of every regional council but one.

The Fall 2005 riots in poor urban neighbourhoods populated by immigrants and first generation French from former French colonies illustrates the current malaise and divisions in France over race and class and the breakdown of the republican universal model for equality. Even prior to the riots the republican approach to racial politics had been in flux. Largely in response to a 2000 EU directive on race discrimination, the right-wing Raffarin government, put into place a new policy and structure, with an unprecedented level of resources to deal with discrimination, based on race, ethnicity, religion and sexuality (Gehring, 2005). Up until 2002, equality policies were focused on gender equality with no attention to other forms of discrimination. The new agency began working with a range of groups – ethnic, religious and sexuality based; women's groups did not participate in this process.

Women's policy agencies: an increasingly institutionalized, yet still marginal role

In the context of the shifting parameters of the state, the women's policy machinery has maintained its presence and has become even more integral to government affairs, taking advantage of the new institutional parameters of French politics. Since the centre-right government created the first Deputy Minister of the 'Feminine Condition' in 1974 to the current Deputy Minister of Social Cohesion and Parity under the right-wing de Villepin government, there has been a ministerial portfolio dedicated to women's rights issues for 25 of the last 32 years under both the Left and Right. Regional and departmental field offices operate under the authority of the Paris-based Women's Rights Service and in 2000, women's policy agencies employed over 500 people. It is important to note that a good share of policy machinery positions are defined by temporary contracts without full civil service status and many of the positions in the territorial administration are part-time and poorly paid. Thus, while the women's policy agencies have solidified their presence vertically and horizontally, they still remain at the relative margins of the state apparatus. A closer look at the operation of the full range of structures demonstrates their institutionalized, yet marginal presence.

Central administration: the ministerial offices and the service

As Table 6.1 shows, although the leadership of the women's policy agencies has varied with the change of government, governments of the Left

Table 6.1:   Evolution of Cabinet Level Offices responsible for women's rights issues since 1995

Year	Governing majority/PM	Cabinet level office/head
1995–97	Right – Juppé	None – an administrative position in a Ministry
1997–98	Left – Jospin	None – Delegation in PM's Office – Fraisse
1998–2002		Deputy Ministry in Ministry of Social Affairs – Péry
2002	Right – Raffarin I	Delegate Ministry of Parity and Equal Employment – Ameline
2004	Right – Raffarin II	Ministry of Parity and Equal Employment – Ameline
2006	Right – de Villepin	Ministry of Social Cohesion and Parity – Vautrin

and the Right have downgraded ministries to administrative offices or lower-level offices and upgraded offices to higher ministerial level positions, usually as a result of feminist outcry over the absence of a separate ministerial portfolio. This occurred in 1997 under Socialist Prime Minister Lionel Jospin and under right-wing Prime Minister Jean-Pierre Raffarin. Prime Minister Raffarin's decision to upgrade the Delegate Ministry of Parity to a fully-fledged Ministry in 2004 was not due to feminist pressure, but was a response to the success of the Socialists in the regional elections. The women's policy office had not reached such a high level of government authority since the Roudy Ministry in 1986.

In contrast to the fluctuating ministerial offices, the women's rights administration has remained quite constant. The current Women's Rights and Equality Service, or Service, was formally recognized under the Roudy Ministry and made permanent by an executive decree in 1990, under the Socialist Rocard government. The Service's mission has remained the same – to oversee the formulation and implementation of feminist policy and more recently to pursue gender-mainstreaming; it is not formally allowed to propose policies. In 2005, there were 51 people working there. While there have been some changes in the size and number of the units of the Service, its overall structure, shown in Table 6.2, has remained the same.

The relatively small administrative Service has remained autonomous from the politically appointed women's ministries; often housed in different buildings. The relationship between the political head and the Service depends on each minister. Under the Péry ministry from

Table 6.2:   Structure of the Women's Rights and Equality Service 1995–2005

Agency Head

Missions	Bureaus

• Studies, Research and Statistics
• European and International Affairs
• Coordination of Territorial
  Network (Regional
  Delegates, Departmental,
  Chargée de Mission and Women's
  Rights Information Centres)
	• Equal Employment
	• Social Rights
	• Human Resources
	  and Communication

1998–2002, femocrats asserted that there was a good working relationship and close collaboration between the ministerial staff and the Service.[4] Under the Ameline Ministry, from 2002–2005, the relationship was quite distant, with the large ministerial staff operating unilaterally. The Service seeks to be present in key interdepartmental decision-making arenas, for example in the Public Employment Service, the formal arena where government representatives from the employment administration come together to oversee administration at all levels of the state. Periodically, the Minister has established formal correspondents in each Ministry that serve as entry points into the sectorized ministerial system. This strategy is highly dependent on ministerial initiative, since most cabinet-level bodies are regulated by statute law. Recent social cohesion legislation, for example, adopted under the Ameline ministry eliminated the formal presence of the Service in employment policy.

Like the authority of the ministerial leadership, budgets have been reduced and increased under both the Left and the Right. The recent budget reforms and the establishment, since 2000, of a separate assessment of state spending on 'women's rights', called the budgetary yellow pages, make it easier to track spending on women's rights. The formal budget of the women's rights administration is under 1 per cent of the total government budget. This does not include expenditures for gender equality programmes outside of the women's policy offices, the wages of the 500 people employed by the women's policy agencies or the operating budget of the ministerial office. With these figures, the total budget for women's rights and gender equality probably approaches 5 per cent. The combined budgets of expenditures on women's rights programmes, but not operations, across the whole government was €46 million, in 2002, in 2003, €45 million and in 2004, €35 million (Jaunes Budgetaires, 2005, p. 59). The budget for activities specifically allocated to the women's rights offices, according to official figures supplied by the current Service, outside of salaries, was at its lowest point since 1982 – €11 million under the Socialists in 1998. It steadily increased until 2003 to €18 million in 2003 and was reduced to €17 million in 2004 and 2005 (Interview Morel, 18 May 2005).

Territorial administration and women's rights information centres

The territorial administration has been under the authority of the Service since the early 1980s, through the mission for the coordination of territorial administration (Table 6.2). Delegates in each region (12) and department (92) are appointed by the Minister and are often replaced when a new Minister arrives. Regional delegates have more permanence and resources than the departmental delegates; they typically have several staff members. Some regional delegations are left vacant, particularly in times of budgetary constraints. Since 2001, the regional delegate positions have been formalized at higher level civil servant positions, paid through the budget of the national administration budget. The '*chargées de mission*' in the departments have a far less permanent status, very few are civil servants, many are part-time positions, and few have secretarial staff. Operating budgets can be supplemented through the regional or departmental coffers, if the delegates have a good working relationship with the administration and government authorities at their level. Decentralization of budgets and services to the regions and the departments has generally given the territorial administration more opportunities. In addition, some municipal governments have set up their own women's rights positions or commissions.

Regional delegates are brought to Paris regularly to meet with the Service and the Minister; the departmental delegates less frequently. Both are required to make annual activity reports to the Service. Their authority comes through formal policy directives issued by the Service. The territorial administrators must also report to the government hierarchy at the regional or departmental levels. Depending on the individuals in the position and the level of resources in each office, the delegates and their staff can play very important roles in introducing a gendered perspective into regional and local policy discussions.

In the region of PACA (Provence-Alpes-Côtes d'Azure) in 2000, the regional delegate and a ten person staff were highly involved with policy discussions on employment, violence and individual rights (Appleton and Mazur, 2000). The delegation as a whole took a gender-mainstreaming approach, which was their principle assignment from the Service. Their goal was to bring a gendered perspective in all policy discussions and to alert mainstream actors to issues of gender discrimination and gender equality. The delegate convinced the regional council to insert an equality clause into the regional plan; an indicator of the success of the work of the delegation as a whole. The departmental delegates in PACA also took a mainstreaming approach, but had more limited resources to pursue the broad-based agenda. The regional case study shows the importance of leadership and individual connections in the success of these quite under-resourced and marginalized offices.

The 120 Women's Rights Information Centres at the national, regional and local levels, also first established in the 1970s and increasingly institutionalized over the years, are formally registered as non-governmental organizations with the state. Their major goal is to inform the public about women's rights issues. Centres typically collect a wide range of information for the public, organize public lectures and are open regularly for public consultation. Despite their formal group status they are also under the authority of the Service, receiving one-tenth of the Service's operating budget each year and a sizeable amount from the European Social Fund: €152,000 in 2003 and €169,000 in 2004. Since 2001, the national Information Centre in Paris has coordinated the regional and departmental centres. The Service is the administrative link between the centre network and the Ministry. All centres are required to submit an activity report to the Service. Most centres collaborate directly with local women's groups, which tend to have representation on their board of directors and provide additional funding. There is also an Association of centres which holds meetings and publishes a monthly information bulletin. Even more than the territorial administration the centres are highly dependent on individual leadership and local community involvement.

The importance of the centres and the territorial administration has been fully recognized in the constant and ever-increasing level of financial support for the women's policy agencies in general. According to the Service femocrat who headed the territorial coordination department for over ten years, these offices have maintained the reputation and legitimacy of the Service in the face of administrative reform and downsizing. Their permanence and reputation inside and outside of the state prevent politicians from eliminating the territorial arm of the policy offices without severe repercussions at all levels (Interview Sylvie Zimmerman, 15 May 2005).

Subsidizing women's groups

A significant part of the Service's budget goes to funding women's groups, through the functional areas of rights, equal employment, and communication and research. Part of the Jacobin system, where the state sought to control independent groups, most groups in France receive some level of state subsidization; few raise their own money. Up until 2001, the funding process was closed and secret, seen as a major political arm of the Ministry, with funding decisions determined by the politics of the ministry. For many women's movement activists the funding is a way for the ministers to co-opt and control the groups; others see the funding as a crucial resource.

Under Socialist Minister Péry, the process of group funding was made more transparent and formal. Starting in 2002, groups were required to submit a formal application, and if funded, were asked to sign contracts with the Service. Typically, the Ministry accepts the recommendation of the Services, but also makes special requests. In funding decisions from 2003–2005 under the right-wing Ameline ministry, the funding process has been rationalized and has moved away from political criteria. In May 2005, under the right-wing government, the applications of several prominent left-wing feminist groups were under reconsideration, but other explicitly feminist groups received funding, often at similar levels over the three year period. Groups associated with the Right received funding during the period, in some cases, reduced funding.

In 2005, roughly 20 per cent of the Service's budget went towards supporting both feminist and non-feminist groups, associated with the Right and the Left. The budget for groups was reduced to €200,000 from 2003 to 2004, but remained the same from 2004 to 2005. From 2003 to 2005, 103 groups received funding; three-fourths of which were funded each year, often with similar levels of funding. Socialist Deputy Minister Péry also asked the Service to improve relations with associational partners to promote the work of the groups, to allow them to better communicate amongst each other, and to promote better collaboration with the women's policy agencies. Two new publications were put out, one for women's groups and other for researchers.

Consultative bodies

From the beginning, consultative bodies have been important instruments for the women's policy agencies to work with women's movement actors – both individuals and groups, in the elaboration of feminist policy and gender-mainstreaming. The Ministers have the formal authority to convene them and the Service oversees administration. Together they provide a unique and respected arena where representatives from different ministries, the Service and interest groups come together with experts to study and discuss policy, to issue a formal report and/or to make key policy recommendations.

Since the Roudy Ministry, there have been two permanent statutory commissions: the Upper Council for Equal Employment and the Upper Council on Sexual Information (*Conseil Supérieur de l'Information Sexuelle*). The Council on Sexual Information focuses on issues related to women's health as mothers, and on reproductive rights. From 1993–1998, neither commission was called into session, since 1998 they have both been convened on a regular basis. The period of inactivity coincides with the absence of a ministerial office for women's rights issues and of any broad-based interest in the commissions from women's movement groups. The Ministers and the Service see these commissions as a major resource for effective policy implementation and interest groups watch carefully the composition of the Councils to assure fair representation. For example, feminist groups complained when Minister Ameline removed several left-wing representatives from the Upper Council, but they were reappointed shortly after the publication of the complaints in a national newspaper. Femocrats in the Service assert that the Sexual Information Council has more influence than the Equal Employment Council partially due to the vitality of women's groups in reproductive rights issues, and the decline of feminist activity in the trade unions.

Departmental-level Commissions Against Sexual Violence with members from the women's rights administration, the police, women's groups and other relevant administration, have played an important role in sensitizing actors to anti-violence measures at the local level since 1989. They have not been systematically supported over the years; the last official policy directive came from the Service in 1997. Certain Commissions have contributed to anti-violence policies at the local level, thanks to the work of activist departmental delegates. Ministers have also appointed temporary commissions to treat specific pertinent policy issues.

The Parity Observatory was created in 1995 by right-wing President Jacques Chirac in response to the rising demands from the groups and individuals pushing for policies to promote equal numbers of men and women in public office, or parity. It is a consultative commission that has a small staff, a tiny budget and a sitting president that creates subgroups of experts to study and make recommendations on specific issues under the parity theme. First administered by the Service, the Observatory has since been attached to the Prime Minister's office. The Observatory played an important part in the development of the parity reforms in 1999 and 2000 (Baudino, 2003; 2005). Its role since has been less clear, partially reflecting the ambiguous role of Observatories more generally in France. Still, it has continued to meet on a regular basis and to produce reports on the implementation of parity. The Observatory's lack of formal authority, distance from the women's rights offices, and partisan agenda has under-mined its effectiveness and clout. Indeed, many critics have argued that it has been used by right-wing and left-wing governments to stall taking authoritative action on parity, both before and after the 1999–2000 parity reforms.

The impact of Europeanization and the UN

In the late 1990s, in response to stepped-up Europeanization, gender-mainstreaming in France has become a major instrument for feminists within the state alongside the EU gender equality directives. Despite the concept being an English term and its links to feminist forces outside of France, gender-mainstreaming has been a touchstone for the Ministers, the Service and the territorial administration. This shift became clear under the Péry ministry and has continued under Minister Ameline. Many of the new policy instruments put into place since 2000 are justified and guided by a mainstreaming logic. Femocrat mainstreaming efforts are also supported by subsidies from the European Social Fund allocated to regions that have put into place mainstreaming measures. The budget of the Service now counts EU money as a permanent budget line. Since 1999, femocrats at all levels have organized numerous conferences and workshops on gender-mainstreaming to educate public officials about the new concept.

Femocrats see gender-mainstreaming as a strategic tool to advance their feminist agenda in recalcitrant policy circles and to convince actors out-side of state feminist circles to implement gender equality policy directives. The annual National Employment Plan, required each year from EU mem-ber states with specific areas of emphasis, one of which is to 'assure equal-ity between men and women', has been a major focal point of this strategy. In one case, a femocrat from the Service was able to convince decision-makers in the employment administration, in the name of the EU require-ments, to insert a concrete target for reducing women's long-term unemployment into administrative orders to territorial employment actors and offices (Interview Natasha Djani, 13 May 2005).

Thus, femocrats have taken advantage of the support for EU measures within government circles. At the same time, the tendency for sectorization between government departments and elitism prevails. Only represen-tatives from the Minister's cabinet and not the Service are sent to Brussels with little communication of any discussions occurring in Brussels. In addition, gender-mainstreaming efforts have remained technocratic, with femocrats at the various levels of territorial administration embracing the idea and actors outside of these arenas unaware of the new concept.

The French public appears to be relatively uninformed about these bureaucratic efforts as well; there is little discussion of gender-main-streaming in the media.

United Nations feminist policy formation has also been a focal point for the women's policy agencies and certain women's movement actors. The 1995 UN Women's Conference in Beijing was the culmination of an emerging transnational feminist movement and an indication of the saliency of global feminism. The governments of many countries, including France, took seriously the process of preparing a formal report for the conference – a society-wide consultation was held in 1994, coordinated by the women's policy agencies at all government levels, in collaboration with women's movement groups and actors. The success and salience of the 1995 UN process led to the call for a follow-up process called Beijing-plus-5; providing a second opportunity for feminists to place pressure on governments and governments to evaluate the progress in gender equality. A second more comprehensive consultation of women's groups throughout the country was made, this time under the coordination of the Deputy Minister of Women's Rights, which gave the process more legitimacy than in 1995.

Policy approaches of the Péry (1998–2002) and Ameline (2002–05) ministries

It is useful to take a closer look at the policy approaches of the left-wing Péry Ministry and the right-wing Ameline ministry to compare the activities of the women's policy agencies in the context of a significant government change; which did not change that much between the two ministries. This continuity provides evidence for the argument that a new gendered approach to public policy is emerging in large part from the impetus of the women's policy machineries. Although the Péry Ministry was not a full-fledged Ministry and Nicole Péry was a Socialist Party activist with few women's movement or feminist credentials, the Deputy Minister elaborated and implemented an active agenda that focused on solidifying and institutionalizing the work of the women's policy machinery. In fact, Minister Péry and her cabinet did not initiate any of the major feminist reforms adopted under the Jospin government. Instead, the focus was on making the administration of feminist policy and gender-mainstreaming more efficient and effective through the various reforms with regards to the commissions, the budget, the territorial administration and relations with women's groups. The focus of the Péry ministry reflected the consensus in the feminist policy community around the need to shore-up the gaps in policy implementation. In addition to the

general administrative reform, implementation was targeted in employment, violence, political representation and reproductive rights.[5] The
Péry ministry also created a new statutory commission in parliament –
the Delegation of Women's Rights, which began hearing testimony and
making reports in 2000; thus creating another state-based arena for the
articulation of women's rights issues by women's movement actors.

Another innovation put into place at the initiative of Minister Péry was
a direct effort to implement gender-mainstreaming – the *jaunes budgétaires*.
A part of the complex budgeting process, yellow budget pages consist of
the formal reports made to parliament from the government about expenditures made in the previous fiscal year in a specific policy sector. The Péry
ministry instituted a women's rights and gender equality version. The
Service was responsible for putting into place the process which involved
contacting all ministries to identify the funds earmarked for gender
equality. Administrative correspondents were identified in each
Ministry by the Service. As the femocrat in charge of putting in place this
new instrument asserted, the very process of creating communication
across the ministries put into place a mainstreaming ethic (Interview
Françoise Philippe-Reynaud, 20 May 2005). Budget reports from the
regional delegates were included starting in 2001. The policy initiatives
undertaken each year across all administrative departments are summarized in the published document as well. The budget report is now a permanent task of the Service, under the responsibility of a budget officer in
the Service, a male femocrat, who indicated that all ministries routinely
provide budget reports to the Service (Interview Jean-François Morel, 18
May 2005). While the yellow pages are seen as an innovation in gender-
mainstreaming in Europe, it is not clear the degree to which femocrats
and policy makers use this tool in formulating and implementing policy;
very few individuals outside of the femocrat arena know that the special
budget pages exist.

When the right-wing returned to power in 2002, particularly following
the strong showing of the extreme right in the presidential elections, most
observers expected the Ministry to disappear, the gender equality budget to
be reduced and the women's rights administration to be forgotten. Nicole
Ameline, an elected official from Normandy and former Deputy Ministry
for the Marine with no formal women's movement credentials, was seen
by many as the ideal agent for this reversal. However, there was no reversal. Instead, Minister Ameline continued the work of the Péry Ministry, the
Service and the Commissions. In 2004, in an interview with the right-
wing women's magazine *Madame Figaro* Ameline talked about the promise
of feminism and called her own approach as Minister feminist.

The minister brought in a large staff that was known to make unilateral decisions without any consultation of the Service. Some of the issues pursued by the Ameline Ministry included violence, employment, the rights of immigrant women, and social inequalities. The major policy innovation of her tenure, the Equality Charter, was a clear continuation of the efforts of the Péry ministry to elaborate a gender-mainstreaming approach through direct consultation with a broad range of groups, administrative actors and experts.

The Service femocrat who worked directly with Minister Ameline on the Charter process, stated that the idea had originated with the long-time director of the Service, Brigitte Grésy (Sylvie Zimmerman, Interview, 15 May 2006). The Equality Charter (*Charte de l'Egalité*) is a 280 page document that outlines detailed government plans for gender equality, by sector and ministry (http://www.social.gouv.fr/femmes/). For the most part, the measures reflect the work of the women's rights administration through its consultative commissions and hence to a certain degree the positions of feminist groups and experts that have been long-time partners with the Service. Over 300 representatives of non-feminist groups, ministries, and agencies signed the final charter. Minister Ameline presented the Charter to the public in March 2004 as the government's response to 'gender-mainstreaming', using the English term.

Women's policy agency–women's movement collaboration in public policy formation

Women's movement groups and individual actors are the major partners of the women's policy agencies; they receive funding for specific projects and research, work with femocrats on the consultative commissions, and are regularly consulted by both the service and the ministerial cabinets. When governments are reluctant to support key feminist policy issues, women's movement groups place pressure on politicians to be more proactive, including, in sustaining the women's policy machinery itself.

The increased institutionalization of the women's policy agencies, as a consequence, must be placed in the context of women's movement resurgence. Beginning in 1992, new groups focused on specific policy reforms including sexual violence, parity, reproductive rights, sexual harassment, and sexism in the media and mobilized a new generation of women and men interested in feminist action; several new groups focused on women of colour. Established groups too were revitalized around specific policy campaigns and gender experts connected to women's studies became more prevalent, with several new women's studies journals being created during the period. Women's groups inside of trade unions and political parties of the Left, important women's rights actors in the late 1970s and 1980s, were quite absent.[6]

The participation of the women's movement groups and actors in the development of feminist policy contributed to making the women's policy machineries more successful in breaking the perennial symbolic trend in feminist policies to produce more authoritative government action. Examining five areas of feminist policy formation during the period illustrates the extent to which women's movement actors worked with, and in some cases led, femocrats in the women's policy agencies to push feminist policies beyond the symbolic imperative.

Reproductive rights

Since the Roudy Ministry provided for state funds to cover two-thirds of the cost of abortions, government policy had been silent on abortion and contraceptive issues (Robinson, 2001). In 1999, with increasing pressure from the powerful *Collectif des Associations pour les Droit de l'Avortement et de la Contraception* – Collective of Associations for the Right to Abortion and Contraception), the Jospin government initiated a new campaign for reproductive rights, issued a report on abortion provision, and promised to reform abortion and contraceptive rights. These new policy efforts responded to many of the demands of the feminist campaign, that had been also elaborated in the state feminist consultative Upper Council on Sexual Information. While implementation was slow, the new legal stipulations engaged public officials in the health administration to comply. Furthermore, in the right-wing Equality Charter, 11 out of 30 detailed measures on women's health targeted implementation and the state feminist commission continued to be an important arena for overseeing implementation.

Equal employment

The 2001 Génisson Law, aimed at addressing the gaps in policies promoting gender equality in the workplace, was also a product of the women's policy agency–women's movement partnership, through the Service and its Bureau of Equal Employment and the Upper Council for Equal Employment. Since the adoption of a 1983 law by the Roudy Ministry, the pursuit of sexual equality in the work place had been relegated to the symbolic arena, with few results and little interest in the various voluntary programmes put into place to promote gender equality at work (Mazur, 1995b). The Socialist government first launched a campaign to promote the revised equality measures with the help of the

Service; the right-wing Ameline Ministry placed equal employment at the centre of its action as well.

With new support from five major firms, the employers unions, President Chirac, the proliferation of new equality plans (Laufer and Silvera, 2005), and a new firm-level women's group to promote gender equality, there has been a renewed interest in making equal employment policy meaningful. In addition, following President Chirac's declaration that pay equity between men and women should be achieved in five years, the Ameline ministry went to work on a new pay equity law aimed to shore-up the gaps in existing legislation. Seen as an opportunity to promote authoritative policy on wage equity by feminist observers, the 2005 law has been criticized for being toothless. Whether the new support for equality efforts breaks the symbolic imperative remains to be seen, particularly given past resistance of organized management and labour and the labour administration to equal employment stipulations and the right-wing government's reluctance to compel employers to pursue the new equality programmes.

'Reconciliation' of work and family

France has some of the most developed family policies designed to boost the birth rate and seated on conventional gender roles where men are the family breadwinners and women are the family caretaker and part-time workers (Revillard, 2006; Morgan, 2002; Heinen, 2004). Part-time work, and the government programmes that promote it, is also seen by non-feminist policy actors as a way for women to reconcile their double-burden and not for men. Women were banned from working at night in most jobs up until 2000, reflecting the continuing salience of the nineteenth-century approach to working women – to protect their child-rearing capabilities.

In recent years, the promotion of policies that provide real choices to working mothers and fathers to reconcile home and work duties has become a part of discussions in the larger family policy community. More than organized feminism, it has been individual feminist experts inside and outside of government and femocrats in the Service that have made strong arguments for including reconciliation issues into family policy, often through the reports of the Upper Council on Equal Employment (Revillard, 2006).

The long held pro-natalist approach of family policy and its highly gender-biased assumptions, have been slow to change. The ban on night work, defended by most trade unions, was only recently lifted with the adoption of a 2000 law, due to increased state feminist lobbying and a 1999 European Court of Justice ruling against France. Recent reforms that reduced the work-week to 35 hours, seen by many feminist labour market experts and the femocrats in the Service as an opportunity to promote shared work and family obligations between men and women, failed to seriously address the reconciliation of work and family responsibilities for men and women (Mazur, 2007).

Still, there has been some progress in the area of parental leave. In response to state feminist calls for a more gender-balanced family policy, in 2001 the Socialist government sponsored the first government effort to promote parental leave for fathers; 50 per cent of new fathers took advantage of the leave in 2002–03 (Revillard, 2006). Minister Ameline's Equality Contract also stressed the importance of a gender balanced work–family relationship for all families regardless of socio-economic class.

Parity

As a wealth of studies on the 1999 amendments to the constitution and the 2000 law show, women's movement groups and actors played a crucial role in getting parity reforms on the books (Baudino, 2003 and 2005; Sineau, 2002; Bereni, 2003; Bereni and Lépinard, 2003, 2004; Lépinard, 2007). The state feminist Parity Observatory was a key arena for the elaboration of the demand for parity reform. The state feminist–women's movement partnership, however, was more successful in putting parity reform on the Socialist government's agenda, than in assuring that the new stipulations would be authoritative. Moreover, parity activists avoided, for strategic reasons, articulating any demands for the inclusion of issues of race, class, and ethnicity in the parity campaign; thus missing the opportunity to overcome larger tensions within the women's movement over issues of race and ethnicity (Lépinard, 2006).

The immediate results of the parity reforms have been mixed. For the 2002 legislative elections, all of the political parties took a reduction in state subsidies rather than present equal numbers of men and women candidates. In 2002, the percentage of women in the National Assembly went from 11 to 12 per cent. After the 2002 municipal elections, 47.5 per cent of city councillors in cities over 3500 were women, with 6.9 per cent of mayors. In March 2004, women on regional councils went from 27.5 per cent to 47.6 per cent. One women regional president was elected. The importance of parity laws is even more clear in light of the results of the 2004 cantonal elections, where parity requirements do not apply; 10.9 per cent of cantonal councillors were women. The executive boards of town collectives are still comprised of 90 per cent men and only 5.7 per cent have female presidents.

It is important to note that it has only been four years since the radical concept that challenges the established balance of power within political parties has been put into place. In this perspective, the regional and municipal election results may be an indicator of the possibility for real change. In addition, the right-wing government continued to take action on parity; a 2003 law addresses some of the gaps and the Ameline ministry, with parity at its core, announced specific parity measures.

Sexual harassment and domestic violence

Underpinned by what many feminist observers identify as Latin, southern European macho attitudes, public responses to sexual violence issues like rape, women battery, and sexual harassment have been less pronounced than other areas of feminist policy with women's movement actor–state feminist collaboration only achieving partial policy success. Anti-sexual harassment policy, first introduced in a 1992 law, has met with a great deal of resistance despite a strong collaboration between the major anti-sexual harassment group, *Association Contre les Violences Faites aux Femmes au Travail* (Association against Workplace Violence towards women) and the women's policy agencies at all levels. Litigation has remained limited due to the reluctance of women to come forward and the assumption in the criminal justice system that sexual harassment is not a serious problem. There have been no costly settlements against the perpetrators of sexual harassment; due in large part to the absence of large collective action lawsuits with large settlements in the French legal system. The issue of sexual harassment in universities was not raised as a public problem until 2002 with little resolution as to whether government policy should actually regulate it (Saguy, 2003). Anti-sexual harassment policy continues to be seen by many as a threat to individual freedoms; described by members of parliament and the mainstream press as an American invasion of 'repressive Puritanism' into private sexual relations.

Up until 2000, issues of domestic violence were rarely discussed in public, much less comprehensively addressed in public policy. A small network of feminist groups and under-funded women's shelters received limited support from the women's policy agencies. Both right-wing and left-wing women's ministers have made violence against women an important issue and pursued limited policies, such as sensitizing administrative actors about violence issues and informing women about ways of dealing with domestic violence. In 2000, the Péry Ministry commissioned the first systematic national study of violence towards women in France and created a National Commission on the issue. The findings of the study released in late 2000 shocked the public, showing that women in couples were the most victimized and that the highest incidence of violence was found in middle-class households. The Ameline ministry continued to support these efforts, in a series of policy efforts and in the Equality Charter. Several high profile cases of women being murdered by their partners in 2003 and the broad-based efforts of the new feminist group, *Ni Putes Ni Soumises* (Neither Whores or Submissive(s)) in the same year made the issue even more prominent. To date, however, the French state has still not developed an authoritative approach to reduce domestic violence.

Conclusion

State feminism in France is certainly alive and well in 2006 in the face of the 'rudderless state'. The emerging new rules of the political game in France have provided more opportunities to the women's policy machineries and their women's movement partners, than constraints. A more open and Europeanized state has contributed to providing unprecedented space for women's interests to be articulated. The women's policy agencies have maintained an institutional presence at all levels of government and a financial base in the face of administrative reform; actually capitalizing on the reform atmosphere to make the women's rights administration more responsive and accountable. Active and loyal femocrats at all levels have made sure that the offices remain intact and even strengthened in the process of decentralization. Europeanization too has seemed to strengthen rather than weaken state feminist action, through a general gender-mainstreaming approach that permeates the administration and through specific policy instruments that incorporate gender-mainstreaming permanently into the operation of the gender-specific ministries. Even the fragmentation of the political party system and the constant oscillation between Right and Left has not damaged the state feminist offices. Issues of co-optation are no longer raised due to the revitalization of the women's movement groups and the less political approach of the ministries and administration to group relations.

To be sure, the state feminist machinery is not as well funded as other areas of administration and many of the positions in the women's rights administration are temporary with very low salaries. Thus, the machinery remains weak and marginalized within the system as a whole. In addition, the Fifth Republic is not completely gendered, also reflecting the dynamic of the rudderless state; the long established gender-biased universalist approach still drives much elite decision-making alongside the more gendered ethic of the women's rights administration.

At the same time, the work of the women's movement–women's policy office partnership delegitimates republican universal arguments against gender equality in government circles. Moreover, formal policy documents must take a more gendered approach, due to stipulations from the EU. Whether the current reforms will produce public policy that effectively deals with gender inequities in all areas of society remains to be seen. It is certainly easier to make a public statement, appoint a commission, adopt a new law, and produce a policy paper than to put the resources and political capital into authoritative implementation of more controversial policies that, at their core, re-allocate resources from men to women. The women's rights machinery may also still be used as a part of a political strategy to pre-empt criticism on an official level without actually addressing the deep-seated gender inequities that are the focus of feminist criticism.

Only time will tell whether the various new feminist reforms backed by a small but dedicated women's rights administration and a supportive women's movement can overcome the formidable obstacles to actually gendering the Fifth Republic. But in this state feminist-guided process the French Republic does appear to be more open to a gendered perspective and to the societal actors who articulate that perspective and in this process, may very well be becoming more democratic.

Interviews

(Open-ended interviews conducted in May 2005)

Cécile Cochy, Women's Rights and Equality Service, Social Rights Mission.

Sandrine Dauphin, Women's Rights and Equality Service, Study and Research Mission, 1998–2003.

Natasha Djani, Women's Rights and Equality Service, Equal Employment Mission.

Christiane El Hayek, Women's Rights and Equality Service, Communications Mission.

Cécile Gineste-Van Haaren, Women's Rights and Equality Service, Communications Mission.

Jacqueline Gottely-Fayet, Women's Rights and Equality Service, Study and Research Mission.

Fabienne Grizeau, Women's Rights and Equality Service, Equal Employment Mission and Study and Research Mission, 1988–2002.

Catherine Laret-Bedel, Women's Rights and Equality Service, Employment Equality Mission.

Jacqueline Laufer. Expert of Equal Employment Policy in Firms.

Nicole Michel, Women's Rights and Equality Service, Social Rights Mission.

Jean François Morel, Women's Rights and Equality Service, Human Resources Mission.

Françoise Philippe-Reynaud, Women's Rights and Equality Service, 1998–2003.

Sylvie Zimmerman, Women's Rights and Equality Service, Territorial Administration Mission.

Notes

1. Thanks go to Claudie Baudino and Anne Revillard for their comments on the chapter and to Johanna Kantola and Joyce Outshoorn for their crucial editorial advice.
2. For an assessment of the Roudy Ministry see Mazur, 1995a, and for analyses of the women's policy agencies by policy sector see Mazur, 2001b; Robinson, 2001; Mazur, 2004; Baudino, 2005; and Mazur, 2007.
3. For analyses of the impact of and the literature on gender-biased universalism in public policy see for example, Baudino, 2005; Mazur, 2001b, 2004.
4. Interviews were conducted with twelve femocrats in May 2005; the list of interviews is presented at the end of the chapter.
5. See the annual reports issued to the public by the Péry Ministry, *Egalité en marche*.
6. For more on the women's movements in the 1990s see for example, Bereni, 2003; Baudino, 2003; Picq, 2002; Gaspard, 2003.

7
Gender Governance in Post-unification Germany: Between Institutionalization, Deregulation and Privatization

Sabine Lang

Introduction: ten years after[1]

When Myra Marx Ferree assessed the conditions of German state feminism in 1995, she employed the metaphor of the 'half-full or half-empty glass' to analyse the mixed success of the women's equality machinery (Ferree, 1995). Positive effects included the institutionalization of communication venues between the autonomous feminist movement and femocrats and the power of the women's offices to keep gender issues on the political agenda, leading to successes like women's studies positions at universities and the preservation of at least some of the extended child care infrastructure in the East. On the downside, Ferree acknowledged that the same machinery was not able to fend off budgetary downsizing in the women's infrastructure, to counteract women's unemployment or to mediate in the communication breakdown between Eastern and Western feminists in the aftermath of unification.

Ten years later, several indicators would suggest the glass is fuller than before. The most obvious of all: between 1998 and 2005, Germany was governed by a coalition of Social Democrats and the Green Party. Both parties had historically backed strong women's policy machineries and equality policies. In Germany, a 16-year conservative ruling coalition was ousted in 1998 to make room for the first Social Democratic/Green coalition on the national level. In fact, gender democracy had been one of the founding principles of the Green Party, and its early quota rule had facilitated a sea change in gender composition of the German parliament. Bündnis 90, the East German alliance that merged with the West German Greens after unification, had been co-founded by the East German Unabhängige Frauenverband (UFV; Independent Women's Association).

124

Thus, one could assume that the Red–Green government might have had substantial positive impact on women's policy agencies and, more broadly, on the advancement of gender equality. Another indicator for a more powerful role of the women's policy machinery could be the tailoring of European Union policies towards gender mainstreaming. Gender mainstreaming as a strategy might strengthen the leverage of the equality machinery because its reservoir of gender knowledge seems essential for implementation. A third positive indicator might be that as of 2005, after the end of this left–centre coalition, Germany for the first time has a *female* Chancellor. Even though Angela Merkel explicitly distanced herself from any 'feminist' label and did not promote a women's agenda, her election was noted as a step in women's advancement in politics.

Yet mapping the terrain of German gender governance today does not support this optimistic reading. Instead, it exposes some of the same ambivalences as a decade ago along with new challenges that threaten the established women's policy agencies. While institutionalization has increased, so have efforts to deregulate, 'download', and reprivatize gender issues. Deregulation is referred to here as softening or abandoning formerly strict legal frameworks or organizational competences. 'Downloading' means the relocation of former federal authority or responsibility to state and local governments (Banaszak et al., 2003, p. 4). Reprivatization points to the transfer of formerly public duties back onto the individual citizen (Lang, 2001). My argument is that it is a combination of these three governance strategies that shapes German gender governance in the early twenty-first century.

State feminism in Germany today consists of an even more complex and multitiered landscape of locations and hubs of women's policy agencies than a decade ago. But its well developed organizational networks are also under attack. Some feminists challenge the effectiveness of a femocratized political infrastructure, especially after seven years of Red–Green government have produced fewer significant advances in gender equality than the female backers of this coalition had hoped for (Kontos, 2004). Moreover, the fiscal crisis of the state and the European Unions' gender mainstreaming initiatives have contributed compelling public rationales for downsizing the women's equality machinery.

What at first sight looks like a well developed and sustainable system of gender governance, describes in fact a precarious set of actors that is increasingly on the defensive in German politics. The following chapter aims to assess the forces that shaped German gender governance since the mid-1990s and the impact of political transformations on the women's policy machinery, on its advocacy role within the state, its relationship with the women's movement and on gender policies. In the first part, three developments will be examined in regard to their effects on the gender equality machinery and women's mobilization: First, post-unification reform agendas, second, the role of the Red–Green coalition government and third, Europeanization. The second part will focus on how the women's equality machineries and women's movements have taken up these challenges and how well equipped they are to address and counter policies of deregulation, downloading and reprivatization.

Shifting political contexts for state feminism: unification, the Red–Green agenda and Europeanization

In the mid-1990s, Germany reeled under rising unemployment and a staggering economy. The former locomotive of Europe delivered the weakest overall economic performance of all EU member states (Wiesenthal, 2004). Political and economic stability, which historically had relied on a consensus between corporatist actors in a system that fostered compromise and stable coalitions, was eroding in the face of an accelerating fiscal crisis (Kitschelt and Streeck, 2004). Business associations lobbied for deregulation of the employment sector and for downsizing active labour market policies and public works programmes. Unions saw their collective bargaining power and their membership base erode. The conservative social welfare and employment regime of West Germany that relied on a male breadwinner model and on employee/employer contributions to the social safety net was put into question. It neither reflected the realities of the new Länder with their high female labour force, nor was it equipped to handle the double crisis of fewer payers and higher spending during the accelerating unemployment crisis. Yet instead of using this reform discussion to examine the gendered foundations of the German welfare state, prominent experts framed the increasing availability of women on the labour market as a 'problem' that fuelled the crisis.[2]

The resulting 'Agenda 2010' reform package lends overall support to the assessment that the German power centres still are 'inaccessible and antithetical to feminist concerns' (Young, 1999, p. 220).

Post-unification reforms

Feminists have analysed unification primarily in terms of its direct effects on women from the former GDR – the emphasis being (i) on *direct* impact and (ii) on the implications for women in the new *Länder*. Concerns about a gendered restratification of the eastern Länder in the transition to capitalism were fuelled by declining birth rates, the reintroduction of the traditional trade off between family and work and the devaluation of female labour as the value of paid labour increased (Rudd, 2000; Dölling, 2005). These processes are still in full swing: while in 1990, 86 per cent of women aged 18 to 59 in the new Länder were employed, in 2004 only 50 per cent had employment (Statistisches Bundesamt 2004). Women leave the eastern states at much higher rates than men to seek paid work and careers in the western part of the country. A second direct effect is that unification has considerably altered state feminism in the new Länder by introducing the western equality machinery (see below and Ferree, 1995). Beyond these direct effects, unification has also contributed to jump start or accelerate reforms with more indirect, but long term implications for women both in the old and new Länder. The two most gender sensitive reform arenas are federalism and the welfare state, the former being in its early stages, the latter being implemented by 2006.

Why and how would federalism reform impact gender governance? After 1990, all eastern states adopted versions of western states' equality laws and equality machinery. Each eastern Land cooperated with a western Land that deployed advisers and senior civil servants to assist with the built up of state bureaucracy and infrastructure. Copying the West German bureaucratic and legal framework included the integration of equality offices into the administration of the new Länder. Typically, the type of women's policy machinery created in the five new states mirrored that of their western partner, fostering a kind of managed 'institutional isomorphism' (DiMaggio/Powell, 1991, p. 70; Sauer, 2005b).[3] Thus, the state of Brandenburg, with its social democratic partner state North Rhine-Westphalia, devised one of the most progressive gender equality laws and a strong women's policy machinery; Saxony, on the other hand, with the rather uncommitted and conservative state of Baden-Württemberg as partner, ended up with a weak legal equality framework and a precarious institutionalization of equality offices. These differences notwithstanding, an infrastructure was established that organized communication between eastern and western states, synergizing local and regional activities around institutionalized hubs.

In the aftermath of unification, German style federalism has been once again put into question. While federalism reform was on the West German agenda long before the GDR imploded, the mounting transaction costs of unification gave it renewed momentum.[4] Federal funds from the West were channelled primarily into the eastern states' civil service, public infrastructure and in job creation programmes. This public sector built up in the East took place under the auspices of co-operative federalism, a governance regime that rests on multilevel and decentralized decision making and is in essence consensus oriented, conservative and rather averse to individual states' experiments and innovation (Wiesenthal, 2004). The western states delivered the blueprints; the new Länder adopted them with slight variations. Cooperative federalism did not just guarantee the adoption of the women's policy machinery in the East. It also provides the framework for enforcing the Basic Law principle of 'equality of living conditions in the federation' in all German states and amounts to substantial yearly transfers from rich to poorer states.

The system of state equality machineries has profited in two ways from cooperative federalism: It has successfully copied an established infrastructure and integrated it into the Eastern states' bureaucratic build up, and its financial transfers have enabled especially economically weak but gender sensitive states to keep financing their equality infrastructures. One of the long-term effects of unification is that demands for revamping this system of cooperative federalism have been gaining momentum. The rich southern states in particular, which happen to be also the weakest in gender policies, have been kindling a movement to restructure relationships among the Länder in terms of a more *competitive* federalism (Wiesenthal, 2004). Competitive federalism would reduce the equalizing power of the federal government and challenge the requirement for equal living conditions while at the same time instilling more room for experimental state policies. Its advocates frame it as a means for generating more 'competition for excellence' in schools, universities and other public infrastructure arenas. Yet introducing more competitive elements into states' governance and squeezing the poorer states even more might, instead of encouraging experimental gender policies, produce a downward spiral of deregulation and de-institutionalization of the women's equality machinery. Several indicators of such negative effects will be addressed below (see section 'Women's Policy Agencies'). As much as cooperative federalism has been deemed as a straightjacket, it accounted for an upward isomorphism in creating a certain standard of women's policy agencies. But a policy environment that does not intrinsically value feminist goals – the majority of German states is now ruled by conservative coalitions – is not likely to compete over the most innovative gender policies or the best funded women's policy agencies.

Another arena in which unification has jump started political and social transformation with considerable gender implications is the ongoing restructuring of the German labour market and welfare state. High unemployment in both West and East Germany has led to calls for a stronger flexibilization of the workforce and for the creation of a low income service sector in extended household and care services. The

Red–Green coalition reacted with a sweeping set of labour market and welfare reforms. These so called 'Hartz reforms' consist of a set of laws revamping the central pillars of the German social system such as unemployment insurance, social assistance and job training. Several cornerstones of the reforms affect women more negatively than men. Critics are pointing towards the renewed 'masculinist constructions' (Roth, 2005) that are embedded in central provisions, such as the effect of so-called *Bedarfsgemeinschaften* (need based relationships). Living in a need based relationship, which means living in a joint household with a gainfully employed partner, whether married or not, now restricts access to the cash subsidy of Unemploymentfund II (Alg II) and, sometimes more importantly, to its related qualification and retraining programmes. Approximately two-thirds of those who do not qualify for Alg II and thus for a basic state subsidy under this new provision are women (Berghahn/Wersig, 2005, p. 90). In effect, what is being re-established through the reforms is more reminiscent of a 'nineteenth century style sexual contract' (ibid.) than of a twenty-first century model of a dual breadwinner society. Indirect gender effects are embedded in so called 'One Euro Jobs' – low wage and state subsidized jobs that are mostly created in service sectors dominated by women. Moreover, publicly sponsored employment in community related jobs threaten to counter initiatives to professionalize and financially legitimize care work (Veil, 2005).

On a more positive note, the Hartz reforms establish the responsibility of the state to guarantee childcare for qualification and retraining initiatives. In sum, these reforms reconstitute a focus on the family as the prime social unit. They perpetuate a gendered dependency model that interferes with the claim to women's autonomy and to the realization of a dual breadwinner society that German feminists have long advocated. They download responsibilities such as childcare provision from the federal level onto cities and counties without transferring adequate funding. They reprivatize (mostly) women's unemployment compensation by renewing dependency on male breadwinners. It is ironic that these reforms carry the stamp of the most women-friendly government that Germany has ever had.

The Red–Green coalition: from mainstreaming to sidelining gender

With the advent of the Red–Green coalition in 1998, hopes for new impulses regarding gender policies were high. For the first time in German government, women headed five out of 14 ministries and made up 32.8 per cent of members in the Federal Parliament. The parties with strict quota rules – the Party of Democratic Socialism (*Partei des Demokratischen Sozialismus* – PDS), the SPD (*Sozialdemokratische Partei Deutschlands* – German Social Democratic Party) and the Greens – had a proportionally much higher percentage of female members of parliament (*Bündnis 90/Die Grünen* 58.2 per cent, SPD 37.8 per cent, PPS 58.3 per cent) than parties without strict quotas (FDP) (*Freie Demokratische Partei* – the Free Democratic Party) 25.5 per cent, the CDU/CSU (*Christlich Demokratische Union/Christlich Soziale Union* – Christian Democratic Union/Christian Social Union) 23 per cent, thus fuelling expectations for a collective femocrat and parliamentary leverage in the arena of women's politics.

Under the previous conservative government, women's policies had been focused on family-friendly measures, like increasing options for women to combine family and work, or, most notably, the 1996 federal law that guaranteed the right to half day care for children three years and older. The downside of this much hailed measure had been that the law stipulated a right only to *half-day* care. This inadvertently encouraged cities and counties with a shortage of facilities to cut their fulltime preschool programmes into two half day sessions and by doing so double available spaces. Also in 1997, a long overdue law was passed that criminalized marital rape. But in other gender policy arenas that needed attention, such as prostitution or the stark under-representation of women in the German business sector, the federal government remained non-committal.

Femocrats and project activists had high hopes for the first Schröder government, its five women cabinet members and, most of all, its Women's Minister, Social Democrat Christine Bergmann, to end the *Reformstau* (reform blockage) in gender politics. Feminists hoped for better access and overall a gender sensitive political culture to become the signature trademark of 'Red–Green'. Initially, even though the German Chancellor had publicly derided women's policies as 'hype', Red–Green delivered by focusing on neglected areas of women's equality while at the same time advancing support for families by specifically addressing mens' responsibilities as partners and fathers. In a first step, monthly child allowance for parents was increased to 250 DM (or €128) in 1999 and then to 270 DM (or €138) per child in 2000 and to €154 in 2002. In 2001, the infamously termed *'Erziehungsurlaub'* (education *vacation*) was not just renamed *'Elternzeit'* (parental leave time) but was also revamped such that both parents could take it at the same time and for a joint maximum period of three years.

Aside from these family oriented measures, a whole set of initiatives and laws signalled the end of the gender reform blockage. With the action platform 'Fighting Violence against Women' in 1999, the federal government institutionalized preventive policies, more encompassing legal rights for women and launched an impressive public awareness campaign. In 2002, a law was passed regulating contact as well as claims to the joint living space for women in case of marital violence. Also in 2002, the Prostitution Act defined prostitution as an independent or dependent labour activity with access to health insurance, social security and pension funds. During the same period, the Civil Marriage Act for Gays and Lesbians took effect, and the Foreign Nationals Act was altered so that non-national women and girls in case of divorce would get an independent residency permit after only two years of marriage instead of four. In all ministries under female leadership, Joyce Mushaben has observed, legislation was enacted that paid tribute to gender equality and the mainstreaming agenda (Mushaben, 2005).[5]

But while these overdue laws were hailed by women's organizations, the real challenge for Red–Green became the passage of two laws that were, first, less cost neutral, and, secondly, that directly affected the business sector – until today the most resilient hold-out against gender equality in Germany.[6] Business associations mobilized early to prevent the two capstone projects of the Red–Green women's agenda: The passing of an Affirmative Action Law for the private business sector and an Antidiscrimination Law in accordance with European Union requirements.

The Affirmative Action Law had been part of the Red–Green coalition agreement and was considered central by feminist politicians of both parties. At the same time, it was highly controversial within the parties. Business oriented Social Democrats in particular, including the Chancellor, publicly toned down expectations regarding its scope and impact. The Women's Ministry received signals early on that an expert evaluation it had commissioned from a feminist legal scholar and ex-state minister advocating forceful compliance incentives for companies was unacceptable. As a result, the Ministry's first draft of the law relied strongly on voluntary compliance by businesses to draft yearly company-wide affirmative action plans and show results in advancing women. But it also included measures in case of non-compliance, ranging from prohibition to compete for state contracts to group action suits that associations could file in lieu of an individual plaintiff.

The Women's Minister came under severe attack from business friendly groups within her own party, most notably from the Chancellor himself. He made it clear that under his chancellorship such a law would not pass; relations between them soured. The compromise that took effect in 2001 signalled a significant defeat for the Women's Ministry, for feminist advocates in the parties and women's organizations that had supported a strong legal framework. Instead of a law, business associations and government signed a non-binding agreement in which business promised to take all necessary steps to foster gender equality in hiring and promotion. Progress would be monitored through bi-yearly reports by the associations. The Women's Minister, in a last attempt to insert some accountability, left the door open to pursuing a legal framework in case of non-compliance (BMFSFJ, 2001). The first of these reports, published in 2003, presents a rhetorical firework of 'best practices', but lacks any systematic effort to devise coherent strategies to advance women. Nevertheless, government and business concluded that the path of voluntary compliance had proven to be effective and would be continued (BMFSFJ, 2003, p. 4).

Several factors contributed to this defeat for the women's policy machinery and women's advocates within the two governing parties. First, the policy environment, dominated at the time by debates about high unemployment and high labour costs, was not conducive to a law that business was able to frame as expensive and bureaucratic. Second, due to a lack of strategic cohesion there was little action by women's organizations to mobilize for an Affirmative Action law. Third, the internal blockage from business friendly parliamentarians, cabinet ministers and the Chancellor himself was too massive to overcome.

The failure to pass this capstone gender law was followed by other setbacks. When the Red–Green coalition won re-election in 2002 after an explicitly family oriented campaign (Lang and Sauer, 2003), the Chancellor offered the Women's Ministry to Renate Schmidt, a Social Democrat with strong commitment to family policies, but much less enthusiasm for gender issues and feminism. Under her auspices, blockages continued, most notably the unsuccessful attempt to pass an Anti-discrimination Law. The need for such a law had long been evident, since four European Union directives on equal treatment had not been implemented nationally. Only after the EU had already started infringement procedures against the German government for non-implementation did the Red–Green coalition finally present a draft of the proposed law in the fall of 2004. In a hearing organized by the Ministry of Family, Youth, Seniors and Women in March 2005, business associations derided the law as a 'job killer' and again pronounced that its bureaucratic costs would augment Germany's fiscal crisis. The most contentious passages included a provision that would have extended legal protection against discrimination based on race, ethnicity or gender beyond public and employment law into private contracts and services, such as rentals and insurances (Wersig, 2005, p. 101).[7] Business associations also mobilized against the introduction of limited group action suits and the establishment of a federal anti-discrimination office that would be in charge of information and facilitation. Even though the coalition parties passed the law in the *Bundestag* (First Chamber of German parliament), the conservative majority in the *Bundesrat* (Second Chamber) rejected it. In 2006, the grand coalition of Conservatives and Social Democrats passed a 'light' version of the law, which has been renamed *Allgemeines Gleichbehandlungsgesetz* (General Equal Treatment Law), and still offers a number of loopholes, for example for landlords and in private insurances.

Summarizing seven years of Red–Green government, the record on gender governance is mixed at best. Despite initial successes, resistance from within the ruling parties and the cabinet as well as strong business interests contributed to an effective marginalization of gender politics. An initially robust equality frame was downsized into a traditionalist equal opportunity frame that centred around provisions helping women – but not men – to combine work and family (Lang and Sauer, 2003). Thus, under the governance of two of the most gender equality committed parties, a paradigm shift occurred from a focus on broader policies of gender justice to a focus on family policy. Lack of party cohesion and of executive support, added by lack of outside mobilization, added to prevent effective gender governance under the Red–Green coalition.

Europeanization

In lieu of strong national mobilization, women's advocates began looking towards the European Union to create the momentum lacking within Germany. Europe, as Petra Kodre and Henrike Müller have recently argued, had not really been on the map of the German women's policy machinery or the women's movement until the mid-1990s. The implementation of EU directives on equality was routinely delayed – in some cases up to 18 years (see Kodre/Müller, 2003, p. 93; Von Wahl, 2005). In 1995 and 1997, when two decisions by the European Court of Justice (ECJ) shook up German state affirmative action laws, public commentators focused on the national implications of the rulings, but downplayed EU influence on the national policies these rulings exposed. While the Kalanke decision of 1995 first provoked insecurity and ultimately legal changes in the laws of progressive German states like Berlin, Bremen and North Rhine-Westphalia, the Marshall decision in 1997 allowed adequate and individual assessment based quotas in state equality laws.[8] Moreover, an intervention by the European Commission declared that combining women's equality measures with public contracts was not in accordance with EU law, putting a stop to attempts by Berlin and

Brandenburg to follow the US example by actively promoting private business responsiveness to an equality agenda. An ECJ ruling in 2000 declared a law excluding women from voluntarily joining the Federal Armed Forces (*Bundeswehr*) as not in accordance with Community Law. As a result, after a revision of the German Basic Law, in January 2001 the first 244 female recruits entered the *Bundeswehr*.

EU policies have since seeped into many arenas of gender policies, women's policy machinery and the women's movement. The gender-mainstreaming paradigm, in particular, has become a central pillar of government action and women's agency concern. The Red–Green coalition introduced gender-mainstreaming in 1999, with the goal to make it a formal component of all policies of the Federal government by 2008. Yet the 'model projects' initiated so far include mainstreaming mostly in governance sectors where gender sensitivity had already been trained before, such as in statistical data offices or in development aid policies.

The Länder have started initiatives to implement gender mainstreaming as well. But their diverse strategies and goals reflect the erosion of cooperative federalism, fiscal pressures and the lack of commitment by some state governments discussed above. A few women's policy agencies, as in the state of Berlin, have used EU leverage to press successfully for money and resources to implement gender mainstreaming. Yet the conservatives are inclined to replace women's policies with gender mainstreaming (Abgeordnetenhaus Berlin, 2005, p. 3945). Two lines of rationalization have emerged: Either it is argued that the crisis of public finances makes spending cuts necessary and that with gender mainstreaming, the women's policy agencies become superfluous; or it is claimed that the EU forces the states to mainstream gender and therefore the women's infrastructure can be downsized.[9] The women's policy agencies seem caught between a rock and a hard place. Embracing the gender mainstreaming principle might mean to face the downloading of responsibilities for gender mainstreaming onto units of the civil service that might neither be willing nor well equipped to perform as gender advocates, and it might threaten the equality office's infrastructure (Lang, 2005). But not embracing gender mainstreaming would mean rejecting the one strategy that is 'en vogue' and has a built in EU leverage for gender advocacy.

Women's policy agencies – between institutionalization and deregulation

Germany still has one of the largest women's policy machineries in Europe. Its organizational base forms the more than 1900 local Women's

Equality Offices in cities and counties and their national association BAG (*Bundesarbeitsgemeinschaft lokaler Frauenbüros*), the Federal Association of Local-Government Women's Offices (BMFSFJ, 2004). A second organizational tier is made up of the Women's Ministries or Women's Departments within Ministries of the sixteen German states. These are in charge of implementing state equality laws and working with the civic women's project infrastructure as well as with state parliaments, parties, business, and unions to advance equality within their states. They are flanked by equality officers in public institutions such as the courts, universities, research institutes, hospitals and public media. The third organizational tier is the Federal Ministry for Family, Youth, Women and Seniors with its mandate to devise and implement laws and regulations as well as to initiate model projects towards more gender equality. But what appears to be a well institutionalized system of women's policy agencies is under pressure on several levels.

At the local level, 'institutional isomorphism' seems to be changing direction: While in the 1990s, many cities and counties were still building or stabilizing their women's policy agencies, recent developments point towards their shrinking in reach, financial stability and staff. Four states in 2005 are in the process of downsizing the number of equality offices or the office's structure by means of reducing costs or legal revisions. In Lower Saxony, for example, a proposed change in the communal law would abolish the threshold of 20,000 inhabitants that so far requires the installation of a women's equality office. In Schleswig-Holstein, a grand coalition of Social Democrats and Conservatives wants to extend the threshold for full time equality officers from 10,000 inhabitants to 15,000 – a step that would reduce the number of equality officers by about half (BAG Press Declaration, 2005/06/07). In the eastern state of Brandenburg, another grand coalition recently downsized equality offices while at the same time extending their mission towards other 'diversity' constituencies, namely seniors, the disabled and migrants. In Saxony, the conservative government contemplates changing the name and tasks of the women's equality officers into 'family officers'. Conservative Baden-Württemberg amended its State Equality Law in October 2005 into an 'Equal Opportunity Law', allowing longer periods between providing statistical equality plans as well as more flexibility to justify personnel decisions that do not correspond with women's advancement principles. Equality Officers on the local level are not, as women's organizations had demanded, required under the provisions of the reformed law (DGB, 2005).

The national coordination organization of equality offices, the BAG, is in no bargaining position to do more than to appeal to the respective state governments to reconsider their decisions. Overall, equality agencies are not altogether abolished but downsized and hollowed out. As a result, their ability to produce substantive policy change and cognitive shifts in the perception of gender shrinks. Ferree's diagnosis of 1995 still stands that, 'at a minimum (the move to institutionalize the women's equality officers) offers a structural mechanism for channelling communication and resources between the autonomous feminist movement and women's caucuses and organizations and between East and West' (Ferree, 1995, p. 112). In many cases women's offices have gone beyond that and were able to contribute to changing gender cultures within bureaucracies and to public awareness of its issues. But their volatile position in times of fiscal crisis, of bureaucratic downsizing and of the predominance of gender mainstreaming calls these accomplishments into question.

Reduction of women's infrastructure takes place not just at the local, but also at the state level. In 2004, 10 of the 16 German states had established women's ministries. In four states there was an ombudswoman for gender equality assigned to the governors office and in two states there was a department within the Ministry for Social Affairs handling women's issues (BMFSFJ, 2004, p. 191). But the trend is towards downsizing. Brandenburg's grand coalition and conservative Hesse recently abolished first their Women's Ministries, then, in a next step, their department for women's issues within the Social Ministry. Instead of a full ministry, there is now one woman in charge of women's issues, situated in the governor's office. The rationale for both states' steps was gender mainstreaming. Hesse has also cut means for women's shelters by one-third, abolished women's qualification and training projects and stopped affirmative action measures introduced in 1993 in the most advanced state women equality law.[10] With this deregulation of legal frameworks for gender equality, implementation on the local level suffers.

Another setback for the institutionalized women's policy agencies was the publicly almost unnoticed abolition of regular meetings of the states' women's ministries, historically a driving force in federal policymaking.[11] (GFMK, 2005) At their last conference in June 2005, the joint Conference of the Women's and Equality State Ministers (GFMK – *Gemeinsame Frauenministerinnenkonferenz*) decided with a majority vote by the conservative states to dissolve itself and in the future address women's issues in the context of the joint meetings of the states' youth and family ministers. Even though the states with left-leaning governments protested against this 'backlash to the sixties'[12] which recognized women only as mothers or wives, the conservative representatives prevailed and insisted that the institutionalization of women's ministries in the German Länder had always been considered a 'temporary' measure (GFMK, 2005, p. 2). Only a procedural miscalculation of the conservatives has as of summer 2006 saved the GFMK, since the Youth ministers could not muster the necessary two-thirds majority vote for incorporating women's issues into their agenda. This leaves the GFMK in limbo. The effects of losing the coordination potential of the Länder ministries through the GFMK would be substantial. First, the isomorphism or adaptation effect between the Länder would decrease; and, second, their internal bargaining power in regard to other ministerial coordination bodies, the national government as well as EU institutions would suffer from lack of a joint political voice. Trying to abandon this instrument in times of heightened Länder influence on the EU level (Börzel, 2002) is a severe setback for the women's equality machinery as well as for gender policies.

Previous research on the efficacy of the German women's policy machinery supports this mixed assessment, pointing to its role in conflictual policy arenas as overwhelmingly symbolic. The women's policy agencies did not take strong positions and had no influence on the outcome of the bioethics debate (Braun, 2007), on issues of women's political representation (Kamenitsa and Geissel, 2005) and on the abortion debates (Kamenitsa, 2001). Do these results indicate an *absolute* lack of efficacy of women's policy agencies? I believe there is sufficient evidence to question such an interpretation. Taking into consideration the multiple points of intervention the agencies have on the local, the state and the national levels, each governance level provides for a number of *relative* successes that often occur under the radar of broader inquiries. Local women's policy agencies provide numerous women's organizations with an institutional hub and with entry points into the political arena. Agencies in some German Länder have become relentless watchdogs over budgets and over instilling gender perspectives in state legislation. And the first four years of the Red–Green women's policy agencies on the federal level exemplify how, under encouraging leadership, such an agency can do more than symbolic gender work. Yet these relative victories are the result of specific constellations: of mostly left-leaning parties in power, of feminists in executive office and of a policy environment that is conducive to gendered change. If the policy environment changes, and if the personnel changes, women's policy agencies can degenerate to merely symbolic entities within the larger bureaucratic structure of German governance. Another key to the agencies' effectiveness is support by the women's movement. Yet the German women's movement tends to exacerbate the sidelining of women's policy agencies.

The NGOized women's movement

The German women's movement today is highly institutionalized and thus has come a long way from its early roots in a separatist and autonomous women's culture. In the early 1970s and 1980s, the movement had largely consisted of grassroots projects that made a point of keeping their distance from the state. Attempts to form long term alliances, strong national organizations or bargains with the institutions of the German corporatist state were perceived as the route to cooptation and loss of power. When the state was being brought into the feminist debates of the 1980s and claims grew louder that women's issues receive a fair share of state interest, public spending and state jobs (Kulawik, 1992), the path from women's project feminism to an NGOized and highly institutionalized feminism was paved. 'Femocrats' began working within state bureaucracies to advance women's issues. Working women decided that the best form to advance their agenda would be within professionally oriented women's organizations. And women's projects started to become more professionalized, to develop strategies to secure their jobs and to provide continuity for their members and constituencies – resulting in what I have previously described as the NGOization of German feminism (Lang, 1997).

Today, this NGOized and institutionalized German women's movement sector is made up of three organizational clusters: the disintegrated and largely state dependent local grassroots project culture, the professionalized women's organizations under the heading of the German Women's Council (*Deutscher Frauenrat*), and the culture of femocrats, feminist and women's advocates within the institutions of the state and the parties. Smaller clusters of feminist activists are situated within the university research community. And while these three clusters interact infrequently, they rarely strategize, develop joint policy goals or mobilize the German women's public together.

In the first cluster, the majority of formerly independent projects is by now semi-institutionalized and receives basic funding for personnel and infrastructure from local or state governments. In Berlin, Germany's capital and a city-state that is governed by a Social Democratic–Socialist alliance and is severely in debt, the 2004 budget included about €9 million for women's projects, which is a total of about 0.07 per cent of the city's budget, and considered very high if compared to other states (Abgeordnetenhaus, 2005, p. 3900). Efforts by the liberals and conservatives to cut these funds for women's projects by about 10 per cent in 2004 were largely fended off – resulting in effective cuts of about 4 per cent. But Berlin is the exceptional city-state, with the most engrained and diverse infrastructure for women. In 2004, state funding went to some 65 women's projects, of which about 20 worked in labour market qualification, 27 in the arena of violence against women, about 15 were engaged in intercultural work and 18 offered women's centres with a multifaceted set of support and other programme activities (ibid.).

A striking contrast to this 'feminist haven' is the southern state of Baden-Württemberg. This conservative and catholic state, one of the richest regions in Germany, has three times the inhabitants of the state of Berlin, but overall in 2004 only spent €1.5 million on women's issues (Staatshaushaltsplan, 2004), which amounts to 0.007 per cent of the state's budget, or 10 per cent of what Berlin spends. Additional funds that its capital Stuttgart provides for women are limited to about €550.000 a year for a women's shelter, approximately €480.000 for mother–child programmes, €150.000 for a cultural women's programme and €50.000 for institutional affirmative action measures in the city (Stuttgart, 2004). This part of the women's movement, while providing essential local women's infrastructure remains almost invisible in national politics. It has become a professionalized and state dependent women's project culture that has altered its mission from feminist consciousness raising to providing services for women, from developing critiques of the masculinist state to becoming its bargaining partner and from organizing feminist publics to providing associational spaces for women.

The second cluster of the NGOized German women's movement is made up of an impressive number of professional and cultural national women's organizations, engaging effectively with women's issues in their fields of expertise. The majority of these women's organizations are members in the German Women's Council (*Deutscher Frauenrat*), which is the only nationally prominent catalyst for women's interests. In 2006, more than 50 German women's organizations were members. Twenty-eight were professional organizations such as the Association of Women Lawyers or the Women Medical Assistants' Organization, six were women's chapters of parties and trade unions, 19 represented social and cultural constituencies or women in bi-national families and three were religious associations such as the Jewish women's organization.[13] The Council is an effective advocacy tool for the liberal spectrum of women's organizations, but it does not represent formerly 'autonomous' women's projects such as the countries' 16 feminist women's health centres, the women's shelter network, or younger women. Yet whenever an aggregate of the German women's civil society is needed, the Women's Council is being brought to the table. A case in point is the public hearing on the above-mentioned Anti-discrimination Law, organized by the Ministry of Family,

Youth, Seniors and Women in March 2005. Feminist stakeholders should have had a vested interest in this issue. Fifty-six relevant social groups and scientists were invited to comment on the proposed law. Of the 37 groups only two were women's organizations, the Women's Council and the Association of Women Lawyers. All in all, the participation of the women's non-governmental sector in this crucial deliberation process on a central piece of legislation was 5.4 per cent. Business interest groups, on the other hand, constituted 29.7 per cent of invited groups and representatives of ethnic and racial minority NGOs constituted 21.6 per cent.[14]

The lack of public visibility of a diverse women's movement is also reflected in declining protest events as well as declining participation rates in protests. The proportion of protests in Germany that were organized by women's movement actors in relation to all other major protest domains has declined from 2.6 per cent between 1970–1979 to 1.7 per cent between 1980–1989 down to 1.2 per cent in the West from 1990–1997 and 0.9 per cent in the East during the same time period (Rucht, 2004, p. 161). Even more striking is the decline in participants of women's movement protests in relation to all protest participants: From 0.8 per cent between 1970–1979 to 0.7 per cent between 1980–1989 to 0.4 per cent between 1990–1997 in the West and 0.3 per cent in the same time period in the new Länder. Dieter Rucht's conclusion that overall in Germany's protest culture 'women's protests are marginal' (ibid., 160), concurs with the organization-based analysis presented here, leaving the majority of mobilization to femocrats and incorporated actors – the third tier of the movement we looked at before – without a major support base in the wider German public.

These different venues of women's movement institutionalization – that is, femocrats *working within* institutions, professional women's organizations *lobbying* institutions and women's projects professionalizing and *being funded* by institutions – have another troubling effect. They privilege women with adequate educational, cognitive, cultural and financial resources to interact in or with these institutions, but tend to marginalize women without these means. Institutionalization therefore does not just lead to a different organizational base of the women's movement, but it also creates new lines of inclusion and exclusion. Mary Katzenstein's observation that women without institutional access are without allies and might even have been better off when they were still considered to be a central constituency of the diverse women's movement (Meyer, 2003) holds for Germany, too. Two of the most fragile female constituencies in German society today are single mothers and migrant women. Both these constituencies, even though for differing reasons, are not well represented even within the existing selective and marginalized women's advocacy. They neither have strong organizational bases, nor solid institutional relationships or media access. This lack of mobilization capacity became evident for example during the recent headscarf debate, in which Muslim women themselves hardly played a public role. Only in 2005, migrant women founded the *Bundesverband der Migrantinnen* (Federal Union of Women Migrants), the first national women migrant association in Germany, with the aim of giving Muslim women a voice in current public debates.

Local feminist cultures remain fragmented and resource-poor, and the national sector of feminist organizations is, compared to other German civic sectors, tiny (Ferree and Gamson et al., 2002, p. 149). In sum, the NGOization and institutionalization of the German women's movement has provided the different parts of the movement with selective access to governance bodies and with a partial insider advantage. But this insider advantage is offset by the movements' lack of mobilization capacity.

Conclusion: state feminism without a public?

In this chapter, I have tried to unravel the reasons for the mixed success of femocratization in Germany and to point to the challenges that state restructuring poses for the women's policy machinery. To make no mistake: this is a mixed success on a comparatively high institutionalized level. Women's policy agencies are by no means in immediate danger of being eliminated. In the favourable policy environment of the first four years of the Red–Green coalition, they were indeed equipped to launch innovative policies. But even though women's policy agencies are in no immediate danger, they have become part and parcel of a restructuring of state and society under neoliberal premises that involves broad strategies of deregulation, downloading and privatization.

Different governance levels and modes intersect to produce deregulation, downloading, and privatization. The more bargaining power the Länder get in relation to the federal government, the more the federal state will withdraw from policy arenas in which before it had provided at least policy guidelines. The organization of the civil service, education, child care, the universities and other arenas might become part of the downloading process from federal state to the Länder – and in all these fields, a more competitive federalism will in all likelihood take hold. Competitive federalism is an asset for policy arenas in which the Länder invest in order to promote business and enhance their international profile. Gender equality, we have to conclude, is not likely to be one of these arenas any time soon.

Länder governments, due to either ideological bias or fiscal pressures, are not prone to invest in the women's policy machinery in the future more than they did in the 1990s; in fact, the trend points in the opposite direction. With gender mainstreaming they have a strategy at hand that might be looked at as a cheaper alternative to an elaborate women's policy machinery. This is not an inherent flaw of the mainstreaming strategy, but it can be exploited that way.

In sum, the established pillars of institutionalization are weakened by deregulation, downloading and privatization. But it is not as though the femocrat structure is crumbling yet. Now the question is whether and how the next generations of, less feminist and less formally equality oriented, women will inhabit and protect the existing spaces. State feminism has contributed much to counteract gender inequality, but it cannot do it alone, and, in particular, not without support and commitment from German women's publics. Yet whether the effects of neoliberal restructuring will revive the women's movement, remains a speculative question.

Notes

1. My thanks go to Katie Rogers for her research support and to Joyce Mushaben and the RNGS group for wonderful comments.
2. Helmut Wiesenthal from the Berlin Humboldt University, for example argued that 'This extreme unemployment – resulting both from the wave of de-industrialization and from higher labour market participation among East German women – constitutes Eastern Germany's basic political-economic problem' (Wiesenthal, 2004, p. 42).
3. I owe the reference to this concept to Birgit Sauer (2005b).
4. The total net financial transfers from West Germany to the *Neue Länder* between 1990 and 2002 reached approximately €800 billion (Wiesenthal, 2004, p. 42).
5. Even though Joyce Mushaben cites gender relevant policy successes for example in the Ministries for Justice and Education, I argue that some successes are not a result of feminist federal secretaries, but the effect of sometimes rather contentious interventions by women's policy machineries or women's organizations *against* bureaucratic intentions. A case in point is the federal effort to revamp university education, including the law on 'Junior Professors' that Mushaben cites. The secretary in charge, Edelgard Bulmahn, had attached strict age caps to this newly created entry level position in the university system – age limits that, so the university equality officers and women advocates argued, would have had strong adverse effects on women in this critical phase of career and family development. Only after a flurry of

protests was the Bulmahn ministry willing to alter these strict age limits in order to accommodate women's career patterns.

6. In 2003, women earned 75.8 per cent of male wages, were largely overrepresented in low paying jobs and among higher management positions made up only 8.1 per cent (BMFSFJ, 2003; 2004; CEDAW, 2003, p. 41).

7. Antidiscrimination law in Germany until 2006 did not extend into private contract law. This resulted in a number of blatantly discriminatory practices, such as higher health insurance tariffs for women than for men (Wersig, 2005).

8. In the 1995 ECJ ruling *Kalanke* v. *Freie Hansestadt Bremen*, the Court struck down a quota provision of the *Land Bremen* on grounds that it created an 'automatism' for promoting equally qualified women over men in the Bremen Civil Service in case of numerical underrepresentation. Two years later, in the *Marschall* decision, the Court acknowledged the lawfulness of the use of positive discrimination and quotas if the hiring process reflected case based decision making and not a simple automatism (BMFSFJ, 2004, p. 214; Wahl, 2005, p. 81).

9. Helga Hentschel, Berlin Senate, Department for Women's Issues, Interview August 2005.

10. Gabriele Wenner, speaker of BAG, at http://www.frauenbeauftragte.de/bag/schlechte%20zeiten.htm (accessed 1 June 2006).

11. Helga Hentschel, Berlin Senate, Department for Women's Issues, Interview August 2005.

12. Berlin's women's state Secretary Harald Wolf, press release 3 June 2005.

13. http://www.frauenrat.de/module/home/start.aspx# (accessed 18 January 2006).

14. Figures compiled from Öffentliche Anhörung des Ausschusses für Familie, Senioren, Frauen und Jugend, 7 March 2005 at http://www.bundestag.de/ausschuesse/archiv15/a12/Öffentliche_Sitzungen/20050307/ (accessed 16 January 2006).

8
Unfinished Business: Equality Policy and the Changing Context of State Feminism in Great Britain

Joni Lovenduski

Introduction

The first women's equality agency, the Women's National Commission (WNC) was established in 1969. Since then sex equality policy in Britain developed from simple prohibitions on sex discrimination in certain narrowly defined fields, to policies based on wider concepts of equal treatment for women and men. It is now to become part of the framework for combined and interacting policies on equalities and human rights. The agendas and powers of the UK agencies are affected by the other equality agencies. The first British equality agency was the Race Relations Board, established in 1965, which was replaced by the Commission for Racial Equality in 1976. In 2000 The Disability Rights Commission was established. New sex equality agencies appeared from 1976, notably the Equal Opportunities Commission (EOC) in 1976, the Women's Unit (WU) in 1997, replaced by the Women and Equality Unit (WEU) in 2001. At the time of writing, in 2006, the whole of the equality policy agency apparatus is on the point of being restructured. Legislation to bring together all the various equality agencies in the UK into a single body was enacted in 2006. A Commission for Equality and Human Rights (CEHR) that also includes the 'new' strands of equality and human rights is scheduled to open for business in 2007.[1]

The creation of a combined agency is a natural development. Over almost four decades, the definitions of sex equality have changed. Initially it was thought of in terms of men and women as categories with relatively little appreciation of differences among men and among women. Gradually the crosscutting nature of inequality became apparent, as feminists and other equality advocates drew attention to the importance of class, race, disability, sexuality and other sources of disadvantage that combined to affect the life chances of individuals. This shift paralleled two related developments in British feminist thinking: the first a change from a focus on sex defined as the biological distinction between women and men to gender defined as the social implications of masculinity and femininity; and the second a growing sensitivity to diversity and intersectionality. Such insights framed consideration of diverse sources of inequality in agency decision-making, and were reflected in the creation of new institutions with combined responsibilities. Over the years, a substantial equality policy community developed, which was characterized by considerable interaction including substantial cooperation and policy transfer between agencies, advocates and NGOs representing the different bases of inequality. As these processes unfolded the priority of treating employment discrimination in equality policy shifted and agencies began to recognize the importance of service provision (Spencer, 2005, p. 31). The growing influence of new-right thinking after 1979 led to significant changes in the machinery of government as succeeding administrations reformed government processes and institutions. Thereafter a key development in the political context was the programme of constitutional reform and government restructuring initiated after the 1997 general election. In this process the civil service, the legislature and the judiciary were all reconfigured. The new constitutional settlement set a political context in which various opportunities were created. With an eye on women's votes and a record number of women in parliament, cabinet and government, the Labour governments were generally much more sympathetic to women's issues. In addition, international actors, notably the UN, the Council of Europe and the EU have affected government thinking on equality agencies.

It is impossible to account for the current configuration of British women's policy agencies without discussing both the wider equality policy communities and the changing policy context that has led to the current reforms. However, the reforms are still under development at the time of writing, hence this chapter, like its subject, is work in progress. To illustrate and account for these various developments, this chapter consists of five parts. First I will consider the changing political context in which, second, institutional changes in state feminism are taking place. Third I will outline the other equality agencies in Britain and explain their significance to state feminism. I will then consider equality policies in terms of their content and their place in women's movement organization and thinking. Finally I will discuss the evolving relationships between the policy agencies and the women's movements since 1995.

Changing political context

The UK is an EU and UN member state, a consolidated European democracy and, in Gøsta Esping Andersen's (1990) terms a liberal welfare state (albeit one which hovers on the border of liberal and social-democratic) subject to the same pressures as other such states. During the 1980s a sustained programme of privatization began that included, inter alia, steel, coal, utilities, water, the railways. The period was characterized by macro economic shifts in which the long decline of the industrial sector that provided well paid and secure men's jobs gave way to a service economy that offered low paid, insecure women's jobs. Welfare state institutions and the programmes of social provision became subject to an ongoing process of review, reform and change from the 1980s.

Institutional change took place against a background of other political changes. The UK constitutional system turns on the convention of parliamentary sovereignty but is animated by the realities of majoritarian party government. Particularly in the delivery of public services, but also across most areas of government activity, the longer-term shift to agencification and the contracting out of public services to NGOs and the private sector affected patterns of decision-making and policy implementation at local, regional and national levels. As a consequence of the resulting vertical and horizontal shifts, the British state has altered considerably since the 1980s (Banaszak et al., 2003; Judge, 2005; Toynbee and Walker, 2001).

State reconfiguration was to some extent paralleled by changes in organized groups, some parts of which became more influential while at the same time becoming more state dependent. In terms of social movements the traditional trade union movement continued its long decline as did other mass membership organizations including the political parties, the churches and the long established women's organizations such as the Women's Institutes. However, changes in the delivery of social provision offered opportunities for participation as adjustments in the policy environment permitted access to decision making by NGOs, think tanks, lobbying and advocacy organizations.

It is difficult to argue that the system has been characterized by welfare state retrenchment. True, successive conservative governments neglected hospital and school building programmes, reduced some benefits and attempted to squeeze public spending. However some benefits actually increased under the Conservatives (e.g. disability payments) and the national social security bill increased. After 1997, although slow to start (following a pledge to honour Conservative spending plans for its first two years of government) successive Labour governments invested heavily in health and education spending and reformed benefit programmes to target children and the working poor as major beneficiaries. These reforms are framed in a new right 'welfare to work' discourse. But rhetoric and reality are dissonant. The more accurate descriptive term is restructuring. Indeed, since 1997 Labour governments have attempted the long overdue task of restructuring much of government activity.

The UK policy environment is comparatively closed, with access limited to certain insider organizations and through the political parties, a configuration that historically presented many obstacles to women's movement actors. Opportunities expanded in the late 1990s. First, successive Labour governments proved more disposed than their predecessors to cooperate with advocacy and lobbying groups. Partly this was a response to 18 years in opposition during which time the party worked closely with many advocacy groups, think tanks and experts to prepare its policies. When Labour entered government those relationships continued as many newly elected MPs and government advisers were drawn from the groups. Second, constitutional reform included devolution and ceded some equality responsibilities to new assemblies and regional governments in Scotland, Wales and Northern Ireland. In the course of the establishment of the Scottish Parliament and the Welsh Assembly in 1999 some equality responsibilities were combined in local committees and agencies. The Northern Ireland Act of 1998 established a single equalities commission for Northern Ireland that by 1999 was responsible for some nine equality strands, having absorbed pre-existing single equality commissions. It was thought by government to offer a model for its revision of equality agency provision in 2005.

Third, the equality agenda itself expanded and women's agencies were able to benefit from expansions of power in other equality sectors.

Fourth, additional bases of inequality requiring different remedies became subject to regulation. The government signed up to the EU 'social chapter' in 1997 and proved willing to make use of the equality provisions in the constitution and citizenship part of the Amsterdam Treaty in the Sex Discrimination Electoral Candidates Act of 2002. Two EU Directives in 2000 extended equal treatment provision to new strands and extended race and ethnic origin equality provision beyond employment and occupation. The Employment or Framework Equal Treatment Directive (FETD) (Council Directive 2000/78/EC) established a general framework for equal treatment in employment and occupation and outlawed discrimination on the basis of religion, belief, disability, age and sexual orientation. The Race Directive (Council Directive 2000/43/EC) prohibited discrimination on the grounds of race or ethnic origin in the areas of employment, social protection, education, goods and services, including housing. In terms of agencies, article 13 of the Race Directive requires that 'member states shall designate a body or bodies for the promotion of equal treatment of all persons . . . These bodies . . . may form part of agencies charged at national level with the defence of human rights'. The article further requires that the competencies of the bodies include the capacity to provide independent assistance to victims of discrimination, to conduct independent surveys concerning discrimination, and publish independent reports on any issue relating to such discrimination.

Fifth, advocates began to make connections between equality and human rights, pointing out that human rights arguments were relevant to some sources of discrimination that were not subject to anti-discrimination law (Spencer, 2005). In addition new 'equalities' and new remedies became subject to regulation. Labour delivered on its manifesto promise to incorporate the European Convention on Human Rights into legislation in the Human Rights Act of 1998.[2] Furthermore, the EU's contribution to equality policy took a new turn with the insertion of Art 13 on non-discrimination into Part Two of the Amsterdam Treaty, on citizenship of the Union. The subsequent race equality directive showed the influence of this 'Human Rights turn' in that its scope extended beyond employment.

Sixth, a major gender shift was marked by the election of 101 women to the 1997 House of Commons, a step change in women's representation. Political parties became more responsive to women when, following shifts in voting patterns, and under pressure from their women members, they began to make policies to appeal to women voters. These changes began in the early 1980s and became effective in the 1990s when the Labour Party introduced quotas of candidates to increase its representation of women in parliament. Despite declining memberships and loss of popularity, political parties continue to be the motor of the political system, hence increases in women's power in the parties marked an improvement of their ability to make the political system work for feminist goals. Important to this chapter, the incoming 1997 government honoured a manifesto promise to institute a Women's Unit 'close to the centre of government'. Taken together, these changes improved opportunities for agencies to expand their mandates and for women's advocates to influence policymaking.

Overall the period since 1995 and especially since 1997 has seen increased consultation and interaction between women's movements, agencies, politicians and government on a significant range of women's concerns.

These have included not only traditional and longstanding women's issues such as violence to women and childcare but also the wider issues of pay, pensions, representation, budgets and indeed the full range of policy. A clear women's agenda was established and patterns of cooperation and coalitions across agencies, movements, parties and government became apparent. An emerging feminist policy network is a considerable force, very effective when it acts in concert. However, it is important to stress that the welcome development of improved feminist policy advocacy and competence is also a product of the widely noted change in the way government does business. The emergence of a system of governance in which policy makers draw on multiple sources of advice and processes institutionalize consultation with stakeholders is congenial to the politics of women's movements only up to a point. Such advocates are included but can rarely trump the employer interests that are prioritized by government.

Institutional changes in state feminism

Prior to 1997 two women's equality agencies existed – the Women's National Commission (WNC) and the Equal Opportunities Commission (EOC). They had mixed success, varying considerably both in their influence with government and the women's movements and also in the issues that they engaged. The Women's National Commission (WNC) was the official voice of women's organizations at Whitehall. Poorly resourced and rather conservative, the WNC was initially slow to include the new feminist groups, which emerged in the 1970s (Lovenduski and Randall, 1993; Stokes, 2003). Moreover, as the official representative of groups with bases in conflicting religious, economic, and partisan organizations the WNC was unable to take a line on such important women's issues as abortion or prostitution (Kantola and Squires, 2004; McBride Stetson, 2001a). On such issues, campaigners found it more useful to work directly with interested MPs (Childs, 2004; Sones et al., 2005). The WNC continues to represent the informed opinion of women to government. It does this by bringing together and consulting women's organizations and experts on women's interests who are its 'partners'.[3] The WNC is headed by a chair and a commission appointed by government and is serviced by a small team of civil servants. In 1998 it was moved to the cabinet office where it worked in conjunction with the Women's Unit. Since then it has followed the Women's Unit from ministry to ministry (see below). In 2003–04 its budget was 305,000 UK sterling.

The *Equal Opportunities Commission* was established as a cross sectional agency with responsibility to oversee the Sex Discrimination Act of 1975

(SDA), which outlawed direct and indirect discrimination on grounds of sex in employment, education and the provisions of goods, facilities and services. The EOC is also headed by a chair and a commission of government appointees but is a 'Quango',[4] in theory autonomous of government. For most of its history the EOC interpreted its mandate narrowly, focusing on employment issues. After 1997 and especially after 2001 it interpreted its brief more widely. Formally, its remit is constrained within a narrow ambit, rendering it unable to intervene in policy debates unless it could identify an employment or financial disadvantage to women. However, although reluctant to take on a wider policy role, the EOC sponsored court and tribunal cases, getting involved in policy to the extent of influencing equal pay debates and promoting good practice among employers. Currently it is accountable via the Minister for Women and the civil service department to which it is attached (which has varied with changes of Minister). In 2004–05 its budget was 9.5 million UK pounds and it employed a staff of 150 (Thiesen et al., 2005; Keter, 2005). By 2005 the amount was 10 million UK pounds. Its funding was cut in 2006 by 10 percent (*Guardian*, 3 April 2006, p. 29).

The third agency, the *Women's Unit* (WU) was established in response to pressure from women's movement advocates for a women's ministry. Its establishment accompanied developments within the cabinet where a sub-committee is responsible for equality issues. From 1986 a ministerial group on women's issues operated under the aegis of the Home Office; in 1992 it became a cabinet committee, its brief to consider women's issues on a cross sectoral basis. A succession of cabinet members were given the 'women's portfolio' in addition to their other responsibilities (Lovenduski and Randall, 1993; Stokes, 2003). In 2005 the Cabinet Committee was, at the request of the Prime Minister, replaced by the Ministerial sub-committee on equality (GenderNet, 2002).

The Women's Unit was created after 1997 to support the Minister for Women. Its remit was crosscutting, with an aim of 'feeding the concerns of women . . . directly into policy making across government' (Women's Unit, 1998). During its four years of operation its priorities were childcare, employment and safety for women. It worked with women's organizations both directly and via the WNC and also commissioned research on women's policy issues. Small, ineffective, and not well respected, the WU moved around government following a succession of women's ministers until 2001. After an intensive campaign by women's advocates and following a government review, it was relaunched as the *Women and Equality Unit* (WEU) with a larger budget, staff and remit, within which its focus was mainly, but not exclusively, on economic issues such as the gender pay gap (Squires and Wickham Jones, 2004). Originally it was located in the Department for Trade and Industry (DTI) headed by Minister for Women, Patricia Hewitt who held the post from 2002 until 2005. This move to a large and well-resourced department led by a competent feminist cabinet member undoubtedly benefited the unit, which prospered throughout the second 'new' Labour government. Its economic emphasis continued, notably with its headline Kingsmill Review, a high powered Commission set up by Patricia Hewitt, to investigate women's pay. After the 2005 election the Women's Ministry transferred to the Secretary of State for Culture, Tessa Jowell. Then in Spring 2006, it moved again after a cabinet reshuffle to Ruth Kelly the Minister for the newly created Department for Communities and Local Government. She is supported by a junior minister, Meg Munn.

As a unit of the civil service, the WEU is responsible for developing and drafting legislation. It managed the consultation process over the Government's Equality Bill and provided the bill team from its staff. In 2005–06 it led the Discrimination Law Review, a review of the sex discrimination legislation, preparatory to a planned revision of anti-discrimination legislation. Organizationally two ministers lead the unit, one a secretary of state and therefore a cabinet member, the other fairly junior. The junior minister's post is very minor and has twice, briefly, – in 1997 and in 2005 – been unpaid, apparently because the Prime Minister 'forgot' to budget a salary for the post. Angela Mason, a well-respected advocate brought in from the gay rights organization Stonewall in 2002, directs the unit. Mason told interviewers that she understood that her job was to see into being a single equalities body, hence her tenure at the Women and Equality Unit is aimed at the dissolution of the current women's policy apparatus. At the time of her appointment observers believed that her priorities were in sexuality discrimination and that she was less interested in issues of gender (Interview with former unit staff member, 11 March 2003). The unit has a staff of 63, mainly civil servants seconded from various departments. In 2004 its budget was 2.5 million pounds (Thiesen et al., 2005).

Separate or partly separate combined equality apparatuses operate in Northern Ireland, Scotland and Wales and include sex equality in their concerns. According to the WNC the devolved governing bodies of Northern Ireland, Scotland and Wales 'have greater regard for equality than the UK government' (WNC, 2005). In its 2005 CEDAW report, the WNC draws approving attention to the equality remit of the Scottish Parliament and Welsh Assembly, both of which have taken measures to improve equal opportunities in education. Both have combined legislative equality committees and make equality policies. However, core responsibility for equality policy has not been devolved, it is a central government matter, hence the women's policy agencies described above have responsibility for, and in the case of the EOC, maintain regional offices in Scotland and Wales. In Scotland there have been considerable improvements in infrastructure aimed at allowing women to participate. A notable innovation is the establishment of a crèche for visitors to the Scottish Parliament. The Welsh assembly features a cross-sectoral Equality Unit which supports the work of its Committee on Equality and had a budget of 655.000 UK sterling in 2004–05. The Scottish Parliament has an all party cross-sectoral Equal Opportunities Committee and there is an Equality Unit in the Scottish Executive with a budget of 6 million UK sterling and 28 staff of whom seven work on women's issues. The Equality Commission for Northern Ireland is also cross-sectoral; it employed 143 staff and had a budget of 6.7 million UK sterling in 2004–05 (Thiesen et al., 2005). The detailed arrangements in Scotland and Wales and in Northern Ireland, with its special priority for religious discrimination and separate structure, are impossible to cover in a chapter of this length (but see Meehan, 2005). However the cross sectoral briefs of these agencies are important indicators of the development of government thinking on the management of equality policy.

In summary, prior to 1997, the agencies were ineffective on many issues, hence women's movement advocates prioritized the direct lobbying of policy makers and MPs or making appeals to the public via the media and direct mobilizing activities such as demonstrations and campaigns. After 1997 the pattern changed as new agencies were established and alterations in the remit and operating procedures of the older agencies increased their policy ambit. During these processes women's organizations became more effective.

Other equality agencies

The equality apparatus of the UK is messy. It is deemed to be complex, inaccessible, unequal, confusing and backward looking in that the enabling legislation provides for remedy after discrimination but does not empower institutions to act to prevent discrimination from happening. Not only is there a huge array of relevant legislation, there are, at the time of writing, three agencies and at least six departmental equality or human rights units with equality policy responsibilities. Moreover, policies and priorities differ between Northern Ireland and the mainland, though the organizations have quite a lot of contact. Prior to the establishment of the CEHR in 2007, age, religion or belief and human rights had no official institutional voice. Different equality strands are provided with different levels of protection and have access to different orders of legal instruments when seeking remedy or redress. Thus the women's policy agencies operate in a complex framework of equality legislation and overlapping institutions. They are part of a set of equality agencies with which they cooperate on various policies and with which they are in frequent communication.

The *Commission for Racial Equality* (CRE) is the ranking and best-funded agency. Despite a troubled history the CRE has been very successful at enhancing its powers and strengthening the law on race since 1997. The Race Relations Amendment Act (2000) established a positive duty on public sector bodies to promote race equality, a significant extension of the legislation. It followed the Stephen Lawrence Enquiry into the failure of the Metropolitan Police to prosecute after the murder by white youths of a black teenager in 1993. The enquiry found the Metropolitan Police to be institutionally racist, a diagnosis that attacked the canteen culture of the police. The underlying idea that institutions have cultures that carry racist values was soon extended to other organizations and other 'isms' by equality campaigners.

The Disability Discrimination Act of 1995 permitted positive discrimination in respect of disability defined as the '(in)ability to carry out normal day to day activities'. The Disability Rights Commission Act of 1999 established the *Disability Rights Commission* (DRC) along the lines of the EOC and CRE though with some variations in powers. The Disability Discrimination Bill (2004) extended the definition of disability and provides for a positive duty to promote equality for disabled people in the public sector. Similar to the duty on race equality, it came into force in 2006. Debates about disability and equality added to pressures to extend equality regulation beyond its traditional employment focus. A substantial proportion (50 per cent) of disabled people is not in paid employment. Similar arguments are currently made about the focus of policies to treat inequalities of aged people (Spencer, 2005). Disability equality policy is especially important in that it firmly establishes that discrimination and remedy are specific to the source and type of disadvantage, hence offers irrefutable evidence that one equality is not pretty much like any other.

Overall, pressure to combine equality institutions and legislation has been growing since at least 1997. Diversity issues were much affected by the organizational structures of equality agencies, which for some years now have been stretched from their original focus on particular inequalities to cover multiple discriminations. However, agencies were frequently frustrated by their inability to act on cross-strand discrimination (Spencer, 2005, p. 35). Although some attention is paid to discrimination on the basis of disability, age and sexuality, the government's priority is racial and ethnic inequality.

Policies

In 2006 the big policy story was the planned institutional changes to the equality agencies. The policy was decided amid claims that a combined agency will have the capacity to address multiple sources of inequality and growing agreement across government that the equality sector was ripe for rationalization. But, at the same time as they were negotiating terms and preparing for amalgamation, the women's agencies continued with business as normal, pursuing a changing range of objectives and taking roles in the implementation of government obligations such as the oversight of gender mainstreaming. Accordingly, in this section I will first consider the policy for an amalgamated equality and human rights commission, second sketch out the priorities of the women's equality machinery and third briefly examine the implementation of gender mainstreaming in Britain.

The Commission for Equality and Human Rights

By 2003 regulatory measures that affected equality and or tackled discrimination in the UK mainland included 26 or 35 major statutes, 52 statutory instruments, 13 Codes of Practice, three codes of guidance and, depending on who is counting, 9 to 16 EU directives and six international treaties[5] (Keter, 2005). Equality officials, in conjunction with movement advocates, became adept at transferring gains made by one equality strand or agency across the sector. Although there was considerable disagreement on specifics, some common concerns about the priorities for reform emerged. These included (1) the establishment of common and clear standards that employers and the public can understand. (2) A positive duty for all public bodies to promote equality for all. (3) Protection on grounds of sexual orientation, religion and belief and age to be extended to goods, facilities and services. (4) A general principle of equality such that it is an overriding principle of UK law that no unjustified discrimination is permissible. Support for change was considerable by the time Labour was re-elected in 2001. Government was responsive to demands for change but was determined also to establish a combined equality agency, which included Human Rights – not least because it was reluctant to establish a separate Human Rights Commission (Spencer, 2005).

Published on 3 March 2005 and reissued with some amendments after the 2005 general election, the government's Equality Bill was prepared after an extensive process of consultation with stakeholders including existing equality agencies, the social partners and advocacy organizations from across the sectors. The consultation process involved interagency and intersectional co-operation and an unprecedented level of consultation and preparation.[6] Plans for the new agency, the CEHR were supported by the EOC but initially opposed by the CRE and the DRC, all of which will be dissolved (or merged into) the CEHR. The DRC and CRE accepted the government's plans only after considerable negotiation and compromise. The CRE compromise is expressed in terms of 'joining' the CEHR at a later date, but not later than the autumn of 2009. In 2005 the combined equality agency budget was 50 million pounds sterling per year. The budget envisaged for the new CEHR, at constant prices, is 70 million UK sterling, which will have to cover the costs of the new equalities and of Human Rights provision. The CEHR will be located in Manchester – away from Whitehall and routine access to government officials.[7] Both the proposed budget allocation and the Manchester location have been the subject of considerable protest, especially from the CRE, which currently enjoys a London location. The Equality Act provides that the new CEHR will be established through a specified transition period in which its institutional structure will be determined and the current equality legislation review will be completed (Keter, 2005; Equality Bill, 2005). Institutional and organizational questions loom large in the ongoing debates about the CEHR. The crucial issues are about how its work will be organized. Will it be a federal agency with parallel units for each strand? How will its concerns be combined? Should it be responsible to parliament or government? If government, then through which department should it be accountable? The CEHR might be more powerful if it is located in one of the great departments of state such as the Home Office. Human Rights campaigners would like it to be in the Department for Constitutional affairs. There are also questions about how implementation will be monitored.[8]

That women's policy agencies played a significant role in the policy processes is well illustrated by their achievements in the negotiations surrounding the government's Equality Bill. Their involvement was partly a function of their prescribed roles and functions, but they were also active and sometimes radical participants. Many feared that gender equality issues would get insufficient attention in an amalgamated agency. These fears were underlined by asymmetric legal provision for the different equality 'strands' according to which women were not as well provided for legally as some other groups. As discussion developed, government improved its proposals for various groups and responded to some but not all of feminist concerns.

In these negotiations the EOC successfully prioritized the inclusion in the legislation of the public sector duty on gender, which was a central demand of the women's movements. The gender duty obliges public sector bodies both to ensure that their actions will promote equality of opportunity between women and men and to make public services more responsive to their different needs (DTI, 2004). In theory it means that every government department, local authority, state agency and service provider will be required to take steps to promote gender equality and that they will be monitored on their performance. The practice may of course be different.

The examination of the process of amalgamating UK equality machinery affords initial insight into the status of state feminism in a combined agency. Not all outcomes coincide with movement wishes. In the consultations surrounding the government's Equality Bill we can see both the positive and negative sides of changes for women who are included and listened to but are not the major stakeholders, hence find their interests trumped by those of employers. The gender duty is limited to the public sector. It is not, despite women's movement pressure, to be applied to the private sector (Fawcett Society, 2006) Even so, during the process the movements increased their purchase on decision-making through the Equality and Diversity Forum and through representation on the task force set up to work out details of the legislation. They were aided in this by the various women's policy agencies.

Agency priorities

British women's policy agencies have extended their initially narrow ambits and have made initiatives on a range of issues such as violence, rape, health and childcare. Across these and other issues, diversity goals have become more important in the work of all the agencies, reflecting both government and movement priorities. Women's policy agencies have made repeated efforts to raise the profiles of their diversity programmes, possibly in anticipation of the new combined agency but also under instruction from government. The WEU sets an example to other government agencies and departments by publishing statistical research that cross tabulates gender, age and ethnicity and claims to integrate minority ethnic data in all its research. It sponsors research on minority women and has established groups of minority ethnic women stakeholders to plan events and publications. Similarly, the EOC collects information, sponsors research and runs campaigns about minority women at work. All three agencies publish information in the languages of the minority communities.

While the EOC prioritized equal pay, the duty to promote gender equality, pensions and updating the sex equality legislation, the WEU prioritized civil partnerships, pay, pensions, public appointments, women in public life and work–life balance. The WNC prioritized consultation and the inclusion of women's movement organizations and actors in government policy discussion. In short, a pattern of MP, agency and movement cooperation has emerged as networks on women's issues and a women's issue agenda has been effectively established.

Most important for the argument of this chapter, the WEU took on other equality strands. As of 31 March 2005 its brief is to 'realise the benefits of diversity . . . [by] . . . taking action to support economic opportunities for women, work across Government, the European Union and the United Nations, reduce barriers to social participation and improve our legislative and institutional frameworks for equality'.[9]

All three agencies have tried to respond to pressure to respond to diversity issues. Initiatives prior to the establishment of the Women and Equality Unit in 2001 were mainly ad hoc interagency initiatives. Since 2001 the WEU and the Women's Minister have been active, organizing occasional receptions and public events targeted at minority ethnic women. More systematically both have organized a number of meetings and networking occasions. For example, the Ministry for Women hosts a bi-annual meeting of top women's organizations. After 2001 the number of invited organizations was increased, for the specific purpose of including minority ethnic women's groups. A six monthly meeting between the Minister and women living in Muslim communities is held to discuss issues specifically affecting Muslim women, such as labour market concerns or religious discrimination. In 2003 the WNC established, at the request of the Minister for Women, a Muslim Women's Network chaired by Farkhanda Chaudry. To date agency work with minority women is mainly top down.

Gender mainstreaming

Gender mainstreaming is government policy in the UK. However, the implementation of gender mainstreaming has disappointed equality advocates and many officials. All three agencies share responsibility for gender mainstreaming. The exact division of labour is unclear. For example, the Women and Equality Unit produced a web-based tool for assessing the gender impact of policies and legislation on women, while the WNC has reported on its implementation and the EOC offers mainstreaming information on its website.

With the exception of the Department for International Development, which takes CEDAW seriously and uses UN gender impact assessment instruments to inform its aid policies, there is little evidence that gender mainstreaming is properly implemented in the big government departments (Daly, 2005). The DTI, the home department of the WEU, during the tenure of Patricia Hewitt as Minister for Women set up a Gender Expert Group on Trade. The Treasury, in conjunction with the Women's Budget Group and the DTI has undertaken gender analyses of government expenditure, but has not institutionalized this as a regular part of the public expenditure review. The DTI and the Department for Work and Pensions (the home department of the DRC) have each undertaken a gender analysis of a programme in their departments. The Foreign and Commonwealth Office has published a document 'Inclusive Government: Mainstreaming Gender into Foreign Policy' which argues that gender mainstreaming has positive benefits for everyone. Some public services, such as the National Health Service run gender mainstreaming pilot projects. One of the few examples of gender mainstreaming of public policy is found in the strategy described in 'Women's Mental Health: into the Mainstream'. However, even this proposal ignores the needs of key groups of women including lesbians, disabled women, ethnic minority women and transgender women, all of whom have mental health needs that arise at least in part from the multiple discriminations on the basis of their multiple identities (WNC, 2005).

However, there are neither means in place for ensuring that Government departments use such a tool, nor any procedures in place to assess the impact of current policies and policy making on women and men and girls and boys separately (WNC, 2005). The problem seems to be, quite simply, that the relevant officials, even where they are willing, do not understand the meaning of gender, hence government officials lack the capacity to implement the policy (Fawcett Society, 2006). The sophisticated theorization of gender that has been such a concern of feminist scholars for the past thirty years has yet to attract the attention of the average official. The implications of difference and equality, multiple discrimination and multiple identities that are central to any gendered reading of policy are not part of their expertise. Thus official statistics are still not presented in formats that show gender difference in conjunction with other social differences. Most civil servants do not understand the term and have received no training in its implementation. In Scotland and in Whitehall the social justice and inclusion agendas are not integrated with anti-discrimination agendas. In short, gender mainstreaming is barely noticeable in UK government at any level. Yet the government has the power to require compliance and to monitor and enforce implementation. For example, the government now requires all legislation to be assessed for its compliance with the Human Rights Act, demonstrating that such an infrastructure is within its imaginative capacity. No equivalent requirement has been made for gender mainstreaming.

Agencies and the women's movement

Since their inception, the relationships of British agencies with the movement varied according to the leadership of the particular agency and by agency type. In its early days the EOC was particularly aloof from the women's movements but relations improved during the 1980s when Joanna Foster became head of the commission. They declined when she was replaced and improved after 1997. After 1997 the EOC worked with women's organizations on a number of campaigns and initiatives. For example the EOC and the Fawcett Society served on the steering committee of and provided resources for the Electoral Commission's 2004 report on Gender and Political Participation and on the task force for the Equality Bill.

Relations between the movements and the WU and later the WEU also varied. The WNC however is a different kind of agency as it is directly involved with the representation of movement interests to government. The main changes here have been of three kinds. First, there has been a gradual increase in the willingness of the WNC to include explicitly feminist advocacy organizations among its partners. Secondly, the WNC has proved willing to work closely with organizations in campaigns on women's issues. Third, with (albeit modestly) increased resources, it has become better at the transmission and representation of its partner's interests.

There is no doubt that after 1997 the government agenda was increasingly feminized. For example feminist experts and issue based movement organizations working on domestic violence, equal pay, childcare and representation in elected and appointed assemblies and commissions were both integrated into government as experts and consultants and active in the lobbies. Professional groups such as Justice for Women, which campaigned on and offered assistance to women accused of murdering violent spouses, both made legal services available to women and made representations to government and media on their behalf. The Women's Budget Group, which brought together experts and advocates on social policy and economics, established a working relationship with the Treasury, reporting on the gender impact of government spending. By 2001 the Women's Budget Group was regularly consulted on financial issues and their impact on women (Himmelweit, 2006). The most prominent campaign was that over political representation, thought by many advocates to be the key to the other issues. That view appears to be justified by the active roles taken by feminist MPs who have taken up such issues as abortion, childcare, violence against women, forced marriages, health issues such as breast cancer screening, equal pay, pensions, rape, traffic and prostitution and the future of the sex equality machinery and legislation (Sones et al., 2005; Childs, 2004). In short, a pattern of MP, agency and movement cooperation has emerged as networks on women's issues and a women's issue agenda has been effectively established.

The network depends partly on personnel and partly on the growing effectiveness of women's movement organizations. Some credit for the emergence of the feminist policy network must go to the Fawcett Society, which is active across the women's issue agenda. This organization, which dates to the suffrage movement, now has about 2000 members. It is a highly effective feminist campaigning organization. Recently it has been particularly well led, by Mary Ann Stephenson and then by Katherine Rake who succeeded her in 2001. Fawcett has an admirable record of success and good, close working relationships with other movement organizations including the single issue or sectoral organizations. Fawcett is important not only because it is effective but also because it is a multi-issue group able to organize different groups of women. Most other visible active groups are either organized around single issues (Rape Crisis, Women's Aid Federation), sectors (Women's Health, Reproductive Rights) or ethnicities.

In the research for this chapter I could find no example of a women's policy agency opposing a high priority movement issue. However, women's policy agencies have been mostly silent on controversial issues such as lone parent benefit and abortion, suggesting that they prefer not to oppose the women's movement organizations, but are nonetheless constrained by their official positions. Moreover the women's policy agencies' positions become more delicate when the women's movements do not agree. For example disagreements about the combined equalities agency divide the movements on racial lines.[10]

By the end of the 1990s there was an appreciable feminist presence in state institutions and movement organizations and actors were able to influence decisions on a range of issues including childcare, domestic violence, the gender duty, government spending, benefit provision and political representation. This increased ability to influence stemmed both from a changed configuration of women's policy agencies and from increased levels of women's representation at Westminster and significant presences of women in the devolved institutions that were established in Scotland and Wales. With the exception of reproductive rights, which are treated as a medical issue by government, priority movement concerns are addressed by one or other of the agencies. There is a great deal of evidence that agencies have advanced the women's agenda.

However, the pattern is not one of unalloyed success. For example, agency activity on movement issues is marred in two important and related respects, neither of which are wholly their fault. First, as government agencies they must reflect government thinking; second, they are better able to reflect the concerns of white than minority women. Women's movement demands are incorporated into agency activity through a filter of government priorities. The agencies have been attacked for excessive tenderness to business interests, a criticism that seems justified. For example, in the consultations over the CEHR, advocacy organizations repeatedly complained about agency complicity in the prioritization of employers over other stakeholders.[11]

To some extent then the two problems are related. Agencies are sensitive to diversity issues but articulate the concerns of minority ethnic women less well, both because black and minority ethnic women have fewer resources and are less well organized than white women and because agencies are constrained by government immigration policies (McLeod et al., 2001; Davis and Cook, 2002). Immigration issues will be excluded from the gender duty and Southall Black Sisters, the black women's organization that campaigns on violence against black women, is not a 'partner' of the WNC.

Conclusions

State feminism in the UK has changed since 1995. Politically, the most important developments are the emergence of a feminist policy network of politicians, women's movement actors and policy agencies, the increased cooperation among equality agencies who are now a substantial policy community and the shift away from simple employment priorities by all the agencies to wider public service concerns. Thus the results for feminists are mixed. On the one hand, feminists have increased their purchase on the state and may benefit from the gains made by other equality advocates in the CEHR; on the other, they will soon lose their separate organizational voices.

Whatever its benefits, the reorganization of the agencies into a large, combined CEHR signals the end of an era in which, finally, women's movement agencies routinely assisted women's movements on a large number of issues and contributed to the extension and radicalization of the women's agenda. It took a great deal of time and a lot of political work to get to that stage. But the jury is still out on the CEHR and will be out for some time to come (Niven, 2006). The women's policy networks described above may be under threat. It may be that in exchange for the positive duty on gender, the women's agencies made a Faustian bargain, giving up their ability to prioritize women. Responsibility for sex equality is now part of an intersectional brief in which it is planned to bring 'diversity to the forefront'. Recent appointments to equality commissions have prioritized individuals with combined equality experience, without protecting 'single voice' appointments. Combined voice appointments will be the norm for the CEHR, perhaps making it ever more difficult to create institutional bases for state feminism or indeed, to identify distinctive women's policy agencies or to identify and analyse state feminism. In this situation the relationship between agencies and movements will, once again, need to be renegotiated.

The analysis offered in this chapter is largely an account of the past. It is too early to assess the success or failure of movement actor interventions in the policy to create a combined agency. It will be important to trace these processes of change both in order to track the strategies of feminist equality advocates and women's policy agencies and to consider what their engagement and participation portends for the substantive and descriptive representation of women.

Acknowledgements

I am grateful to Deborah Mabbett, Judith Squires and Alan Ware for their comments on a draft of this chapter and for conversations with and help from equality officials in all the agencies

Notes

1. The opening is scheduled for October 2007.
2. However the government was reluctant to establish a separate Human Rights Commission (Spencer, 2005).
3. In 2005 the WNC listed over 300 'partner' organizations covering a 'diverse range of women's activities and interests across the UK'. These included cross-sectoral multiple issue groups such as the Co-operative Women's Guild with 3,200 members; networking groups such as City Women's Network (160 members) and Engender (200 members) as well as numerous single issue groups such as Abortion Rights, and sectoral groups such as Rights of Women. A substantial number of partners are professional or work based organizations. Their earliest foundation date was 1866 and most recent one in 2003 (WNC 2005). Many of these organizations are part of the voluntary sector; either directly organized around women's concerns, or with significant women centred units, branches or activities. Such organizations now regularly intervene on women's

issues and seek to promote women's substantive and descriptive representation either via the WNC or directly. Partner organizations included both direct membership organizations such as the Fawcett Society with about 2000 individual members and the Federation of Women's Institutes with 8000 members, as well as projects, networks and charities that campaign for, or provide services to, women.

4. Quasi-Autonomous Non-Government Organization.
5. CEDAW was signed by UK in 1981 and previously excluded protocols were agreed in 2004.
6. See www.womenandequalityunit.gov.uk/cehr for full descriptions of the consultation processes and links to the CEHR task force and to participating organizations. (Accessed 25.07.2006.)
7. There will also be a London presence, the exact configuration of the two offices has not been finalized.
8. Consultation on these and other issues is scheduled for completion in January 2006. http://www.womenandequalityunit.gov.uk/cehr/gender_duty.htm (Accessed 25.07.2006.)
9. See www.weu.gov.uk. (Accessed 25.07.2006.)
10. Here, of course, the agencies are also divided, as the CRE has been a vociferous opponent of the government's proposals (CRE, 2004). The 1990 Trust, an umbrella organization of black and Asian campaigners rejects the single commission and protests that this is yet another trick to dilute the evil of white racism. The Equality Bill has generated differences in emphasis within the movements and among the agencies. To some extent the differences reflect different briefs.
11. Such criticisms were not confined to women's advocates. For examples from across the equality spectrum, CRE, 2004; Fawcett, 2004.

9
Women's Policy Machinery in Italy between European Pressure and Domestic Constraints

Marila Guadagnini and Alessia Donà

Introduction

In comparative studies, Italy is considered as having a 'Mediterranean welfare state regime' (Ferrera, 1993; Esping Andersen, 2000) based on the central role of the family as an institution which ensures social protection with a minimum state intervention (Naldini, 2003; Saraceno, 2003). Recent data concerning EU countries before enlargement confirm the shortage of resources earmarked for family policies in Italy (about 4 per cent of overall expenses) as compared with a European average of 8 per cent (Eurostat, 2005).

The lack of a family policy in the form of services for children, care, monetary transfer and measures to reconcile professional and family life (Saraceno, 2003) was the result of a political context peculiar to the consensual model of democracy based on an ideological cleavage (Fabbrini, 1999). Catholic culture on one side and Marxist and socialist culture on the other coexisted in an attempt to reconcile the concept of gender equality with that of the centrality of the family. This explains why, even though relatively advanced gender-equality legislation had been adopted (mainly in order to comply with European directives), the gendered division of labour remained unchanged. The percentage of women with jobs remains one of the lowest in Europe.[1] Women's income from work is on average 24 per cent lower than that of men, occupational segregation remains high (CNEL, 2003) and the sharing of work within the family continues to penalize women workers, who devote twice as much time as men to family work (Arcidonna, 2003).

Most indicators of gender equality show that Italy is one of the most backward countries in Europe (World Bank, 2005). Even though women have reached high levels of education and their participation in the labour market can no longer be considered as sporadic, maternity is still an event that obliges a large number of women to retire from professional life. Italian women have to contend with a schizophrenic social policy which, on the one hand, gives them guarantees as workers (in accordance with the regulations adopted under European pressure) and, on the other hand, penalizes them when they decide to have children. This explains the apparent Italian paradox of the coexistence of a low female employment rate together with a low fertility rate.

The reasons for the difficulties in reforming the Mediterranean welfare regime to meet the new demands of a society that began changing in the 1970s can be found in a number of factors. These include: a highly male-dominated decision-making arena (the percentage of women elected to Parliament over the last decade was only 11 per cent) and a gender-blind culture which is little inclined (and indeed unwilling) to promote women's rights. The idea of the woman as responsible for the family rather than occupied in a professional career is a hangover from a past which is still present in the political culture.

In this type of context, the development of a gender-equality policy was largely influenced by EU membership (Donà, 2006). As from the 1970s, implementation of European directives on gender equality profoundly changed the Italian legal framework centered on the 'woman-mother' and helped overcome cultural and social resistance. The influence of Europe was also crucial in the set up of a women's policy machinery at national (and local) level, while the women's movement greeted it with some distrust (Guadagnini, 1995; Donà, 2006). Even so, over the last decade, women's policy agencies became an arena through which women were able to convey their demands in policymaking. State feminism developed in Italy from the mid-1990s. Previous research has examined women's policy agencies' role in different policy debates. The findings show that out of twelve policy debates examined (three on abortion, two on job training, three on prostitution, three on political representation, and one on constitutional reform), in no fewer than five cases an alliance was formed between members of the women's movements and women's policy agencies, which made it possible to obtain policies favorable to enhancing women's rights (Danna, 2004; Guadagnini, 2005; 2006).

This chapter provides an overview of Italian women's policy machinery in the period – from the mid-1990s up to the present-day – in which the structure of women's policy agencies has been consolidated at both national and local level. First, it examines the changes in the political-institutional context. Second, it shows the institutional changes in women's policy machinery at the national level, partly in response to EU pressure, and the implications they had on the working agenda and on relation-ships with the women's movements. Third, it discusses the new issues addressed by the agencies, such as the gender mainstreaming approach and the degree of its implementation. Finally, it examines the develop-ment of state feminism at the local level.

The reconfigured state as a new challenge for state feminism

Several changes have affected the Italian political system over the past decade, and three in particular have had an important bearing on gender-equality policies. The first is both institutional and political. The profound crises which hit the political system in the early 1990s opened up a period of ongoing institutional reforms (Gundle and Parker, 1996). These pro-vided for new rules for the election of the municipal, provincial and regional councils and for the national parliament, for which the propor-tional system was abandoned in favour of a mainly majority system. The quota system, which was introduced to counterbalance the negative effects of a mainly majority system, was abolished by the Constitutional Court in 1995. Since then the issue of improving women's access to elective posts has been given top priority both by the women's movements and by women's policy agencies.

The electoral reforms led to a bipolar-type competition between the parties, with the creation of two alternative blocs, the left-wing coalition of the *Ulivo* (Olive Tree – now called *l'Unione*, or The Union) and the centre-right coalition of the *Casa della Libertà* (House of Freedom) (Verzichelli and Cotta, 2003). At the national level, from 1994 to today, there was first the victory of the centre-right (the first Berlusconi government in 1994–1995), then the centre-left (1996–2001), then again a right-wing government (the second and third Berlusconi governments, 2001–06) and lastly, after the 2006 political elections, a centre-left coalition led by Romano Prodi took power.

The national governments that held power between 1996 and 2006 were different in terms of policy in almost all areas, reflecting the different ideology that inspired their actions: the centre-left governments acted in favour of the gender-equality agencies and policies while the centre-rights governments were more committed to a neoliberal economic agenda.

The second change concerns the entry of Italy into the single European currency area. The commitment to the Growth and Stability Pact was an external constriction that had a profound influence on domestic economic and financial policy since it has required considerable effort to reorganize and control the national budget (Dyson and Featherstone, 1999). The centre-left and centre-right governments have adopted different approaches to the problem: the former reduced public spending in a number of areas, including health and security, while introducing new taxes (on property and independent workers) and even adopting a special tax (referred to as the 'tax for Europe'). The Berlusconi (2001–06) governments partly relieved tax pressure, with a very slight enlargement of the no-tax area and a reduction in taxation on higher-bracket incomes, but it also introduced greater cuts in social spending. For example, the resources of the National Fund for Welfare Policies to be given to local governments for the management of important services such as health, assistance and education, were halved. In a country with a historic lack of social services, these further cuts applied to an already modest level of welfare spending made the situation for families with pre-school children and with old people to support (36 per cent of all families in Italy have at least one old person aged 65 or over to support) even worse, further aggravating women's position.

The third change concerned the decentralization of administrative and policy power to the local governments. As in other European countries, the crisis of the central welfare state, coupled with the process of European integration and the demands made by pro-autonomy forces (the Northern League) have induced national government to rethink the set-up of the State. The devolution of policy powers was achieved through a series of reforms adopted in 1997–8 and two constitutional reforms that were approved only with the vote of the centre-left majority in 2001 (Guadagnini 2006). After these reforms, equal-opportunities policies became the responsibility of regional governments, and this led to the consolidation of women's policy agencies at the local level.

Changes in the women's policy agencies . . .

Right from the outset, the structure of women's policy machinery provided for a division of responsibilities between those agencies that worked on gender equality at the workplace and those involved in enhancing women's rights in all other sectors. The former included the 'National Committee for the implementation of the principles of equal treatment and equal opportunities for workers of both sexes'[2] at the Ministry of Labour. It had the task of monitoring implementation of the Law on equality (Law 903/1977) and of promoting affirmative action by selecting, funding and monitoring affirmative action projects submitted by private and public actors, trade unions, job training centres and associations, according to the Law on affirmative action (Law 125/91). Both laws were adopted in order to implement European directives and recommendations. As from the 1990s, the Committee was allocated €516,000 and a secretarial staff of between 8 and 14 people: it had a special fund to finance affirmative action projects. While the Committee's tasks have remained unchanged over the past ten years, the role of the second agency aimed at implementing the laws on equality at the workplace, the Councillors for Equality, has been reinforced. They now have the task, at regional and provincial level, of implementing and monitoring the application of the principle of equal rights and non-discrimination, including recourse to actions before a court. In 2000,[3] the National Network of Equality Councillors was created at the local level, presided over by the National Councillor for Equality, in order to coordinate local activities and ensure the exchange of information and best practices.

For all matters not concerning employment and work, the National Commission for Equality and Equal opportunities (*Commissione Nazionale per la parità e le pari opportunità* – CNPPO), an advisory body attached to the Prime Minister's Office, was set up in 1984. The CNPPO was to be made up of representatives of the political parties, both sides of industry, the most representative associations in the country, and other members of society. Its resources remained limited: in the mid-1990s it managed to reach an allocation of 2 billion lire (just over €1 million). The number of staff in the secretary's office rose to 13.

In 1996, under the left-wing government headed by Prodi (1996–98), a new agency was created to implement European directives. This was the Minister for Equal Opportunities with the executive function of preparing governmental gender-equality policy, implementing the gender-mainstreaming strategy, representing Italy in the EU arena and adoption such measures as may be necessary to adapt the Italian legal system to the requests of the EU.[4] In 1997 a DPO (Department for Equal Opportunities)[5] was also set up to provide support for the Ministry's activities. Overall financial resources amounted to €15,798,569 in 2004.

In 2004 came yet another reorganization of the national agencies, with the abolition of the CNPPO and the creation of a consultative committee Commission for Equal Opportunities between Men and Women (*Commissione per le Pari Opportunità fra Uomo e Donna*) as a mouthpiece for the Minister and under her presidency (Ministero Pari Opportunità, 2004b).

Lastly, in accordance with EU Race Directive 43/2000/EC (on the equal treatment of people regardless of race and ethnic origin), the government set up UNAR (*Ufficio Nazionale Antidiscriminazioni Razziali*, Italian National

Office Against Racial Discrimination) within the DPO in 2003. Its aim was to promote equal treatment and to fight against discrimination based on racial or ethnic origin, with the task of handling complaints by victims of discrimination. In contrast with the status of institutional autonomy and operational independence provided for by the EU, the head of UNAR is under the political control of the President of the Cabinet Council or the

Table 9.1:   Women's Policy Agencies in Italy at the national level 1996–2006

Institution	Main functions
Prime Minister' Office Commission for Equality and Equal Opportunities (operational from 1985 to 2004)	Political-advisory function, cross-sectional mandate (all fields, except employment); collecting and disseminating information and data on the situation of women, studying and drafting the modifications to be made to the law in order to ensure gender equality, and promoting the adequate representation of women in decision-making posts
Minister for Equal Opportunities (created in 1996)	Executive function, cross-sectional mandate Represents the country in EU and international arenas Monitors the adoption of EU legislation
Department for Equal Opportunities (operational since 1997), which includes:	Aid to the Minister drafting government equality policies and implementing gender mainstreaming
• The Commission for Equal Opportunities for Men and Women (since 2004)	Advisory functions, law-making schemes, monitoring and assessment of the state of implementation of equal-opportunities policies
• The UNAR (operational since 2003)	Gathering of complaints, and legal assistance
Minister of Labour National Committee for Equal Treatment (since 1983; reinforced as from 1991)	Law-enforcing function, monitoring antidiscrimination legislation at the workplace Approval, financing and monitoring of affirmative-action programmes Proactive work in the field of equal opportunities in the labour market
National, regional and provincial Equality Councellors (since 1991; reorganization since 2000)	Supervising compliance with the Law on equality through inspection activities in cooperation with Labour Inspectors Bringing action before the court

Minister delegated by the President. Furthermore, the financial resources (€2,035,357 a year) and staff (10–12 people as permanent staff and six experts) do not seem to be sufficient to ensure the adequate legal assistance that victims of discrimination need, as was made clear by the last report on the activities carried out by UNAR (2005). The report also pointed to the lack of an intersectional approach able to go beyond discrimination based on race or ethnic origin, as a factor which weakens an effective antidiscrimination policy. To solve this problem, it was suggested that UNAR should be transformed into an all-embracing office to protect any victim of discrimination. To this day no reform has been adopted.

To sum up, over the past decade both the executive and law-enforcing agencies have been institutionally strengthened under European indications. On the contrary, the CNPPO, which was an autonomous political-advisory body, has been abolished. The functional distinction between the employment sector and other policy areas has been maintained. It remains to be seen how effective the current fragmentation of responsibilities between the agencies is, with each one responsible for only some aspects of discrimination. The opportunity to bring together in a single, consistent manner all the various legislative measures concerning women's policy agencies was lost in May 2006, with the publication of the Code for Equal Opportunities between Men and Women (*Codice per le pari opportunità tra uomo e donna*) drafted by Minister Stefania Prestigiacomo (*Forza Italia* – the party of Berlusconi), a young businesswoman with no links to the feminist movement. The Code turned out to be a 'cut and paste' of previous laws and, as such, did not help improve inter-agency coordination. The current Minister, Barbara Pollastrini (The Union), appointed in May 2006, has announced her intention to modify the Code.

. . . make the Italian role in EU gender policy-making more effective . . .

In the last decade the reorganization of the women's policy machinery has been considerably influenced by the EU. However, in more recent years, these women's policy agencies have shown the capacity of making the Italian role in EU policy-making both visible and effective. A study into the role of Italian actors in EU equal-opportunities policy-making shows that the EU has become a new arena in which the national women's policy agencies can take the initiative to promote the rights of women (Donà, 2004).

As mentioned above, it is the Minister and the DPO who prepare and represent the Italian position on gender issues at EU level. The draft law presented by the European Commission is submitted to the members of the Italian permanent delegation. In particular, in the case of gender equality directives, it is the staff specialized in social matters who have the task of passing on the proposal to the competent International Relations Division of the DPO and to the legislative office of the Ministry of Labour. The proposal is then examined together with the administrative offices concerned and, where necessary, both sides of industry are consulted. Also the Department for EU Policies takes part in the preparatory meetings to coordinate institutional communication at domestic level, and between the domestic and EU levels (with the permanent delegation in Brussels). As concerns the case of the recently approved Equality Directive 2002/73/EC on equal treatment between men and women, DPO officials participated directly in the bargaining within the Employment and Social Affairs Community workgroup,[6] while officials of the Ministry of Labour prepared and coordinated inter-ministerial meetings at the national level. The preparatory meetings have mainly been of an administrative nature, principally consisting of meetings between officials from the Ministry of Labour, from the Department for Equal Opportunities and from the Department for EU Policies. The Italian women's policy actors conducted the negotiations and were able to present Italian policy preferences in such a way as to accommodate them in the final European draft. According to the study, both the Minister and, especially, the DPO, have been able to build up a good level of policy expertise and technical competence, thus enabling the latecomer Italian women's policy agencies to interact with institutions of other European countries with a far longer tradition in the field of equal opportunities. Moreover, a relatively stable community of equal-opportunities policy makers was created, consisting of officials with experience in European issues and in equal-opportunities issues.[7] In addition, the direct link between officials in the DPO and the Ministry of Labour on the one hand, and members responsible for social issues in the Permanent Delegation on the other, encouraged efficient cooperation and coordination between the government actors who, at both domestic and European level, promote and defend Italian interests in the field of equal opportunities.

The study revealed the lack of influence of domestic women's groups to the ministerial meetings for the elaboration of the Italian policy preferences to be submitted at the EU level. However, some women's associations gained a direct route (i.e. without the national government intermediation) to the EU policy-making via the European Women's Lobby, which, since 1991, has gained increasing ability in conducting its lobbying activity within the European institutions.

. . . with mixed effects on domestic state feminism

The strengthening of women's policy machinery at the domestic level had mixed results, depending on the type of agencies and policy areas involved and on the political colour of the government. In relation to the agencies in the employment sector, the strengthened role assigned to the national and local Equality Councillors has helped make the fight against gender discrimination at the workplace more effective and visible. Also the promotion of affirmative action has acquired increasing visibility over the years: as from the early 1990s, the funds used by the Committee at the Ministry of Labour to finance affirmative-action projects amounted to 10 billion Italian lire (over €5 million) and many women's associations have benefited from these resources. On the other hand, there has been no significant commitment by the Committee to gender the debate on the most important pieces of legislation concerning the reorganization of the labour market adopted either during the left-wing governments (Guadagnini, 2001) or during the ones headed by Berlusconi.

In relation to the other women's policy agencies, the coexistence, until 2004, of the CNPPO and of the Minister and the Department for Equal Opportunities, with responsibilities for the same policy areas, produced both positive and negative effects, depending on which government was in power: during the left-wing governments, all these agencies increased their effectiveness and visibility, involving women's movements actors in their activities. On the contrary, during the Berlusconi governments, the CNPPO and the Minister for Equal Opportunities came into conflict (see below).

Over the past decade the only issue on which there has been a large consensus between these agencies, across the political colour of the governments, has been that of the empowerment of women and the promotion of balanced representation of women and men in elective offices, an issue which was given high priority by most of the women's movements.

During the centre-left governments (1996–2001), the CNPPO, chaired by Silvia Costa (Christian Democratic party), intervened in the debate that led to the adoption, in 2001, of the constitutional reform laws on devolution (Laws 2/2001 and 3/2001) (CNPPO, 1999, 2001, 2003). The laws included provisions that require all regions to adopt measures to remove all obstacles to full equality between the sexes and to promote equal opportunity of access to elective posts in regional councils (Guadagnini, 2006). Moreover, the CNPPO and the Ministers for EO supported the proposal submitted by centre-left women MPs to modify another article of the Constitution, art. 51,[8] in order to make it possible to adopt quotas in all the electoral laws. The proposal was finally approved during the centre-right government in 2003, when the Minister Prestigiacomo successfully managed a cross-party alliance of women MPs (Guadagnini, 2005).

The commitment of both the CNPPO and Minister Prestigiacomo on the issue of the empowerment of women continued with the implementation of the constitutional reform. Results have so far been limited.[9] In 2005 during the debate on the national electoral law (a return to a proportional system with fixed lists of candidates and a majority bonus for the successful coalition), the Minister unsuccessfully presented a legislative initiative for the introduction of a quota system in the candidate party lists.[10] Up until today, quotas have only been adopted for the 2004 European Parliament elections and only four regions out of twenty implemented a quota system.

The centre-left governments: the consolidation of state feminism (1996–2001)

While the ministries of both governments have seen eye to eye with the CNPPO on the subject of empowerment, on all other issues the political colour of the government coalitions has had an important influence both on the Ministers' policies and on relationships with actors in the women's movement.

Due to the proximity of the movement to the Left, during the left-wing governments some feminists cooperated and became involved in the creation of the new DPO, even though a more radical part of the movement continued to remain at a distance (Calloni, 2002, p. 128). The issues on which the ministries and the DPO were particularly active were: the sharing of family-care responsibilities between men and women, reconciliation of work and family care, children's rights, family policies, trafficking of women, the development of women's business activities and the implementation of gender mainstreaming strategy (see paragraph below) (Ministero per le pari opportunità, 2004a).

The instability of the governments, with the change of three ministers (Angela Finocchiaro, Laura Balbo and Katia Bellillo) in just five years, weakened the role of the ministers and allowed neither continuity of action, nor stable cooperation with women's groups or individuals, even though this did take place in some cases. For example, on the issue of the trafficking of women, a number of women's associations were involved in the policy-making process that led to the adoption of the law on immigration (Law 40/1998), which provided for a series of provisions in favour of women (Danna, 2004).

Much of the policy agenda of the Ministers and the DPO was influenced by EU legislation. The law on parental leave (Law 53/2000) was introduced to implement a European directive. As well as measures on parental leave, it also contained a series of articles to promote the reconciliation of work and family care, including the obligation for local governments to draw up 'urban timetables' in order to make the duration and opening hours of public, commercial, school and employment services more flexible (Presidenza del Consiglio dei Ministri, 2000).[11] In addition, many financial benefits were provided by the State budgets of 1999, 2000 and 2001, including the extension of maternity benefits to mothers without access to other forms of income, tax allowances and paid leave for up to two years for parents with children. Funds were made available for local projects to provide services for children and for school integration for handicapped children.

Another subject at the centre of the ministers' agenda was the promotion of women's entrepreneurial activities. On the Minister's initiative, a Women's Entrepreneurship Monitoring Centre (*Osservatorio sull'imprenditoria femminile*) was set up and a law was passed which introduced the obligation for all local and national administrations to facilitate access to public funds by companies run by women. Local offices were set up for this purpose (the 'Bersani package' of 29 April 1999) (Presidenza del Consiglio dei Ministri, 2000).

Finally, on the initiative of Minister Laura Balbo in particular, a feminist and university professor, measures were adopted for the implementation of teaching and research programmes in the field of equal opportunities and for developing activities to increase the number of women in the scientific sector.

The centre-right years: the paralysis of state feminism (2001–2006)

Cooperation between the women's movement and the minister and the DPO was broken off by the right-wing Berlusconi government when Stefania Prestigiacomo was appointed Minister for Equal Opportunities. Disagreements between the Minister and the DPO and various sectors of the women's movement emerged on a number of issues, as can be seen in the Shadow Report (2004) presented in New York at the 49th session of the CSW (28 February–11 March 2005) in opposition to the Report drafted by the DPO.[12] The Shadow Report critized the Minister and the DPO for abandoning the gender mainstreaming approach, for promoting initiatives aimed to push women back into their family role and for cutting back their commitment in development cooperation programmes for women. The Minister was also reproached for her support for the Berlusconi government's policies, which had harmful effects on women, including the White Paper on welfare, the university and school reform, the labour reform (Biagi Law 30/2003) and the new law on immigration (the Bossi-Fini Law 30/2002), which made the rights of immigrant women even more insecure and discouraged victims of trafficking from following programmes to escape exploitation.

The toughest battle between Minister Prestigiacomo and a considerable part of the women's movements came about when the law on in-vitro fertilization was discussed in Parliament and approved in 2004. The Minister voted in favour of one of the most restrictive laws in Europe (Law 40/2004) but when a referendum was called in June 2005 to repeal some parts of the law, the Minister supported it. The referendum did not reach the quorum and the law remained in force. At the end of her mandate, Minister Prestigiacomo showed greater attention and willingness to take action on women's issues, such as the defence of the existing law on abortion and the introduction of a quota system into the electoral laws. But when faced with her initiatives, her own government came out heavily against her.

The national women's policy machinery as an agent of Europeanization: the gender-mainstreaming approach

Unlike northern European countries, where state feminism has been consolidated over many years and where a gender-mainstreaming approach has long been adopted even though under a different name, gender mainstreaming was a complete novelty in Italy both for the agencies and for the women's movement. For this reason, the CNPPO has been active in disseminating this new concept through conferences and seminars, while the Minister and the DPO were given the task of implementing this new strategy. Indeed, the first initiative taken by the very first Minister appointed (Angela Finocchiaro) was the approval of the programme for a mainstreaming strategy at governmental level in the form of a Directive (Prodi-Finocchiaro Directive of 7 March 1997). The Directive was addressed to all members of the government and stated that a gender perspective should be introduced in the policy-making process, in all policy areas, in order to achieve the objective of the improvement of women's lives and conditions. The Directive only listed the actions to be undertaken, but did not contain a plan for implementing them, nor did it provide indications about the financial and staff resources required to implement them. The effectiveness of the gender-mainstreaming strategy in the national government was in practice entrusted to the willingness of the Minister for equal opportunitites to promote initiatives and veto any measures that ran counter to the strategy. At the level of central government, no methodology has been applied to assess gender impact, even though this was drafted by the DPO in 1999. In contrast, a gender impact assessment methodology has been developed at regional level, once again in response to pressure from Europe. When planning the use of EU Structural Funds, the methodology drafted by the DPO has provided the model to be followed by many regional governments when planning and monitoring their action programmes.

The implementation of a gender-mainstreaming approach at national level was then interrupted during the Berlusconi governments. We have already seen how isolated Minister Prestigiacomo was within her own government. Moreover, implementing a gender mainstreaming strategy requires financial resources and skills greater than those at the disposal of the minister and the DPO. Its application requires not only the development of special technical instruments and the presence of several skills, but it also involves a process of radical and time-consuming reorganization.

Consolidation of the national women's policy machinery does not always involve the fragmented women's movement

Over the past ten years, the national women's movement has maintained its traditional internal fragmentation in an array of groups, associations and individuals that work in different areas of interest with little or no coordination. First of all, there is a group of women who are involved in the political arena and who have strengthened their positions in the parties and trade unions. This is the area which has been most involved in consolidating a form of state feminism, which more than others has viewed the women's policy agencies as an instrument for empowerment. Priority issues for this area have been those of gender equal representation, reconciliation of work and family care and, more recently, civil rights such as the recognition of *de facto* couples, the right to in-vitro fertilization, and the use of the abortion pill.

Then there is another, smaller but expanding area made up by women in the universities. As from the second half of the 1990s, women's study centres were created in some universities to develop gender studies and to apply pressure to obtain curricula recognized as part of university studies. Also this part of the movement has provided the women's policy machinery with know-how and expertise.

No particular changes have taken place, however, in the main national associations since the early 1990s. There continue to be active associations such as *UDI, Arcidonna,* the *Casa Internazionale delle Donne* (International Women's House) in Rome, the numerous *Casa delle Donne* (women's houses) and collectives of women in various cities in Italy. Some networks which arose during the second half of the 1990s to promote political representation of women such as *Emily* enjoyed rapid growth. All these associations are close to the Left and some of them have cooperated with the Ministers and the DPO during the centre-left governments.

Then there is the cultural part of the movement, which works on women's identity and difference and consists of the groups and associations set up in the 1970s and 1980s (*Libreria delle Donne* (The Women's Library) in Milan, the *Orlando* association, the *Libera Università delle Donne* (Free University of Women) the *Società delle storiche* (Women Historians), and the *Società delle letterate* (Women in Literature). Together with journals dating further back (DWF – *Donna Woman Femme*), some online journals (*Donne in viaggio* – Women on the move; *Il Paese delle Donne* – Women's Country; *DeA-Donne e Altri, Marea*) are channels for making the movement's positions and initiatives known. This part of the movement has always remained removed from the activities of the women's policy agencies.

At the national level, the fragmentation of the movement prevents the development of close-knit lobby groups capable of imposing their own agenda on the women's policy agencies (except in the case of equal gender representation, in which there is still great pressure by all the groups). For as long as the CNPPO was active, it provided an arena in which the demands of the movement – or at least of those associations and groups which had representatives in the commission – could be heard. After its abolition, it was the Minister herself who decided which groups and associations should be consulted and involved. The left-wing government ministers involved experts and feminists from a number of associations, while a rift was created between much of the movement and Minister Prestigiacomo.

On civil rights issues (for example, the controversial regulations concerning in-vitro fertilization and the proposed law on the regulation of *de facto* couples, mentioned above) there was great mobilization by the national associations and left-wing party members and trade unions. The latter organized a protest demonstration against attempts to modify the 1978 law on abortion, which brought 250,000 people into the streets of Milan in January 2006, under the banner *Usciamo dal silenzio* (Let's emerge from our silence). The lack of attention for women's rights demonstrated by the centre-right government, the position adopted by the Catholic Church against abortion and in favour of the traditional family and marriage, gave new impetus to a movement that for years had been absent from the streets.

Unlike in other European countries, the gender/diversity issue has been little discussed within the movement. There has been no debate, for example, on the right of muslim women to wear a veil, as there has been in France. There are associations, especially at the local level, consisting of native and migrant women which work on intercultural issues, such as *Almaterra* as well as international associations which fight for peace and to develop relationships with women in difficult places (*Donne in Nero* – Women in black). There are also associations of immigrant women, but their mission is limited to providing assistance and services for immigrant women. The fact that no debate has yet started up on this issue is possibly due to the fact that Italy is a country with more recent immigration. So far, the only proposal to tackle a number of areas of discrimination with a intersectional approach is the one presented, as mentioned above, by the recently founded UNAR.

The emergence of state feminism at the local level

At the local level there is a quite lively archipelago of women's groups. Many of them are institutionalized not-for-profit associations with a degree of professionalization. They work in the field of social services and in a vast array of policy areas: women's health and culture, women's labour and violence against women (Della Porta, 2003). Many associations organize cultural or professional courses, guidance courses for problems of the family, legal assistance, counselling, music, and so on. They provide intercultural mediation services and help-lines on violence against women. Many associations have benefited from European funds and participation in programmes launched by the EU (Daphne, Urban, Equal).

In recent years there has been increasing cooperation between these associations and local governments, which has fostered a sort of political exchange: the women's groups receive material and symbolic resources while the local governments obtain social services provided by women's voluntary associations at lower costs (Della Porta, 2003).

The creation of a local-level women's policy machinery was considered by the groups and associations as an opportunity to obtain resources in exchange for services provided for the agencies. During the course of the past decade, equal-opportunities commissions were set up in almost all regions and provinces (Ministero per le pari Opportunità, 2006). They are advisory bodies and have their own financial autonomy for managing a number of initiatives (conferences, publications, studies and participation in European projects). In addition, in recent years, local government departments and delegations for equal opportunities have been set up in many regions.

From the few available studies, it seems that the development of local state feminism differs from one region to another, depending on the political colour of the local government and on the geographical location. In some areas of the South, for example, the equal-opportunities departments are mainly concerned with family policies. In the 'red' regions of central Italy, in Veneto and in northern Italy in general, equal-opportunities departments have promoted initiatives in favour of gender friendly working hours in offices, shops, and schools, to combat violence against women and in favour of immigrant women (Del Re, 2004). In Piedmont for example, the Department of Education of the City of Turin, with equal-opportunities responsibilities, has set up a 'city committee to combat violence against women', which includes almost twenty local women's associations, in order to foster greater cooperation among those who work in the sector and promote more effective policies.

Even though the devolution of responsibilities to territorial authorities is a recent phenomenon, some indicators suggest that this process is going to reinforce local state feminism. Firstly, the number of equal opportunities departments is on the rise. Secondly, regional charters (*statute*) adopted after the devolution reforms have given greater power to the regional equal-opportunities commissions and regions are taking initiatives to reform their welfare systems towards more gender-sensitive social services provision (in Puglia the reform has been approved in June 2006). Thirdly, there has been considerable interest on the part of women's associations in ensuring that the women's policy machinery becomes consolidated in order to have a direct contact within the institutions. There still remains the risk, however, of accentuating the disparity that already exists between the richer and the poorer regions of the country.

Conclusions

This chapter has discussed the main changes that have taken place in Italy over the past decade. Women's policy machinery has undergone a process of reinforcement at the central and local levels in response to the European pressure and to the transfer of responsibilities from the State to local governments. It would, however, be unrealistic to think that the EU alone is capable of correcting the resistance that are inherent in the Italian system and in particular in a welfare regime based around the figure of the woman-mother. EU directives and national legislation to implement them have certainly had the merit of adding the image of the 'woman-worker', but the political elites have continued to resist any process of change that might alter the welfare system and lead to a true family policy. The influence of the EU on women's policy agencies has been filtered by the political colour of the government: under the centre-left government, the agencies were strengthened and they contributed to national policy-making, while under the centre-right they were halted in their tracks. The EU is also a new arena in which women's policy agencies can act, and they have proved capable of sitting at the negotiation table and acting with the same level of competence and preparation as those of other countries. At the national level, the agencies have improved over the years in terms of organization and influence. Even so, in the light of the experience of the alternation of government coalitions between 1996 and 2006, it can be said that the government support to women's policy agencies, in particular the Minister and the DPO, is a necessary precondition for their actions and results on domestic policy. One need only think of how the strategy of gender mainstreaming has been abandoned during Berlusconi's governments.

Encouraging signals have however emerged at the local level. First of all, the consolidation of the local women's policy agencies has brought about increased cooperation with the existing array of women's groups and associations. The gender mainstreaming strategy, while slowed down at national level, has made important steps forward at regional and provincial level. It has been implemented by many regions in structural-fund planning (and some of them have taken the initiative to extend the gender-sensitive monitoring system to all policies managed at the local level). Regional governments (encouraged by the new responsibilities they have acquired) have promoted initiatives in areas of women's interest such as the recognition of *de facto* couples and the adoption of the abortion pill, areas in which national politics is having difficulty in intervening. The regions have thus taken the lead in the path towards the recognition of equal opportunities and the safeguarding of rights and, as we had seen, the involvement of groups and associations takes place more at the local than at the national level.

To conclude, the joint action of European pressure and the constraints which are inherent in the political, institutional and social context of Italy have made both steps forwards and backwards regarding issues of gender equality, but the march towards equal rights has never stopped.

Notes

1. Only 42 per cent of women aged between 15 and 64 are employed (the European average is 55.6 per cent): the percentage decreases 37.7 per cent when one considers employed women against the total population (Eurostat, 2005).
2. The Committee, chaired by the Minister of Labour, consists of representatives of trade union and industrial organizations, of the cooperative movement and women's associations, as well as the equal opportunities counsellor, and includes participants without the right of vote, such as external experts and officials from the Ministry of Labour and other ministries. The members are nominated by the Ministry of Labour and hold their posts for three years.
3. Dlgs (decree) 196/2000.
4. The Minister had the right to introduce discussions in the Council of Ministers regarding deeds considered to be in conflict with the strategy of gender mainstreaming, and she can also veto them. The Minister assists the President of the Cabinet Council during appointments involving equal-rights issues.
5. With DPCM of 28 October 1997.
6. The work of the Cabinet Council is carried out by sector-based work groups consisting of members of the Permanent Delegation, representatives of the Commission and delegations of national executives.
7. Some executives of the DPO had previously worked in the Department for EU Policies.
8. The reform modified art. 51 of the Constitution by adding to the existing paragraph stating that 'All citizens of either sex can have access to public offices and elective posts under equal conditions' a new sentence stating that 'For this purpose, the Republic promotes, by means of special measures, equal opportunities for women and men'.
9. Chaired by Marina Piazza, a renowned sociologist, the CNPPO launched a campaign to gather the 50,000 signatures needed to promote a popular-initiative law to be discussed in Parliament. The proposal provided for the presence of 50 per cent of men and women candidates in the electoral lists in all polls. The signatures were collected, but parliament never discussed the proposal.
10. Despite this, the result of the most recent elections in 2006 showed an increase to 16 per cent in the number of women elected, a percentage still far from the European average of 20 per cent.
11. All the legal measures concerning protection and assistance for maternity and paternity later came together in Consolidation Act no. 151 of March 2001.
12. The Shadow Report was prepared by important women's associations (*Arcidonna, Candelaria, Caucus delle donne-Comitato romano, CGIL-Politiche delle pari opportunità*, the Italian Committee of the European Women's Lobby, *Cooperativa Generi e Generazioni, Paese delle Donne*, ABCD-*Ateneo Bicocca Coordinamento delle Donne*), signed by some feminists including the president of the CNPPO, Marina Piazza, and it was circulated on the Internet.

10
Dutch Decay: the Dismantling of the Women's Policy Network in the Netherlands

Joyce Outshoorn and Jantine Oldersma

Introduction

In comparative research on women's movements and women's policy agencies, the Netherlands gained the reputation of having a rather successful movement and an effective women's policy agency willing to advance movement goals and enhance access of women into decision-making arenas (McBride Stetson and Mazur, 1995; McBride Stetson, 2001a; Outshoorn, 2004a; Lovenduski et al., 2005; Hausmann and Sauer, 2007). Over the years the agency employed many women who had strong ties with various branches of the movement, making for an open attitude towards feminist demands, which were often directly incorporated into its policy papers. Although relations between women's movement groups and the agency were never free from tension, numerous women's initiatives and institutions were funded generously by the agency, ranging from the indispensable International Institute and Archives of the Women's Movement (IIAV) to organizations against sexual violence, feminist publishing and film ventures and small-scale cultural projects (IPM, 1986).

However, since the mid-1990s there has been an unmistakable dismantling of the once well-institutionalized women's policy network and an indisputable decline of the women's movement itself. Over the last two years there has been an open debate about abolishing the agency altogether, as supposedly women's equality policy is now well-integrated into mainstream policy. This has taken place in a context of the drastic shift to the right in Dutch politics, after the rise and the assassination of the populist Pim Fortuyn in 2002. The shift has been disastrous for most gender sensitive discourses. Toughness is being advocated on all fronts, gender discrimination and inequality are no longer issues which motivate politicians. In this discourse, only migrant and minority women, especially when they are from Muslim countries, are oppressed and need to be aided, suggesting gender inequality among ethnically white Dutch has been eliminated. This chapter will discuss the changes in the women's policy network and the shifts in the political context over the last decade, which have led to an ideological shift in which the problem of women's unequal status has been reduced to a problem of 'only migrant women'. How have relations between the women's policy agency and the women's movement developed in this period and what policy outcomes favourable to women have emerged?

The starting point of our analysis is the women's policy network in 1994, the year in which an unprecedented cabinet, the so-called Purple cabinet, took power. It bridged the left–right divide in Dutch politics by allying Social Democrats with Conservative Liberals and Social Liberals, excluding the Christian Democrats from power for the first time since 1918. The women's policy network had reached its zenith shortly before this accession (Outshoorn and Swiebel, 1998). Central to it was the women's policy agency itself, the Department for the Coordination of Equality Policy (*Directie Coordinatie Emancipatiebeleid* – DCE), located within the Ministry of Social Affairs and Employment, headed by a junior minister. The agency had a cross-sectional mandate and a coordinating role, enabling it to intervene in policy areas of other ministries. It also had its own budget, allowing the funding of women's movement organizations on a wide range of issues. It chaired the Interdepartmental Committee for Women's public policy (*Interdepartementale Coordinatiecommissie Emancipatie* – ICE) which consisted of civil servants from all the other ministries, intended to coordinate policy and to offer the opportunity to integrate gender aspects into mainstream policy. In addition, many ministries had a section or at least a couple of civil servants responsible for women's affairs.

Outside the national bureaucracy the network included the Permanent Standing Committee for Women's Public Policy of the Second Chamber of Parliament. There was also an informal All-Party Women's Caucus (*Kamerbreed Vrouwenoverleg*) which united women MPs across party political divides. Of major importance was the Emancipation Council (*Emancipatieraad* – ER), an official advisory body to the cabinet, which had to be heard on issues pertaining to women, but could also initiate its own reports. It consisted of both experts and representatives of political parties. Members sat for a five-year period; it had a small but highly qualified staff; many were feminists. Underlying the whole network was a basic consensus about the goals of women's equality policy, which had not been altered since the adoption of the Emancipation Green Paper of 1985 (*Beleidsplan Emancipatie*, 1985).[1]

Women's movement organizations were highly institutionalized and specialized in the mid-1990s. They no longer staged public protests and therefore lost the visibility of previous decades. Many depended heavily on state funding; including those of migrant women. After the mid-1990s there was little new mobilization and the once controversial issues of feminism had been adopted by the mainstream, including issues around sexual violence and abortion. Public debate was mainly about combining work and care. This was also the major women's policy goal of the Purple cabinets, which were in power until 2002. The continuity and complacency of the Purple era, however, were drastically challenged with the rise of the new populist leader Pim Fortuyn during the election campaign of 2002. After his assassination shortly before the national elections of 2002, his party, the List Pim Fortuyn (*Lijst Pim Fortuyn* – LPF) won no less than 26 of the 150-member Second Chamber of parliament, an unprecedented victory in electoral history.

The swing to the right

The Netherlands was until the twenty-first century politically a quiet backwater in Europe where the major societal conflicts were adroitly depoliticized and integrated into the existing political landscape. Oppositional groups and movements were usually invited to discuss their grievances by the political elite, a strategy characterized by the three 'c's: compromise, consensus and co-optation (Duyvendak et al., 1992, p. 213). In this way opposition was institutionalized in the elaborate networks of the Dutch corporatist state. The three most important parties on the political stage were the CDA (*Christen Democratisch Appèl* – Christian Democrat Appeal) (16–30 per cent), the conservative liberals VVD (*Volkspartij voor Vrijheid en Democratie* – People's Party for Freedom and Democracy) (15–25 per cent) and Labour (*Partij van de Arbeid* – PvdA, 15–30 percent). With the 2002 landslide victory of Fortuyn's party, the LPF became essential for a majority coalition of the right. The new cabinet allied the LPF, the VVD and the Christian Democrats. After nine months, it was clear that the LPF harboured too many conflicting personalities and the cabinet fell. In the elections of 2003, the LPF was reduced to a third of its size and the CDA, after nearly a decade in the opposition, once more became the largest party. The ensuing coalition government (Balkenende II, VVD/CDA/D66) was again right-wing. Among political observers, it is contentious as to how far politics are 'back to normal'; with De Vries (2002) we hold that even if the electoral balance of power has been more or less restored, there has been a major shift in discourse.

The LPF is a populist party which has a high profile on issues like migration and crime. Integration of Muslim immigrants was and is problematized in relation to traditional right-wing issues such as law-and-order, but also in relation to progressive issues like gay rights and sexual equality (Pels, 2003). Studies of voting behaviour, however, show that the voters were mainly motivated by Fortuyn's right-wing anti-migration and tough on crime rhetoric (Van Praag, 2003). Fortuyn and his successors clearly unleashed a backlash against lenient policies on migration and progressive policies on crime previously typical of the Netherlands. The LPF discourse on these issues has largely been adopted by mainstream right-wing parties that stress the need for maintaining 'traditional Dutch values' and for migrants to adapt to the 'national culture'.

The success of a new nationalist discourse may have been aided by changes in the institutional structure of the state during the 1990s on the supranational, the national as well as on the local level. The Netherlands has been a loyal supporter of European integration, but the rejection of the constitution in the 2005 referendum showed that negative feelings towards the European Union have become dominant. On a national level the shift of power to the EU and to local authorities seem to leave politicians in a void, unable to deal with the consequences of international developments. In the following, we will record the most important changes in state institutions and their consequences for gender equality policy.

An important feature of Dutch national politics is the proportional electoral system which guarantees access to parliament for many small groups and translates votes directly into parliamentary seats. Dutch governments consequently are necessarily coalitions and were never extreme in their discourse (Andeweg and Irwin, 2002). The '*Regeerakkoord*', the agreement between coalition parties at the start of a new parliamentary period, has become more important during the 1990s and the prime minister has taken on a more pronounced role as the primary spokesperson for the cabinet. In addition, the national civil service was reformed; a 'pool' of higher civil servants is expected to change seats regularly in order to loosen their ties with sectoral interests and to make them more responsive to the general policy line. Another change was the fashion of 'New Public Management' that inspired governments to privatize a number of state services and to create quangos for many others.

The new importance of the coalition agreement did not immediately curb the ambitions of the women's movement. In 1994, child care policies to combine work and family and shop closing hours were high on the cabinet's agenda. On two other issues, widow's pensions and social assistance, new arrangements (both in 1996) were detrimental to women's interests. A new group Widows in the Cold (*Weduwen in de Kou*) protested against the new pension law which discriminated against women; the National Committee of Women on Social Assistance (*Landelijk Comité Vrouwen in de Bijstand*) organized resistance against a new rule forcing women to search for a job when their youngest child is five years old. Women's movement organizations, however, were divided on these issues. In 1995 women's groups were able to persuade the Minister of Health to keep birth control pills in the standard package of nationally financed health care. In 2004 this battle was finally lost when it was decided that only those under twenty-one could get them free under the national health insurance (Outshoorn, 2000; Koekebakker and Van der Tol, 2005).

In 1998 the coalition agreement of the second Purple cabinet (Kok II) decided on a new gender mainstreaming device: every department was obliged to produce three targets and to report regularly on the progress made to attain them. An evaluation of this operation showed that it had been successful in some departments, but others had just recycled old targets. Attention to structural dimensions of gender discrimination, however, had not been accomplished (Tecena, 2000). In 2002 gender issues disappeared completely from coalition agreements of the right-wing parties and they did not return in the 2003 version. The main reason for the Purple cabinets in pursuing gender equality policies was to increase women's labour market participation, in order to maintain the welfare state. With the advent of right-wing governments, this objective remained; the secondary status of migrant women was added as a second priority.

The civil service reform has been largely detrimental to gender issues because at its introduction, gender mainstreaming had not yet been translated into formal arrangements within the departments (Koekebakker and Van der Tol, 2005). Its success therefore depended on personal interests of civil servants and if they moved to other departments or left the civil service altogether, initiatives were simply abandoned (Interview femocrat, 14 January 2005).

Privatization and quango-ization relevant to gender issues has been prevalent in child care and in social security arrangements. The already relatively high costs of child care (compared to other European countries) were increased by the right-wing cabinet in 2005 in a manner that makes parents the prime administrators and organizers of an elaborate system of subsidies. In the social security sector, the role of social partners has been curbed; a closing of opportunities for women as they had become well represented in the trade union movement over the last decade. Retrenchment policies in disability and unemployment are detrimental to women while movement demands to ameliorate the situation of women in the matter of pensions have been largely neglected (Outshoorn, 2000; Koekebakker and Van der Tol, 2005).

Decentralization of state power resulted in the delegation of responsibility to local authorities. This impaired women's movement organizations as they are often better organized at the national level. However, decentralization has also resulted in organization of networks at the local level in many municipalities where subsidies for socio-cultural work and for black and migrant women's groups are still available. In some municipalities women's centres are still functioning (Bureau Boven, 1998; Outshoorn, 2000; Koekebakker and Van der Tol, 2005).

European Directives on women's equality have had a major impact on national law (Van der Vleuten, 2001). The Netherlands was very slow at implementing equality legislation because of the extra costs; it even tried to obtain an exemption to equal pension rights after the Barber arrest in the Maastricht Treaty.[2] Dutch women's movement groups have been slow to take up the EU channel, partly because of the intricacies of the Brussels policy process, but also because several major issues are still decided at the national level. The Dutch Council of Women (*Nederlandse Vrouwenraad –* NVR) and the now defunct Women's Alliance (*Vrouwenalliantie*) supply the candidates from the Netherlands for the board of the European Women's Lobby (EWL). The Netherlands is a member of CEDAW; it signed the treaty in 1980 and ratified it in 1991. The CEDAW requirement of five-yearly reports on the state of affairs have provided women's groups with a new opportunity. In 1997 a first report to CEDAW was made; followed by a shadow report made by women's movement actors in which criticism of government policies were more pronounced (Groenman et al., 1997). CEDAW and the follow up on the UN Beijing Women's World Conference Beijing 10+ again served as rallying points for movement actors in 2004–05 (Koekebakker and Van der Tol, 2005) to highlight the shortcomings of the two cabinets since 2002. The 2006 Shadow Report on CEDAW also points out the breakdown of the national machinery, the inadequacies in gender mainstreaming and social-economic policy, and the stereotypical treatment of migrant women in policy (De Boer and Wijers, 2006).

The mid-1990s had seemed to provide a window of opportunity with the advent of the Purple cabinet. The new cabinet was more progressive on ethical issues and in favour of women's equality. They kept, however, the 'managerial style' of government with an emphasis on efficiency and the market and maintained the commitment of its predecessors to welfare state retrenchment. Purple-I (1994–8) Labour politician Ad Melkert was the Minister of Social Affairs and Employment; he also took equality policy into his portfolio. He appointed a new head to the DCE, former communist and Green Left politician Ina Brouwer, who had no ties to the women's movement. The ousting of the Christian Democrats was a blessing for the women's movement in as far as ethical issues were at stake; shop closing hours could at last be liberalized, so that working women no longer had to rush to shop before six p.m. However, the new coalition limited gender policy to a 'work, work, work' philosophy; the reconciliation of work and family life was high on the political agenda, but other parts were neglected.

During Purple-II (1998–2002), when D66 minister Annelies Verstand was junior minister for women's public policy, this policy line received more criticism; like Melkert she did not have a network in the movement, but unlike him she also lacked a network in parliament. Some maintain that Purple-I was a break with the past and point out it had a vision of gender mainstreaming that was successful until the right-wing electoral swing (Interview gender expert, 13 December 2004). At the same time, the gender neutral discourse of the Purple coalition made it hard to reframe women's problems, as it made any distinction between the sexes appear discriminatory (Outshoorn, 2000, p. 43). Under Balkenende-I (2002–03) a desperate search for a politician to take charge of equality policy in the end brought Khee Liang Phoa (LPF) as junior minister to power. In Balkenende-II (2003–) Aart Jan de Geus (CDA), formerly leader of the Protestant trade union movement, became the minister in charge of equality issues as well as of Social Affairs and Employment. Neither will be remembered as enthusiastic defenders of equality policy.

The demise of equality policies cannot be blamed on a lack of women in politics. From the 1970s on women have entered parliament in a gradual progression, and they now occupy 35–40 per cent of the seats in the most important body, the Second Chamber. Our research showed that in 1995 approximately half of these seats were occupied by female parliamentarians with links to either feminist or traditional women's organizations. Leaders of (most) political parties and journalists expect cabinets to have some 20–40 per cent of women; the 2002–03 right-wing cabinet Balkenende-I was a much criticized exception, having only one woman minister. The stormy entrance of the List Pim Fortuyn (a nearly all male list) into parliament in 2002 and the loss of seats by the VVD (where most women were at the lower end of the list) led to a decline of the number of women in parliament for the first time in thirty years (Leyenaar, 2004, pp. 190–1).

Women's organizations of the political parties on the left had been important movement allies in the 1970s and the 1980s. However, in 1995 the women's movement lost a major ally when the Red Women, the women's organization of the PvdA, disbanded and continued as a loose network, *Rosa*. The CDA-women's organization (CDA *Vrouwenberaad*), on the other hand, gained influence as the party was forced to reconsider its party programme and ideology by its electoral losses. It developed a friendlier stand on women's status going beyond the traditional family and housewife discourse, taking into account the importance of women's care work. The VVD is the party with the largest gender gap in electoral support, being favoured by male voters. A highly visible media campaign by prominent female parliamentarians caused the list to be drastically 'feminized' for the 2003 elections. Ayaan Hirsi Ali, an outspoken black former Somali refugee and advocate of the liberation of Muslim women, transferred from the PvdA to the VVD and became a controversial spokesperson in and outside parliament.

The decline of the national machinery

The elaborate women's policy network developed by assiduous and persistent femocrats and feminists since the late 1970s started to crumble in the mid-1990s. The Standing Group in parliament was abolished when the Second Chamber streamlined its standing group system in 1994. The All-Party Women's Caucus in parliament suffered a quiet death around the same period. The Commission for Equal Treatment m/f (*Commissie Gelijke Behandeling m/v*) was reformed in 1995 into a Commission which had to deal with all forms of discrimination (Outshoorn, 2000). Although it was feared at the time this would mean less attention to women's discrimination, this has not been the case; at least half of the cases brought to the Commission still concern sex discrimination. This can be ascribed to the highly respected Chair, Jenny Goldschmidt, a committed feminist, but also to the reputation of its predecessor. Women also know how to find their way when faced with sex discrimination, partly because verdicts of the Commission on this issue continue to receive much publicity in the media.

The still existing provincial and local women's units were subject to far reaching cuts in funding; this resulted in the abolishment of all save two of the provincial Emancipation Bureaus (*Emancipatiebureaus*), while the attention to gender issues in municipalities dwindled when local femocrats lost their mandate or job. The very active Emancipation Council vanished at the end of 1996 in the reform of the advisory structures to the government. To salvage its legacy, the Council, some feminist MPs and several femocrats were able to push for the formation of a temporary commission for women's public policy in the new advisory body system, Tecena

(*Tijdelijke Expertisecommissie voor Emancipatie in het Nieuwe Adviesstelsel*) in 1998, for a period of three years. Its goal was to incorporate women's policy goals into the new system, and ensure the appointment of women on the new boards. It was reasonably successful on both scores, but in its final report Tecena pointed to the vulnerability of this progress: only with continual pressure and political commitment, can this be sustained (Tecena, 2000, p. 31).

These events left the Department for the Coordination of Equality Policy as the only important actor of the former network; the ICE being neither very prominent nor very active. The DCE had emerged more or less unscathed by budgetary cuts; its administrative resources remained fairly stable until the mid-1990s. At the beginning of the 1990s the budget was approximately 13 million Euro a year (on a total government budget of 86 billion euros). The agency had about 28 full time equivalents (fte) of staff at its disposal. During the 1990s the total budget plummeted to €7 million (on a total budget of *c.* 100 billion) mainly because part of the responsibility for gender policies and related subsidies was shifted to other ministries. Staff was reduced to about 24 fte in 1993, but at the end of the decade the volume had risen again to about 34 fte. The budgetary loss, however, was more than compensated when in 1998 €27 million went into the new Daily Routine Incentive Scheme (*Stimuleringsmaatregel Dagindeling*), later succeeded by a budget of approximately €24 million from the European Social Fund Objective 3 and again €100 million from the ministries of Education and of Social Affairs and Employment.

When in the 1990s the EU was becoming interested in gender mainstreaming, the DCE started to take advantage of the growing money stream emanating from Brussels. This, of course, limited the autonomy of the agency to decide on its own priorities, but this was counterbalanced by good access to decision-making circles in the EU. When the national budget became smaller, this was more than offset by funding from the European Social Fund, used for projects like promoting women in decision-making and men to take up caring roles (Interview femocrat, 14 January 2005).[3] The DCE, however, is not the principle body setting the gender agenda for EU policies or representing the Netherlands when it comes to gender policies. As it is relinquishing its coordinating role, it does not feed the policies of the various ministries whose civil servants and minister represent the Netherlands in the EU. This is in contrast to the situation at the UN, where DCE members represent the Netherlands on the Committee on the Status of Women, and a representative from the Netherlands Council of Women (*Nederlandse Vrouwenraad*) is included in the official delegation to the General Assembly.

The framing of the issue of women's status in the official policy documents of the various cabinets, drafted by the DCE, surprisingly has not shifted over time since the 1985 *Beleidsplan* (Beleidsplan, 1985). The main aim of gender policy was (and is) to promote a society in which individuals, regardless of sex or marital status, can achieve an independent existence, and in which women and men have equal rights, opportunities, liberties and responsibilities. Its main focus was on equal rights and on structural change so that the traditional gender order would no longer determine the organization of society, as well as challenging the cultural meanings of femininity and masculinity. Policy papers of the 1990s elaborated on these themes, sometimes rearranging priorities, such as increasing women's representation in decision-making, the redistribution of paid and unpaid work between women and men and changing the images of masculinity and femininity. For the rest policy papers resembled more a shopping list of good intentions than a logical plan for action. They all attempted to broaden the scope of public policy beyond the issue of women's participation on the labour market, the favourite framing of successive cabinets, which they justified by the necessity of maintaining the welfare state. Sexual orientation has always been an issue in DCE policy, and since the mid-1980s policy papers incorporated ethnicity; the funding of projects and organizations of migrant women dates back to the same period.

In 2001 a new paper was presented, the Ten Year Plan for women's public policy (Meerjarennota, 2000). It more or less retained the aims of the *Beleidsplan*, but with more regard for diversity among women, taking in different life courses. Five central areas for policy intervention were outlined: work, care and income, power and decision-making, human rights, information technology and gender, and day-planning (*dagindeling*).[4] That same year a white paper on gender mainstreaming was adopted (Ministerie SZW, 2001). Following the Council of Europe's conception of gender mainstreaming, the white paper was quite explicit about the factors making for success of this strategy, such as commitment of the political and civil service leadership, well-delineated policy goals, gender expertise and both financial means and policy instruments for implementation. It also gave a blueprint for the organization for mainstreaming. It proposed setting up a Commission for the Assessment of Women's Public Policy (*Visitatiecommissie Emancipatiebeleid* – VCE) to be appointed by the cabinet. The VCE's mandate was to check the progress made by the various ministries in mainstreaming gender policy; it meant that the task of the coordinating Minister, which was both to facilitate and to monitor the activities of the ministries, is split. The Commission was officially appointed in April 2004 and came up with its final report in January 2007.[5] Its final report shows that gender mainstreaming is not progressing and that many ministries lack the political will and know-how to implement this strategy (VCE, 2007). The report also took diversity into account, and showed that only a couple of ministries have set out policies on this issue.

With its tradition of cross-sectional policy, the DCE seemed well-placed to take up gender mainstreaming when this was adopted at the UN Beijing International Women's Conference in 1995, as it provided the mandate to intervene in other policy areas and to coordinate gender policies across the board. Under the new director Brouwer, however, the strategy of the agency turned to forming new alliances with other social actors such as employers, with the consequence that it began to neglect its traditional role. Previously, the DCE had had sections on key policy areas and a civil servant assigned as a permanent liaison to all other ministries, to provide advice and also to function as a 'watchdog'. This system fell into neglect, leading to less contact with the other ministries. One interviewee stated: 'The positive side to gender mainstreaming is that it is an incentive to choose another strategy; the negative side is that a lot of expertise is needed to develop that strategy and that was not available or not sought. You need expertise, feminist knowledge, to get gender mainstreaming going and there was no interest in and no money for that any more' (Interview gender expert, 13 December 2004).

It also led to a loss of expertise about other policy areas within the agency. This was not compensated by a stronger ICE, which increasingly was only attended by junior civil servants, losing status in the process. As another one of our interviewees commented: 'In the early nineties the same people were always present and they could be counted on. At a certain point in time this game was spoiled. People were given other jobs, others came etc.' (Interview femocrat, January 14, 2005).

Under Brouwer new civil servants were recruited, with other networks and a different way of working which fitted with the strategy of attracting new allies. The organizational culture became more informal and less focused on civil service procedure. The Commission Daily Routine (*Dagindeling*), with members from 'inside' and 'outside', typifies the new approach; it was successful in setting the issue of combining work and care on the political agenda. When Brouwer was ousted by junior minister Verstand in 2000, her successor, Gabriele Bekman, appointed for two years, attempted to reassert the DCE's coordinating role. But this was severely hampered by the fact that it could no longer rely on counterparts within the other ministries; the relations with other ministries had become increasingly strained (Interview gender expert, 13 December 2004). The expertise within the ministries, essential for gender mainstreaming, dwindled. Turnover is high, and many previously well-trained civil servants in women's affairs, have transferred to other work or exited altogether.

After the right-wing shift in politics of 2002–03, the situation deteriorated even further. As one femocrat of the DCE commented:

> If gender mainstreaming means activating other layers of government and civil society organisations, then quite a lot was happening, albeit in a limited amount of policy sectors. If gender mainstreaming means influencing the big dossiers of other departments, then the view shifts. That has not been very successful. Attempts have been directed at the Treasury (tax system), integration of migrants, economic affairs and home affairs, but they died at the end of the '90s and came to a complete standstill under Balkenende-I. (Interview femocrat, 14 January 2005)

The DCE did achieve that the other ministries each formulated three policy priorities for gender policy in its domain. In general, however, the DCE has become less involved in other policy areas, leaving issues to the other ministries. Moreover, with another shift in its leadership (Bekman was replaced by the first male director, Ferdy Licher, in 2003), the coordinating role of the DCE itself is at stake. It has disappeared quietly from its formal mandate in 2004 (*Staatsblad*, 28 October 2004), taking both the interdepartmental committee and the new assessment committee VCE by surprise. Part of the task of the VCE is to advise on the future structure for gender policy; the change in the formal mandate of the DCE can be read as an attempt to foreclose the recommendations of the VCE.

The relationship between the DCE and women's movement actors

One of the strengths of the Dutch organization of gender policy has always been the strong ties between the DCE and the various women's movement organizations. Although the relationship was never unproblematic or cordial, the funding strategies of the DCE had provided the women's movement with a strong financial backbone (Outshoorn, 1995). This had included groups from the autonomous women's movement as well as the traditional women's organizations allied within the National Women's Council (*Nederlandse Vrouwenraad* – NVR), and the Women's Alliance (*Vrouwenalliantie*). The latter two have a membership of over a million and they became increasingly proficient at lobbying for gender issues.[6] The NVR lost its subsidy in the late 1990s and is now a volunteer organization. The Women's Alliance funding was ended in 2004 and its member-organizations no longer were willing to finance the general staff. Continuing as an organization financed on a project-base was cut short by conflicts within the executive (Interview director, 11 February 2005).

Other women's movement organizations had been forced to merge and 'professionalize' since the early 1990s, while remaining subsidies were more and more issued for single projects only, and not for permanent staff or overhead costs. This enabled government to influence priorities and to persuade the organizations to pay more attention to prevailing policies. This has led to an erosion of the permanent staff of these organizations and a lack of money to invest in new projects or take up issues not on the government agenda.

In 1996 the DCE initiated another drive to force movement organizations into a larger conglomerate. This met with vehement opposition, but in 1998 the Institute of Women and Work (*Instituut Vrouw en Werk*), Arachne (lobby- and advice bureau), the Women's Exchange Programme International (WEP-I) and Aisa (black, refugee and migrant women's organization) merged into E-quality, an expertise centre for the women's movement. It received less funding, however, and its terms of reference were severely limited (Koekebakker and Van der Tol, 2005). The documentation centre and library IIAV (*Internationaal Informatiecentrum en Archief voor de Vrouwenbeweging*), the *Clara Wichmann Institute* (expertise on gender and law), the Foundation against Trafficking of Women (*Stichting tegen Vrouwenhandel* – STV) and *Transact* (Centre for gender and health) remained independent, as they were funded by other ministries than the DCE. This change in funding was inspired by the concept of gender mainstreaming; the second Purple cabinet managed to transfer a number of subsidies to other departments.

After 2003, however, most subsidies stopped altogether. This forced many organizations like the Red Thread (*Rode Draad*), an organization of sex workers, and the Dutch Society for Women's Studies (*Nederlands Genootschap Vrouwenstudies*) to go on as volunteer organizations, while the Clara Wichmann Institute had to close its doors. Organizations still receiving longer term subsidies were the IIAV, E-quality and the Women's Alliance. The Alliance was disbanded in 2004; the IIAV and E-quality faced severe budget cuts and had to restrict their activities (Koekebakker and Van der Tol, 2005, p. 8). From 2004 on, applications for funding have to target women in marginal positions, mainly women and girls from minority backgrounds, if they are to receive subsidies. This has enabled the platform organization of migrant women's groups, Tije International, to survive as a volunteer organization. Further government priorities are rights and security, labour market participation, economic independence and politics and decision-making (Meerjarenbeleidsplan Emancipatie 2006–10, 2005).

With these changes, the support structure of the women's movement which came into being in the early 1980s, has now been largely dismantled. Its disappearance has diminished the relations of the DCE with women's movement organizations but also between movement experts and lobbyists and parliament. Movement organizations have maintained their access to party spokeswomen in parliament, who became increasingly critical of consecutive cabinets. But movement actors have few ties to national government institutions left, including the DCE, and on the whole one can conclude that they have become effectively marginalized in the policy process. The *rapport* established between MPs and the DCE in the earlier period has also disappeared. As noted by one of our interviewees, critical MPs are out to score in the media, with less emphasis on negotiating with the coordinating minister and benefiting that way (Interview femocrat, 14 January 2005).

State restructuring and offloading of state activities to civil society has hit the older and the professional branch of the women's movement hard. Surprisingly, political activities by women's movement organizations have not shown real decline over the past years, and a wide array of cultural and educational activities are still organized in many towns and local communities (Post, Oldersma and Outshoorn, 2006). Its lobbies during the 1990s became more and more centred around the political calendar. The lobby organization Arachne started the '*Prinsjesdagborrel*' (Prince's Day Drinks – after the opening of the parliamentary year when the national budget is presented) where new policy initiatives are criticized from a gender perspective. Now E-quality organizes this yearly event. The DCE commissions the biannual Emancipation monitor (*Emancipatiemonitor*), which manages to incite public debates on the direction of equality policy each time it is published. As mentioned, the mandatory CEDAW reports have been a rallying point for debate and critical comments on national equality policies. At the local level, the International Women's Day on 8, March, still serves as a mobilizing and networking event for many feminists from the older and the younger generation. The resources for lobbying, however, have undoubtedly decreased.

While the former mass organizations are waning, websites and chatrooms on feminism, and more generally on women, are booming. In the second half of the 1990s many organizations started websites. In 1995 the Women's House Amsterdam started the first one, followed in 1996 by Women's Interests (*Vrouwenbelangen*), an organization that had just celebrated its hundredth jubilee. Many organizations have since then created websites,[7] the most important of which is Emancipatie.nl (2000), with up to date information on political activities and links to major women's policy dossiers of governments. Other portals are operated by the Women's Net (*Vrouwennet*), Women's Square (*Vrouwenplein*) (2000) and Women on the Web (formerly Webbgrrls) (all started in 1996), and the Website of the NVR (1998).

Despite this proliferation of women on the web, the feminist press is still in demand; *Opzij* has a circulation of around 75,000 (was 80,000). There are also still women's groups within the labour unions and at most universities. Many networks organizing women in management and women in the professions are still active, but since a coordinating agency is missing, it is difficult to keep track of the precise state of affairs. Migrant and minority women such as the growing group of young Muslim women, are also important new players in the field. Many bookshops, cafés and other types of entertainment are still available for a feminist and/or lesbian public. Another development is the proliferation of organizations, small businesses and authors offering workshops or advice on psychological and spiritual matters that seem to have replaced the consciousness raising and radical therapy groups of early feminism (Van Voorthuizen, 1996).

These new developments pose problems for the DCE; it no longer seeks the support of the older women's organizations and deliberately changed its relationship with these, partly because they were indeed old, partly because they were too critical of government policy. As one of our interviewees said:

> The traditional movement often did not understand what was happening. They felt abandoned and advertised that equality policies were in the wrong hands. The gallery of the Second Chamber was always filled with elderly women (. . .) The relationship turned into a cash relationship and under Balkenende-II it was not even that any more. (Interview femocrat, 14 January, 2005)

Attempts at making contact with younger movement actors, however, has not succeeded, because they are not organized as formal organizations but as informal networks which are not interested in or equipped for gaining influence in 'traditional' politics.

The demise of feminist and of women's organizations, however, is not paralleled by shifts in public opinion on feminist issues to date in general.

The Dutch public, both male and female, was relatively quick in adopting the central tenets of feminism, but difference of opinion among the general public still exist about the importance of work for women's emancipation. The ideology of motherhood is still strong and women are divided on the issues of child care centres and part-time work. The debate has been reinvigorated by the demographic shift; many experts hold that increasing women's labour market participation is vital for maintaining pensions and health care for the elderly. Discussion about feminism took a grim turn after the success of the Fortuyn movement. The swing to the right put the spotlight on migrants and especially on problematic gender relations among Muslim groups. These had already been the subject of a play, *Aisha*,[8] which was not performed because radical Muslims threatened with violence. The feminist magazine *Opzij* paid attention to growing dissatisfaction about Muslim men refusing to deal with female civil servants and problems of gay teachers in schools. The controversial VVD-parliamentarian Ayaan Hirsi Ali blamed the oppression of Muslim women on the 'backwardness' of Islam as a religion and pleaded for a better protection of women threatened with violence, but also for a suppression of mosques, Muslim schools, veils and other paraphernalia of religion in public space. Muslimas, however, protested against her views and felt overruled by her staunch Enlightenment discourse. Her television film *Submission*, made with filmmaker Theo van Gogh, was a catalyst for his murder by a young radical Muslim in 2004. The focus on the problems of migrant women highlights practices of an extremely serious nature and it is beginning to lead to mobilization of women who have been silent for too long. This new turn of events feeds the tendency by politicians, however, to regard the problems of non-migrant women as nonexistent and feminism for white women as a relic from the past.

Conclusions

In the Netherlands the women's policy network created in the 1980s has more or less disappeared. Many of the institutions providing access of women's movement organizations into decision-making arenas have been abolished. The ties between movement organizations and the women's policy agency have shrunk, and relations between women's movement organizations and parliament have also shrunk, partly due to fewer MPs willing to take up gender issues, who also tend to be backbenchers. The major shift in gender policy has been the turn to gender mainstreaming, aimed at integrating gender policy in all policy areas. It is open to question as to how far the conditions for success for this strategy are present, such as political and administrative commitment, gender-expertise in the various ministries and clear and well-cut policy aims. The women's policy agency, the DCE, gradually relinquished its coordinating role, which was confirmed by the discrete removal of this role from its policy mandate in 2004. Many politicians and bureaucrats see its demise as a logical step in implementing gender mainstreaming.

Formally speaking, there is little shift in framing of the issue of women's status, as the 1985 *Beleidsplan* still provide the general ideas for policy. New priorities have been set, but they have not offset the tendency to reduce gender policy to issues pertaining to women's participation in the labour market. The recent rediscovery of violence against women not only reverts to a gender neutral framing of domestic violence, but also redefines it as a problem of non-white ethnic women, especially Muslim women, excluding ignoring the persistent problem of violence against women of all ethnicities. The only innovation in the violence frame has been the inclusion of violence against women in war and conflict situations in foreign and defence policy.

It is as yet difficult to establish whether movement success is also on the decline in the Netherlands. Many of its issues have become mainstream and have been incorporated into regular policy; so have many issues become part of a public consensus about gender equality. There is a general feeling, however, that equality has been achieved, making the problem lose urgency and making feminist claims seem redundant and out of date. The women's movement itself is undeniably in decline. There are fewer organizations now than at the beginning of the 1990s, and most of these are not able to mobilize new generations of activists. Some foresee a new wave of feminism emerging from communities of non-white women, but others point out that facilitating factors, such as resources, unity and leadership for a new wave are lacking. Feminist debates are not lacking, though, most recently on the issue of migration and diversity.

The shift to the right, with its focus on Dutch nationalism, suspicion of the EU, the rejection of multiculturalism and the general anxiety about internationalization, has not been conducive to new mobilization of groups of women. At the same time, the expanding funds of the EU for projects and research and the activities concerning CEDAW support movement actors with ties to international networks; the DCE made ample use of EU–ESF funding. The fact that equality policies are more and more part and parcel of multilevel governance may prove to be a blessing in times of nationalist backlash.

The decline of gender policy can thus be ascribed to several factors. First of all, there is the decline in political commitment to gender equality, save for the issue of the labour market. Secondly, the decline of women's movement actors makes for a less effective lobby and pressure from mobilized public opinion. Movement organizations have not been able to keep women's issues on the political agenda or mobilize a new constituency. Thirdly, the framing of equality policy in terms of ethnic and cultural differences is detrimental to feminist mobilizing. Though it attracts right-wing allies, it alienates the left and leaves the issue largely in limbo. Finally, some of the strategic decisions of the women's policy agency have proved to be unfortunate, especially the choices in alliance structures, losing contact with women's movement organizations, and in letting go of its coordinating role with concomitant loss of gender expertise for other policy areas.

Interviews

Monique Leijenaar, political scientist and gender expert, Amsterdam, 13 December 2004.
Hella van de Velde, femocrat DCE, Leiden, 14 January 2005.
Thera van Osch, Former director VrouwenAlliantie, Leiden/Nieuwegein, 11 February 2005 (e-mail).

Notes

1. The Beleidsplan Emancipatie was a government white paper analysing in extenso the problematic aspects of women's plight in Dutch society.
2. The Barber arrest refers to Case 262/88 of the European Court of Justice (17 May 1990) about equal pension rights for men and women.
3. The initial budget of €27 million was spent in four years (Daily Routine Incentive Scheme, 140 projects, 1999–2003), The ESF-3 financed the follow-up: €24 million (175 projects, 2002–07). During preparation of another follow-up under the title Day Arrangements and Combination of Functions (*Dagarrangementen en combinatiefuncties*) the Ministry of Social Affairs and Employment unexpectedly closed the possibility for sending applications to the Agency. €100 million for the period 2004–07 were then supplied jointly by the ministries of Education and Social Affairs and Employment. Eighty municipalities applied for 111 projects for in total €48,7 million, so only 50 per cent of this budget will be used. (Source: Ms J. Roemeling, former project manager Daily Routine ESF-3 (2001–05).
4. The idea of daily routine is that the organization of daily life, with opening hours of shops, schools, organizations, etc. as well as public holidays, interferes with the combination of work and family life for both women and men. In 1996 a Committee was set up by the DCE to chart the problems in this area; later its work was continued by the Steering Committee Daily Routine.
5. It is headed by an ex-chair person of the CDA, a number of academic gender experts, a former top civil servant and two people from social organizations.

It has an experienced secretariat run by a former DCE femocrat. One of the authors of this paper, Joyce Outshoorn, is a member.

6. The National Women's Council (*Nationale Vrouwen Raad* (1898); the Platform for Economic Independence (*Breed Platform voor Economische Zelfstandigheid* (1982) merged in 1994 with the Association for the Redistribution of Paid and Unpaid Work (*Associatie voor Herverdeling van Betaald en Onbetaald Werk* (1978)) into the Women's Alliance (1994–2004).

7. Websites are operated by organizations as diverse as the Association of Women Academics (*Vereniging van Vrouwen met een Hogere Opleiding* – VVAO, 1999, 5000 members), Black and Migrant Female Academics (1998, 50 members), Catholic Women's organization (1998, 25,000 members), Older Women (WOUW-Amsterdam 1997), Women on Social Assistance (80 groups of 6–10 women, 1999) and Maroc Girls (2000).

8. Aisha was the Prophet's fourth wife, only nine at the age of her marriage.

11
The Evolution of Spanish State Feminism: a Fragmented Landscape

María Bustelo and Candice D. Ortbals

Introduction

Spanish feminism has been typified by fragmentation during the last decade between women's policy agencies and women's movement actors. During the 1980s and 1990s, Spain experienced federalization and became part of the European Community. In this chapter, we describe these institutional changes and their implications for state feminism. We highlight national and subnational equality institutions and policies, concluding that the mix of national, regional, and international politics holds both advantages and disadvantages for Spanish feminism.

On one hand, this conclusion is counterintuitive: more women pursuing equality in more arenas should yield a greater voice for feminism. Although we demonstrate that Spanish feminists and politicians seek equality measures at multiple administrative levels and that expanding policy realms often serve as opportunities for the women's movement, we also note disadvantages. A greater voice for equality does not ensure that policies across the entire nation reflect a rich definition of state feminism; rather, diversity yields some policy discourses and outcomes which can be evaluated positively and others which can evaluated negatively. Societal activism also defies simple conclusions, for the Spanish women's movement includes many actors with diverse goals, some of whom benefit from federalization and others who are dismayed about regional politics. While finding that feminists reacted more positively to the socialist party than to the conservative party, we conclude that relations between feminists and bureaucrats are highly nuanced.

A rapidly changing political context

Spain transitioned from a right-wing, closed dictatorship to a modern, European-oriented democracy in approximately ten years. Franco died in November 1975 and Spain entered the European Economic Community (EU today) in 1986. Within these ten years, the national women's policy agency, the Women's Institute (*Instituto de la Mujer*, WI), was created. The 1983 establishment of the WI marks the beginning of state feminism and gender equality public policies in Spain (Gil, 1996). From this moment, gender equality public polices, and the institutional frameworks around them, have developed very quickly. The WI is an important 'tool' in equality policymaking, and even though it was established approximately ten years later than comparable institutions in other advanced industrial democracies, by 1994 it was similar in terms of goals, budget, and human resources (Valiente, 1995). The late arrival of Spanish equality policies is also reflected in the development of regional equality agencies, beginning in the late 1980s, approximately five years after the WI was created. Regional developments proved to be even more rapid and strong than those at the national level (Bustelo, 1998). Therefore, in terms of gender equality policies and 'women's machinery' at different governmental levels, Spain has experienced one of the quickest growth patterns in European countries in the last twenty years.

According to Valiente, the main factors for the creation of the WI were the Socialist Party's (*Partido Socialista Obrero Español*, PSOE) presence in government and the socialist party feminists who fought for equality measures (Valiente, 1995). Gender policies became identified with the socialist party because it governed Spain from 1982 until the mid-1990s. When the People's Party (*Partido Popular*, PP) took office in 1996, the new Cabinet supported equality institutions and gender policies though the party had been categorically against them. The Fourth World Conference in Beijing and European Union resources for gender policies are key factors that explain conservative support for gender policies. After eight years of conservative government, an important political change took place at the national level. In March 2004, the PSOE won the national elections and has since led the country in equality matters.

The regional political landscape today is also much more favourable to the PSOE than in the 1990s. For example, in 1998, 11 of the 17 regions were in PP hands, whereas the PSOE now governs 10 of the regions. It is important to note that the political sub-systems in the regions have varied dynamics and in many cases are different from the national system. For example, regional or nationalist political parties sometimes form coalitions with a major party – or another regional party – which consequently impacts regional governance (see Table 11.1). Therefore, the regional political contexts in Spain vary enormously from one another.

Policy priorities

Socialist state feminism from 1983 to 1996 sought policies related to abolishing discriminative legislation remaining from the Franco era, fighting against violence against women, furthering parity discussions, advancing gender research and instituting programmes for prostitutes and single mothers. Socialists also promoted policies related to coeducation, health and employment.

Although the policy priorities of the PP diverged from those of the PSOE, the WI between 1996 and 2004 maintained many policy programmes. The prioritized goals of the conservative party included fighting violence against women, assisting rural women, offering job training and helping women balance work and family responsibilities. The PP-led WI was noticeably quiet about important issues, especially the gendering of education reform in the 2001 Quality Law (*Ley de Calidad*, LOCE). During the late 1980s, the socialist-led WI helped to introduce feminist ideas into education debates and the resultant 1990 Law on the General Organization of the Education System (*Ley de Ordenación General del Sistema Educativo*, LOGSE) became the legal benchmark for non-sexist education programmes. The LOCE, unlike the LOGSE, does not mention the importance of equality between the sexes and its text is not written in gender inclusive language.

The PP has also challenged certain advances in gender violence policy. Gender violence has become a public issue of concern to Spanish society and not only feminists (Valiente, 2005a; Bustelo, Valiente, and Villavicencio, forthcoming). Spanish feminists, traditionally concerned with violence, have suggested multiple solutions, many of which the PSOE began to address in the 1980s.[1] On one hand, the PP governments did not 'noticeably cut back' services. Moreover, the WI addressed the issue through two specific plans against violence from the Women's Institute (Valiente, 2005a, p. 110) and the party claimed that its actions, such as education initiatives and research, raised awareness and prevented violence (Valiente, 2005a). Although vocal about violence, the PP was unconditionally against the PSOE-proposed gender violence law[2] which they rejected twice, in 2000 and 2002, when they had an absolute majority in the National Parliament.

The PP also opposed quotas and rejected any initiative to reform electoral systems. Whereas the PSOE enacted a 25 per cent party quota in

Table 11.1: Spanish National and Regional Equality Institutions 2006

Level/Region	Type of Organization and date of creation	Party in Government	Governmental area	Equality Plans
National	*Instituto de la Mujer (1983)*	Socialist Party (2004)	Employment and Social Affairs	I Plan 1988–1990 II Plan 1993–1996 III Plan 1997–2000 IV Plan 2003–2006
Andalucía	*Instituto Andaluz de la Mujer (1988)* Andalusia Woman's Agency	Socialist Party	Presidency Equality and Social Affairs (2004)	I Plan 1990–1992 II Plan 1995–1997 Equality & Gender Unit (2000)
Aragón	*Instituto Aragonés de la Mujer (1993)* Aragón Woman's Agency	Socialist Party/Regional Party (PAR)	Presidency Social Affairs and Family (2003)	I Plan 1994–1996 II Plan 1997–2000 III Plan 2001–2004
Asturias	*Secretaría Regional de la Mujer (1989)* *Dirección General de la Mujer (1993)* *Instituto Asturiano de la Mujer (1999)*	Socialist Party	Presidency (since 1999)	I Plan 1989–1991 II Plan 1993–1995 III Plan 1996–2000 IV Plan 2001–2005
Baleares	*Comisión Interdepartamental (1990)* *Instituto Balear de la Mujer (1999)*	Conservative Party	Presidency	I Plan 1991–1993 II Plan 1996–1999 III Plan 2002–2005
Canarias	*Instituto Canario de la Mujer (1994)*	*Coalición Canaria* in coalition	Employment and Social Affairs	I Plan 1995–1996 II Plan 1997–2000 III Plan 2003–2006
Cantabria	*Agencia de Promoción de la Mujer (1986)* *Dirección General de la Mujer (1997)* Woman's Directorate General (D.G.)	Socialist Party/Regional Party (PRC)	Institutional Relations and European Affairs	I Plan 1991–1993 II Plan 1998–2001 III Plan 2003–2006

Castilla-La Mancha	*Dirección General de la Mujer (1990)* Woman's Directorate General *Instituto de la Mujer de Castilla-La Mancha (2002)*	Socialist Party	Institutional Relations (presidency)	I Plan 1990–1994 II Plan 1995–1999 III Plan 2000–2003 IV Plan 2004–2008
Castilla-León	*Secretaría Regional de la Mujer (1994)* *Dirección General de la Mujer e Igualdad de Oportunidades (1999)* Woman's Directorate General and Equal Oportunities	Conservative Party	Family and Equal Opportunities	I Plan 1994–1996 II Plan 1997–2000 III Plan 2001–2005 Equality Law (2003)
Cataluña	*Comisión Interdepartamental de Promoción de la Mujer (1987)* *Institut Català de la Dona (1989)* Cataluña Woman's Agency	Socialist Party in coalition with two nationalistic – regional parties	Presidency	I Plan 1989–1992 II Plan 1994–1996 III Plan 1998–2000 IV Plan 2001–2003 V Plan 2005–2007
Comunidad Valenciana	*Dirección General de la Mujer (1997)* Woman's Directorate General (D.G.)	Conservative Party	Social Welfare	I Plan 1989–1991 II Plan 1997–2000 III Plan 2001–2004 Equality Law (2003)
Extremadura	*Dirección General de la Mujer (1991)* *Instituto de la Mujer de Extremadura (2001)*	Socialist Party	Culture	I Plan 1991 II Plan 2000–2003 III Plan 2006–2009
Galicia	*Servicio Galego de Promoción da Igualdade del Home y la Muller (1991)* Agency for the Promotion of Equality between Woman and Man	Socialist Party/BNG (Nationalistic Party)	Equality and Welfare	I Plan 1992–1994 II Plan 1995–1997 III Plan 1998–2000 IV Plan 2002–2005 Equality Law (2004)

(Continued)

Table 11.1: (Continued)

Level/Region	Type of Organization and date of creation	Party in Government	Governmental area	Equality Plans
La Rioja	*Dirección General de Bienestar Social (1988)* *Dirección General de Familia y Acción Social (2003)* *Dirección General de Servicios Sociales*	Conservative Party	Youth, Family and Social Services	I Plan 1991–1995 I Plan Integral 1996–1999 II Plan Integral 2001–2004
Madrid	*Dirección General de la Mujer (1989)* Woman's Directorate General (D.G.)	Conservative Party	Employment and Woman	I Plan 1989–1991 II Plan 1993–1996 III Plan 1997–2000 IV Plan 2001–2005
Murcia	*Dirección General de la Mujer (1991)* *Dirección General de Política Social y Familia (1995)* *Dirección General de Juventud, Mujer y Familia (1997)* *Instituto Murciano de la Mujer (2002)*	Conservative Party	Presidency (2002)	I Plan 1993–1995 II Plan 1997–2000 III Plan 2003–2005
Navarra	*Subdirección General de la Mujer (1991)* *Instituto Navarro de la Mujer (1995)*	Conservative Party	Social Welfare, Sports and Youth	I Plan 2006–2010 Equality Law (2002)
País Vasco	*Instituto Vasco de la Mujer – Emakunde (1988)* Basque Woman´s Agency	PNV *(Partido Nacionalista Vasco)*	Presidency	I Plan 1991–1994 II Plan 1995–1998 III Plan 1999–2004 Equality Law (2005)

1988 and proposed political parity in a 2001 bill (no more than 60 and no less than 40 per cent of candidates from one sex), the PP rejected the bill. According to Valiente, the PSOE-led WI made political representation a 'top priority' but under PP leadership it became a 'very low priority' (Valiente, 2005b, p.186). In fact, the PP appealed to the Constitutional Court (*Tribunal Constitucional*), claiming that two regional parity laws – from Castile-La Mancha and the Balearic Islands – were unconstitutional.

The new socialist government led by Rodríguez Zapatero has already substantially impacted gender policies. From the beginning of his government, clear signals of change were evident: a parity government, the creation of the 'Equality Policies General Secretariat' (with a higher rank than the WI), the approval of the gender violence law (December 2004), a set of measures to promote equality between women and men which involve all the Ministries (March 2005), the reform of the Civil Code which allows homosexual marriage (July 2005), the *Plan Concilia*, reconciling the personal and work life of civil servants inside the national public administration (December 2005), the 'Dependency Law' (December 2006), and a new national Equality Law (March 2007). Other issues are to be accomplished soon, including the approval of a new national Equality Law, a new Dependency Law and the re-inclusion of gender equality aims in a reformed Education law. Further reform of the abortion law,[3] however, has not yet been prioritized.

Fragmented state: changes in the national and subnational agencies

As noted above, the women's national machinery in Spain during the last decade has been the WI, led by the People's Party (PP) from 1996 to 2004. During this period, no apparent institutional changes transpired, with the exception that the Ministry of Social Affairs, created in 1988 and to which the WI was affiliated, gained work and employment competencies in 1996 and thereafter became the Ministry of Employment and Social Affairs (*Ministerio de Trabajo y Asuntos Sociales*). This change might have affected equality measures because, as explored above, the PP-led WI stressed the policy area of employment, which was logical considering European programmes offered resources related to that area.

As a consequence to the Socialist Party ascendance to government in 2004, an 'Equality Policies General Secretariat' was created in the national administration, positioned above the WI in the Ministry of Employment and Social Affairs (this Secretariat depends directly on the Ministry). Because this institution has been created *ex-novo* and has had such a short lifespan, its impact on the gender policies institutional framework cannot yet be fully assessed. However, we can conclude that it is playing an important role regarding some issues, such as gender violence. For example, in March 2005, the 'Special Governmental Delegation against Violence toward Women' was created by the Secretariat. The Secretariat is also playing an important role in the proposal of the future Equality Law and has assumed a great deal of the WI's leadership role.

However, the national level alone does not offer a complete picture of gender policies in Spain because regional machineries now shape Spanish state feminism. The Spanish Constitution of 1978 set an original model for territorial organization (a quasi-federal one), which established political and administrative autonomy for the regions (*Comunidades Autónomas*, Autonomous Communities). In all their constitutive laws (*Estatutos*), general equality rights and powers related to 'woman's promotion' were established, even for the slow-track regions.[4] The regions institutionalized these powers through different organizational forms. At first, the WI represented an institutional model for the regions (Valiente, 1995; Martínez, 1997), which set up women's agencies approximately around 1988 (see Table 11.1). The regional governments created equality institutions or 'women' specific agencies, which are in charge of coordinating and encouraging gender equality policies, exactly as the WI has been. The political debates concerning the establishment of institutions and the agencies' degree of impact on policy outcomes have varied over time. For example, in Andalusia, a socialist parliament easily approved a women's institute, whereas in Galicia, a more conservative community, the regional parliament failed several times to establish an institute, therefore resulting in a later start to equality policies. Moreover, fast-track communities (such as Catalonia, Galicia, Basque and Andalusia), received policy competencies in areas such as health and education at an earlier point than the so-called slow-track communities. Health and education, important competencies for gender policies, were finally devolved in the late 1990s to the slow-track communities.

Even though the basic purpose of regional agencies is the same, two important organizational factors demonstrating institutional strength must be examined: type of agency and department or governmental area where they are located (Bustelo, 1998; 2004). We assume here that the best type of agency is an 'autonomous organism,' like the '*institutos*' which have their own budget and are created by law (as opposed to the '*direcciones generales*' which depend directly upon a governmental department and its decisions). Moreover, the preferable governmental area for agencies is the 'presidency' area because, first, this area's competencies span across other governmental areas and, second, it gives femocrats a better position for persuading colleagues in other governmental departments (as opposed to, for example, the 'social affairs' area, which might imply that (in)equality is mainly an issue for marginal women).

Changes in the institutional positioning of regional agencies have also taken place over time. Some regions began with interdepartmental commissions and later established autonomous institutes. The general trend has been to establish more 'autonomous organisms' and to move them into the presidency area (see Tables 11.2 and 11.3). However, recent changes in the opposite direction have occurred. Some regional governments have changed 'women's agencies' from the presidency area to a 'Family and Social Affairs' Department (for example, Castile-Leon ruled by the People's Party and Aragon ruled by the Socialist party), or to a specific Department of 'Equality and Social Affairs,' as in Andalusia. Due to recent political change in Galicia towards the left,[5] the Galician

Table 11.2: Institutional framework of Spanish Regional Gender Policies 1998

Governmental area/Type of organism	Presidency	Welfare/Social affairs	Culture	Family, Women and Youth
Autonomous organisms	88 *Andalucía* (PSOE/PA) 93 *Aragón* (PP/PAR) 89 *Cataluña* (CiU) 88 *País Vasco* (PNV-EA)	94 Canarias (CC/PP) 91–95 Navarra (UPN-PP)		91 Galicia (PP)
Woman's General Directorates (or similar structures)	86–97 Cantabria (PP/PRC) 90 Baleares (Interdepartmental Commission) (PP)	89 Castilla-La Mancha (PSOE) 89 Madrid (PP) 88–97 Comun. Valenciana (PP/UV) 94 Castilla y León (PP)	88–91 Extremadura (PSOE) 88–95 Asturias (PP)	
Other non-specific structures	91–97 Murcia (PP) D.Gnal. Youth, Women and Family	88 La Rioja (PP) D. Gnal. Social Welfare		

Table 11.3:　Institutional framework of Spanish Regional Gender Policies 2006

Governmental area/Type of organism	Presidency	Welfare/ Social affairs	Others
Autonomous organisms	89 Cataluña (PSC/ERC/ICV) 88 País Vasco (PNV) 90–2000 Baleares (PP) 89–2002 Castilla-La Mancha (PSOE) 91–97–2002 Murcia (PP) 88–95–99 Asturias (PSOE)	88 Andalucía (PSOE/PA) 93 Aragón (PSOE) 94 Canarias (CC/PP) 91–95 Navarra (UPN-PP) 91–2005 Galicia (PSOE/BNG)	88–91–2001 Extremadura (PSOE) (Culture)
Woman's General Directorates	86–97 Cantabria (PSOE/PRC)	88–97 Comunidad Valenciana (PP/UV) 94 Castilla y León (PP)	89 Madrid (PP) (Work and Women)
Other non-specific structures		88–2003 La Rioja (PP) D. Gnal. Family and Social Action	

Equality Service (*Servizo Galego de Igualdade*, SGI) moved from the old department of family to the new Department of Equality and Welfare, which is held by the vice-president of the Galician government. The impact of these recent changes, along with that of the national level 'Equality Policies General Secretariat,' remains to be assessed.

Equality plans have been the main tool for articulating gender equality policies at the national and regional levels in Spain.[6] Regional women's policy agencies have developed their own equality plans which involve several governmental departments in the administration's effort to advance equality. Equality plans are a set of aims, objectives and actions, approved by the Cabinet (both at the national and regional levels), to be carried out in a concrete period of time by the different governmental departments involved in each action. The plans vary regarding the number of actions, the concrete nature of actions, the relative importance given to each set of actions and their corresponding budget allocations.

All regions have approved equality plans (see Table 11.1). Some regional agencies are now developing their fourth or even fifth plans (Catalonia). Unlike other Spanish regions, Andalusia never approved a third general plan, thus the region's second plan (1995–97) was its last. Nevertheless, the Andalusian Women's Institute (*Instituto Andaluz de la Mujer* – IAM) has remained an active policy agency in the areas of gender violence, employment, education, health, social policies and cultural activities. At the national level, specific plans on gender violence were also approved from 1998. These plans emerged as a result of gender violence becoming an extremely hot issue in Spain. Many regions have also approved violence-specific plans which normally coexist with the general equality plans.

After twenty years, equality plans are still the main instruments that articulate equality public policies in Spain. However, the policy instruments of 'gender units' and equality laws have recently been introduced. The former may be defined as programmes or structures for implementing gender mainstreaming within public administrations. Both instruments are analysed below.

In addition to the national equality law, which was approved in March 2007,[7] five regional equality laws have already been approved since 2002 in the regions of Navarre, Castile-Leon, Valencia, Galicia and the Basque Country.[8] The most recent and complete is the Basque 'Law for the Equality of Women and Men'. From our point of view, using laws as a policy instrument allows for more comprehensive public actions regarding gender issues than equality plans. One limitation of equality plans is that gender policies tend to remain almost exclusively in the executive branch. Conversely, laws permit gender action to fully enter the legislative and the judicial branches (for the latter, if sanctions are imposed when the law is broken). The introduction of laws is a step forward in Spanish gender policies, at least formally, and may turn Spanish state feminism's historical 'power of persuasion' (see Valiente, 1995) into a 'power of sanction'. In other words, a change from 'soft' to 'hard' measures and legislation may be occurring. In fact, some femocrats view equality laws as a new opportunity in gender public policies. The director of the Basque Women's Institute (*Emakunde*) considers laws part of an evolutionary process and, in her view, and especially for the feminists who decided to 'enter' the state, they constitute the next step in the conquest for recognition and legitimization of the term 'positive action' (Bustelo and Peterson, 2005). In our view, socialist femocrats are now far more conscious than before of the need for stronger instruments after being in government from 1982–1996 and out of government from 1996–2004.

Many variables come into play when assessing equality laws, including the laws' preparation, articles and relationship to previous equality plans. The equality law's length of preparation and elaboration is crucial. For example, in the case of the Basque law, a long preparation period signalled greater participation of the different actors and stakeholders involved. There are other significant differences between the Basque law and the other four laws. Differences in the law's articles are quite striking: from the two very general articles of the Navarre law to the well-defined principles and well-organized five general titles, eighty-three articles, and sixteen final dispositions of the Basque law. Indeed, the Basque regional gender policies have the reputation of being the most advanced and developed in the Spanish scenario.

The first four regional laws are quite general and 'soft'[9] compared to the Basque law, meaning that if they are substituted for equality plans and solely remain in the symbolic realm, they might even be an excuse to relax concrete and specific actions. Therefore, the overall impact of laws in promoting a more equal society depends on their relation to equality plans. For example, in the case of Galicia, the approval of an equality law seems to be a good excuse for interrupting an equality plan.[10] In contrast to a concrete equality plan, the Galician law is written in quite general terms, thus meaning the law could be interpreted as a step backwards in gender policies. Interestingly enough, the Basque law is not only supposed to be compatible with past plans, but the very law obliges regional and local powers to have equality plans of their own. Castile-Leon's law, similar to the Basque one, establishes – although not in obligation terms as in the Basque Law – equality plans for the regional and local levels (as well as for other public institutions). The other existing regional laws have no mention of equality plans. The (in)compatibility of the new laws with the former equality plans is certainly a worthy topic for future research.

The second new instrument developed in Spain is the so-called 'gender units'. Andalusia and Cantabria have gender units (created in 2000 and 2005 respectively) and the Basque law has considered the establishment of small 'gender units' in the different governmental departments and institutions of the Basque public administration. The oldest unit – the Equality and Gender Unit – was created by the Andalusian Women's Institute in cooperation with the Andalusian Directorate General of European Funds. This unit provides the Administration with a stable support structure to implement and consolidate gender mainstreaming in the region. Its main aim is to facilitate the integration of a gender perspective in the formulation, implementation, monitoring and evaluation of the plans, programmes and services developed by the Andalusian regional government (*Junta de Andalucía*). This unit has been quite successful at offering gender training and creating teams to introduce a gender perspective within different programmes and services inside the region's public administration. However, because the unit was created with

European Funds, which will no longer be as generous in Spain due to the entrance of the new East European countries, and because it is a programme run by an external consultancy agency and not a stable structure, its continuity during the next years is yet to be seen.

Gender units are a direct product of the gender mainstreaming discourse which is strongly encouraged by European and international actors. European institutions have greatly impacted gender policy in Spain since the early 1980s. During Spain's negotiations to enter the European Community, feminists in the Socialist Party used the need to be European as an argument for the establishment of the Women's Institute (Valiente, 1995). The WI represented Spain at the EU level from its establishment in 1983 until 2004 when the new Equality Policies General Secretariat assumed this role.

The European Union has mostly impacted Spanish gender policy by providing a legal framework for gender equality policies. The EU framework gives legitimacy to Spanish women's demands, accelerates reforms of Spanish gender policies through transposition of EU gender legislation into national law, and encourages the creation and development of women's governmental and non-governmental equality organizations (Lombardo, 2003, pp. 164–5). However, some inaccurate transpositions such as the parental leave Directive into the Spanish Conciliation law of 1999[11] suggests that the 'Europeanization' of Spanish gender policies, although clear, has its limits, both in regard to the limits of the EU gender policy itself, mainly focused on employment, and in the very implementation process of gender policies by the Spanish governments and their attitude towards gender issues (Lombardo, 2003; 2004).

In addition to international influences on policies, the development of gender policies at the local level must be taken into account. In 1985, through the Basic Law on Local Government (*Ley Reguladora de las Bases de Régimen Local*), municipal powers were established. The following year, the WI and the Spanish Federation of Municipalities and Provinces (*Federación Española de Municipios y Provincias*) jointly recommended that municipalities should create interdepartmental commissions, or even independent institutes, to promote equality between women and men. Municipalities often publish equality plans and offer services such as temporary childcare services, computer and language classes, and recreation. Although some municipal services for women existed in the 1980s, municipal agencies became more common throughout the 1990s (see Valiente, 1998; Ortbals, 2004).

Discussing the evolution of institutional frameworks, instruments, and policy outcomes is not sufficient for explaining variation between regions.

Policy discourses have also evolved in a differentiated way, depending not only on political ideology, but also on institutional strength and the issues addressed. Interpretations of gender equality are multiple and sometimes even contradictory. The discourses in the Basque Plan and the Madrid Plan (regarding the issues of family policy, politics, and violence) demonstrate great variation in the interpretation of gender equality from region to region (Bustelo and Peterson, 2005). The two regions are remarkably different in how they conceptualize gender and inequality. While both represent gender dimensions with a focus on the social categories of women and men, power relations are absent in the Madrid policy discourse while the Basque country does pay attention to power. For instance, gender inequality in politics is represented by the Basque plan as a problem of male domination in politics while the Madrid discourse attributes the problem to women, emphasizing that women should be encouraged to participate the way men do, hence adapting to the male norm. Generally speaking, structural inequalities that cut across gender are almost entirely absent in the Madrid policy discourse. This contributes to the impression that women's interests and needs are conceptualized as essentially fixed disregarding class, race, ethnicity, sexuality, etc. Although references to diversity in Spanish gender discourses are still quite rare, the Basque Country policy discourse includes some explicit references to other structural inequalities that intersect with gender at least in two of the three issues analysed; family policies and domestic violence.

Fragmented relationships: women's movements and the state

Although the landscape of institutional frameworks, policy instruments, and discourses informing Spanish gender policies is fragmented and more research about such themes is necessary[12] (Bustelo, 2003), enormous gains in Spanish gender policies in the last two decades must be applauded. Feminist activism has also diversified and expanded since the transition to democracy. During the transition to democracy, feminist goals included abortion rights, divorce, sexuality, education, and equality in the workplace.[13] In the 1980s, feminists gained many rights, including divorce and abortion options, and they began interacting with newly established women's policy agencies. Initial feminist opinions regarding the national Women's Institute ranged from supportive to 'very sceptical' (Valiente, 1995, p. 223). Relationships between Spanish women's agencies and feminist organizations have typically been weak, with collaboration limited to subsidies and the latter giving advice about equality plans through women's councils (*consejos*) (Valiente, 1995).

Scholars note that feminism has become 'boring' in recent years (Camps, 1998, p. 13) and/or has quieted due to feminist organizations' desire to obtain subsidies from the WI (Valiente, 2001a). The health of the national women's movement is indeed questionable due to its broad discourse on feminism and the sporadic nature of national feminist meetings during the 1990s and 2000s. Whereas the transition era produced a lively women's movement fighting for the above-mentioned policy goals, the current movement is highly fragmented, with movement organizations proffering discourses of difference feminism, Muslim feminism, lesbian feminism, equality feminism, and recreational associationalism. Moreover, in the past fifteen years, the Spanish feminist coordinator (*Federación de Organizaciones Feministas del Estado Español*) has held only two national meetings, in 1993 and 2000.

Although movement fragmentation is substantial, we argue here that diversity in the movement yields many active women's organizations that pursue various goals and maintain relations with the state. To demonstrate this argument, we explain three dynamics. First, we explain feminist scepticism in the last decade due to conservative party governance. Second, we document the mixed record of women's policy agencies regarding lesbian, religious, and ethnic identities. Finally, we discuss relations in regions and municipalities, concluding that collaboration between organizations and agencies is stronger at the subnational than the national level, but that friendly relations depend on the women's organization and the political context at hand.

As noted above, the PP-led WI was an active agency between 1996 and 2004; yet its impact was questionable in debates about gendered violence, parity laws, and non-sexist education. Feminists were aligned with the PSOE on its 1999 comprehensive law against gender violence, thus they were frustrated when the PP voted it down. The 2004 change of government made possible the comprehensive law against violence, which passed in 2005, without PP objections, and to the satisfaction of many feminists.

The 2004 return of the PSOE also advances parity goals. Women's organizations that fight for parity (e.g. Lobby of Europe; Federation of Progressive Women) are often affiliated with the socialist party (Valiente, 2005b; Jenson and Valiente, 2003), whereas the PP's strong discourse against positive discrimination and quotas (Bustelo, 2004) means that it has not been able to embrace the movement. As noted above, the PP-led WI did not pursue parity measures (Valiente, 2005b). However, Rodríguez Zapatero immediately formed a gender-balanced cabinet and the new equality law will maintain a national quota.

Feminists were also dismayed with the PP's LOCE education policy. The Spanish feminist coordinator, education unions, and the United Left political party converged to protest against the LOCE in a campaign called 'For a quality education for all girls and boys' (*Por una educación calidad para todas y todos*). Furthermore, in late 2003, feminists criticized the WI for firing a top femocrat who had worked on education policy since the 1980s, arguing that few feminists were even left at the agency. When returning to power, the PSOE vowed to reform education and allowed the rehire of said femocrat.

Each of these policy areas demonstrates frustrations on the part of feminists; yet, the most symbolic and outrageous breakdown of relations occurred in 2003. The WI director, Miriam Tey de Salvador, had publishing interests[14] in a book about prostitutes, entitled *All Women are Whores* (*Todas Putas*). The book enraged feminists; they mocked the Women's Institute and asked that the director step down. Instead of celebrating the 20-year anniversary of the WI, feminists argued that the director 'caused a great damage to the Women's Institute . . . with respect to [its] public image . . . [and its] credibility' (*Red Estatal de Organizaciones Feministas contra la Violencia de Género*, 2003). Despite criticisms, Tey remained the WI's director until 2004, whereupon the incoming PSOE government appointed a new director. Improvement in relations since the return of PSOE governance is demonstrated by the questionnaire response of one feminist organization. The respondent states, 'our opinion of the [current] WI is very positive . . . but relations during the eight years of the People's Party government had been practically void'.[15]

One should note, however, that parts of the women's movement, primarily rural women and businesswomen, were pleased with policy outcomes of the PP-led WI. Rural women, removed from adequate social services and recreational opportunities, often feel alienated. Empowering rural women requires state assistance, and accordingly they desire better childcare options, assistance for aging persons, and job training (AFAMMER, 2006). Rural women collaborated with the PP-led WI on several occasions, most notably when the WI helped organize and fund the III Worldwide Conference of Rural Women in Madrid in 2002. Moreover, rural women have participated in European Union employment programmes, which the PP-led WI supported. In fact, one prominent rural women's organization reported that the PP is the party that does the most to create equality between the sexes in political, economic and social life.[16]

Although women's policy agencies, both national and subnational, have attended to the interests of rural women, they have not privileged other identities. In fact, some lesbian organizations have perceived state feminism as a negative influence. At the 2000 national meeting of feminists, a Catalan lesbian organization suggested that the current women's movement was more conservative and heterosexual than earlier stages of Spanish feminism. They presumed that this was partially due to feminism's incorporation into state institutions and its inclusion of activists who do not wholly embrace lesbianism. The group also cited their goals of legal recognition, shared motherhood, and marriage rights. The 2005 PSOE law permitting same-sex marriages helped achieve these goals, though some lesbian voices claim the law benefits gays more than lesbians.[17] Finally, equality plans have largely discussed sexuality in a heteronormative way, solely relating it to issues such as maternity and menopause, thus lacking an 'intersectional perspective on gender and sexual orientation' (Platero, 2005a; 2005b, p. 3). Even the latest WI equality plan (2003–06) is silent on these matters.

Spanish women's policy agencies have also responded awkwardly to Muslim women's identities. Although the latest WI equality plan (2003–06) acknowledges multiculturalism, it does not mention Muslim identity. Moreover, equality plans largely portray immigrant women as an unempowered and endangered group that is subject to sex trafficking and in need of education (Instituto de la Mujer, 2005). The 2002 debates about whether a Moroccan girl could be barred from a *concertado*[18] school for wearing a headscarf manifested these uneasy dynamics. The PP education minister argued that the headscarf was a symbol of discrimination; the WI was not vocal on the matter, and some feminists concurred that the scarf 'represents the submission of women' (*El País – Nacional*, 20 February 2002). However, when the region of Madrid[19] permitted the girl to attend school wearing the headscarf, the Muslim women's organization *An Nisa* (The Women) was pleased, arguing that the headscarf is 'voluntary' and a 'fundamental right of one's own image' (Rodríguez Aparicio, 2002). Activists at a 2005 international congress on Islamic feminism in Barcelona concurred that Muslim womanhood does not necessarily connote submissiveness and inequality and asserted that 'feminisms must be more inclusive' (International Congress on Islamic Feminism, 2005). The WI funded the Barcelona conference and its new director expressed her support for its themes (*ABC Cataluña*, 28 October 2005), therefore suggesting that the current WI is embracing a more empowering view of Muslim women.

Initial evidence shows that subnational agencies respond better to diversity. The Andalusian Women's Institute (IAM), for example, embraces Gitana feminists, who are active through the ROMI women's organization. ROMI holds the IAM in high regard (Asociación de Mujeres Gitanas ROMI, 2002). Regional and municipal administrations have also recognized sexual orientation, with the Basque Country and Catalonia notably utilizing an intersectional approach. The former discussed sexual orientation in its latest equality plan (1999–2005), promotes activities that persuade against discriminatory attitudes, and incorporated references to 'multiple discriminations' (e.g. race, ethnicity, disability, sexual orientation, etc.) in its new equality law (Platero, 2005b, p. 15).

Subnational women's policy agencies offer women's movement actors several additional advantages. Collaboration between subnational agencies and organizations is often greater than has historically been the case at the national level. Questionnaire data from Andalusia and Galicia indicate that regional women's agencies have interacted with more women's organizations than the national Women's Institute. In 2002, 37 of 47 women's organizations reported that none of their members had attended activities, such as conferences and job training, hosted by the WI, yet only three organizations report that none of their members had attended activities hosted by their respective regional policy agency (Ortbals, 2004). Face-to-face communication with subnational femocrats is more likely because women can meet with them at regional and municipal agency locations.

The regional cases of Andalusia and Galicia further demonstrate subnational relations. The Andalusian women's movement is loosely knit, with organizations located in the cities of Seville, Granada, Cordoba, and Montilla since the 1970s.[20] The Andalusia Women's Institute has assisted many feminist organizations through subsidies. For example, the IAM has financed and published a book about single parenthood authored by *Acaná* (Association of Women that Confronts Maternity Alone) and it contributed funds to the 2000 national feminist meeting hosted by the Assembly of Women – *Yerbabuena* in Cordoba. Questionnaire data confirm the positive impact of the IAM. In Andalusia, 27 of 30 organizations either 'agreed' (24) or 'very much agreed' (3) that the IAM helps women in the Andalusian community (Ortbals, 2004). Despite these positive data, one must note that some feminists, while viewing the institute positively, recognize it as a bureaucratic agency that is not as radical as their own feminist organizations.

Galician feminist organizations, though grouped into several organizations, have shared many goals including the promotion of Galician nationalist culture (Ocampo, 2002). Galician feminists have not preferred institutional feminism and, in the late 1980s, argued that a regional women's institute would dampen the women's movement (*Mulheres Nacionalistas Galegas*, 1989). The Galician parliament rejected propositions for an 'institute' in the late 1980s and later established the Galician Equality Service (SGI) in 1991. Feminists especially disapproved of the conservative (PP) regional administration's family policies (Santos, 1992; Ortbals, 2004). The regional family ministry was deeply concerned about the region's declining demographic growth and proposed measures to assist families with many children, thereby potentially encouraging women to have more children. Given that the women's policy agency was ascribed to the family ministry, feminists were angered that the region was promoting women's traditional identity as mothers and pronatalism, rather than feminism.[21] The Vigo municipal Women's Department, unlike the SGI, maintained strong, positive relations with Galician feminist organizations during the 1990s. The department, under leftist leadership for much of the 1990s, financed an education booklet featuring Galician women, compiled statistics about Galician women, and worked alongside feminists to enact a non-sexist toy campaign. The nationalist feminists of Galicia, without close relations with regional administrators during this time period, sincerely valued the Vigo women's policy agency.[22]

Relations with feminists in Galicia, though strikingly poor throughout PP governance, should not be extrapolated to describe relations with all women's organizations or current relations with feminists. Twelve of 17 Galician organizations responded to a questionnaire stating that they either 'agreed' (10) or 'very much agreed' (2) that the SGI helps women in the Galician community (Ortbals, 2004). Moreover, the SGI has documented in its magazine the many conferences and activities it has held with rural and housewives associations. SGI relations with feminists are likely to change in the near future due to the 2005 Galician election which resulted in a leftist coalition government.

Although certain municipalities have furthered feminist goals, they are not all ripe with feminist activism. In the absence of feminist organizations in smaller municipalities, cultural[23] and rural associations are the women's movement *vis-à-vis* women's policy agencies. Cultural associations are easy to dismiss; yet, their goals are complex, they far out-number feminist organizations, and they capture the attention of women's policy agencies.[24] The goals of cultural associations include integrating themselves in their communities, pursuing culture, sharing one another's anxieties, and paying attention to senior citizen women. Although they hold the more feminist goals of pursuing equal opportunities and professional development, their activities consist of cultural trips, handicrafts, coffee breaks, and informal chats.[25] The salience of such activities may be linked to socialist feminist thought in the 1980s which favoured recreation as a means to bring women out of the private sphere and raise feminist consciousness (Partido Socialista Obrero Español, 1980). The growth of associations may also be attributed to women's policy agencies, for agencies often express that women should participate publicly through associations and throughout the 1990s and 2000s they offered associations subsidies and hosted recreational events for them (Ortbals, 2004).

Similar to numerical growth in subnational associations, growing international connections of the women's movement should be recognized as a significant trend. The Spanish Coordinator for the European Women's Lobby's (*Coordinadora Española para el Lobby Europeo de Mujeres*, CELEM) most important goals – to further equality in political and social representation, seek equal employment conditions for women, and fight gender violence – hinge on national and international factors. The new PSOE national administration, on account of its comprehensive violence law and equality law, positively influences the organization's goals. CELEM's goal of improving women's employment, however, greatly depends on the European Union's employment insertion programmes. Because the PP emphasized job training and favoured such EU programmes for women, this movement goal is less dependent on party governance. Even in the conservative region of Galicia, EU employment programmes have benefited women, particularly rural women who face limited employment opportunities.

Conclusion

Spanish institutional feminism quickly developed over the last twenty years, thereby leading to a diverse and fragmented institutional landscape not only at the national but also at regional and local levels. The last decade at the national level was characterized by People's Party leadership of the WI, which did not drastically reduce what the socialists had accomplished during the first decade of Spanish state feminism. Nonetheless, the March 2004 arrival of the socialists has already yielded a stronger bureaucratic commitment to feminist goals, both at the institutional level through the creation of the Equality Policies Secretariat and in terms of outcomes related to parity government, equality programmes, the violence law, and the future equality law.

At the regional level the landscape is even more uneven. Although the overall landscape today is much more favourable to the PSOE than in the 1990s, each regional political context in Spain is quite specific in impacting regional machineries, thus Spanish state feminism, in unique ways. Although there has been a tendency for creating autonomous institutes under the governmental area of presidency, regions differ according to new policy instruments, such as equality laws and 'gender units,' and in terms of discourses, which inform gender policies. Through the general discourse of programmes and services detailed in equality programmes, the gender mainstreaming discourse has greatly impacted national and regional Spanish policies. However, the gender mainstreaming strategy has been practised in various ways, with some regions utilizing the new policy instrument of 'gender units'.

The Spanish women's movement is also fragmented, with goals pertaining to sexual identity and parity democracy as well as rural identity and recreation. As a result, relations between policy machinery and the women's movement depend on movement actors, political parties, and administrations. Andalusia, with a leftist administration, yields satisfactory relations between femocrats and women's movement actors. Alternatively, Galician feminists had strained relations with the PP-led regional agency (1991–2004) even when many non-feminist actors approved of the agency. The Galician and Andalusian cases, though contrasts in terms of feminist and agency relations, indicate that more interactions occur between movement actors and agencies at the regional level than the national level.

Gender violence policy at the national level also demonstrates the complex impact Spanish parties have on state relations with the women's movement and policy outcomes. The final approval of the comprehensive violence law at the end of 2004, which is internationally recognized to be one of the most advanced laws of its kind, can be considered a great victory of the feminist movement. Although feminists were aligned with the PSOE and other left parties about the issue, one cannot discount the fact that the PP had maintained public attention, programmes, and resources about violence through an official 'domestic violence frame'. While the PP frame is a *degendered* one, it helped keep alive the alternative *gendered* frame held by the feminist movement (Bustelo, 2004).

Because PP-led policy agencies and discourses have at times been beneficial to women, it is tempting to identify all equality instruments and all policy discourses in current Spain as 'state feminism'. Moreover, it would be easy to label any Spanish women's activist, politician, or bureaucrat, who favours equality and takes a policy stance about it, as feminists. We, however, conclude that recognizing Spain's new diverse landscape does not mean that feminist progress is everywhere. We applaud the proliferation of policy agencies and diverse activism among Spanish women, acknowledging that Spain's strides have largely been in a forward direction. Nevertheless, we recognize that some policy styles and movement actors do not approach politics in the most feminist-gendered way, allowing for pockets of conservatism within Spain and leaving some feminists asking whether an institutional approach to feminism is sufficient. A quotation by one women's organization aptly explains our generally positive yet realistic understanding of Spanish equality policies after more than twenty years of rapid and diverse developments:

> Right now we are in good times, for equal opportunity politics in Spain has strengthened the role and activeness of the women's institute and has considerably improved relations with women's organizations. Moreover, the work of some feminist organizations in recent years has strengthened the social position of all women's organizations and their capacity to impact the design of policies, although difficulties persist in certain contexts.[26]

Notes

1. Feminist strategies included the punishment and rehabilitation of perpetrators, violence prevention, and improved bureaucratic responses to victims. The PSOE administration raised awareness about violence, trained police officers, and opened centers for victims (see Valiente, 2005a).
2. The *integral* (comprehensive) law defined violence as a woman's issue and recommended stiff penalties for male perpetrators.
3. In Spain, abortion is only legal 'when women have been raped; when pregnancy seriously endangers the physical and psychological health of the mother; and when the fetus has malformations' (Valiente, 2001b, p. 115).
4. The 1978 Constitution established two tracks to autonomy. The fast-track regions received competencies – including education and health – from the very beginning.
5. In June 2005, after more than 20 years of conservative PP governance, the PSOE and the BNG (a nationalistic left-centre party) are governing in coalition.
6. The WI issued its first equality plan in 1988.
7. Ley Orgánica 3/2007, de 22 de marzo, para la igualdad efectiva de mujeres y hombres (Organic law for the effective equality of women and men).
8. Navarre approved the first law in 2002 (*Ley Foral 33/2002*). In 2003, Castile-Leon (*Ley 1/2003*) and Valencia (*Ley 9/2003*) approved laws. Galicia approved a law in 2004 (*Ley 7/2004*) and the Basque law was approved in 2005 (*Ley 4/2005*).
9. Although more analysis is needed, the non-Basque laws are different in their general content and vague terminology such as 'to promote' and 'to stimulate'.
10. The former director of the SGI, when asked about the budget devoted to the law's implementation, said that the budget assigned to that IV equality plan could be used because they could 'interrupt' it after the law's approval (answer of SGI director Marta González to a participant's question in the Conference on Beijing + 10, Madrid, 4–8 March 2005).
11. The parental leave Directive into the Spanish Conciliation law of 1999 was interpreted not as an individual right, but as a leave linked to the mother who can transfer up to eight weeks to the father. Thus, and contrary to the

European Directive spirit, it has been understood as a right exclusively of the mother who can, if she wants, hand it over in part to the father.

12. Evaluations of Spanish gender policies commissioned by the national and regional agencies so far have conceptual and methodological limits.

13. For information on feminism during democratization, see Escario, Alberdi, and López-Accotto, 1996; Valiente, 2001a.

14. Tey was a 'professional with a previous career in the private publishing sector' (Valiente, 2005b, p. 190).

15. The authors administered a brief questionnaire to approximately ten organizations during 2006. Statements taken from the questionnaire remain anonymous.

16. One rural organization indicated its preference for the PP on the aforementioned questionnaire.

17. Some voices are critical due to the lack of debate about how marriage impacts lesbians. Lesbians are concerned that marriage, as a heterosexist institution, privileges men (thus gay men). They also do not want to be represented as feminine versions of male homosexuality (i.e., gay women). See Platero, 2005a; 2005b; 2006.

18. *Concertado* schools are private schools that receive public funds.

19. Regions have education policy competencies, thus the ultimate decision was of the Madrid region.

20. For example, Seville feminists are organized through a municipal coordinator. The Assembly of Women – *Yerbabuena* of Cordoba is also a prominent regional organization because it hosted the 2000 national meeting of Spanish feminists. Finally, the Assembly of Women – Granada have actively protested and explored feminist theory since the early 1980s.

21. Such policies included family plans of action, family education initiatives, and family centres.

22. Personal interview with *Mulheres Nacionalistas Galegas*.

23. Another way to identify cultural associations is by their own identification with *lo lúdico* or *lúdico-recreativas*, which in English translates poorly to recreation (Ortbals, 2004).

24. In 1994, cultural associations constituted 46 per cent of women's organizations in the Madrid region whereas feminists groups accounted for only 20 per cent (Colectivo IOÉ, 1996). Well over 1,000 women's organizations are present in Andalusia, yet only two are feminist affiliated with the national coordinator.

25. Goals and activities of associations are samples from 2002 questionnaire responses (Ortbals, 2004).

26. This quotation is an anonymous response to the authors' 2006 questionnaire.

12
Swedish State Feminism: Continuity and Change

Christina Bergqvist, Tanja Olsson Blandy and Diane Sainsbury

Introduction

In an international context, Sweden and the other Nordic countries have attracted attention because of their policies to combat inequalities between women and men and their high rankings on various gender equality indicators. Central to the countries' gender policy regime have been policies to encourage women to become earners and men to become carers, such as individual taxation, provision of affordable childcare, and generous paid parental leave with rights of leave for mothers and fathers. Women have further benefited from the social democratic welfare regime, which has promoted equal social rights. The countries also established women's policy agencies – or gender equality agencies in Scandinavian parlance – at an early date (Bergqvist et al., 1999; Sainsbury, 1999).

As the policies took shape, Helga Hernes (1987) formulated the concepts of state feminism and the woman-friendly state. These concepts have been important for three reasons. First, they provided a handle for understanding an aspect of gender politics, previously ignored, as well as the new policies emerging in Scandinavia since the 1960s. Second, the concepts offered an alternative to anti-statist feminist theorizing that precluded thinking about feminist politics inside the state; and third they broke with a universalist view of the patriarchal state, underlining that the state and state policies were variables and not constants.

Ironically, the initial explanations of the rise of woman-friendly policies failed to consider or even rejected women's activism or gender politics as a factor. Instead the major explanations emphasized an egalitarian political culture, the dominance of the Social Democratic party and its ideology of equality, and state–society relations (Adams and Winston, 1980; Ruggie, 1984). The failure can also be traced to the picture of the Swedish women's movement in the international literature, stressing that co-optation, partisan loyalties and corporatist arrangements made the movement ineffectual (Eduards, 1981; Gelb, 1989; Elman, 1995). Recent feminist research has challenged this interpretation, documenting the importance of women's collectivities and individual actors in shaping gender equality policies (Bergqvist, 1994, 2004; Hobson, 1999; Sainsbury, 1999, 2004).

However, in contemporary literature the picture of a weak movement survives as researchers rely on earlier scholarship, unaware of the re-vitalization of the Swedish women's movement. The resurgence of the movement has involved generational renewal, a strengthening of radical feminism and a broadening of its strategic repertoire to include new forms of protest politics, various types of networking and even forming a feminist party.

This chapter examines change and continuity in Swedish state feminism during the past decade – focusing on gender mainstreaming and EU membership. Initially we outline the political context, and then we describe the gender policy machinery and developments since the mid-1990s. Subsequently we analyse the relationship between the machinery, gender equality policies and the women's movement. We are interested in the role of movement actors in shaping policies but also the feedback effects of policies on movement politics. What role did femocrats and the women's movement play in putting gender mainstreaming on the policy agenda? And how has gender mainstreaming affected the gender equality agencies and other state agencies – and more broadly the opportunity structure? We also analyse the dynamics of EU membership and how the EU has shaped the opportunity structure. Although many women feared that EU membership would undermine welfare state and gender equality policies, feminists and femocrats have also seen the possibilities for Sweden to have an impact on the EU's gender equality policies and in turn that EU policies could influence Swedish legislation in a positive direction.

The political context

The 1990s were a decade of neoliberal discourse and reforms to restructure the state. Restructuring consisted of welfare state retrenchment, with experiments in privatization of public services and monopolies, the introduction of New Public Management (NPM), increasing deregulation and decentralization, and the weakening of corporatism. Ten years on, many observers concluded that the retrenchment measures of the 1990s did not fundamentally alter the defining properties of the welfare state, and since the early 2000s expansive reforms have again been on the policy agenda.

The gender policy regime has also been strengthened through improvements in childcare and parental leave (Sainsbury, 2000; Lindbom, 2001; Bergqvist and Nyberg, 2002).

The most profound change in the institutional arrangements of the state has instead stemmed from Sweden becoming a member of the European Union in 1995. In joining the EU, a unitary state, with strong local and regional government by European standards, was grafted onto a system of multilevel governance. There were also several changes in legislation to bring Swedish laws into accord with the body of existing EU law, the *acquis communautaire*.

The decision to join the EU generated much controversy, dividing the country and creating strains on the party system. The EU referendum produced a narrow majority of 52 per cent for membership. After membership, opposition and negative sentiments have remained strong, as witnessed in the first election to the European Parliament in 1995 when half of the elected MEPs were EU critics, and the defeat of the referendum to join the Economic and Monetary Union in 2003. Although pro-EU attitudes have increased, there was still no majority for EU-membership in 2006 (SCB, 2006); and of all the member countries Swedish opinion has consistently ranked among the most negative before the 2004 enlargement.

The issue has also fuelled internal party disagreement, with the deepest divisions in the Social Democratic, Centre and Christian Democratic parties. The lack of support for the EU among many voters and members of the Social Democratic party has posed a special challenge to the party leadership. In attempting to deal with these difficulties, party leaders have pursued a two-prong strategy. To hold the party together, they tolerated opposition to the EU within its ranks. The first elected Social Democratic delegation to the European Parliament consisted of outspoken critics and enthusiastic advocates; critics were also included in the government and have held high positions in the party. The second prong of the strategy has been to attempt to influence the EU in policy areas assigned high priority by the Swedes, including gender equality.

A rightward swing in the electorate in the early 1990s seemed to portend further change; but this trend was reversed in the next election. In 1994 the Social Democrats returned to power, gaining 44 per cent of the vote, and backed by a left majority in the parliament (*Riksdag*). Until September 2006, they formed minority governments, headed by Göran Persson from early 1996 onwards, and supported by the Left Party and the Greens. After the failure of the right-centre parties to win the 2002 election, they, and especially the Moderates, toned down neoliberalism, veering toward the centre of the political spectrum. This strategy led to a victory in the 2006 election; and a four-party government, with the Moderates holding the position of Prime Minister, was formed.

A final change of the past decade has been the increased salience of immigration as a political issue. Compared to the other Nordic countries, immigration began earlier; and Sweden has a much larger share of foreign-born persons in its population. In 1991 the New Democrats entered the *Riksdag* on an anti-immigration platform with racist overtones. However, the popularity of the New Democrats, who had won 7 per cent of the vote, evaporated in the next election, and an anti-immigration party has failed to emerge, at the national level. Nevertheless, the election campaign statements since 1991 reveal increasingly unfavourable representations of immigrants, and in the 2002 election immigrants' integration was an issue (Boréus, 2006).

Policy machinery, gender equality policies and mainstreaming

During the 1970s and 1980s gender equality was transformed into a distinct policy area with its own agencies and legislation, and by the mid-1980s the core institutions were in place. Gender equality had already been integrated into Swedish welfare state policies and the labour market regime, and the establishment of the gender equality machinery did not change that, but rather complemented it. Here we briefly describe the organization of the gender equality machinery, policies and priorities and how they have changed since the mid-1990s. Then we go deeper into how gender mainstreaming has been pursued and its impact on existing arrangements.

Organization

Table 12.1 outlines the organization of Swedish gender equality machinery according to four different functions: the political function, administrative function, policy-advisory function and law-enforcing function.

Political function

Since 1976 the overarching responsibility for gender equality has been in the hands of the *Minister for Gender Equality*, who is a full-fledged member of the government. The existence of a minister signals that this area is of importance, although the minister in charge of gender equality has always had additional areas of responsibility but often no portfolio. The minister has a press secretary, a political adviser and an under-secretary.

Table 12.1: The organization of the Swedish gender equality machinery: national level 2006

Political function	Administrative function within the ministerial hierarchy	Policy-advisory function	Law-enforcing function	Ministerial location
Minister for Gender Equality • Press secretary • Political adviser • Under secretary	Division for Gender Equality (*Jämställdhetsenheten*)	Gender Equality Council (*Jämställdhetsrådet*)	Equal Opportunities Ombudsman (JämO) Equal Opportunities Commission (*Jämställdhet-skommissionen*)	Ministry of Industry, Employment and Communication and Ministry of Justice

Source: Adapted from Borchorst, 1999, p. 168.

The visibility and significance of the position has thus largely depended on the person holding it (Borchorst, 1999, p. 173).

Administrative and policy-advisory functions

The Gender Equality Division (*Jämställdhetsenheten*), established in 1982, assists the minister in the development of principles of gender equality policy, the preparation of gender equality legislation, and the co-ordination of this legislation with the other ministers. The Division's role in policy co-ordination has been strengthened by the principle of the collective responsibility of the government, as laid down in the constitution. This principle has resulted in the joint preparation of bills (*gemensam beredning*) and consultation on bills (*delning*). The Division is also responsible for special projects to promote gender equality and international contacts. It was originally placed in the Ministry of Labor Market Affairs and has since been moved to different ministries depending on the minister in charge.

There is also the Gender Equality Council (*Jämställdhetsrådet*) that meets with the Minister of Gender Equality four times a year. Initially the Council consisted of representatives from the women's movement; but when Anita Gradin became Gender Equality Minister in 1982, she broadened its membership to include the political parties, NGOs and the social partners. The Council has an advisory role; it is mainly an information clearing house and sounding board (Borchorst, 1999, p. 72). The exchange of ideas has flowed in both directions, and the Council has been consulted on controversial issues, like quotas and EU membership (Prop. 1993/94: 147, p. 19). In addition, special ad hoc advisory groups with think tank functions (*idégrupper*) have been set up, such as the masculine roles group, the daddy group, and the women in low paid jobs group (Pikkarainen, 2000, pp. 39–46).

Law-enforcing function

The Act on Equality between Women and Men at Work (hereafter the Equal Opportunities Act) came into effect in 1980. An Equal Opportunities Ombudsman (*Jämställdhetsombudsman, JämO*) and an Equal Opportunities Commission (*Jämställdhetskommissionen*) were then set up with the mandate to oversee the observance of the new anti-discrimination law. This legal turn took place after the first non-social democratic government in 44 years had come to power in 1976, and largely on the initiative of the Liberals. Centre-right governments governed until 1982 and backed the new legislation, which met with resistance from the social partners and the Social Democrats.

The scope of these agencies was limited, because they were mainly responsible for discrimination issues on the labour market not covered by collective agreements, which excluded most of the workforce. Eventually the Equal Opportunities Act and the role of JämO have been strengthened by expanding the scope of the law and positive measures. In 1994 collective agreements no longer could have precedence and all workplaces with more than ten employees have had to have a plan on how to improve gender equality.

To sum up, in an international perspective, gender equality policies have had a high political profile through the existence of a ministerial post at an early date; in a Nordic perspective, the policy area had a stronger administrative organization. Still, there has been a discrepancy between its organization and the encompassing goal of gender equality policies – to ensure that women and men have equal opportunities, rights and responsibilities in all major areas of life. As distinct from many other policy areas, there has been no central administrative agency to implement policies. This has stemmed from the co-ordinating role of the gender policy machinery. Finally, there has been an interesting institutional relationship between gender and diversity policies. Frequently the Gender Equality Minister has also been the Minister for Immigrant Affairs; and gender equality machinery and policies to some extent have served as a model for ethnic equality policies. In 1986 an ombudsman to combat ethnic discrimination, especially in the labour market, was created; and legislation eventually adopted in the 1990s prohibited discrimination against ethnic minorities and provided for positive measures. That the same minister has been responsible for gender equality and immigrant affairs led to an awareness of women immigrants' difficulties and their representation in the Gender Equality Council already in the 1980s.

The structure of the gender equality machinery at the national level has remained quite stable after the early 1980s, but since 1994 two significant changes have been introduced. First, the principle of mainstreaming has clarified that the national goals for gender equality are the collective responsibility of the Swedish government; each minister has a responsibility for gender equality issues in his or her own area. This means that each ministry is supposed to have its own organization for promoting gender equality. However, the Minister for Gender Equality has retained the main responsibility to co-ordinate and monitor the Government's gender equality policies with the help of the staff at the Division for Gender Equality and advice from the Council on Equality issues.

Second, a new level in the gender equality machinery has been introduced. There are now 21 gender equality officers attached to the county administrative boards that serve as an extension of central government authority. The municipalities also play an important role in the implementation of the national policies, but local authorities to a large extent can decide themselves how to deal with the issue of gender equality. In addition, two major changes under debate in 2006 were the establishment of a central administrative agency for gender equality and the creation of a single ombudsman office dealing with all types of discrimination, which we discuss in more detail later.

Policies and priorities

Initially in the 1970s and early 1980s gender equality was related to labour market issues. Thus, Sweden has been seen as a laggard concerning issues of violence towards women (Elman, 1995; Lindvert, 2002; Weldon, 2002a). However, since the mid-1990s a principal policy change occurred with a much stronger focus on issues about violence against women and sexual exploitation, leading to new legislation. In 1998 the government presented a bill called Women's Inviolability (*Kvinnofrid*), which included several measures to combat violence against women and prostitution (Wendt Höjer, 2002).

Besides a greater emphasis on the gender based power structure of society, there have also been improvements since the mid-1990s in the gender policy areas of longstanding concern, but no fundamental policy changes. For the most part, the policies can be characterized as more of the same. The so-called 'daddy month' in the parental leave scheme has been extended to two months. Many feminist activists, individual party women and men as well as the Equal Opportunities Ombudsman see the two months as a step towards a fully individualized parental leave legislation, which would give the mother and the father the same amount of time with no possibilities to transfer any time to the other parent (Borgström, Eriksson and Klinth, 2003). Similarly, the right to a place in pre-school has been strengthened through an Act on Childcare that clarifies the municipalities' obligation to provide childcare for all who need it. As a result public childcare provides places for a larger share of pre-school children today than in the early 1990s (Bergqvist and Nyberg, 2002).

The five priorities (focus areas) of the national action plan on gender equality for 2003–06, drawn up by the Social Democrats and their parliamentary allies – the Left party and the Greens – were an amalgam of women's longstanding demands, a radical feminist perspective, and gender equality focusing on both sexes. The first two were 'equal access to positions of power and influence' and 'equal pay for equal work and work of equal value'. The third reflected radical feminism and includes measures to combat 'violence *committed by men* (our emphasis) against women, prostitution and trafficking in women for purposes of sexual exploitation' and the identification of 'sexualization of the public sphere' as a problem that undermines gender equality. An additional priority was 'men and gender equality' (RS 2002/2003: 140, p. 4). Here the action plan emphasized two points: firstly, that a gender equal society would not be achieved unless men and women work together to transform the conditions that govern the lives of both sexes and, secondly, that men must acknowledge that existing relations of power serve to perpetuate an undemocratic system and the subordination of women (ibid., p. 8).

Gender mainstreaming

The Social Democratic government that took over in September 1994, after a three-year period with a centre-right government, declared that gender equality would be a top priority during the coming years, and that gender mainstreaming was a key strategy. In his governmental declaration Prime Minister Ingvar Carlsson stated: 'For the first time in the history of Swedish democracy the newly appointed government consists of an equal number of women and men. Through this decision I have deliberately wanted to create a model for gender equality efforts in all areas of society. The deputy Prime Minister will have the overarching responsibility to scrutinise in advance the government's policy and ensure that it contributes to gender equality in working life and the community' (Ds 2001: 64, p. 7). The appointment of a 'gender equal' government had a strong symbolic value, and subsequent governments have been composed of a more or less equal number of women and men.

How mainstreaming came onto the political agenda

The impetus behind gender mainstreaming in Sweden came from two domestic sources, and international influences – the adoption of gender mainstreaming in the 1995 Beijing Platform for Action at the UN Women's Conference and in the 1997 Amsterdam Treaty of the EU – added momentum. The first domestic source was the Liberal Minister of Gender Equality, Bengt Westerberg, and femocrats who launched the term in the government bill on gender equality presented in the spring of 1994. The second source was women's activism and the pressure it put on the Social Democratic party. In partisan terms the rise of gender mainstreaming reflected a recurring political constellation distinctive to gender politics in Sweden. Once again the Liberals and Social Democrats were vying for the role as the champions of gender equality.

The term 'mainstreaming' first entered official Swedish parlance in Westerberg's gender equality bill of 1994, which noted the existing mainstreaming functions of the Gender Equality Division; it acted as a co-ordinator and promoter of gender equality policies vis-à-vis the ministries by examining government bills and inquiry commission directives. Of the main instruments mentioned, several measures – gender statistics, funding gender equality research, and special women's projects – had long been in existence. The innovations were a proposal to set up gender equality machinery at the regional level and an effort to gender management by objectives. The bill also pointed out that the public sector reform of management by objectives instead of detailed regulations necessitated a stronger formulation of gender equality as an objective whose fulfilment determined budget allocations (Prop. 1993/94: 147, p. 77). In short, mainstreaming, as presented in the bill, contained elements of codification and new thinking. The bill also underlined a dual strategy, that mainstreaming needed to be complemented by selective measures.

Equally important was the resurgence of the women's movement in the early 1990s. The threat of major welfare state restructuring, women's scepticism towards EU membership and the drop in women's political representation in the 1991 election led to a mobilization of the women's movement. The issue of gender equality and plans to establish a women's party figured prominently in the 1994 election campaign. With the feminist network – the Support Stockings (*Stödstrumporna*) – taking the lead, women mobilized across the political spectrum to increase the number of women in elected office. After the election women's share in parliament rose from 34 to over 40 per cent (Sainsbury, 2005).

Furthermore the disastrous results of the Social Democrats in the 1991 election – their poorest election since 1928 – altered the opportunity structure, providing new possibilities of influence. Party women – both the women's organization and high ranking party members – stepped up the pressure. They urged the Social Democrats to demonstrate that they were a women's party so that there would be no need for the Support Stockings to form a party. Among their demands was that a feminist perspective pervade all policy areas, and this demand was written into the programme adopted by the 1993 party congress (SD, 1993, p. 20). In the 1994 election the Social Democrats pledged to integrate gender equality in a wide range of policies. More specifically, the Minister of Gender Equality in a new Social Democratic government would have the overarching and co-ordinating responsibility for gender equality issues, just as the finance minister has had for economic matters (SD, 1994, p. 4).

Mainstreaming measures

Among the first mainstreaming measures introduced by the Social Democratic government were gender training for members of the government, strengthening the requirement of integrating a gender equality perspective in the work of inquiry commissions, and inserting a gender equality perspective in key steering documents, such as budget directives and operating instructions of the national administrative agencies.

Obviously gender training is a prerequisite for implementing mainstreaming since decision makers and administrators responsible for all policies are to integrate a gender equality perspective in their work. The initial courses were for all the members of the cabinet, but gender training has gradually been extended to other staff members of the ministries and administrative agencies – and eventually to persons preparing materials that form the basis for decisions (Ds 2001: 64, p. 26, pp. 30–2).

Inserting a gender equality perspective into the work of the inquiry commissions is especially important because of their crucial position in the Swedish policy making process. In some cases the commissions actually draft legislation, and usually their reports form the basis of government bills. The Division of Gender Equality initially formulated a special directive that was attached to the instructions given to the inquiry commissions, and the special directive was incorporated into the general instructions issued to all inquiry commissions in 1998. Nonetheless, a follow up study showed that around one third of the commissions had adopted a gender equality perspective, one third had given reasons for not including a gender perspective in their work, and the remaining third had totally ignored gender (ibid.).

Gender equality was included in the general ordinance (*verksförordningen*) regulating the activities of all central administrative bodies. The other important steering documents are specific instructions concerning the responsibilities of a particular administrative body (*myndigheters instruktioner*) and budget directives, in which a gender equality perspective was inserted for several agencies. In 2004 roughly half of the agencies had special instructions, but the agencies dealt with a limited number of policy areas.

Among the most important recent steps has been the adoption of a long term plan to mainstream the ministries and increasing attention to the budget process and management by results (SK, 2005, p. 1). Each ministry formulated a plan to mainstream its work and appointed gender equality coordinators. The coordinators, together with the Division of Gender Equality's officer in charge of mainstreaming, formed an inter-ministerial working group for gender equality and monitored the implementation of the ministries' plans. Efforts to gender the budgetary process concern two crucial facets: 1) the allocation of funds and 2) performance management. Gender outcome analyses were conducted for all policy areas used in the budgetary process, resulting in the identification of 50 goals and several indicators, and 60 directives requiring agencies to report the gender equality activities to the ministries (Prop. 2005/06; GO 2006).

Nonetheless, two independent evaluations concluded that there was a lack of coherence and consistency in the government's steering and oversight of the agencies in the area of gender equality (Ds 2001: 64, pp. 35–6; SK, 2005, p. 1). In response to such assessments, the 2006 government bill on gender equality proposed the establishment of a new national administrative agency for gender equality to carry out the implementation of gender mainstreaming at all levels of government (Prop. 2005/06, p. 155). Parliament approved the bill, and the agency was scheduled to be established during 2007. However, the four opposition parties voted against creating a new agency, criticizing it as a bureaucratic and ineffective measure.

In summing up the developments of the last decade, the following definition of gender mainstreaming – the systematic incorporation of a gender equality perspective in all policies, at all levels, and at all stages of the policy making process – offers a useful handle. A gender equality perspective has successively been applied to an increasing number of *policies* since 1994: higher education and research (the appointment of women university professors), violence against women, prostitution and trafficking. The 2003–06 national plan for gender equality specifically extended the goal to the judicial system – the police and courts; integration, minorities and migration policies; and transport, IT and environmental policies (RS 2002/03, p. 140). By the mid-2000s a gender perspective had been inserted in all policy areas covered by the budget.

The most important innovation with respect to *levels* of policy making during the past decade was the introduction of gender equality officers at the regional level in 1994. At the local level, special projects have been started in several municipalities, but developments are uneven. The unevenness has been exacerbated by decentralization tendencies of the 1990s and budget pressures on local governments which are increasingly responsible for funding services. The 2006 government bill put renewed emphasis on gender mainstreaming at the regional and local levels.

Of critical significance were intensified efforts to insert a gender equality perspective into the preparatory and implementation *stages* of the policy making process. Most importantly, a gender perspective has been included at a new stage of the preparation of government bills through gender main-streaming of the ministries; and new coordination and monitoring bodies have been created. The budgetary process through performance management offers an additional tool for implementation.

The dynamics of EU membership

Sweden's joining the EU is often described as a significant event for the development of the EU's gender policy (Hoskyns, 1996; Hantrais, 2000). Many observers noted that the 1995 enlargement added momentum to the importance of gender equality issues in the EU, because of a greater number of women in parliament and the Commission. The entry of Austria, Finland and Sweden boosted women's representation in the European parliament from 24 to 27 per cent. In addition, as Sonia Mazey, points out Sweden and the other Nordic states were of vital importance in the process to successfully acknowledge and include gender equality in the Amsterdam Treaty (Mazey, 2001). A more recent example of the Swedish commitment to influence the EU gender policy were efforts to make equality between men and women a general objective in the draft constitutional treaty (Bergqvist, 2004).

Although the Swedish government has assigned high priority to influence the EU gender policy, more Swedish women than men voted against joining the EU and the EMU. In general, women have been more negative than positive, fearing that EU membership would undermine the welfare state and gender equality policies (Oskarson, 1996, p. 224). Hence, the general picture of the Swedish EU membership is that Sweden can contribute more to the development of the EU gender policy, than it actually can learn from it.

In this section we offer a more complex picture that takes account not only of adverse effects on domestic policy but also instances when EU membership has strengthened Swedish gender equality policies. Sweden has had to strengthen its Equal Opportunities Act several times in order to match stronger EU regulations. Furthermore, from a state feminist viewpoint, it is equally noteworthy that national gender equality agencies have perceived EU regulations as a new opportunity structure, and as we will see, femocrats have developed different strategies to influence the domestic policy process.

Levelling down policies

Looking first at examples of the 'levelling down' of domestic gender policy due to the EU, the most striking case is perhaps the European Court of Justice's ruling on the so-called 'Tham professors'. The Minister of Education, Carl Tham, introduced gender quotas to increase the number of female professors at Swedish universities. However, since the quotas gave women *automatic* precedence if they had sufficient qualifications, even when a man had higher qualifications, the ECJ rejected the preferential treatment for women, arguing that it conflicted with the EU definition of equal treatment that prohibits all forms of discrimination (Nyström, 2002, p. 226).

Another issue that provoked criticism and was seen as a setback for the Swedish gender equality principles was the implementation of the 1992 Pregnant Workers Directive. The directive introduced two weeks compulsory maternity leave following a child's birth. In Sweden, the parental leave legislation has had a gender-neutral design and according to the opponents of the adaptation to EU legislation the change did not improve the situation of women. The stipulation of maternity leave in the EU policy was thus considered as conflicting with the principle of gender equality and Swedish legislation (Sunnius, 2003, p. 238).

Strengthening policies

In contrast to the above cases, which were lively debated in the media and in the Parliament, much less attention has been given to instances when Sweden has had to sharpen its legislation in order to comply with EU rules and regulations (see Bergqvist and Jungar, 2000; Fransson, 2000; Nyström, 2002). There are major differences between the legislation in the EU and in Sweden. One important distinction is that the EU law promotes a strong anti-discrimination policy, while positive action has characterized the Swedish Equal Opportunities Act.

The discrepancy has been most obvious in the field of equal pay. The EU's equal pay approach emphasizes strong laws, individual rights and non-discrimination, whereas Sweden has traditionally regulated equal pay in collective agreements between the social partners, and not through legislation (Borchorst, 1999; Nielsen, 1996). Hence, the law and the courts are assigned a significant role in the EU, whereas active measures and collective bargaining rights are emphasized as the primary means of regulating equal pay in Sweden. Thus, prior to the adaptation to the EU legislation, there was a low level of individual protection and anti-discrimination provision in the Swedish Equal Opportunities Act.

The Equal Opportunities Ombudsman (JämO), who is responsible for the enforcement of the Equal Opportunities Act, played a crucial role in bringing about change. Shortly after Sweden had joined the EU, JämO began to take wage discrimination cases to the Labour Court, which is a special court dealing with conflicts in collective agreements and mainly composed of representatives of the employers and trade unions. Previously court cases had involved job discrimination – hiring and promotions – and JämO had never taken any wage discrimination cases to the Court. She argued that the adaptation of the Swedish Equal Opportunities Act to EU law permitted wage cases in the Court, even though the necessary changes were not yet enforced in the national law (*Göteborgs-Posten*, 17 October 1995).

However, since JämO won only one out of six cases, she started to call attention to discrepancies between Swedish and EU law and to criticize the Labour Court. Besides arguing that the Court lacked competence (in EU law) and it needed a more gender equal representation, she also claimed that the wage discrimination cases clearly illustrated the risk of a biased court. Since the social partners had already agreed on the wage in collective agreements, neither of their representatives in the Court wanted to declare the agreement invalid (Olsson Blandy, 2005). Finally, JämO argued that wage discrimination cases ought to be decided by ordinary courts, and not a specialized court where the social partners were in the majority.

JämO's actions helped produce a comprehensive revision of the Equal Opportunities Act to bring it in line with the EU law. Among the most important changes were prohibiting indirect discrimination, a definition of 'equal work', easing the burden of proof, and a definition of 'sexual harassment'. JämO's criticism also led to a questioning of the future role of the Labour Court in wage discrimination cases and eventually changes in the Court's composition so that the representatives of the social partners no longer formed a majority (Olsson Blandy, forthcoming; SOU, 2006: 22, p. 64).

Using the EU to influence domestic policy

The discussion above illustrates how the EU has provided new instruments and opportunities that JämO has used in the domestic policy process. There are, however, different ways in which the EU can provide domestic actors with new opportunities. The subsequent example demonstrates that when the EU Commission was preparing the first draft of the new equal treatment directive in the access to and supply of goods and services, the Swedish Division for Gender Equality perceived it as an opportunity to get a more inclusive anti-discrimination legislation in Sweden. In other words, the Division saw the EU as an arena to influence its *own* domestic policy.

The 2004 Equal Treatment Directive was a response to the important 2000 Racial Equality Directive, which not only prohibits discrimination in employment, but also in education, social protection (including social security and healthcare) and access to goods and services. As a result, the EU Commission's first draft proposal of the new equal treatment directive contained a clause that prohibited using sex as a basis to calculate insurance premiums and benefits. Since Sweden has no gender equality legislation in the private social-security sector, the Gender Equality Minister, Margareta Winberg, actively supported Commissioner Anna Diamantopolou. Winberg sent a letter to Diamantopolou supporting her draft proposal of the directive; she wanted to make sure that the commission's proposal on the equal treatment directive was as strong and comprehensive as the racial directive (Interview with Marianne Laxén, 2 December 2003). However, due to the opposition of several member states and intensive lobbying from the insurance industry, the final equal treatment directive was not as comprehensive as the racial directive in relation to insurance.

Nonetheless, it is interesting to note that the domestic equality agencies wanted to influence the EU gender policy *because* it would have an important effect on the Swedish gender policy. According to a division femocrat, the proposed directive was regarded as a great opportunity for Sweden to introduce anti-discrimination in the field of private social security insurance. 'We have tried to influence [the EU] precisely with the idea that it was a way for us to influence Sweden' (Interview with Cecilia Asklöf, 6 November 2003). This example clearly illustrates that the impact of the EU not always works in one direction (top-down), and that the multilevel government system in the EU can enhance the role of women's policy agencies.

One Ombudsman for all discrimination?

JämO is one of several ombudsmen in charge of combating discrimination, and the role of the ombudsmen and a more coherent anti-discrimination legislation came under debate when the commission on discrimination (SOU, 2006, p. 22) presented its report in February 2006. The main task of the commission was to review and consider a consolidation of Swedish anti-discrimination legislation in connection with implementing two EU anti-discrimination directives, the Racial Equality Directive prohibiting 'discrimination on the grounds of racial and ethnic origin', and the 2000 Employment Equality Directive against 'discrimination on the grounds of religion or beliefs, disability, sexual orientation and age'. The commission recommended that the different laws against discrimination should be combined into one more effective and comprehensive act. It also proposed that the existing four Ombudsmen – JämO, the

Ombudsman against Ethnic Discrimination, the Disability Ombudsman and the Ombudsman against Discrimination because of Sexual Orientation – should be merged into one authority, the Office of the Ombudsman against Discrimination (SOU, 2006, p. 22).

Of the four ombudsmen only JämO opposed an amalgamation. Both the current and former JämO claimed that the work for gender equality would lose ground and that gender equality would be less prioritised if JämO lost its current status. They argued that existing gender structures discriminated against women as a group and that women were not a minority. Accordingly sex discrimination was not comparable with other kinds of discrimination grounded on minority status, and the task of JämO was different from the other ombudsmen. Although they admitted that sex/gender was interrelated with ethnicity, they insisted that sex discrimination and gender equality required a separate organization. Many critics also argued that if an amalgamation were implemented it was important to establish a new central administrative agency for gender equality (Lundin, 2006). Opposition to an amalgamation was shared by representatives of Left Party, the new feminist party, Feminist Initiative (*Feministiskt initiativ*, FI) founded in 2005 and the two largest union organizations, the LO (The Swedish Trade Union Confederation) and the TCO (The Swedish Confederation for Professional Employees). Most of the political parties favoured one ombudsman for all kinds of discrimination. Their main argument was that one agency was more efficient and would be able to consider intersectionality.

Women's movement actors, femocrats and gender equality machinery

Women's movement actors and femocrats, as we have seen, were instrumental in putting gender mainstreaming on the political agenda. Movement actors were decisive to its adoption as the government's strategy, while femocrats have been key actors in implementing gender mainstreaming. In turn, the government's policy of gender equality and mainstreaming has created a new opportunity structure, opening up possibilities for feminists and movement actors. Feminist researchers from the universities and feminist statisticians from Statistics Sweden have been involved in gender training. Femocrats, feminist scholars and feminists who have started consulting firms were involved in developing methods for gender mainstreaming; and feminist academics have carried out policy evaluations assessing the implementation of gender equality policies and mainstreaming. To the extent that gender mainstreaming results in the proliferation of gender equality experts and officers in the public administration it could contribute to a further feminization of the state. Paradoxically, given its goal of permeating the entire administration, gender mainstreaming might result in stronger specialized women's policy machinery since the current administrative unit is under-dimensioned to handle such a formidable task. Women's movement actors and femocrats on inquiry commissions have suggested strengthening policy machinery, and the commission on gender equality policies recommended the establishment of a central administrative agency (SOU, 2005, p. 66), which the government included in its 2006 gender equality bill, despite criticism from several important administrative agencies and lukewarm or divided support among women's party organizations. In the run-up to the 2006 election, Feminist Initiative launched the most ambitious proposal to improve gender equality machinery. The party advocated strengthening the minister by creating a ministry, establishing an administrative agency, and setting up a parliamentary committee; it also defended JämO (FI, 2006, p. 5). The argument for strengthening the policy machinery is not to promote gender mainstreaming but to achieve major feminist policy goals.

Gender mainstreaming has both its advocates and critics in the women's movement, and disagreements undermine the prospect of its adoption as a movement strategy. The pros and cons revolve around a series of tensions. The first is the transformative potential of gender mainstreaming versus its susceptibility to being reduced to a variety of techniques. Proponents of gender mainstreaming emphasize its transformative capacity. According to them, incorporating a gender perspective reveals the male norm in structures and processes, thus disclosing the androcentric design of institutions, cultures and organizations. Proponents also claim that gender mainstreaming brings women's issues, which have been on the sidelines and marginalized, to the centre of the stage, elevating them to major policy issues (Rees, 1998; Jahan, 1995). Critics complain about the lack of transformative results of gender mainstreaming, stressing the difficulties of implementation and the possibility of integration into existing power structures. For many of them, gender mainstreaming has generated a discussion of methods and techniques – but little more. A second tension concerns the supposed pervasiveness of gender mainstreaming in its aim to encompass all decision-makers and all policies versus accountability and priorities. As aptly expressed, 'If gender is everybody's responsibility in general, then it's nobody's responsibility in particular' (Pollack and Hafner-Burton, 2000, p. 452). Similarly, if gender mainstreaming pertains to all policies then it is not necessary to designate priorities. More concretely, critics have expressed concern that gender mainstreaming is the focus of too much attention and will divert resources from special projects for women.

Special measures

Women movement actors have continued to utilize the second prong of the official dual strategy, the focus on women and special measures directed to them. For the women's movement in the 1990s the issues of violence against women, sexual abuse, prostitution and trafficking became of utmost concern. During at least the last 20 years the feminist movement, especially the shelter movement, has linked the issue of violence to sex, gender and power. Until the 1990s an explicit feminist perspective was rarely represented in public policy debates and legislation. In a study of the policy discussions since the 1930s Maria Wendt Höjer finds that an individualistic perspective on violence against women 'in part gave way to a feminist one, in which gender is the central analytic category' (2002, p. 213). Crucial for the reframing of the debate was the mobilization of the women's movement (including party women from left to right) and a commission on women's inviolability (*Kvinnofrid*) in 1995. The resulting legislation included a new kind of offence called *gross violation of a woman's integrity*, a wider definition of rape and the prohibition to purchase sexual services. The last measure is perhaps the most unusual and controversial as it only criminalizes the person (almost always men) who buys sex (Svanström, 2004; Erikson, 2005).

Another example is the inquiry commission on women and power which represented an enormous academic mobilization of over a hundred gender scholars and feminist researchers (SOU, 1998: 6, pp. 234–56). The commission made feminist research visible in the public debate; and, importantly, by engaging a number of younger scholars, help to assure the renewal of the feminist research community.

Additional special measures have been subsidies to women's organizations largely to improve women's political representation. From the early 1990s onwards women's organizing has assumed new forms. As put by Gunnel Gustafsson, a main feature of the women's movement has been its increasing diversity both in terms of who organize and how they organize (Gustafsson et al., 1997; cf. Rönnblom, 2002). The growing importance of networks has posed a challenge because the system of subsidies is tailored to formal organizations. Movement actors have called for a revision of the system to include networks; and a proposal to this effect is under consideration. In addition, gender mainstreaming of grants to other organizations, by inserting a gender equality perspective into the subsidies regulations, has been proposed. Organizations that receive funding would have to report on their gender equality efforts (SOU, 2004, p. 59).

In short, these examples demonstrate the importance of retaining a dual approach rather than substituting mainstreaming for special measures directed at women to rectify existing inequalities between the sexes. At the same time we find a close relationship between feminist politicians, femocrats and women movement actors. Some individuals move in and out of these different roles.

Conclusions and reflections

As distinct from several countries in this book, women's policy machinery has not been under attack in Sweden. The explanation of this involves several factors. The early establishment of the Minister for Gender Equality in the mid-1970s enjoyed the support of all the political parties. The ministerial position signalled the importance that the government, irrespective of its composition, has assigned to gender equality policies. The increased presence of women in parliament and party elites, along with the growing significance of women's votes and a resurgent women's movement, virtually make it political suicide to dismantle existing gender equality machinery. Opponents could accuse the government of failing women and undermining efforts to work for a gender equal society, which has been a national goal since the 1970s.

Nor has gender mainstreaming resulted in a weakening of the policy machinery. On the contrary, gender mainstreaming has become a major justification for strengthening the machinery and the government's proposal for a national administrative agency for gender equality. However, the change in government after the 2006 election may end the plans for a new agency. Moreover, the Swedish experience reveals the difficulties of fully implementing gender mainstreaming, even in a favourable setting; and it underlines the necessity of retaining a dual strategy.

The major impending change in the machinery was triggered by the implementation of EU directives. If the recommendations of the inquiry commission on discrimination come into force, a comprehensive anti-discrimination administration will supplant the gender equality ombudsman. The effects of such a reform are difficult to predict, especially without knowledge of the organizational details. A pessimistic scenario entails the realization of JämO's fears. A more optimistic scenario hinges on femocrats continuing to staff the new administration and the allocation of increased resources. Then the reform may be more formal than substantive, and the staff will be armed with stronger anti-discrimination legislation.

Despite possible amalgamation, the adverse ruling of the European Court on the Tham professors and the general scepticism of many Swedish women – women, femocrats, women politicians and the Swedish Women's Lobby have worked to influence the EU. Since joining the EU, women's share of MEPs has ranged from slightly over 40 per cent to nearly 60 per cent, and the Swedish commissioners have been women. Just as feminists viewed the state as a crucial arena, they – including the critics of membership – have transposed this view and their strategic repertoire to the EU. As shown in our analysis above, the impact of EU membership is complex, entailing gains and losses, and it is dynamic. The gains have included legal adjustments strengthening Swedish anti-discrimination legislation and a new opportunity structure. Femocrats, especially JämO and the Gender Equality Division, have attempted to utilize the EU in order to influence domestic policy. Thus the phrase 'the impact of EU membership' is a misnomer in that it implies a one-way process; in reality membership involves reciprocal influence.

The resurgence of the Swedish women's movement suggests a paradox that runs counter to the conventional wisdom – movement success has not resulted in complacency or deradicalization. Despite high rankings using various indicators of gender equality and the gradual strengthening of gender equality machinery, the feminist debate is robust and the movement is in the midst of a cycle of mobilization. Besides a dynamic of party competition, a contributing factor to the mobilization would seem to be rising expectations given the prominence of gender equality in the general debate and the fact that all the parties claim to be feminist. In turn this heightens feminist consciousness and expectations. The recent backlash in the media, attacking radical feminism and the feminist party, has embittered many feminists and strengthened their convictions that Sweden is a male dominated society that needs to be changed. An additional point is the problematic relationship between the movement and the state based on movement theory that emphasizes a strict demarcation between the two. Movement actors move in and out of the state, especially in the Swedish case given the strategic significance feminists have assigned to the state. For example over time several of the Support Stockings have acted as autonomous feminists, prominent gender researchers and femocrats. According to movement theory feminists are no longer movement actors when they are active in the state, but once outside the state they are movement actors.

Finally, state feminism has highlighted that the state is potentially a vehicle and arena for women's activism. Nevertheless, until fairly recently the state feminism literature has largely not problematized state variations and state–society relations. Instead it has focused on a single variable – the existence of and variations in women's policy agencies across post-industrial states. In working on this chapter, we discovered the importance of state structures to gender mainstreaming. On the one hand, the collective responsibility of the government and the lack of ministerial rule promoted embryonic forms of gender mainstreaming. On the other hand, the dual state – the division of the executive into ministries and semi-autonomous central administrative agencies – currently poses a problem in implementing gender mainstreaming, and it has prompted a discussion of the organizational reforms that are necessary for implementation. In other words, both existing state structures and shifts in the institutional terrain have contributed to the changing face of state feminism in the Swedish case.

13
Women's Policy Agencies and Climate Change in the US: the Era of Republican Dominance[1]

Dorothy E. McBride

Since the 1960s, the US government, like those in Western Europe, has responded to demands from the women's movement for policies to achieve sex equality, gender equity, and improvement in the status of women. However, US policy makers have never thought of women's policy agencies as the first step toward achieving those goals; thus, there has never developed a permanent cross-sectional agency assigned responsibility for women's issues and status.

Possibly the most famous commission in the US is the Equal Employment Opportunity Commission (EEOC) established to enforce Title VII of the Civil Rights Act of 1964. Rather than the product of women's movement activism, EEOC was a target of lobbying by activists to enforce the anti-discrimination law. EEOC has the power to investigate complaints, conciliate between employers and complainants, and file suits against employers. Since sex discrimination was one of a long list of prohibited employment practices in the Act, there is some question whether the EEOC qualifies as a women's policy agency.[2] Nevertheless, it has had a major impact on women's legal rights through its responsibility to issue guidelines interpreting the law principally in the 1970s. Then, under the leadership of Eleanor Holmes Norton, EEOC was a pioneer in developing the doctrine of indirect discrimination (called *disparate impact*) and established sexual harassment – both *quid pro quo* and hostile environment – as a prohibited form of discrimination in US employment policy (Meehan, 1985). Both EEOC and government advisory commissions with more specific mandates to study and make recommendations to improve the status of women played important roles in the emergence of the second wave women's movement in the US. Following President Kennedy's lead in 1961, all 50 states established commissions on women and, during the 1970s, each President formed his own version of a national commission.

These had multi-issue mandates and were largely advisory to the Chief Executives. Presidents of the Right and Left appointed feminists, but there were uneasy relationships on a political level when commission recommendations seemed to depart from Presidential priorities and perspectives. From time to time there have been proposals to establish, through Congressional statute, a commission that is independent of the President. However, there is no unified support for such a commission. The US women's movement is diverse – some might say fragmented – and is riddled with ideological divisions. Many activists are not feminist.[3] Thus, there is great concern that a national commission would become the captive of one or another ideological wing of the movement and, under the institutional authority of Congress, support policies opposed by the others. Whether cross sectional national women's policy machinery comes about continues to depend on the interests of each President.

State feminism in the 1990s

In the absence of a permanent multi-issue national agency, US women's policy machinery at the federal level in the 1990s was characterized by small, single issue committees and agencies scattered throughout the bureaucracy without any central coordination. Some of these have been established by specific legislation (as far back as 1920). Others have been created by executives – the President or by Secretaries or undersecretaries of major executive agencies. At the federal level, therefore, femocrats work in a variety of offices remote from power, ranging from those that are quite permanent with statutory authority to those that disappear with a change in presidential administrations or majorities in Congress.

One exception was the White House Office of Women's Initiatives and Outreach established by President Bill Clinton initially to develop support for his re-election. Later it played a key feminist role in the partial-birth abortion debate (McBride Stetson, 2001c). The other was the Congressional Caucus for Women's Issues (CCWI) composed of all women members of Congress. The CCWI reached its greatest success in the 1980s and early 1990s when it sponsored a series of bills to address pensions, insurance, child support, day care, tax reform, and family leave. It was also a partner for movement actors attempting to limit the harsh impact of the 1996 welfare reform (McBride, 2007).

Many state governments had federally mandated Sex Equity Coordinators in vocational education offices. Nevertheless, the dominant pattern at the state level remained the women's commissions, either advisory to the executive or stand alone, inspired by the commission movement of the 1960s (Parry, 1998; Stewart, 1980). The pattern of women's commissions has varied with shifting political conditions. Several of the state-level machineries and a handful in the larger cities and counties on the coasts have conducted research, disseminated information, and advised policymakers for decades, sometimes in overtly feminist ways (e.g., the Michigan Women's Commission). All such units are supplemented by, though not necessarily coordinated with, the activities of hundreds of offices, committees, and councils dedicated to specific policy areas including rape and domestic violence, women's health, early childhood development, and workforce development.

Previous research on policy making about abortion, political representation, prostitution, job training, and welfare has shown that effective alliances between women's movement actors and these national and state agencies have been rare: in only two policy debates (of 13 studied) did femocrats help women's movement activists achieve their policy goals (McBride Stetson, 2001b; 2001c). One was the role of the Office of Initiatives and Outreach in President Clinton's veto of a ban on abortion procedures. In the other, vocational education sex equity coordinators in the states banded together to lobby Congress to keep special programmes for women in a reauthorization of federal funding (McBride Stetson, 2001b). Both successful alliances occurred in the 1990s, at the federal level, when women's movement organizations formed a permanent lobby in Washington and Democrats held either the Presidency or one house in Congress (Boles, 1993).

Specific agencies for specific issues in the 1990s

The Women's Bureau of the Department of Labor presents itself as the oldest women's policy agency, established by Congress in 1920 to advance the interests of working women. It typifies the US approach to women's policy machinery – a small office within one of the departments of government with a mandate limited to one issue. In the 1970s, the Women's Bureau became the administrative core of an equal employment policy campaign for stronger enforcement of anti-discrimination laws and ratification of the Equal Rights Amendment to the constitution. In 1978, the Director, who is appointed by the President and must by statute be a woman, became part of the Office of the Secretary. For many years the Bureau had authority to review all policy proposals in the Labor Department relating to women and equality in the workplace. The activities, influence, and effectiveness of the Women's Bureau depend a great deal on the perspectives of White House staff and the President's agenda. From 1992–8, the Director was a feminist and a union activist. She promoted the interests of all sorts of women in the workforce and was determined to keep the question of 'what does this mean for women?' at the forefront of policy debates.

The *Defense Department Advisory Committee on Women in the Services* (DACOWITS) was established in 1951 by Executive Order of the President. Composed of 15 civilian members, it has authority to make recommendations only to the Defense Department relating to the recruitment and retention, treatment, employment integration and well-being of women in the Armed Forces. From time to time it has turned out to be an advocate for equality for women in the military and since the 1950s, many of the barriers to their participation have been removed. In the 1990s, DACOWITS also weighed in on issues of status and promotion, retention, health care, child care, training, and sexual harassment.

After a campaign by women's health movement activists, in 1991 the Department of Health and Human Services (DHHS) set up the *Office on Women's Health* (OWH) 'to improve the health of American women by advancing and coordinating a comprehensive women's health agenda throughout the DHHS to address health care prevention and service delivery, research, public and health care professional education, and career advancement for women in the health professions and in scientific careers' (US DHHS, 2005). Well funded and enjoying bi-partisan support, the OWH quickly accrued a relatively large (for a US women's policy agency) staff and a budget to fund model health programmes and conferences. It established women's health coordinators in the Food and Drug Administration, the Centers for Disease Control and Prevention, National Institutes of Health and other agencies in DHHS, a network of regional coordinators and liaisons with women's health offices in the states. It also had a mandate to present policy initiatives.

These agencies represented the state of women's policy machinery in the US in the mid-1990s. Since then, such agencies have been subject to quite momentous shifts in political and state alignments which came to fruition over the late 1990s and early 2000s. These changes – commitments to international agreements, reconfiguration of state/regional arrangements, and dominance of a right-wing party – are similar to changes in many European countries. The remainder of this chapter examines these changes, their effects on US femocrats, and the implications for women's movement activism and influence.

The context: climate changes in the state and politics

There are three changes in the state and politics that are important for the relations between women's policy agencies and women's movement organizations in US policy making since 1995. The first relates to a rare incursion of international institutions into the mix. Domestic opposition to any role for the United Nations in US policy making and the historic reluctance of the US Senate to ratify international treaties, such as the Convention on Elimination of All Forms of Discrimination Against Women (CEDAW), have meant that any significant shift in the authority of the federal government to supranational institutions is unlikely. At the same time, with the expansion of transnational communications, non-governmental organizations have used the UN agencies as forums for advocacy, which in turn provides additional political resources to domestic women's movement actors as well as femocrats. It was just this situation that occurred after the Fourth World Conference on Women at Beijing in 1995, providing an opportunity for a slight expansion of state feminism.

The second state change in the decade was the devolution of national responsibilities to states and localities especially in areas of welfare and job training policies. Despite the constitutional provision that delegates only a few policy powers to the federal government and reserves policy issues such as labour, family, education, criminal and civil law and policy to the states, since the 1930s Congress has used its powers to spend money and to regulate interstate commerce to dominate the domestic policy agenda. The build-up of federal policy eventually provoked a backlash. As far back as the Nixon administration in the 1970s, right-wing leaders have called for a *New Federalism* which would reduce the federal reach and reposition the states as the prime movers and laboratories for policy making and administration. What is involved in the new federalism is to reduce federal rules and requirements and let the states use the money as they see fit. The idea of transferring federal government policy responsibilities to the states appeared to resonate with the public, enough so that Bill Clinton claimed to be representative of 'New Democrats' who were willing to consider ideas that would reduce government spending, balance the budget, and empower the states. As governor of Arkansas in the 1980s, he had come to national prominence through his leadership in revamping welfare and education policies (Osborne, 1990). He also led the way for development of the National Governors Association as a powerful lobbying group. These forces – ever more popular Republicans, the New Democrats and the National Governors Association – combined in the 1990s to fashion a dramatic shift in welfare policy: the Personal Responsibility and Work Opportunity Reconciliation Act of 1996. PRWORA eliminated the federally enforced entitlement to the poor and gave a great deal of discretion to the states to achieve the general goal of reducing welfare rolls by pushing recipients (mostly lone mothers) into the workforce (McBride, 2007). This triumph of devolution set the stage for continued decentralization for the next decade.

The third shift is both political and institutional: the entrenchment since 2001 of a solid Republican party majority in national executive, legislative, and judicial institutions committed to a neoliberal economic system and a social regulatory agenda.[4] This change is more than just alternation of governing parties. The Republican leaders have been united by a set of beliefs about the role of government to an extent unprecedented in American politics. On the one hand, they envisioned reduced taxes, individual and private solutions to social and economic problems, devolution to the states, and support for market mechanisms. On the other, they maintained that government must embody particular moral values founded on traditional Christian teachings. They are supported by a strong network of foundations, lobbying organizations, scholars, and think tanks. In governing, the White House has used the President's vast appointment powers to place people pledged to promote the party 'line' in every executive and administrative office and, where possible, among Congressional staffs and in the judicial branch. The victory of the right-wing in US policy making is arguably the most significant shift of the early 2000s.

Even before its full success, Republicans showed their disdain for what they considered 'special interest' agencies and the growing power of the right-wing had had a chilling effect on women's policy machinery. As early as the 1980s, President Reagan went after the women's policy offices in the Department of Education. Those that were not eliminated were starved of funds. At the same time, they made little effort to establish agencies that focus on women. In Congress, the Congressional Caucus for Women's Issues (CCWI) had flourished when the Democrats had the majority; when Republicans took over in 1995, all 'legislative service organizations', including the CCWI, lost official support. Members of Congress could continue to join, but their staffs were forbidden from promoting or coordinating caucus-sanctioned actions. Like most of its peer caucuses, the CCWI reincorporated as a private, non-profit think tank of sorts: Women's Policy, Inc. (Gertzog, 1995). It remains in existence but is composed only of women members of the House of Representatives, not the Senate.

The effect of climate change on agencies and femocrats

International influences: commitment to the UN plan of action

Although a federal comprehensive women's policy agency had not been put in place for nearly 20 years, the UN Beijing Conference prompted

President Clinton to establish the President's Interagency Council on Women (PICW) in August 1995, just before the conference convened. Rather than a new body, the council was a mechanism for launching projects across the major departments of government: Health and Human Services (DHHS); Justice; State; Labor; and the Agency for International Development. First Lady Hillary Rodham Clinton took the position as Honorary Chair giving the agency a high profile in the administration. After the first few years when DHHS Secretary Donna Shalala was the executive chair, Secretary of State Madeleine Albright took the position and moved the PICW to the State Department.

The PICW worked through interagency groups on specific issues, most with an international, rather than a domestic, focus: women and the global economy; women and prisons; rural women (in developing countries); trafficking in women and girls; gender and institutional change; micro-enterprise development. Vital Voices, promoting women in democracy around the world, got its start through the PICW (Vital Voices, 2006). The anti-trafficking initiative had the most lasting effect on US policy. President Clinton made the issue a top priority in 1998 and the PICW working group on the issue found allies in Congress to enact a comprehensive statute strengthening the judicial and social resources to prosecute trafficking and protect its victims. However, in the process, the policy debate frame shifted from a focus on women victims of trafficking toward gender neutral references: as a result the Trafficking Victims Protection Act of 2000 referred to victims as 'any person coerced into labor or sex' but not identifying the victims as women and girls (except in the preamble to the law).[5] Nevertheless, the act did define sex trafficking to include both coerced and non-coerced prostitution although only coerced prostitution was subject to serious prosecution (McBride Stetson, 2004).

As a women's policy agency, PICW had more political resources than administrative ones. It was, essentially, a Cabinet committee which established a group of sub-committees composed of bureaucrats and femocrats from within its member agencies. There was no separate staff or budget and a very general mandate to 'make sure that all the effort and good ideas [of the Beijing Conference] get implemented when we get home' (PICW, 2000). Whatever clout it had came because it comprised the most prominent women in government – First Lady Hillary Rodham Clinton, Secretary of State Albright, Secretary of Health and Human Services Shalala, Attorney General Janet Reno, Labor Secretary Alexis Herman – all with a feminist commitment to the letter and spirit of the Beijing Plan of Action. Despite the high powered membership, the PICW served at the discretion of the President.

Others in the women's movement were inspired to implement the Plan of Action in the United States. Former Congressional representative Bella Abzug and Leslie Wolfe, President of the Center for Women's Policy Studies, developed the 'Contract for Women in the United States' endorsed by over 80 women's movement organizations. It came as close as anything in the US political discourse to the idea of gender mainstreaming: 'to adapt major recommendations from the Platform for Action to a national grassroots campaign to make women's concerns central to policy making at federal, state and local levels' (Onyango, 1996). The PICW was not an ally in this effort probably because its mandate was primarily to deal with international issues.

The PICW did try to reach out to the grass roots by holding a series of regional meetings and a large national satellite-networked conference in 1996 to obtain recommendations for the Beijing + Five report on the US for 2000. However, when it came to assessing the leadership provided by the PICW for promoting the Plan of Action in the US, movement actors gave it low grades for failing to act decisively to attack problems of women's poverty and rated other efforts in education, health, and economic status, mediocre at best. The most progress was in placing women in power and decision making positions, as reflected of course, in the PICW itself (US Women Connect, 2000).[6]

In this instance, influences from the international level spurred the government to establish a women's policy agency which promoted a policy agenda largely supported by the women's movement organizations. The high status of the members brought visibility to the Beijing Platform into domestic politics. The primary achievement was a stronger policy on trafficking. The moment was brief and had no lasting effect on the strength of US women's policy machinery.

Devolution of policy authority: the New Federalism

There were trends toward establishing this new state form in the 1980s, led by the Reagan administration: (1) the Job Training Partnership Act of 1984 which pushed the private sector to take leadership in providing job training and decentralized the administration to the states; and (2) the Family Support Act of 1988 which empowered the states, for the first time, to develop policies that did not follow the federal policy of Aid to Families with Dependent Children (AFDC also referred to as 'welfare'). An exception to this trend was the Vocational Education Act of 1984 which maintained a strong federal role in directing federal funds to help special groups, including women (McBride Stetson, 2001b).

With the passage of PROWRA in 1996, devolution was entrenched in national policy. Thus, the reauthorization of the Carl D. Perkins Vocation and Applied Technology Education Act in 1998, called Perkins III, followed suit by eliminating many federal mandates, especially those relating to lone parents, displaced homemakers, and gender equity. Also left up to the states was the option to provide their own funds for the full time Sex Equity Coordinators who had successfully promoted gender equity since the 1980s. The immediate effect of Perkins III was that only a few states continued to fund a women's policy office for vocational education, losing important women's movement allies in the states (McBride Stetson, 2001b).

Whereas devolution may close some federally supported doors for women's policy agencies, the new social and economic responsibilities of the states have the potential to open doors for leadership by their women's policy agencies. They long have been most active in tackling issues related to the economy because, relative to controversial issues like reproductive rights and affirmative action at least, the debates over work and education tend to be less ideologically charged and are thus 'safer' subjects for advocates positioned *inside* the government itself (Parry, 1998). By framing welfare reform in terms of expanded educational opportunity, child care availability, and equal pay enforcement, women's agencies could direct policy in a pro-woman direction without arousing the suspicion of the Right.

Further, the shift of policy authority to the states has drawn the attention of interest groups and policy analysts. The recent studies by the Institute for Women's Policy Research (IWPR, 2004) provide, for the first time, a wide range of comparative data on the status of women in the states. Nevertheless, my review of the state women's policy agencies websites documents only 35 agencies out of 50 states. Of these, 25 report that they have statutory authority, most based on laws passed in the 1970s. At the same time, 10 or 40 per cent of these 25 agencies list special activities for helping welfare mothers get job training and jobs and/or programmes for training, often in non-traditional occupations. This survey shows a great deal of variation in size, mandate, and activities among the structures. One of the most interesting, in the context of devolution, is the Tennessee Economic Council on Women. Established in 1998, in the wake of welfare reform, its powers include reporting and recommending to the state government in areas of job training, educational opportunities, pay equity, and domestic violence. Its 2005 report on job training directed attention in part towards problems of gaining self-sufficiency for welfare recipients (Tennessee Economic Council on Women, 2005), moving into a gap left by devolution of welfare policy.

Overall, devolution has closed more doors for state feminism than it has opened. It has changed policy processes and substantive outcomes in the very areas of policy that are important to the status of women: welfare, job training, and education. Devolution has reduced the reach of federal agencies, and few state commissions have moved to fill the vacuum.

The era of Republican dominance: 2001–2007

With the Republicans in power, the Congressional Caucus for Women's Issues continued to organize as a members' organization in Congress and work in a bipartisan way on a variety of issues. The issues that draw such bipartisan support often pertain to violence and sexual assault. In 2003–04, for example, the CCWI sought to require the Pentagon to have a comprehensive policy regarding sexual assault of women in the military. Another initiative involved attention to women small business owners and increases in US support for the UN Development Fund for Women (UNIFEM) an agency that also foregrounds prevention of violence. In the 109th Congress which ran from 2005–07, CCWI added international sex trafficking to their agenda. These issues – violence, trafficking and small business – are the only ones that find some support in the Republican majority.

The Bush administration dismantled the President's Interagency Council on Women, removing any top level systematic attention to compliance with the Beijing Plan of Action and multi-issue policy machinery. Bush is also the first president with no White House office or staff assigned to communicate with organizations interested in women's issues. Thus, the Republican dominance has severely restricted the already limited US women's policy machinery that has a multi-issue scope. Have femocrats in specific offices for specific issues in the departments of government met the same fate? The answer is mixed; there are three types of machinery in this Republican-infused cold climate: 1. Dead and Frozen Agencies; 2: Chilly Femocrats; and 3: Warmer Offices.

Dead and frozen agencies: Women's Bureau; DACOWITS

The Women's Bureau has always been a tiny agency, but its Directors are Presidential appointees, they have had a direct line to the Secretary of Labor, and many took the opportunity to promote equity for women at work aggressively. One of the most important functions of the Bureau was to provide information on the status of women in the workforce and to inform women of their legal rights. Since 2001, there has been a dramatic shift in the mission and scope of the Bureau. While there used to be over 20 fact sheets documenting the changing status of women in the workforce freely available, by 2005 there were only two, although the WB does provide access to reports on women workers from the Bureau of Labor Statistics.[7] The top Bureau initiative is 'Strengthening the Family' rather than promoting women's rights and equality. Another effort focuses on women small business owners. Under the Bush WB, a topic such as 'better jobs' includes initiatives in nursing, mentoring programmes in science and engineering, and training military spouses while the goal of 'better earning' points women towards information on managing their money rather than earning more of it or getting equal pay. The Bureau was charged with providing training in non-traditional occupations under the WANTO (Women and Apprenticeship in Non-Traditional Occupations) Act of 1992, but the Republican Congress shut down the programme in 2002, relieving the Bureau of this obligation. For those who remember the activist Bureaus of the past three decades, it is difficult to lose an insider advocate for working women. The Bureau, established by Congressional statute, still has 10 field offices in the regions which the Bush administration has tried unsuccessfully to eliminate.

Unlike the Women's Bureau, DACOWITS did not have the protection of statutory authority (it had been established by Presidential order at the request of Secretary of Defense George Marshall in 1953). In 2001, Defense Secretary Donald Rumsfeld tried to eliminate DACOWITS, considered by some in the right-wing as 'insubordinate' for recommending the removal of barriers to women's service in the Navy and Special Forces. Saved by the intervention of military veteran Representative Heather Wilson (a Republican), DACOWITS' mission was recast. It is no longer the agency to promote the status and equality of women in the military; instead, its current directive limits its attention to health care for service women and the effects of deployment to Iraq and Afghanistan on family life. It still does its annual report to Congress on gender representation in the military.

Chilly femocrats at health and human services

Under the Republican hegemony, the climate is chilly for femocrats at the Department of Health and Human Services (DHHS), although they continue to retain their mission and resources. The largest public bureaucracy in the world (according to former secretary Donna Shalala) has a network of offices on women's health led by the Office on Women's Health (OWH). These date from the early 1990s, when activists from the women's health movement made a big fuss about the kind of research and services DHHS was turning out. In short, all we seemed to know about health was based on studies of men, not women. The mission has not changed since 1991; officially the charge is to insert attention to women in all aspects of federal health policy and to establish networks through-out other national agencies and in the states (US DHHS, 2005). The OWH also advises the Secretary and Assistant Secretary for Health on scientific, medical, ethical and policy issues related to the advancement of women's health in the US and internationally. The idea of inserting attention to women in health policy resembles European gender main-streaming, although it does not always focus on comparisons between women and men, but treats women as a special group.

By 2005 there was a rather impressive (by US policy machinery stan-dards) array of offices for women's health coordinated by OWH in the DHHS Secretary's office (the head is a Deputy Assistant Secretary for Women's Health) including at the Center for Disease Control and Preven-tion (CDC); Food and Drug Administration (FDA); Office of Research on Women's Health (ORWH) at the National Institutes of Health (NIH); Regional Health Coordinators in the 10 regions of the DHHS; Office of Minority and Women's Health in the Health Resources and Services Administration and liaisons for women's health in all other HHS agen-cies. OWH initiatives are wide ranging. There is a National Women's Health Information Center (NWHIC), established in 1998, which has a website and newsletter making a vast array of information available to women. There are campaigns for improving health, especially of minority women. OWH lists the following as the specific areas of women's health on its agenda: girl and adolescent health; breastfeeding; heart health; older women's health; violence against women; reproductive health; HIV/AIDS in women; breast health; environmental health; international health.

Despite this apparent activism, the femocrats at the OWH have to walk a careful line in one area central to women's health, that is, repro-ductive issues. Early in the Bush administration feminists found bogus studies on the DHHS website that showed a link between abortion and breast cancer or undermined the use of condoms to prevent HIV/AIDS (National Council for Research on Women, 2004). These are no longer on the website; in fact one can find information on what are termed 'birth control methods'. Further, charges that the Bush administration promotes abstinence masked as scientific research is not borne out in the materials available through OWH and the NWHIC. Still, there is no information on abortion as a health matter for women.

The frustration of working in a women's policy office in the era of Republican dominance is often borne in silence by femocrats who do what they can for women within the constraints. For some, however, the burden becomes too great. This was the situation in August 2005 when Dr Susan F. Wood resigned her position as head of the OWH at the FDA to protest the way agency officials stonewalled efforts by health professionals and women's advocates to make Emergency Contraception (EC, or Plan B) available over the counter in drug stores. There is evidence that the policy bosses responded to the dominant right-wing belief that EC is a form of abortion despite scientific authority to the contrary (Harris, 2005).

The legal status of the health policy machinery is mixed. Some of the offices were established in congressional legislation, while others could be removed by the President. Since the late 1990s, women in Congress have filed the Women's Health Office Act, legislation to give the OWH statutory authority. The bill would essentially institutionalize the OWH and the other offices at HHS in their present form. This effort reached its greatest success in 2002 when the House of Representatives approved the bill (H.R.1784). The Senate has never considered it. In January 2005 it was introduced again but was not taken up by a committee.[8]

Warmer offices: Office on Violence against Women and International Women's Issues

The Office on Violence Against Women (OVAW) was established in the Department of Justice by the Violence Against Women Act (VAWA) in 1995. The result of a successful feminist strategy, the VAWA placed the issue of rape and domestic violence solidly on the national agenda. It strengthened federal laws and authorized substantial federal funds to promote services, protections, and prevention programmes for victims; these projects have had a major impact on the way states treat domestic violence (Laney, 2004). At first, the Office was in a central location at the Department of Justice where it focused on policy issues as well as administering grant and information programmes. However, by the end of the Clinton administration, it was demoted to the Office of Justice Programmes and limited to technical aspects of grant making. Despite the overwhelming majority of Congress that reauthorized the VAWA in 2000, the Bush administration made no changes in the Office location.

In 2002, Senator Joseph Biden (D-Del) who has long championed a strong federal role on the issue of violence against women, won approval of a bill to establish the Office of Violence Against Women as a permanent, separate and independent office in the Justice Department (42 USC 3796).[9] Under this law, the Director is appointed by the President with Senate confirmation and reports directly to the Attorney General.

The law also set forth the duties and functions of the office to include development of policy, development and management of grant programmes, and leadership in coordinating federal policy under VAWA. VAWA gave also gave policy mandates to the US Attorneys, the Immigration and Naturalization Service, FBI, Health and Human Services (Office on Women's Health), civil and criminal divisions at the Justice Department and part of Housing and Urban Development, Labor and Defense Departments. There was a bit of a hiccup in the implementation of the new law when Attorney General Ashcroft failed to comply at first. After complaints from the bill's sponsors, he placed the OVAW as a separate and independent part of the Justice Department in 2003.

The OVAW is one of the rare women's policy offices whose status and influence have increased under the Republican majority. Congress reauthorized the VAWA in late 2005. In Fiscal Year 2005 Congress appropriated $369 million to the Office for grants and special projects. At the same time, feminists criticize the Bush administration for cutting appropriations each year and the 2006 budget was no exception. In addition, the Office is not immune from the great American abortion debate. In September 2004, the OVAW released the first National Protocol for Sexual Assault Medical Forensic Examinations, a detailed handbook to regularize the treatment of rape victims in hospitals nationwide. Missing from the Protocol, however, was the recommendation to inform victims about emergency contraception (EC). Only five states presently require hospitals to do so. Availability of EC, which anti-abortion activists consider to be an abortifacient, has been one of the most controversial issues in the reproductive rights debate.[10] Members of Congress, nursing organizations, law enforcement officials, and other groups have protested the omission of EC information from the National Protocol and Senator Hillary Rodham Clinton and Representative Carolyn Maloney among others have filed what are mostly symbolic bills to require OVAW to include this information.

The other Office where femocrats find themselves in a relatively warm environment (for the Bush administration) is in the State Department: the Office for International Women's Issues (OIWI). In 1994, The Foreign Relations Authorization Act directed the State Department 'to designate a senior advisor to promote international women's human rights within the overall human rights policy of the United States Government' (P.L. 103–230, sec 142). Soon after, this office was overshadowed by the higher profile PICW led by Hillary Clinton. Bush eliminated the PICW, but his State Department gave the OIWI a prominent role in policy toward Afghanistan and Iraq.

The head of the office is the Senior Coordinator for International Women's Issues appointed by the Secretary of State. She has responsibility for coordinating a variety of projects and policy positions, including working with the US delegation to the UN Commission on the Status of Women. In 2005, the initiatives foreground support to increase health, education, and political participation of women in Afghanistan and Iraq during the post-war reconstruction period. The Middle East Partnership Initiative had a $218 million budget with a Women's Empowerment Pillar. Other areas on the OIWI agenda are support for micro enterprise development, anti-trafficking in persons, HIV/AIDS, women in post-conflict situations, refugees and international cooperation/UN Beijing Platform of Action.

Any administration would use this office to put a positive face on its foreign policy by outlining funding that helps women. Clinton focused on women's human rights. Bush (along with first lady Laura Bush) uses political empowerment of women as one way of justifying military actions in Afghanistan and the Iraq war and a forum for anti-abortion rhetoric. This policy places feminist movement activists in the position of being firm critics of the war and the administration stance on reproductive rights, yet supportive of the overall goals of improving women's political roles and economic status. This contradiction was front and centre at the 2005 UN conference on the Beijing Plan of Action. Called as essentially a symbolic reaffirmation of the Plan, the meeting was dominated by the insistence of the US delegation (which comprised three Republican business women) that the conference declaration include language that did not incorporate any 'new international right to abortion'. While the leader of the American delegation, Ellen R. Sauerbrey, US representative to the UN Committee on the Status of Women (CSW), eventually backed down, the message was clear that the Republican opposition to reproductive rights for women will undermine whatever efforts the Republican administration makes to promote women's status.

In general, despite these exceptions, the dominance of the Republican party in the federal government has limited the range and type of activities undertaken by women's policy agencies to conform to the ideological agenda. Of course, any party in the majority gets the opportunity to make its mark but the extent of ideological control throughout the bureaucracy is unusual. The social conservatives equate feminism with what they consider the excesses of the sexual revolution and equate special programmes for women's interests with supporting these feminists.

Diversity

There has been little change in the way agencies treat diverse constituencies. Despite much discussion among scholars (led by Crenshaw, 1998) about the need to approach policy in terms of intersectionality – that is considering the interaction of individual sources of oppression such as race, gender and disability – the US government treats discrimination one group at a time. Thus, EEOC and the courts consider cases about sex discrimination separately from those charging race discrimination. The Americans with Disabilities Act, also enforced by EEOC, does not classify its constituencies in terms of gender or race. The Department of Labor has both a Women's Bureau and an Office of Disability Employment Policy. There are no policies at the federal level that distinguish minorities in terms of sexual orientation.

The Office of Women's Health and its offices throughout the Department of Health and Human Services are the only women's policy agencies that recognize ethnic and racial minority women. There are special research programmes and the OWH directs information to the four government-recognized categories of ethnicity in the US: African American women, Hispanic women, Asian/Pacific Islander/Native Hawaiian women and American Indian/Alaska Native women. The OWH also works with activist organizations such as the Black Women's Health Initiative.

Effect of changes in women's agencies on women's movement activists

The advent of the Republican majority in the early 2000s with its radical social conservative agenda ramped up the threats to women's rights and equality. The most public struggle is over reproductive rights; pro-choice leaders are faced with the possible end of legal abortion through appointment of Supreme Court justices endorsed by anti-choice groups. They have waged major campaigns, through lobbying, litigation and petition drives, to protect legal abortion. There are other threats as well that demand response: to affirmative action, lesbian rights, child care support and gender equity in education and sports. This situation stretches the energies and resources of activists but at the same time has tended to encourage formation of coalitions especially with the Democratic party to end the Republican era once and for all. A bridge in this coalition is EMILY'S List, a PAC (Political Action Committee) that raises money for pro-choice Democratic women candidates for the House and Senate.

A few activists for women's interests have benefited from the Republican domination. Since the mid-1990s, there has been an increase in the visibility of women's movement organizations that support policies of neoliberalism, moral conservatism and oppose most campaigns of the second wave movement actors. Prominent among them is the Independent Women's Form (IWF) whose mission is 'advance the American spirit of enterprise and self-reliance and to support the principles of political freedom, economic liberty, and personal responsibility . . . provide a voice for American women who believe in free markets and who seek equality of opportunity rather than equality of outcomes' (http://www. iwf.org/specialreports). They oppose federal sexual harassment rules, affirmative action, education equity, welfare, and child care. On reproductive issues Feminists for Life and the Susan B. Anthony list, a PAC which supports anti-choice women candidates, campaign against pro-choice activists. These conservative groups support the Bush administration policies and have benefited from the Republican dominance in policy outcomes and through appointments of their members and allies to top positions in the government.

Despite the strong organizational resources at the federal level, national movement actors can not claim to speak for all women. They have to contend with the diversity of activist women including, but not limited to, the intersection of race, ethnicity, gender, and class identities. This diversity is more noticeable at the state and local levels. There, activists form policy coalitions and networks on an informal basis. This strategy has been especially characteristic of African American and Native American activism. State networks are likely to become increasingly important because many of the debates – over abortion, welfare, job training, lesbian rights – play out in state legislatures and referendums.

In general, women's movement actors have not depended on women's policy agencies, even in the best of times, to advance their agenda. Instead, they take advantage of any alliances that come along. Changes in politics and the state since the mid-1990s have had a mixed effect on women's policy agencies and their relationships with women's movement actors. Increased attention to international agreements at the UN resulted in a new high level agency committed to achieving the goals of many of the women's movement organizations. However, the PICW did not open any new avenues for participation by the women's lobbying organizations in Washington. There were few consultations and, in the case of the major anti-trafficking campaign, activists were disappointed at their reception (McBride Stetson, 2004).

Devolution of job training and vocational education policy eliminated the few femocrats who were effective allies of the movement. By leaving it up to the states whether to fund positions of Sex Equity Coordinators, the act called Perkins III dropped the national commitment to overcome gender-based segregation in job training and employment. Activists working on this issue had to regroup to focus on 50 state governments. The ability to find allies in women's policy agencies at that level varies greatly; in only 10 states have agencies taken up the slack left by devolution of welfare and job training policies.

Women's movement leaders have mixed responses to the effects of Republican dominance on women's policy agencies. The reactions of feminists range from sceptical – with respect to the warmer agencies working on violence and international democracy – to fury and dismay about the silencing of their allies in Health and Human Services, Labor and Defense Departments. At the same time, many groups find it necessary to maintain relationships with femocrats and to take advantage of the financial support available in the area of women's health and for victims of domestic violence. While abortion rights activists remain at war with the administration, organizations that focus on trafficking or violence can find allies inside the government.

The feminist/moralist alliance that developed on the trafficking issue in the 1990s is a recurring one in debates about women's sexuality and has continued into the era of complete Republican dominance. In 2002, the Bush National Security Presidential Directive adopted a strong position against legalized prostitution, denying US grant funds to foreign NGOs that support prostitution as sex work: 'Prostitution and related activities, which are inherently harmful and dehumanizing, contribute to the phenomenon of trafficking in persons, as does sex tourism, which is an estimated $1 billion per year business worldwide. The exposure of trafficked people to abuse, deprivation and disease, including HIV, is unconscionable' (US White House, 2002). In 2004, the State Department asserted: 'Prostitution is not the oldest profession, but the oldest form of oppression.' Even the most radical feminist finds it difficult to disagree, while remaining suspicious of the political motives of such statements.

Conclusion

The changes of the last decade in the state structure and policy have had mixed effects on the US women's policy machinery. Compared with European countries, the US policy makers show very little enthusiasm for transferring policy authority to international agencies. Thus the high level of attention the Clinton administration gave to the US compliance with the Beijing Plan of Action in the late 1990s stands out. While the women's policy office Clinton established did not survive, it had a long lasting impact on policy (especially in trafficking) and in connections to transnational feminist networks (Vital Voices). At the same time, it opened few new doors for movement activists.

Having had a head start with its federal structure, the US has gone further than most of its European counterparts in devolving power to regional governments. The shift of policy discretion in welfare and job training policies to the states multiplied the policy arenas for those seeking to promote women friendly policies and gender equity. The local and state policy networks also find reduced federal support for Sex Equity Coordinators leaving a vacuum that has been filled by only a few state women's agencies.

The 2000 election established Republican party dominance of federal institutions and with it strong support for neoliberal ideologies. But the party is not motivated only by interests demanding transference of state responsibilities for socioeconomic well being to the private sector. It is also in favour of strengthening government's role in some areas. The Republican party's majority is due to the alliance between the pro-business neoliberals (or conservatives and neoconservatives in American discourse) and evangelical Christian organizations united around an agenda that emphasizes traditional gender roles (code-word: pro-family) and opposition to legal reproductive choice (code-word: morality). These ideologues want the state to use its power to enforce their moral agenda. Thus, the Republicans have not led a full-scale attack on women's policy machinery. Rather, they have used the machinery to promote their own policy agenda.

The changes in state feminism since the mid-1990s in the US have resulted in a revised set of policy priorities. By 2000, trafficking and violence issues had come to the top of the agenda. After 2000, gender equality in work, education, and vocational education and support for lone mothers dropped to the bottom. The neoliberal and morality ideologies that hold sway in the 2000s combine to affect the policy initiatives that women's policy agencies are permitted to articulate. The forbidden themes are: reproductive rights, positive discrimination in education and employment, women's studies in education, workers' rights, and pay equity. The permitted themes are: women small business owners, women's democratic participation in foreign countries, support for families, women's health (excluding reproductive health), fighting violence against women, and sex trafficking. The effect on women's movement activists depends on their agendas: some work within the new system; others have given up on the femocrats and moved to the trenches to fight against what they see as a full scale attack on women's rights and feminist goals that can only be fixed by a defeat of the Republican majority.

Notes

1. This material is based upon work supported by the NSF under grant 0084580. Any opinions, findings and conclusions or recommendations expressed in this material are those of the author and do not necessarily reflect the views of the NSF.
2. EEOC is responsible for protecting groups based on age, disability, national origin, race and religion in addition to sex. Nothing in the enabling legislation or the mission statements of EEOC and its counterpart in the Department of Education, the Office of Civil Rights, designates these agencies explicitly to promote sex-based equality. At the same time, they have responsibility to enforce anti-discrimination laws in employment and education.
3. Feminist is used here to denote a discourse that includes all of the following elements: identity with women; be explicitly gendered; represent women; improve the status of women; challenge gender hierarchies (see McBride and Mazur, 2005; Ferree and Mueller, 2004).
4. In fact, the majority was not *solid* until 2003: between 2001 and 2003 the Democrats had an one vote majority in the Senate but depended on Republicans to enact any legislation. Between 2003 and 2007, Republicans enjoyed governing majorities in both houses.
5. As a result the State Department established an advisor on Trafficking in Persons, not a women's policy agency.
6. US Women Connect is an organization intended to network women's movement organizations with NGOs working on women's issues globally. In its 'report card', it praised the PICW as a 'giant step forward' as the first federal-wide women's body since 1978. Yet it criticized it for not 'adequately integrating a gender perspective in legislation, public policy, programs, and budgets. No overall policy for gender mainstreaming, collection of gender disaggregated data, time bound targets' (US Women Connect, 2000).
7. The BLS decided in 2005 to stop gathering data of the number of women workers in private employment claiming that this was too great a burden on employers. 'Departments of Labor, Health and Human Services, and Education, and Related Agencies Appropriations Act, 2006', signed into law on 30 December 2005, included a provision that requires the BLS to reinstate the collection and publication of data on the number of women workers by industry.
8. The co-sponsors are Carolyn Maloney (D-NY) and Deborah Pryce (R-Ohio). They are former co-chairs (in 1999) of the CCWI. Maloney was in the US delegation to Beijing and foregrounds women's health and sexual assault issues on her website.
9. This was helped by the small Democrat majority in the Senate.
10. In August 2006, the FDA approved EC for over the counter sale to women over 17 years of age.

14
Assessing Changes in State Feminism over the Last Decade

Joyce Outshoorn and Johanna Kantola

In the mid-1990s most countries in this research had national women's policy agencies with a broad mandate, often in conjunction with a policy network around gender equality issues. Not all of these were strong or effective; sometimes they were dependent on political incumbency, such as in Italy, Austria and France, or relatively new and less experienced, as in Spain or Belgium. The Netherlands and particularly Australia had well-established units, the latter's cross-sectional model and instruments such as gender budgeting were actually feminist export products in the 1970s and 1980s. Thus, it is not a coincidence that the word 'femocrat' was coined in Australia, the term denoting those feminists who entered the state bureaucracy to work in these institutions. Finland, Germany and Sweden all had well-developed gender units, with those of Germany extending to the regional and the local level. In addition, several of these countries, including, for example, Sweden and the Netherlands, had an advisory policy council, in which women's movement organizations were represented, along with a commission monitoring sex discrimination law. Often the women's policy agencies had close ties to the women MPs, as in Finland, and strong support from party women's organizations, as in Austria.

Only the US and Great Britain had no agency at the national level with an overall responsibility for improving women's status at the time. Rather, both countries had several other institutions such as the EOC and the Women's National Commission (WNC), an advisory body, in Great Britain, and a President's Office along with several specialized agencies, such as the Women's Bureau, DACOWITS and the Office on Women's Health, in the US.

The central question for this study was to analyse how these women's policy agencies have fared over the last decade. Have they been able to

maintain or enhance their roles, keeping women's issues on the transformed political agenda? And have they been able to preserve their
alliances with women's movement groups, as well as making use of possible new opportunities arising from the changes? In order to answer
these questions, the empirical findings of the previous chapters will be
analysed on each of the major changes over the last decade as discussed
in the Introduction. First of all, what have been the shifts in political power
at the national level: which parties formed the incumbent government?
Second, what has been the impact of the supranational level, more
specifically, that of the UN and the EU? Third, with respect to regionalization: where did it occur and what has been its impact on the women's
policy agencies? Fourth, what has been the impact of the New Public
Management, welfare state reform and state institutional changes?

We then discuss the changes within the women's policy agencies and
assess the effects of changes in gender equality policy, in particular gender mainstreaming and diversity. Has gender mainstreaming affected
women's policy agencies? How have they dealt with increasing diversity –
which has complicated the issue of accountability to women's movement organizations which have also diversified? Finally, we assess the
shifting relationship between the women's policy agencies and women's
movement groups: are there still alliances and for which movement
groups do agencies actually stand?

Shifts in political power

All the countries studied in this book have experienced major political
changes over the last decade. The several elections which changed incumbency and composition of the legislatures have been important turning
points. Australia and the US were faced with strong right-wing majorities: in Australia John Howard's Liberal government has been in power
since 1996, and from 2000 on the US had a solid Republican majority in
Congress and a Republican president. A 'grand coalition' between Socialists
and the ÖVP rules Austria, but after elections in 2000 the ÖVP formed a
coalition with the extreme FPÖ of Jörg Haider, to general European dis-
approval. In Spain the conservative *Partido Popular* won the 1996 elections
after twenty years of Socialist rule. Unprecedented 'purple' cabinets, without the Christian Democrats, were formed in the Netherlands (1994–2002)
and in Belgium (1999–); the Netherlands were later faced with two political assassinations and a rightist populist electoral upheaval in 2002.
Furthermore, many European countries, such as Austria, Belgium, France,
Italy and the Netherlands, were faced with the rise of extreme right parties

capitalizing on the feelings of unease caused by immigration. Australia was also faced by a racist party where the right attracted voters on the issue of refugees and illegal immigration.

In contrast to this rise of the right, in Great Britain the 1997 victory of the Labour party at the polls put an end to nearly twenty years of Conservative rule. France elected a Socialist parliament in 1997, and a right-wing one in 2002, and had shifting left/right majorities in the National Assembly and Senate. Sweden was ruled from 1994 to 2006 by a left majority in parliament. In Germany, a 16 year conservative ruling coalition was ousted in 1998 to make room for the first Social Democratic/Green coalition on the national level.

However, in general most countries encountered a rise of neoliberal ideas, with emphasis on the market, privatization, efficiency and innovation. Reforming the welfare state and the introduction of principles from the New Public Management was an issue in all the countries (save perhaps Germany and Spain) studied. In Germany many resisted NMP and other structural reforms to retain the Rhineland welfare state model. The country also still faces the social and financial consequences of the reunification in 1991. The French government, with its strong state intervention in socio-economic life, faced massive resistance when attempting to cut public spending. Finland and Austria, along with Sweden, joined the EU in 1995, a landmark decision which deeply influenced all three states. One dimension of this was the emphasis on neoliberal forms of governance. Furthermore, all the EU member states joining the EMU had to go through the continual and substantial cuts in public spending, with budget discipline imposed, which further exacerbated these tendencies.

Nevertheless, other political issues dominated public debates as well: constitutional reform leading to decentralization and the shift of power to the regions in Belgium, Italy and Spain, and the process of devolution in Great Britain, increasing the autonomy of Scotland and Wales. After 11 September 2001 terrorism and war became dominant on domestic political agendas in many of the states studied.

The impact of the rise of supranational governance

All countries studied in our research have experienced positive effects from the UN, not only because of the UN Women's World Conference in Beijing in 1995, the ensuing Platform of Action and the follow-up of Beijing 5+ in 2000, but also from CEDAW. The Beijing proceedings encouraged feminist civil servants and women's movement organizations

(WMOs) to pressure their governments and formed important rallying points for collective activities. The five-year reports required by CEDAW confront governments with the state of affairs on gender equality, and the shadow reports they elicit present a fine opportunity to femocrats and movement activists alike to criticize the shortcomings of gender equality policy. CEDAW had already shaped the Finnish Equality Act of 1986, and it formed the basis on which Austria criminalized marital rape. It strengthened anti-discrimination legislation in the Netherlands. In addition, the UN trafficking protocol influenced national legislation on the issue, for example in Austria and the US. However the US, being highly critical of UN institutions and very sensitive about its sovereignty, has not ratified CEDAW, and the Howard government of Australia has still not signed the Optional Protocol to CEDAW. The US has also not complied with the Plan of Action under the Bush administration.

The idea of gender mainstreaming (discussed in more detail below), emanating from the UN (after previous pioneering work by the Council of Europe) was set on the agenda in several countries, such as Australia (which had originally influenced UN thinking on this point in the 1980s), and Belgium, especially Flanders. Even in the US, Beijing had a positive effect on women's movement organizations, with the visibility provided by the high-level PICW, a Cabinet task force on the Plan of Action, albeit not very successfully given the increasingly hostile environment to feminism.

For the European countries, the EU has been of huge importance in several ways. Firstly, all countries have had to comply with the various Directives on equality, equal treatment, including social security and pension rights, childcare, parental leave and pregnancy. It can be said that the EU had vital impact on the anti-discrimination laws in all its member states. Great Britain finally signed the Social Chapter in 1997 and the Amsterdam Treaty with its gender paragraph. EU legislation has also strongly influenced equal treatment of other forms of discrimination, the more so when Great Britain incorporated the European Convention of Human Rights (ECHR) into its national legislation. Even Sweden, with its well-developed gender equality policy and strong anti-EU sentiment, had to sharpen its policies on equal pay and equal treatment, which had been opposed by employers prior to joining in 1995. Its national agency, JämO, was adroit in using the policy window opened by accession. Countries have leeway in implementation of the EU directives, but women's movement groups can use the European Court of Justice to press their governments to comply, as has happened in Britain, Germany and the Netherlands. The latter two were slow to implement the Directives from the 1970s and 1980s, with the employers opposed as they maintained equal treatment was too expensive.

Secondly, ideas about structuring gender equality institutions and policy instruments have had important impact on the member-states. Gender mainstreaming was set on the agenda by the EU in the late 1990s and early 2000s; the effect has been marked in Austria, Belgium, Germany, Italy and Spain. In Belgium and Italy gender mainstreaming also inspired recent strengthening of the women's policy agencies. Thirdly, EU funding, by way of the European Social Fund (ESF) was utilized in France and Spain to set up regional gender policy units; the Netherlands used it to fund projects 'day planning' as part of reconciliation of work and family policy. It has not helped pro-EU sentiment, as both France and the Netherlands voted against the plans for the European Constitution in referenda in 2005. Another positive effect has been that the EU made the French state more open to outsiders such as women's movement organizations. Not all countries, such as Finland, were able to utilize EU funds, as the women's policy agencies simply did not have the initial resources to benefit from them and found the system too bureaucratic and cumbersome.

Not all national women's policy agencies have established links with EU institutions, although indirectly they can access the minister who has gender equality in her/his portfolio and who attends the Council of Ministers' meetings. In Italy and Finland this communication works well, although through lack of resources in the latter country is not judged as very effective. In France and Germany feminist civil servants have become smart in using EU regulation to exercise leverage on the domestic level. Belgian feminist civil servants do not seem to use the advantages of location to gain access to the EU bureaucracy.

It can be concluded that supra-nationalization, both on the UN and EU level, has provided new opportunities for gender equality policy and both women's policy agencies and women's movement organizations have been able to use international regulations as leverage in their own country to improve women's status. Australia and the US miss the positive effect of the EU with its binding Directives and treaty clauses; the lack of pressure from this supranational level may be one of the reasons women's policy agencies have been less able to maintain themselves over the last decade. The positive effect of the EU should be qualified in one important respect: for countries joining the EMU, it meant accepting budget discipline and large cuts in public spending, with consequences for both women's policy agencies and women as clients of the welfare state.

The impact of regionalization and decentralization

Many states have decentralized power to the regional level over the last ten years, making these more autonomous, or shifted responsibility for welfare state provision to a lower level of government. The effects on the women's policy agency are very much in evidence. In no less than half of the countries studied, such transfer processes took place, and in all of these the women's policy agencies have grown in strength over the last decade. This has occurred in Belgium, Finland, Great Britain, Italy (under the Left), Spain and Sweden. France and Austria also experience regionalization; in France the position of the women's policy agency remained more or less stable, while in Austria it fluctuated during the period, but it has currently regained its mid-1990s strength.

Looking at this process in more detail, during the process of federalization of the Belgian state the regions set up their own policy units, Flanders first and foremost. Despite a high turnover of responsible ministers, it is the most successful agency within the country, with a decent budget and well-developed cross-sectional policy plans. The other regions lag behind, leading to an asymmetrical situation in the country. In Sweden local level gender units were established and they were able to extend their activities. Both Sweden and Finland have also downloaded welfare services to the local level. In Finland this has given more power to the local councils, but not more budget. It should be noted, however, that the attention paid to gender quotas at the lower level has led to the neglect of other gender issues.

In Britain devolution of the state led to separate women's policy agencies in Northern Ireland, Scotland and Wales. After the constitutional reforms of the 1990s in Italy, the regions have gained in power, including the provision of welfare services. New gender units were established at the regional level, which has provided new points of access to women's movement groups.

The impact is also very much in evidence in Spain, where the regions have attained varying degrees of autonomy over the last decade. After the right-wing *Partido Popular* took power in 1996, the national machinery remained intact. But there has been a vast expansion of regional gender units. The political context and the units' mandates create different types of institutions; sometimes they are in the president's office or under family affairs with their own policy plans. Despite these differences, they have strengthened the overall gender equality machinery in Spain.

It can therefore be concluded that regionalization has provided important opportunities for gender policy: in some countries where national states transferred power to the regions, women's policy agencies were able to use the new opportunities and gain in strength. Not all types of decentralization were positive though: in Finland and Sweden, in contrast to Italy, shifting welfare provision to the local level was detrimental for local agencies. It should also be kept in mind that disparities among and within countries continue to exist. Exceptions here are Finland and the US, where decentralization has so far not improved the scope and resources of states' policy machineries.

Welfare state reform and the New Public Management

At the outset we expected that welfare state reform and the reorganization of state bureaucracies along the lines of the principles of the New Public Management (NPM) would have a negative impact on women's policy agencies. Nearly all the countries studied were strongly influenced by neoliberal ideas about the minimal state, the need to reform the welfare sate and to cut back public spending. These ideas often run counter to the prevailing ideas of social justice, including a fair deal for women. In the cases where neoliberalism was not the dominant discourse, other concerns were pressing, as in Belgium and Spain, where regionalization and its threat to the unitary state dominated public debate. In some countries, including France and Germany, neoliberal approaches to welfare state reform were debated, but did not gain the upper hand, and many reforms on these issues were stalled.

Welfare state reform affected women's policy agencies directly when their budgets were cut, and indirectly when they had to confront the issue of defending women's social rights. However, it appears that welfare state reform was less of an issue in the last decade for the agencies than we had expected to find. When we look at the issues they were addressing, we do find that social inequality, social security and pensions and family policies, including childcare, were key concerns. But increasingly violence against women, trafficking of women, migration-related issues such as headscarf debates, genital mutilation and honour killings, equal representation (parity), IVF (*in vitro fertilization*), legalization of same-sex marriage, and men's status, fill the agenda of the agencies, along with an old-time favourite, abortion, in the US. This suggests that in many states the major welfare state reforms had been completed by the end of the 1990s, and perhaps, the women's policy agencies ceased to fight against it and accepted the neoliberal discourse as a harsh reality. Another explanation could be that the agencies had given up on welfare state issues and shifted their attention to other concerns. It may also in part be a consequence of a more limited mandate and the fact that a number of agencies still have relatively marginal positions in 'hard' policy areas such as socioeconomic affairs.

Bureaucratic restructuring informed by ideas from the New Public Management also took place in most states. Sometimes, as in Sweden, feminists tried to use performance management to make the agencies more accountable to introduce gender equality measures, and to make gender equality a requirement for funding other movement groups. Bureaucratic restructuring also aimed at curbing corporatism; in the Netherlands this has undermined the women's policy machinery. We have found no privatization or outsourcing of activities of women's policy agencies in the countries studied. However, in several states NMP confronted agencies with new requirements about budgeting, monitoring and the funding of women's movement groups. This has decreased their autonomy and has endangered the relationships many had established in the period previous to this study. In the next paragraph we will compare the impact of state-institutional changes in more detail.

Changes in the position of women's policy agencies

From our research it emerges that at the end of the period studied (2006), state feminism has actually become stronger in half the countries studied. This has occurred in Belgium, Finland, Great Britain, Italy (under the Left), Spain and Sweden (see Table 14.1). The strengthening has occurred at the national level, but notably also at the regional and local level. In Belgium, both are in evidence: the federal Unit for Equal Opportunities managed to increase its scope and achieve an autonomous position, even if it still receives a relatively small budget and staff. The new regional

Table 14.1:   Strength of state feminism, compared to situation in the mid-1990s

Weaker	Consolidated	Stronger
Australia	France	Belgium
Germany	Austria	Finland
The Netherlands		Great Britain
United States		Italy
		Spain
		Sweden

units helped to strengthen the overall policy machinery. In a wish to emulate the record of Sweden and Norway, Finland adopted their 'model' for gender equality policy and added an advisory political council with a law-enforcing body to its executive Gender Equality Unit in 2001. The advisory body, the Gender Equality Council, which has good links with women's movement organizations, was maintained, but after the reform it became less well resourced than the other agencies.

Changes in Great Britain came with the victory of Labour in the elections of 1997, after which a new Women's Unit was set up within the cabinet office, with a Minister for Women, which works with the WNC. In 2003 the Women and Equalities Unit was expanded, given more budget, staff and a larger mandate. As mentioned, separate women's policy agencies were established in Northern Ireland, Scotland and Wales. The Equal Opportunities Commission is to be merged into a Commission for Equality and Human Rights which is to encompass all types of discrimination, leading to debate how gender will fare.

Under the left in Italy a Ministry for Equal Opportunities was established with a cross-sectional mandate in 1996, which represents Italy at the EU and monitors EU legislation, alongside the existing advisory committee (CNPPO), under the Prime Minister. The women's unit in the Ministry of Labour on employment issues remained intact, strengthening the executive and law-enforcing branches of the national machinery. In 1997 a department to aid the Ministry of Equal Opportunities was set up. However, the CNPPO was abolished by the right-wing Berlusconi government in 2004 and an attempt to end the fragmentation of agencies failed just before its fall. In Spain, despite the increasing autonomy for the various regions, the national unit, the *Instituto de la Mujer*, maintained its position after the right-wing *Partido Popular* took power in 1996; as in the previous decade, periodic national policy plans remain important for progress. Along with the major expansion of regional women's units, it can be concluded that overall the gender equality machinery in Spain has made important advances. In Sweden too the national machinery is stable, but with an extension of regional and local gender units. JämO, the Minister and the Gender Equality Division have made good use of the opportunities offered by Sweden's joining the EU and have maintained both specific gender policies as well as gender mainstreaming.

The factor that stands out for accounting for the gain in strength of state feminism, is regionalization. All these states decentralized powers to the regional level and/or shifted responsibility for welfare state provision to a lower level of government, and feminists and femocrats were able to seize these windows of opportunities to expand their scope or to establish new agencies. The conventional wisdom has it that Nordic countries have strong state feminism, but with Spain, Italy and Belgium also developing strong machinery, traditional categorization may well have to be revised.

In the intermediary league we find Austria and France; state feminism here has more or less consolidated itself. Both countries have had to cope with changes in political incumbency in the past, leading to refurbishing of the women's policy machinery. In Austria the status of the agency is dependent on the party in power; under Socialist or 'grand coalition' cabinets, it built up a good record as an ally for women's movement organizations, but after the 2000 right-wing victory it was submerged in the Ministry of Social Welfare, Family and Generations. When the Socialist Party returned to power in 2004, the office, which had kept its cross-sectional mandate, regained its strength and was relocated within the Ministry of Health. France's agencies were also dependent on political incumbency; under the right the agencies were weak and budgets fluctuated. But the Women's Rights And Equality Service, which oversees formulation and implementation of gender equality policy, has retained its minister under the right and is now free from politically appointed women's ministries. One can say that French agencies have become a permanent part of the state's landscape. It is very likely that CEDAW and EU requirements about gender equality institutions have enabled both to become more independent from incumbency and maintain their scope and budgets. Like the countries with strong state feminism, decentralization also provided opportunities for creating local and regional agencies in France and Austria.

In the final group of countries studied, consisting of Australia, Germany, the Netherlands and the United States, women's policy machineries have been weakened considerably. The most striking cases are Australia and the US. Under the hostile attitude of the Liberal federal government of Howard, the Australian women's policy machinery has been largely dismantled. The Women's Bureau (working on employment) disappeared in 1997; after severe budget cuts the Office of the Status of Women was demoted in 2004 from the Prime Minister's Department to the Department of Family and Community Services as the Office for Women, losing its cross-sectional mandate in the process. Also lost were important instruments such as gender budgeting and gender analysis. Several programmes for gender equality have disappeared in the course of the decade. Recently the Howard government has attempted to weaken the Sex Discrimination Act. There have been some positive changes at the state level, usually under a Labor government. In the US the rise of the right has led to the bleak picture of frozen, chilly and warmer agencies. Since the George W. Bush presidency, the Women's Bureau's scope was narrowed and DACOWITS' mandate shrunk. The women's health machinery survived, but cannot work on reproductive rights under the Bush administration. The Office on Violence Against Women has gained in status, as have parts of the administration catering for international women's issues, save again for reproductive rights. At the state level the picture is very mixed, depending on political incumbency and state traditions in the area of service provision.

In the Netherlands the national machinery was already eroded in the mid-1990s, under a coalition between the Left and the Liberals, which introduced NPM style reforms, a trend which became stronger under a right-wing government after 2002. The central unit, the DCE, lost its expertise and much of its work to other ministries in the process; its contacts with the professionalized women's movement became tenuous and irregular. In 2005 it also lost its coordinating cross-sectional mandate because of gender mainstreaming and currently its coordinating minister is at risk. At the local and regional level few women's units have survived years of budget freeze and bureaucratic reform.

The fourth case, Germany, is more complex. Here the Left was in power for seven years (1998–2005), and women's policy agencies as such were not in danger, but many of the local level women's units have been faced with state downsizing. Given the fiscal crisis, downsizing is now also threatening many of the women's policy units at the Länder level, the majority of which are run by conservative cabinets. The meetings of women from the Länder offices for gender policy, which are the driving force for the Federal level, are at risk of being suspended. The Federal unit's work has dissolved into an unit of family and youth affairs and although it does provide access to women's movement groups, it mainly serves a symbolic function.

What the four cases therefore have in common was right-wing government (also in the Netherlands where the Liberals and Social Liberals shared power with the Social Democrats until 2002, and in Germany where the majority of Länder governments was also right-wing) focusing on curbing state expenditure along with a persistent conservative family policy.

It can be concluded that in the majority of the countries studied, women's policy machineries were able to strengthen or consolidate their institutions over the last decade, especially in countries undergoing decentralization, both territorially, as in Italy, Spain and France, and functionally, as in Sweden. When this did not occur, right-wing government also emerges as a strong explanatory factor.

Changes in gender equality policy

In the course of the past decade, women's policy agencies were confronted with two challenges directly impinging on their work: the introduction of gender mainstreaming as a major policy instrument and the increasing recognition of the diversity of their constituency, among women. What has been the impact?

Gender mainstreaming

All countries except the US have adopted a gender mainstreaming approach, inspired by the UN or the EU. For a number of countries, notably Australia, Finland, Germany, the Netherlands and Sweden, it was not really a totally new approach, as they had already been following a dual strategy for gender equality policy, combining specific policies for women with a cross-sectional approach. In those cases the new commitment served to reinforce the latter, along with the use of new policy instruments such as gender impact analyses or gender budgeting. For others, gender mainstreaming was innovative, providing an opportunity for improving the infrastructure of the national machinery, as happened in Austria, Belgium (although it is not firmly anchored in the policy-making process), France (which also institutionalized gender budgeting), Italy and Spain. It opened access for feminist civil servants from the national women's policy agencies to expand their mandate and intervene in other policy areas. In those countries, as well as in Germany, gender mainstreaming was also introduced at the regional level.

For several countries, there are also unmistakable cases of gender mainstreaming threatening the existing women's units, as has occurred in Australia at the federal level, in Austria (under the right-wing government), Germany (where the conservatives also oppose it) and the Netherlands. There are also other problems with the gender mainstreaming strategy coming to the fore in the analysis, such as the lack of expertise among civil servants on gender issues and scant commitment of the higher echelons of government. Meagre or lack of funding, without which gender mainstreaming cannot be successful, is delaying a proper implementation in Finland, Great Britain, Italy, the Netherlands and Sweden. In Great Britain gender mainstreaming remains a formal exercise, lacking serious implementation due to low awareness and know-how of the civil servants. Under Berlusconi Italy abandoned gender mainstreaming, which only receives symbolic support from the male political elite. The instrument is also at odds with earlier traditions of gender equality policy as well as being alien to Italian women's movement groups. In Sweden there was scepticism in the women's movement; one reason for this is the fear that gender mainstreaming will lead to a situation in which no one is responsible any more for the overall process of gender equality policy. Despite this doubt and despite processes of decentralization which risks subverting gender mainstreaming, it has actually strengthened the machinery.

Finally, the US, with the predominance of single-issue women's policy agencies, does not employ gender mainstreaming strategies. The closest it came to such an approach was when women from a broad section of the women's movement, inspired by the Beijing Plan of Action, came together for the Contract for Women which aimed at inserting women's concerns into all policy.

In conclusion, we find that at the current stage of implementation, the blessings of gender mainstreaming are mixed and its use raises serious questions about the coordination of gender equality policy in the absence of well-marked responsibilities. At the same time it can also be concluded that gender mainstreaming has become an important device for women's policy agencies to rejuvenate the issue of gender equality policy, and in some instances has led to the strengthening of the machinery. However, in several countries gender mainstreaming is seen as a strategy which does away with the need for gender equality policy, and in this way provides grounds for downsizing the national machinery as no longer necessary. It also emerges that requirements for successful gender mainstreaming, such as expertise, sufficient funding and political will, are usually not in place. These outcomes suggest that much of the theoretical debate on gender mainstreaming lacks empirical reference: current practices do not easily fit into a theory dichotomizing integrationist or agenda-setting forms of gender mainstreaming, and given the very different national contexts in which gender mainstreaming occurs, it seems unwarranted to generalize about the potential transformative capacity of the process.

Diversity

Many women's movement groups and sometimes women's policy agencies had already faced differences among women relating to class, race, ethnicity and sexual orientation prior to the period studied. It was in the 1990s, however, that these categories were increasingly subsumed under the formal category of diversity; creating a new sense of urgency, especially concerning the position of migrant women. By the 2000s, there was a wide range of women's movement organizations based on these differences, with heightening awareness of the intersectionality of these identities. The differences in ethnicity, sexuality, age and disabilities in gender equality policy not only make it more difficult to speak of 'women', or in the name of 'all women', but have also made the linkages between women's policy agencies and movement organizations more complex. It raises the question of accountability: to which organizations do agencies hold themselves to be accountable and with which parts of the movement do they establish alliances? This complexity is reinforced when women's movement organizations do not take on the same issues or disagree on specific ones.

On the whole, different governments and agencies have been slow to recognize diversity among women and to take it into account in policy. Australia, Austria, Finland, France, Germany, Italy and Spain (save for the Basque country which has made intersectionality a cornerstone of its gender policy) have little eye for diversity in their policies. For example, in Australia the Howard government has abolished funding to strengthen minority women's groups' voices, but has singled out rural and family-oriented women in its gender policies. In Austria diversity has hardly been a point in public debate. In France the dominant universalist republicanism stands in the way of taking gender and ethnicity seriously, as well as other grounds for discrimination. The US government continues to treat sex, race, ethnicity, disability, and religion as separate categories in its anti-discrimination policies. The Republican administration in the US tends to see diversity as a source of special interests which are considered illegitimate. This contrasts with the Netherlands and the region of Flanders in Belgium which have incorporated diversity in their gender equality plans and developed specific policies addressing minority group women. This has led to the ethnicization of gender, a phenomenon also occurring in the Netherlands where Islamic women are becoming the major markers of the 'otherness' of migrants. In Sweden gender stood as the model for the development of policy and institutional design against other types of discrimination. The Women's Equality Unit in Great Britain has also taken up diversity in its policies.

The recognition of other forms of discrimination has led to a series of proposals to reform equality institutions, with the intent of setting up one body to cover all form of discrimination. This leads to the fear that attention to gender will be displaced by other concerns, and is on the whole opposed by feminist civil servants and women's movement organizations. The Commission for Equality and Human Rights opens its doors in October 2007, under the chairmanship of Trevor Phillips, former head of the Commission for Racial Equality and chair of the government's Equalities Review of equality policy. At the time of writing (Spring 2007) some commissioners and a chief executive have been appointed but arrangements for the internal organization of the CEHR are not yet known. Although it was strongly opposed by the Commission for Racial Equality and the Disability Rights Commission expressed reservations, the Equal Opportunities Commission was broadly supportive of the measure. At the instigation of the EU Austria merged its Equal Treatment Commissions to cover all types of discrimination in 2000. In the Netherlands such a merger was already enacted in 1995, but there it did not lead to ignoring gender, mainly due to feminists within the commission and the status of its predecessor. It should be pointed out that in these two cases it was not the policy units merging, but the legal body supervising equal treatment legislation. There have been plans and debates on similar mergers in Belgium, where women's movement organizations strongly opposed the plans (which have not materialized because of other factors), and in Sweden, where the decision is still pending. The women's policy agency JämO is opposing the bill.

It can therefore be concluded that many agencies still tend to take women as an undifferentiated category as their point of reference, with the attendant danger of paying too little heed to minority voices. Given the strong impact that the EU has had on the gender equality policies of most of its member states, it will be interesting to see how far the grounds for discrimination in Art. 13 EC (sex, racial and ethnic origin, disability, age, religion and sexual orientation) will be influential in the gender policies of the member states.

The relationship between agencies and women's movements

What has also emerged from our research is that the strength of women's movement organizations is important to maintaining or strengthening women's policy agencies, not surprisingly as weaker movements cannot exert pressure on state policies (see Table 14.2). In two countries, Australia and the Netherlands, the women's movement was undeniably in decline over the last decade. In Australia it lost visibility, despite the fact there are still a number of feminist organizations, such as the Women's Electoral Lobby (WEL). The only organizations which flourished were rural women's organizations, which were supported under conservative rule. Organizations of indigenous and migrant women are in existence, but lead an uncertain life. The decline of the overall women's movement can be linked directly to the 'fall of the femocrat'; there was little opposition

Table 14.2: State of women's movement organizations, compared to situation in the mid-1990s

Decline	Consolidated	Resurgence
Australia	Austria	France
The Netherlands	Belgium	Italy
	Finland	Sweden
	Germany	
	Great Britain	
	Spain	
	United States	

to the incremental dismantling of the national machinery. There is also a men's backlash movement in the area of divorce and child custody undermining feminist legitimacy. Although the Netherlands still has plenty of movement events, women's movement groups no longer go in for public protest. Many of them had become very dependent on state funding; when funding on the basis of projects became government practice, many could not manage this shift and were unable to develop alternative ways of financing. Links to the women's policy agency have become strained and distanced, partly due to gender mainstreaming, partly due to change in strategy of the agency itself. As in Australia, Dutch migrant women's organizations on the whole are shaky and lack continuity. The decline of women's movements in the Netherlands and Australia has gone hand in hand with the weakening of the women's policy machinery. Both had 'old' women's policy agencies, suggesting a link to the life-cycle of the issue of gender equality.

In a number of countries – Austria, Belgium, Finland, Germany, Great Britain and Spain – women's movements have been able to consolidate their positions. In Austria the large women's organizations and the women's unit maintained a fruitful co-operation. Under the right-wing government of 2000–04, right-wing parties attempted to disqualify the whole movement, but with the return of the Socialists in power, funding of women's groups – on the basis of concrete projects – resumed and the old co-operation was re-established. Autonomous feminism is in decline, however, and there is little organization by migrant women. In Belgium women's movement organizations managed to consolidate themselves, becoming more of a partner for policy-makers. The traditional pillarized women's organizations are still going strong and some of the autonomous movement has become institutionalized. Many younger feminists organize in a loose network but also join the more established feminist groups. The relationship with women's policy agencies has become more bureaucratized as financing is also mainly through separate projects, entailing much paper-work. Movement groups have also become more dependent on state-funding, which did not exist in earlier periods.

In Finland women's movement organizations are well integrated in decision-making and are maintaining their organization; since the recession of the early 1990s relationships with the bureaucracy and women politicians have become loosened, but all are still sound allies. Outcomes have come to depend on the person in leadership or minister. There is some organization of minority women. Like Australia, Finland also has a reactionary men's movement focusing on divorce and child custody and attacking policy on violence against women.

In Germany women's movement organizations are highly institutionalized at all levels: the fear of the state, which was traditionally very strong into the 1980s, has disappeared. There are many professionalized women's movement groups, a lively culture of femocrats within the institutions, competent party organizations of women and a continuing grass roots feminist culture. However, there is little grass roots support for women within the state agencies, and on the whole German women's movement groups lack visibility, staging little public protest. Many receive funding from the *Land* level; relationships are complex and multi-layered. The organized movement is one for the privileged, not reaching migrant women or solo mothers, the two most vulnerable groups of women. In Great Britain women's movement groups have become increasingly competent in lobbying; on political representation and employment they were particularly successful but also perhaps a bit too well incorporated, losing public presence. The WEU has not eschewed feminist priorities and advances a feminist agenda. Moreover, the issues taken up are mainly those of white women, as a result of weaker organization of migrant women. These are on particular identities, constructed along religious, ethnic and diaspora lines, making for fragmentation. The exception here is the black women's organization Southall Black Sisters which has been fighting for granting legal status of immigrant women subject to domestic violence. In Spain ties between the national Women's Institute and the movement remain traditionally weak, and under the rule of the PP remained hostile, partly on the matter of education. Organization among migrant women is still embryonic. However, this is compensated by the closer and fruitful contacts that have developed between movement groups and regional agencies.

For the United States the picture is more mixed. The women's movement is highly diversified and ideologically divided. As McBride points out, some feminists work within the system, others 'in the trenches'. There are several well-resourced organizations of a moderate character, at the federal level, but they cannot claim to speak for all women, with the increasing diversity of women's mobilization. There are many ethnically based women's movement groups with their own agenda. Feminism maintains a high profile on reproductive issues. In the 1990s there were several alliances of feminists with moralists on issues of (sexual) violence. Alliances with women's policy agencies are rare.

Regarding those countries where women's movements are well-established, one can conclude that all, save Germany and the US, have women's policy agencies which have fared well over the last decade, either gaining in strength, or maintaining their position. Germany's position can be qualified, as it is mainly the local women's policy agencies that have encountered decline, with an uncertain future at the federal and Länder level. The US has a lively and divided movement, but at the federal level women's policy agencies have not fared well, mainly to be accounted for by the hostility of conservative Republicans to gender equality and feminism.

Three countries have actually experienced a resurgence of feminism over the last decade and tellingly, all three countries have either consolidated their women's policy machinery or strengthened it: France, Italy and Sweden. In the early 1990s women in France rallied round the cry for parity, equal representation of women in politics, with legal changes enacted in 1999/2000. Other mobilizing issues were reproductive rights and sexual violence. New mobilization occurred among women of colour with new women's movement groups, the best known being *Ni Putains, Ni Soumises* opposing sexual oppression and violence. Women's movement organizations are able to obtain funding at various levels; the funding process has become more transparent, although party politics still play a role. Several organizations are regularly consulted by the commissions for gender equality. Europeanization and the fragmentation of the party system are factors leading to a more open state in France, providing new opportunities for movement actors. Their activities have provided backing to the work of the women's policy units and enabled them to establish themselves more firmly within state bureaucracies. In Italy it was the attempt to modify the 1978 abortion law which sparked off the revival of street demonstrations in 2006; before it was the parity issue that led to a resurgence of feminism in the 1990s. At the national level women's movement groups remain fragmented but remain strong in the left parties, the trade unions and in the universities; there is still a lively women's culture. The fragmentation prevents a good lobbying network taking off. Due to state funding, there is an emerging state feminism at the regional level, around issues of social service. Among the women's movement groups there is little debate about diversity and the emergent migrant women's organizations mainly focus on the provision of services to their constituency. Sweden also experienced a resurgence of feminism in the 1990s, with a strengthening of radical feminism with a strong platform on anti-violence, and in 2005 with a women's party, *Feministiski Initiativ*. The revitalization of the movement can be ascribed to the threats to the welfare state, the opposition to the EU and the decline of women MPs for the first time in the 1991 elections. Overall, it seems to be country-specific factors that can account for revived strength.

Conclusions

Feminist researchers on the whole tend to belong to the category of people who are more likely to note that a glass is half empty than half full. Being committed to social change and gender equity, improvements are never fast enough and are often thought to hide a snake in the grass. Looking at the impact of the important changes in the context of women's policy machineries, on the whole these have fared better than many of us thought at the outset of our research. Agencies have been able to make use of the rise of multilevel governance, using supra-national regulation as a lever at the state level, and decentralization as an opening to set the agenda with gender issues at regional and local levels. The onslaught of neoliberal ideas and welfare state reform has had deleterious consequences for several agencies, notably in Australia, the Netherlands and the US, but on the whole most have survived and consolidated or even improved their position within the national bureaucracies, while Great Britain actually developed a national unit in the same period. Gender mainstreaming, promoted by the UN and the EU, has provided the opportunity to open agendas to gender issues and to rejuvenate gender equality policies, although its potential dangers, such as the loss of a coordinating and monitoring unit, are in evidence in some countries. On the downside it has to be concluded that diversity has not been taken into account by most women's policy agencies. Where minority groups have mobilized, issues such as sexual orientation and migrant women's issues are on the women's agenda. Finally, the existence of strong women's movement organizations emerges as central to the well-being of state feminism in general. Without this, there is too little pressure on governments to maintain a solid women's policy machinery, little gender policy innovation and a decline of feminist discourse as the necessary critique of the still existing gender bias in state institutional arrangements, policies and politics. Yet, the presence of lively movement activism is no guarantee of agency strength, as the US case shows.

Acknowledgements

We would like to thank our authors for their critical reading and comments, especially Dorothy McBride, Petra Meier, Jantine Oldersma and Diane Sainsbury.

Bibliography

Aalto, Terhi (2003) *Kuka vie? Naiset, politiikka ja päivähoitolainsäädäntö. Tapaukset päivähoidon subjektiivinen oikeus 1994 ja kotihoidon tuen leikkaus 1995*, Master's thesis (Helsinki: University of Helsinki).

Aalto, Terhi and Anne Maria Holli (2007) 'Debating Daycare in Finland in the Midst of an Economic Recession and Welfare State Down-sizing' in Melissa Haussman and Birgit Sauer (eds) *Gendering the State in the Age of Globalisation. Women's Movements and State Feminism in Post Industrial Democracies* (Lanham MD: Rowman and Littlefield).

AAP (Australian Associated Press) (2006) *Women just as Violent as Men: Survey*, 20 August.

Abgeordnetenhaus Berlin (2005) 15. Wahlperiode, 48. Session, 18 March. Parliamentary protocol.

Adams, Carolyn Teich and Kathryn Teich Winston (1980) *Mothers at Work: Public Policies in the United States, Sweden and China* (New York: Longman).

AFAMMER (Asociación de Familias y Mujeres del Medio Rural) (2006) http://www.afammer.es (Accessed 4 February 2006).

Ahtela, Karoliina (2001) *Työpaikan tasa-arvotyö. Sukupuolten välisen tasa-arvon edistäminen ja siihen liittyvä lainsäädäntö Suomessa ja Yhdysvalloissa*, Licenciate thesis (Helsinki: University of Helsinki).

Amazone et al. (2002) *De toekomst begint vandaag. Perspectieven voor de vrouwenbeweging. Referaten / Rapport. 58* (Brussels: Amazone).

Andeweg, Rudy B. and Galen A. Irwin (2002) *Governance and Politics of the Netherlands* (Basingstoke: Palgrave MacMillan).

Appelt, Erna (1995) 'Frauen und Laeninteressen im korporatistischen System' in *Bericht über die Situation von Frauen in Österreich. Frauenbericht 1995* (Vienna: Bundesministerin für Frauenangelegenheiten) pp. 610–18.

Appleton, Andrew and Amy Mazur (2000) 'Un cas d'étude complémentaire: La Région Provence-Alpes-Côte d'Azure' in Amy Mazur et al. (eds) *Appareils Gouvernementaux Chargés de la Politique en Direction des Femmes* (Paris: Ministère de l'Emploi et de la Solidarité) pp. 96–113.

Arbeitsgruppe Gender Mainstreaming im BMF (2001) *Ist das österreichische Steuersystem tatsächlich 'geschlechtsneutral'? Ergebnisse eines Lohn- und Einkommenssteuer-Vergleichs Männer – Frauen* (Vienna: Bundesministerium für Finanzen).

Arcidonna (2003) *La donna sommersa* (Palermo: Arcidonna).

Arcidonna et al. (2004) *Shadow Report sulla situazione italiana a 10 anni dalla Conferenza ONU sulle donne (Pechino, 1995)* (Rome: Arcidonna).

Asociación de Mujeres Gitanas ROMI (2002) Questionnaire response.

Australian Women's Organizations Conference (AWOC) (2001) Media Release, 25/26 August.

Bacchi, Carol and Joan Eveline (2003) 'Mainstreaming and Neoliberalism: a Contested Relationship', *Policy & Society*, 22, 98–118.

Banaszak, Lee Ann, Karen Beckwith and Dieter Rucht (2003) 'When Power Relocates: Interactive Changes in Women's Movements and States' in Lee Ann, Banaszak,

Karen Beckwith and Dieter Rucht (eds) *Women's Movements Facing the Reconfigured State* (Cambridge: Cambridge University Press) pp. 1–29.

Basu, Amrita (with C. Elizabeth McGrory) (eds) (1995) *The Challenge of Local Feminisms: Women's Movements in Global Perspective* (Colorado and Oxford: Westview Press).

Baudino, Claudie (2003) 'Parity Reform in France: Promises and Pitfalls', *Review of Policy Research*, 20, 3, 365–84.

Baudino, Claudie (2005) 'Gendering the Republican System: Debates on Women's Political Representation in France' in Joni, Lovenduski, et al. (eds) *State Feminism and Political Representation* (Cambridge: Cambridge University Press) pp. 85–105.

Beckwith, Karen (2000) 'Beyond Compare? Women's Movements in Comparative Perspective', *European Journal of Political Research*, 37, 31–68.

Beleidsplan Emancipatie, Handelingen Tweede Kamer, 1984–1985, 19502, nrs 1–19.

Bell, Mark (2003) 'The Right to Equality and Non-Discrimination' in Tamara K. Hervey and Jeff Kenner (eds) *Economic and Social Rights under the EU Charter of Fundamental Rights: A Legal Perspective* (Oxford: Hart Publishing) pp. 91–110.

Bereni, Laure (2003) 'Le mouvement français pour la parité et l'Europe' in Sophie Jacquot and Cornellia Woll (eds) *Sociologie Politique des Usages de l'Intégration Européenne* (Paris: l'Harmattan) pp. 25–45.

Bereni, Laure and Eléonore Lépinard (2003) 'La parité, contre sens de l'égalité? Cadre discursive et pratiques d'une réforme', *Nouvelles Questions Féministes*, 22, 3, 12–31.

Bereni, Laure and Eléonore Lépinard (2004) 'Les strategies de Légitimation de la Parité en France', *Revue Française de Science Politique*, 54, 1, 71–98.

Berghahn, Sabine and Wersig, Maria (2005) 'Vergemeinschaftung von (Ehe-)partnern durch die Reformen der Agenda 2010 – eine Rückkehr zum "Geschlechtervertrag" des 19. Jahrhunderts?' *femina politica*, 14, 2, 84–95.

Bergman, Solveig (1999) 'Women in New Social Movements', in Christina Bergqvist et al. (eds) *Equal Democracies? Gender and Politics in the Nordic Countries* (Oslo: Scandinavian University Press) pp. 97–117.

Bergman, Solveig (2002) *The Politics of Feminism. Autonomous Feminist Movements in Finland and West Germany from the 1960s to the 1980s* (Åbo: Åbo Akademi University Press).

Bergqvist, Christina (1994) *Mäns makt och kvinnors intressen* (Ph. D. thesis), (Uppsala: Acta Universitatis Upsaliensis.

Bergqvist, Christina (2001) 'Jämställdhetspolitiska idéer och strategier', *Arbetsmarknad & Arbetsliv*, 7, 1, 15–29.

Bergqvist, Christina (2004) 'Tillhör framtiden enbart männen? En analys av EU, framtidskonventet och jämställdheten', in Christina Florin and Christina Bergqvist (eds) *Framtiden i samtiden. Könsrelationer i förändring i Sverige och omvärlden* (Stockholm: Institutet för Framtidsstudier) pp. 324–43.

Bergqvist, Christina et al. (eds) (1999) *Equal Democracies? Gender and Politics in the Nordic Countries.* (Oslo: Scandinavian University Press).

Bergqvist, Christina and Ann-Cathrine Jungar (2000) 'Adaption or Diffusion of the Swedish Gender Model?' in Linda Hantrais (ed.) *Gendered Policies in Europe: Reconciling Employment and Family Life* (London: Macmillan) pp. 160–79.

Bergqvist, Christina and Anita Nyberg (2002) 'Welfare State Restructuring and Child Care in Sweden', in Sonya Michel and Rianne Mahon (eds) *Child Care*

Policy at the Crossroads. Gender and Welfare State Restructuring (New York: Routledge) pp. 287–307.

Beveridge, Fiona and Sue Nott (2002) 'Mainstreaming: a Case for Optimism and Cynicism', *Feminist Legal Studies*, 10, 299–311.

BMFSFJ (2001) *Vereinbarung zwischen der Bundesregierung und den Spitzenverbänden der deutschen Wirtschaft zur Förderung der Chancengleichheit von Frauen und Männern in der Privatwirtschaft* (Berlin: BMFSFJ): http://www.bmfsfj.de/ Politikbereiche/gleichstellung,did=6408.html (Accessed 2 February 2006).

BMFSFJ (2003) *Bilanz 2003 der Vereinbarung zwischen der Bundesregierung und den Spitzenverbändern der deutschen Wirtschaft zur Förderung der Chancengleichheit von Frauen und Männern in der Privatwirtschaft* (Berlin: BMFSFJ).

BMFSFJ (2004) *Frauen in Deutschland* (Bonn: BMFSFJ).

Boer, Margreet de and Marjan Wijers (2006) *Taking Women's Rights seriously? Shadow report by Dutch NGOs; an examination of the Fourth Report by the Government of the Netherlands on the implementation of the UN Convention on the Elimination of All Forms of Discrimination against Women, 2000–2004* (Utrecht: NJCM).

Boles, Janet (1993) 'Form Follows Function: the Evolution of Feminist Strategies', *Social Policy*, 23, 38–49.

Borchorst, Anette (1999) 'Equal Status Institutions' in Christina Bergqvist et al. (eds) *Equal Democracies? Gender and Politics in the Nordic Countries* (Oslo: Scandinavian University Press) pp. 167–89.

Borchorst, Anette and Birte Siim (2002) 'The Women-Friendly Welfare States Revisited', *NORA: Nordic Journal of Women's Studies*, 10, 2, 90–8.

Boréus, Kristina. 2006. *Diskrimineringens retorik: En studie av svenska valrörelser 1988–2002.* Stockholm: Ministry of Justice.

Borgström, Claes, Eriksson, Holger and Klinth, Roger (2003) 'Gör föräldrapengen helt individuell', in *Dagens Nyheter*, 13 February.

Börzel, Tanja A. (2002) *States and Regions in the European Union. Institutional Adaptation in Germany and Spain.* (Cambridge: Cambridge University Press).

Braun, Kathrin (2007) 'Women, Embryos, and the Good Society. Gendering the Bioethics Debate in Germany' in Melissa Haussman and Birgit Sauer (eds) *Gendering the State in the Age of Globalisation. Women's Movements and State Feminism in Post Industrial Democracies* (Lanham, MD: Rowman and Littlefield).

Buchanan, James and Gordon Tullock (1962) *The Calculus of Consent* (Ann Arbor: University of Michigan Press).

Buchinger, Birgit and Siegline Katharina Rosenberger (2001) 'A Women-Friendly Employment Administration Pursues Symbolic Policies in Austria' in Amy G. Mazur (ed.) *State Feminism, Women's Movements, and Job Training. Making Democracies Work in a Global Economy* (New York/London: Routledge) pp. 65–76.

Bundesministeriengesetz (2003) Bundesministeriengesetz-Novelle, *Bundesgesetzblatt für die Republik Östereich*, 25 April.

Bureau Boven (1998) *Mini-onderzoek Emancipatiecentra in Nederland. Advies 'Meeting Point'* (Amsterdam: Bureau Boven).

Bustelo, María (1998) 'Regional Public Policies for Gender Equality in Spain: Analysis and Evaluation', Paper presented at ECPR, Warwick, 23–8 March.

Bustelo, María (2003) 'Gender Mainstreaming Evaluation: Ideas from a Meta-Evaluation Study of Eleven Evaluation Processes of Gender Equality Policies in Spain', *Evaluation*, 19, 4, 383–403.

Bustelo, María (2004) *La evaluación de las políticas de género en España* (Madrid: La Catarata).

Bustelo, María, Emanuela Lombardo, Raquel Platero and Elin Peterson (2004) *Country Study Spain. MAGEEQ Report* (Vienna: Institut für die Wissenschaften des Menschen).

Bustelo, María and Elin Peterson (2005) 'The Evolution of Policy Discourses and Policy Instruments within the Spanish State Feminism. A Unified or Fragmented Landscape?' Paper presented at ECPR, Granada, April.

Bustelo, María, Carmen Valiente and Patricia Villavicencio (forthcoming) 'Domestic Violence in Spain' in *Encyclopaedia of Domestic Violence* (New York: Routledge).

Calloni, Marina (2002) 'From Maternalism to Mainstreaming: Femocrats and the Reframing of Gender Equality Policy in Italy' in Ulrike Liebert (ed.) *Gendering Europeanisation* (New York: Peter Lang) pp. 117–48.

Camps, Victoria (1998) *El siglo de las mujeres* (Madrid: Cátedra).

Caul, Miki (1999) 'Women's Representation in Parliament: the Role of Political Parties', *Party Politics*, 5, 1, 79–98.

CEDAW (2003) *Consideration of reports submitted by States parties under article 18 of CEDAW. Fifth periodic report: Germany* (New York: CEDAW).

CEDAW (2004a) *Consideration of reports submitted by States parties under article 18 of CEDAW. Sixth periodic report: Austria* (New York: CEDAW).

CEDAW (2004b) *Consideration of reports submitted by States parties und Article 18 of the Convention on the Elimination of All Forms of Discrimination against Women. Austria* (New York: CEDAW).

CEDAW (2006) *Concluding Comments of the Committee on the Elimination of Discrimination against Women: Australia* (New York: CEDAW).

Celis, Karen (2001) 'The Abortion Debates in Belgium 1974–1990' in Dorothy McBride Stetson (ed.) *Abortion Politics, Women's Movements, and the Democratic State: a Comparative Study of State Feminism* (Oxford: Oxford University Press) pp. 39–62.

Celis, Karen and Petra Meier (2006) *De macht van het geslacht. Gender, politiek en beleid in België* (Leuven: Acco).

Chappell, Louise (2002a) 'The Femocrat Strategy: Expanding the Repertoire of Feminist Activists' in Karen Ross (ed.) *Women, Politics and Change* (Oxford: Oxford University Press) pp. 85–98.

Chappell, Louise (2002b) *Gendering Government: Feminist Engagement with the State in Australia and Canada* (Vancouver: University of British Columbia Press).

Childs, Sarah (2004) *New Labour's Women MPs* (London: Routledge).

CNEL (2003) *Rapporto sul mercato del lavoro 2002* (Rome: CNEL).

Colectivo IOÉ (1996) *El Asociacionismo femenino en la Comunidad de Madrid* (Madrid: Consejo de la Mujer).

Commissione Nazionale per la parità e le pari opportunità, Presidenza del Consiglio dei Ministri, Consulta delle Elette della Regione Piemonte (1999) *La riforma della pubblica amministrazione: la parola alle donne* (Turin: Presidenza del Consiglio dei Ministri).

Commissione Nazionale per la parità e le pari opportunità, Presidenza del Consiglio dei Ministri (2001) *Relazione al Presidente del Consiglio dei Ministri sull'attività svolta (1997–2000)* (Rome: Presidenza del Consiglio dei Ministri).

Commissione Nazionale per la parità e le pari opportunità, Presidenza del Consiglio dei Ministri (2003) *Regioni: quali statuti e quali leggi elettorali* (Rome: Presidenza del Consiglio dei Ministri).

Cooper, Davina (2004) *Challenging Diversity: Rethinking Equality and the Value of Difference* (Cambridge: Cambridge University Press).

Council of Europe (1998) Gender Mainstreaming. Conceptual framework, methodology and presentation of good practices. Final Report of the Group of Specialists on Mainstreaming (Strasbourg: Council of Europe).

Cram, Laura (2001) 'Governance "to Go": Domestic Actors, Institutions and the Boundaries of the Possible', *Journal of Common Market Studies*, 39, 4, 595–618.

CRE (2004) *Fairness for All: a New Commission for Equality and Human Rights: a Response* (London: Commission for Racial Equality).

Crenshaw, Kimberle (1998) 'Demarginalizing the Intersections of Race and Sex: a Black Feminist Critique of Antidiscrimination Doctrine, Feminist Theory, and Antiracist Politics' in Anne Phillips (ed.) *Feminism and Politics* (Oxford/New York: Oxford University Press) pp. 314–43.

Dackweiler, Regina-Maria (2003) *Wohlfahrtsstaatliche Geschlechterpolitik am Beispiel Österreichs. Arena eines widersprüchlich modernisierten Geschlechter – Diskurses* (Opladen: Leske und Budrich).

Dahlerup, Drude (1987) 'Confusing Concepts – Confusing Reality: a Theoretical Discussion of the Patriarchal State' in Anne Showstack Sassoon (ed.) *Women and the State* (London: Routledge) pp. 93–127.

Dahlerup, Drude (2006) *Women, Quotas and Politics* (London: Routledge, Taylor and Francis).

Daly, Mary (2000) *The Gender Division of Welfare* (Cambridge: Cambridge University Press).

Daly, Mary (2005) 'Gender Mainstreaming in Theory and Practice', *Social Politics. International Studies in Gender, State and Society*, 12, 3, 433–50.

Daly, Mary and Katherine Rake (2003) *Gender and the Welfare State: Care, Work and Welfare in Europe and the USA* (Cambridge: Polity).

Danna, Daniela (2004) 'Italy: the Never-ending Debate' in Joyce Outshoorn (ed.) *The Politics of Prostitution. Women's Movements, Democratic States and the Globalisation of Sex Commerce* (Cambridge: Cambridge University Press) pp. 165–84.

Davis, Sonia and Veronica Cooke (2002) *Why do Black Women Organise? A Comparative Analysis of Black Women's Voluntary Sector Organisations in Britain and their Relationship to the State* (London: Policy Studies Institute).

Dearing, Albin and Birgitt Haller (2000) *Das österreichische Gewaltschutzgesetz* (Vienna: Verlag Österreich).

Del Re, Alisa (ed.) (2004) *Quando le donne governano le città. Genere e gestione locale del cambiamento in tre regioni italiane* (Milan: Franco Angeli).

Della Porta, Donatella (2003) 'The Women's Movement, the Left, and the State: Continuities and Changes in the Italian Case' in Lee Ann Banaszak, Karen Beckwith and Dieter Rucht (eds) *Women's Movements Facing the Reconfigured State* (Cambridge: Cambridge University Press) pp. 48–68.

Deutscher Gewerkschaftsbund (2005) *Stellungnahme zum Entwurf des Chancengleichheitsgesetzes* (Stuttgart: DGB).

DiMaggio, Paul J. and Walter Powell (1991) 'The Iron Cave Revisited: Institutional Isomorphism and Collective Rationality in Organizational Fields' in Paul J. DiMaggio and Walter Powell (eds) *The New Institutionalism in Organizational Analysis* (Chicago: University of Chicago Press) pp. 63–82.

Dölling, Irene (2005) 'Ostdeutsche Geschlechterarrangements in Zeiten des neoliberalen Gesellschaftsumbaus' in Eva Schäfer, Ina Dietzsch, Petra Drauschke et al. (eds) *Irritation Ostdeutschland. Geschlechterverhältnisse in Deutschland seit der Wende* (Münster: Westfälisches Dampfboot) pp. 16–34.

Donà, Alessia (2004) 'Italy as Negotiator in the EU Equal Opportunities Policy', *Modern Italy*, 9, 2, 173–87.

Donà, Alessia (2006) *Le pari opportunità. Condizione femminile in Italia e integrazione europea* (Rome/Bari: Laterza).

Donaghy, Tahnya (2006) *Death of the Australian Femocrat*: http://www.unisa.edu.au/hawkeinstitute/hpw/documents/donaghy-death.doc (Accessed 11 January 2006).

Ds (2001) *Ändrad ordning. Strategisk utveckling för jämställdhet* (Stockholm: Ministry of Industry, Employment and Communications).

DTI (2004) *Commission for Equality and Human Rights: Government response to the consultation* (London: DTI).

Duyvendak, Jan Willem, Hein Anton van der Heijden, Ruud Koopmans and Luuk Wijmans (eds) (1992) *Tussen verbeelding en macht. 25 jaar nieuwe sociale bewegingen in Nederland.* (Amsterdam: SUA).

Dyson, Kevin and Kenneth Featherstone (1999) *The Road to Maastricht* (Oxford: Oxford University Press).

Eduards, Maud (1981) 'Sweden', in Joni Lovenduski and Jill Hills (eds) *The Politics of the Second Electorate* (London: Routledge and Kegan Paul) pp. 208–27.

Eisenstein, Hester (1996) *Inside Agitators: Australian Femocrats and the State* (Philadelphia, PA: Temple University Press).

Elman, Amy (1995) 'The State's Equality for Women: Sweden's Equality Ombudsman' in Dorothy McBride Stetson and Amy G. Mazur (eds) *Comparative State Feminism* (Thousand Oaks, CA: Sage Publications) pp. 237–54.

Erikson, Josefina (2005) 'Framing feminist policies – the case of prostitution and pornography in Sweden', paper presented at ECPR, Granada, April.

Escario, Pilar, Inés Alberdi and Ana Inés López-Accotto (1996) *Lo personal es político: El Movimiento Feminista en la Transición* (Madrid: Ministerio de Asuntos Sociales, Instituto de la Mujer).

Esping-Andersen, Gøsta (1990) *The Three Worlds of Welfare Capitalism* (Cambridge: Polity).

Esping-Andersen, Gøsta (2000) *I fondamenti sociali delle economie post-industriali* (Bologna: Il Mulino).

Eurostat (2005) *European Social statistics, Expenditure and Receipts. Data 1994–2002* (Brussels: European Union).

Fabbrini, Sergio (1999) *Quale democrazia. L'Italia e gli altri* (Rome/Bari: Laterza).

Facon, Pedro et al. (2004) *Gelijke kansenbeleid onderweg. Een internationaal vergelijkend onderzoek* (Bruges: die Keure).

Falkner, Gerda (2005) *Frauen sind anders . . . Männer auch! Gender Mainstreaming (GM) Projekte in der Bundesverwaltung* (Vienna: Bundesministerium für Gesundheit und Frauen).

Fawcett Society (2004) *Response to Government White Paper 'Fairness for All: a New Commission for Equality and Human Rights'* (London: Fawcett Society) http://www.fawcettsociety.org.uk/documents/Fawcett%20response%20to%20CEHR%20white%20paper.pdf (Accessed 24 October 2006).

Fawcett Society (2006) *Response to Advancing Equality for Men and Women: Government Proposals to Introduce a Public Sector Duty to Promote Gender Equality* (London: Fawcett Society) http://www.fawcettsociety.org.uk/documents/

Fawcett%20response%20to%20Advancing%20Equality_Jan%20061.doc. (Accessed 24 October 2006).

Ferree, Myra Marx (1995) 'Making Equality: the Women's Affairs Offices in the Federal Republic of Germany' in Dorothy McBride Stetson and Amy, Mazur (eds) *Comparative State Feminism* (London: Sage) pp. 95–113.

Ferree, Myra Marx, William A. Gamson, Jürgen Gerhards and Dieter Rucht (2002) *Shaping Abortion Discourse. Democracy and the Public Sphere in Germany and the United States* (Cambridge: Cambridge University Press).

Ferree, Myra Marx and Carol Mueller (2004) 'Feminism and the Women's Movement: a Global Perspective' in David A. Snow, Sarah A. Soule and Hanspeter Kriesi (eds) *The Blackwell Companion to Social Movements* (Malden, MA: Blackwell Publishing) pp. vii–ix.

Ferree, Myra Marx and Aili Mari Tripp (2006) 'Preface' in Myra Marx Ferree and Aili Mari Tripp (eds) *Global Feminism: Transnational Women's Activism, Organizing and Human Rights* (New York: New York University Press) pp. 576–607.

Ferrera, Maurizio (1993) *Modelli di solidarietà* (Bologna: Il Mulino).

FI (2006) *För en feministisk politik* (Stockholm: Feministiskt initiativ) http://www.feministisktintiativ.se.

Flood, Michael (2006) *Misrepresentation of violence by current or previous partners in the Personal Safety Survey's Executive Summary*, Postings to Ausfem-polnet, 14 and 15 August.

Franceschet, Susan (2003) 'State Feminism and Women's Movements: the Impact of Chile's Servicio Nacional de la Mujer on Women's Activism', *Latin American Research Review*, 38, 1, 9–40.

Fransson, Susanne (2000) *Lönediskriminering* (Uppsala: Iustus förlag).

Fraser, Nancy (1993) 'Clintonism, Welfare, and the Antisocial Wage: the Emergence of a Neoliberal Political Imaginary', *Rethinking Marxism*, 6, 1, 9–23.

Galès, Patrick le (2005) 'Reshaping the State? Administrative and Decentralization Reforms' in Alistair Cole, Patrick le Galès and Jonah D. Levy (eds) *Developments in French Politics*. (Basingstoke: Palgrave Macmillan) pp. 122–38.

Gaspard, Françoise (2003) 'Où en est le feminisme aujourd'hui?' *Cités*, 100, 9, 59–71.

Gelb, Joyce (1989) *Feminism and Politics* (Berkeley: University of California Press).

Gehring, Jacqueline (2005) 'One European Directive, Two Dramatically Different Responses: Explaining the Divergence in French and German Racial Anti-discrimination Policy after the Race Directive', paper presented at the American Political Science Association Annual Meeting, Washington DC.

Gertzog, Irwin N. (1995) *Congressional Women: Their Recruitment, Integration, and Behavior* (Westport, CT: Praeger).

Geschäftseinteilung (2006) *Wiederverlautbarung* (Vienna: Bundesministerium für Gesundheit und Frauen).

GFMK (2005) *Beschluss 'Zusammenlegung der GFMK mit der JMK'* (Schwerin: GFMK).

Gil, Juana María (1996) *Las políticas de igualdad en España: Avances y retrocesos* (Granada: Universidad de Granada)

Gladdish, Kenneth (1991) *Governing from the Centre: Politics and Policy-making in the Netherlands* (London: Hurst/The Hague: SDU).

Goetz, Anne Marie (2003) 'National Women's Machinery: State-based Institutions to Advocate for Gender Equality' in Shirin Rai (ed.) *Mainstreaming Gender,*

Democratizing the State? Institutional Mechanisms for the Advancement of Women (Manchester: Manchester University Press) pp. 69–95.

Goetz, Anne Marie (2004) 'Advocacy Administration in the context of Economic and Political Liberalisation', A paper prepared for the United Nations Division for the Advancement of Women conference, Rome, 29 November–2 December 2004.

Government Programme (2003) *The Government Programme of Prime Minister Matti Vanhanen's Government*, 24 June.

Groenman, Louise et al. (1997) *Het vrouwenverdrag in Nederland anno 1997: Verslag van de commissie voor de eerste nationale rapportage over de implementatie in Nederland van het Internationaal Verdrag tegen Discriminatie van Vrouwen* (The Hague: Ministerie van Sociale Zaken en Werkgelegenheid).

Guadagnini, Marila (1995) 'The Latecomers: Italy's Equal Status and Equal Opportunity Agencies' in Dorothy McBride Stetson and Amy Mazur (eds) *Comparative State Feminism* (Thousand Oaks: Sage) pp. 150–67.

Guadagnini, Marila (2001) 'Limited Women's Policy Agencies Produces Limited Results in Italy' in Amy Mazur (ed.) *State Feminism, Women's Movements and Job Training. Making Democracies Work in a Global Economy* (New York/London: Routledge) pp. 131–54.

Guadagnini, Marila (2005) 'Gendering the Debate on Political Representation in Italy: a Difficult Challenge' in Joni Lovenduski (ed.) *State Feminism and Political Representation* (Cambridge: Cambridge University Press) pp. 131–52.

Guadagnini, Marila (2007) 'The Reform of the State in Italy' in Birgit Sauer and Melissa Haussman (eds) *State Feminism in Post Industrial Democracies* (Lanham, MD: Rowman and Littlefield).

Gundle Stephen and Simon Parker (eds) (1996) *The New Italian Republic. From the Fall of the Berlin Wall to Berlusconi* (London/New York: Routledge).

Gustafsson, Gunnel, Maud Eduards and Malin Rönnblom (1997) *Towards a New Democratic Order? Women's Organizing in Sweden in the 1990s* (Stockholm: Publica).

Gustafsson, Malin (2006) *'En plan för jämställdhet borde kanske utarbetas, men förekommer det ett behov?'– en kartläggning av 26 svenskspråkiga kommuners främjande av jämställdhet*, Master's thesis (Helsinki: University of Helsinki).

Haataja, Anita (2004) 'Yhden tai kahden ansaitsijan malli: vaikutukset ansiotyön, hoivan ja tulojen jakoon' in Heikki Räisänen and Reino Hjerppe (eds) *Hyvinvointi ja työmarkkinoiden eriytyminen*, VATT-julkaisuja 40, pp. 162–86.

Haegendoren, Mieke van, et al. (1994) *Onderzoek naar de financieringsmiddelen van vrouwenorganisaties* (Diepenbeek: LUC).

Halsaa, Beatrice (1991) *Policies and Strategies on Women in Norway: the Role of Women's Organisations, Political Parties and the Government*, Skriftserien nr. 74 (Lillehammer: Oppland Distriktshøgskole).

Hantrais, Linda (ed.) (2000) *Gendered Policies in Europe : Reconciling Employment and Family Life* (London: Macmillan).

Harris, Gardner (2005) 'Report Details F.D.A. Rejection of Next Day Pill', *New York Times*. (15 November), A1.

Hart, Joop de (2005) *Landelijk verenigd. Grote ledenorganisaties over ontwikkelingen op het maatschappelijk middenveld* (The Hague: Sociaal en Cultureel Planbureau).

Haussman, Melissa and Birgit Sauer (eds) (2007) *Gendering the State in the Age of Globalisation. Women's Movements and State Feminism in Post-Industrial Democracies* (Lanham, MD: Rowman and Littlefield).

Hayward, Jack and Anand Menon (eds) (2003) *Governing Europe* (Oxford: Oxford University Press).

Heinen, Jacqueline (2004) 'Genre et politiques familiales' in Christine Bard, Christian Baudelot and Janine Mossuz-Lavau (eds) *Quand les femmes s'en mêlent* (Paris: Éditions de la Martinière) pp. 283–99.

Heiskala, Risto (2006) 'Kansainvälisen toimintaympäristön muutos ja Suomen yhteiskunnallinen murros' in Risto Heiskala and Eeva Luhtakallio (eds) *Uusi jako: Miten Suomesta tuli kilpailukyky-yhteiskunta?* (Helsinki: Gaudeamus) pp. 14–42.

Hernes, Helga (1987) *Welfare State and Women Power. Essays in State Feminism* (Oslo: Norwegian University Press).

Hiilamo, Heikki (2002) *The Rise and Fall of Nordic Family Policy? Historical Development and Changes During the 1990s in Sweden and Finland* (Helsinki: Stakes).

Himmelweit, Susan (2006) 'Making Policymakers more Gender Aware: Experiences and Reflections from the Women's Budget Group in the United Kingdom' in Heidi Hartmann (ed.) *Gendering Politics and Policy* (New York: Haworth Press) pp. 109–22.

Hobson, Barbara (1999) 'Women's Collective Agency, Power Resources and the Framing of Citizenship Rights' in Michael Hanagan and Charles Tilly (eds) *Extending Citizenship, Reconfiguring States* (Lanham, MD: Rowan and Littlefield) pp. 19–78.

Holli, Anne Maria (1991) *Miehisestä tasa-arvosta kohti naisten käsitteellistä tilaa. Tasa-arvoasiain neuvottelukunnan tasa-arvopoliittinen diskurssi vv. 1972–86* Licenciate thesis (Helsinki: University of Helsinki).

Holli, Anne Maria (1992) 'Kunnalliset tasa-arvotoimikunnat tasa-arvolain jälkeen', in Ritva Reinboth (ed.) *Naiskuntavaaleihin*. Tasa-arvojulkaisuja, sarja B: Tiedotteita 1/1992 (Helsinki: Sosiaali- ja terveysministeriö) pp. 71–8.

Holli, Anne Maria (1995) 'Tarvitsemmeko kahta valtiollista tasa-arvoelintä?' *Politiikka* 4, 279–82.

Holli, Anne Maria (2001) 'A Shifting Policy Environment Divides the Impact of State Feminism in Finland', in Amy Mazur (ed.) *State Feminism, Women's Movements and Job Training: Making Democracies Work in the Global Economy* (New York/London: Routledge) pp. 183–212.

Holli, Anne Maria (2002) 'Suomalaisen tasa-arvopolitiikan haasteet', in Anne Maria Holli, Terhi Saarikoski and Elina Sana (eds) *Tasa-arvopolitiikan haasteet* (Helsinki: WSOY and Tasa-arvoasiain neuvottelukunta) pp. 12–30.

Holli, Anne Maria (2003) *Discourse and Politics for Gender Equality in Late Twentieth Century Finland* (Helsinki: Helsinki University Press).

Holli, Anne Maria (2004) 'Towards a New Prohibitionism? State Feminism, Women's Movements and Prostitution Policies in Finland' in Joyce Outshoorn (ed.) *The Politics of Prostitution. Women's Movements, Democratic States and the Globalisation of Sex Commerce* (Cambridge: Cambridge University Press) pp. 103–22.

Holli, Anne Maria (2006) 'Strong Together? A Comparative Study of the Impact of the Women's Movement on Policy-making in Finland' in Sirkku K. Hellsten, Anne Maria Holli and Krassimira Daskalova (eds) *Women's Citizenship and Political Rights* (Basingstoke: Palgrave MacMillan) pp. 127–53.

Holli, Anne Maria, Eeva Luhtakallio and Eeva Raevaara (2003) *Gender and Local Management of Change. National Report of Finland*, http://webappo.sh.se/ C1256DA9002F395F/0/C4A304639821BFACC1256DE5004C1698/$file/report %20finland.PDF (accessed 24 October 2006).

Holli, Anne Maria and Johanna Kantola (2005) 'A Politics for Presence: State Feminism, Women's Movements and Political Representation in Finland' in Joni Lovenduski (ed.) *State Feminism and Political Representation* (Cambridge: Cambridge University Press) pp. 62–84.

Holli, Anne Maria, Eeva Luhtakallio and Eeva Raevaara (2006) 'Quota Trouble. Talking about Gender Quotas In Finnish Local Politics', *International Feminist Journal of Politics*, 8, 2, 169–93.

Hondeghem, Annie and Sarah Nelen (2000) 'Een beleid op weg. Situering van het gelijke-kansenbeleid in België', *Tijdschrift voor Genderstudies*, 3, 1, 36–48.

Hooghe, Marc (1994) 'De organisatiestructuur van de Vlaamse vrouwenbeweging. Autonomie en integratie in een gesloten politieke cultuur', *Sociologische Gids*, 41, 2, 144–61.

Hooghe, Marc (1997) *Nieuwkomers op het Middenveld. Nieuwe sociale bewegingen als actoren in het Belgisch politiek systeem. De milieubeweging en de vrouwenbeweging in Vlaanderen, 1970–1990*, Doctoral thesis (Brussels: Vrije Universiteit Brussel).

Hoskyns, Catherine (1996) *Integrating Gender: Women, Law and Politics in the European Union* (London: Verso).

House of Commons (2005) *The Equality Bill*. House of Commons Research Paper 05/28. 24 March.

Howard, John (1995) *The Role of Government: a Modern Liberal Approach*. The Menzies Research Centre, National Lecture Series, 6 June.

Institute for Women's Policy Research (2004) *The Status of Women in the States 2004* (Washington DC: IWPR) http://www.iwpr.org/States2004/SWS2004/index.htm (accessed 24 October 2006).

Instituto de la Mujer (2005) *Estudio comparativo de los planes de igualdad de oportunidades entre mujeres y hombres autonómicos y nacional* (Madrid: Ministerio de Trabajo y Asuntos Sociales).

International Congress on Islamic Feminism (2005) *Conclusions*: http://www.oozebap.org/text/feminism_islam.htm (Accessed 30 October 2006).

IPM (1986) *Emancipatie en Subsidie* (The Hague: Ministerie van Sociale Zaken en Werkgelegenheid).

Jahan, Rounaq (1995) *The Elusive Agenda: Mainstreaming Women in Development* (London: Zed Books).

Jauhola, Marjaana (2005) 'Sotilaallinen kriisinhallinta ja suvaus' *Tasa-arvo*, 4, 8–9.

Jaunes Budgétaires (2005) *Projets de loi de finances pour 2005: Etats des crédits qui concourent aux actions en faveur des droits des femmes* (Paris: Imprimérie Nationale).

Jenson, Jane and Celia Valiente (2003) 'Comparing Two Movements for Gender Parity: France and Spain' in Lee Ann Banaszak, Karen Beckwith and Dieter Rucht (eds) *Women's Movements Facing the Reconfigured State* (Cambridge: Cambridge University Press) pp. 69–93.

Judge, David (2005) *Political Institutions in the United Kingdom* (Oxford: Oxford University Press).

Julkunen, Raija (2001) *Suunnanmuutos. 1990-luvun sosiaalipoliittinen reformi Suomessa* (Tampere: Vastapaino).

Julkunen, Raija (2002) 'Timanttejakin parempi ystävä? Hyvinvointivaltion murroksen sukupuolittuneet seuraukset', in Anne Maria Holli, Terhi Saarikoski and Elina Sana (eds) *Tasa-arvopolitiikan haasteet* (Helsinki: WSOY and Tasa-arvoasiain neuvottelukunta) pp. 32–49.

Kamenitsa, Lynn (2001) 'Abortion Debates in Germany' in Dorothy McBride Stetson (ed.) *Abortion Politics, Women's Movements, and the Democratic State. A Comparative Study of State Feminism* (New York: Oxford University Press) pp. 111–34.

Kamenitsa, Lynn and Brigitte Geissel (2005) 'WPAs and Political Representation in Germany' in Joni Lovenduski (ed.) *State Feminism and Political Representation* (Cambridge: Cambridge University Press) pp. 106–29.

Kantola, Johanna (2002) 'Rooman valtakunnan tuho: parisuhdelaki-keskustelua eduskunnassa', in Anne Maria Holli, Terhi Saarikoski and Elina Sana (eds) *Tasa-arvopolitiikan haasteet* (Helsinki: WSOY and Tasa-arvoasiain neuvottelukunta) pp. 287–304.

Kantola, Johanna (2006a) *Feminists Theorize the State* (Basingstoke: Palgrave Macmillan).

Kantola, Johanna (2006b) 'Transnational and National Gender Equality Politics: the European Union's Impact on Domestic Violence Policies in Britain and Finland' in Sirkku Hellsten, Anne Maria Holli and Krassimira Daskalova (eds) *Women's Citizenship and Political Rights* (Basingstoke: Palgrave Macmillan) pp. 154–78.

Kantola, Johanna and Hanne Marlene Dahl (2005) 'Feminist Understandings of the State: From Differences Between to Differences Within', *International Feminist Journal of Politics*, 7, 1, 49–70.

Kantola, Johanna and Judith Squires (2004) 'Prostitution Policies in Britain, 1982–2002' in Joyce Outshoorn (ed.) *The Politics of Prostitution: Women's Movements, Democratic States and the Globalisation of Sex Commerce* (Cambridge: Cambridge University Press) pp. 62–82.

Katzenstein, Mary (2003) ' "Redividing Citizens" – Divided Feminisms: the Reconfigured U.S. State and Women's Citizenship' in Lee Ann Banaszak, Karen Beckwith and Dieter Rucht (eds) *Women's Movements Facing the Reconfigured State* (Cambridge: Cambridge University Press) pp. 203–18.

Kaye, Miranda and Julia Tolmie (1998) 'Discoursing Dads: the Rhetorical Devices of Fathers' Rights Groups', *Melbourne University Law Review*, 22, 162–94.

Keck, Margaret E. and Kathryn, Sikkink (1998) *Activists Beyond Borders: Advocacy Networks in International Politics* (Ithaca/London: Cornell University Press).

Keebaugh, Shannon (2003) 'Discounting Care: Shared Care and Social Security Policy', *Australian Feminist Law Journal*, 18, 152–78.

Keter, Vincent (2005) The Equality Bill. Bill 72 of 2004–5. Research Paper 05/28 (London: House of Commons Library).

Key, Stephanie (2005) 'State Government Embarks on Equality Drive for SA', *Media Release*, The Hon. Stephanie Key MP, 28 October.

Kingdom of Belgium (2004) *Response to the questionnaire on implementation of the Beijing platform for action (1995) and the outcome of the twenty-third special session of the general assembly (2000).* http://www.un.org/womenwatch/daw/Review/ responses/ BELGIUM-English.pdf. (Accessed 30 June 2006).

Kitschelt, Herbert and Wolfgang Streeck (eds) (2004) *Germany: Beyond the Stable State* (London: Frank Cass).

Kodre, Petra and Henrike Mueller (2003) 'Shifting Policy Frames: EU Equal Treatment Norms and Domestic Discourses in Germany' in Ulrike Liebert (ed.) *Gendering Europeanisation* (Brussels: Peter Lang).

Koekebakker, Welmoed and Wendy van der Tol (2005) *Zijn de verwachtingen van Beijing uitgekomen? Nederlandse NGO-Schaduwrapportage* (Amsterdam, Tijd voor Actie! Initiatief Beijing+ 10 Nederland).

Kogoj, Traude (ed.) (1998) *Lauter Frauen. Hintergründe und Perspektiven des Frauenvolksbegehren* (Vienna: Turia und Kant).

Kontos, Silvia (2004) *Grüne Frauen- und Geschlechterpolitik in Regierung und Partei – Stand und Perspektiven* (Wiesbaden: GLOW) http://www.glow-boell.de/media/de/txt_rubrik_2/Kontos.pdf (Accessed 9 September 2006).

Köpl, Regina (2001) 'State Feminism and Policy Debates on Abortion in Austria', in Dorothy McBride Stetson (ed.) *Abortion Politics, Women's Movements, and the Democratic State* (Oxford: Oxford University Press) pp. 17–38.

Köpl, Regina (2005) 'Gendering Political Representation: Debates and Controversies in Austria', in Joni, Lovenduski et al. (ed.) *State Feminism and the Political Representation of Women in Europe and North America* (Cambridge: Cambridge University Press) pp. 20–41.

Kriesi, Hanspeter, Ruud Koopmans, Jan Willem Duyvendak and Mario Giugni (eds) (1995) *New Social Movements in Western Europe. A Comparative Analysis* (Minneapolis: Minnesota Press).

Krook, Mona Lena and Judith Squires (2006) *Gender Quotas and Gender Mainstreaming: Competing or Complementary Representational Strategies?* Paper presented at the PSA Women and Politics Conference, Edinburgh 11 February.

Kuhl, Mara (1998) *Belgische overheidsstructuren voor vrouwenbeleid*, Thesis (Antwerp: University of Antwerp).

Kulawik, Teresa (1992) 'Autonomous Mothers? West German Feminism Reconsidered', *German Politics & Society*, 24/25, 67–86.

Laney, Garinne P. (2004) 'Impact of the Violence Against Women Act', *Congressional Research Service*, Washington, DC (5 March).

Lang, Sabine (1997) 'The NGOization of Feminism' in Joan W. Scott, Cora Kaplan and Deborah Keates (eds) *Transitions, Environments, Translations. Feminisms in International Politics* (London: Routledge) pp. 101–20.

Lang, Sabine (2001) 'Reprivatisierungen im neoliberalen Geschlechterregime', *femina politica*, 14, 2, 91–104.

Lang, Sabine and Birgit Sauer (2003) ' "Doris ihr'n Mann seine Partei." Die Reduktion von Frauen- auf Familienpolitik im bundesdeutschen Wahlkampf', *Österreichische Zeitschrift für Politikwissenschaft*, 4, 329–442.

Larner, Wendy (2000) 'Neo-liberalism: Policy, Ideology, Governmentality', *Studies in Political Economy*, 63, 5–25.

Laufer, Jacqueline and Rachel Silvera (2005) *Accords sur l'Egalité Professionnelle Suite à la Loi du 9 mai 2001: Premiers Eléments d'Analyse* (Paris: Timetis).

Law 609/1986 'Laki naisten ja miesten välisestä tasa-arvosta' (Helsinki: Säädöskokoelma).

Law 206/1995 'Laki naisten ja miesten välisestä tasa-arvosta' (Helsinki: Säädöskokoelma).

Law 232/2005 'Laki naisten ja miesten välisestä tasa-arvosta' (Helsinki: Säädöskokoelma).

Lehto, Juhani and Kauko Blomster (2000) 'Talouskriisin jäljet sosiaali- ja terveyspalvelujärjestelmässä' in Hannu Uusitalo, Annit Parpo, and Anni Hakkarainen (eds) *Sosiaali- ja terveydenhuollon palvelukatsaus*. Raportteja 250 (Helsinki: Stakes).

Lehtonen, Heikki (2000) 'Voiko suomalainen hyvinvointimalli muuttua?', *Sosiologia* 37, 2, 130–41.

Leyenaar, Monique (2004) *Political Empowerment of Women. The Netherlands and Other Countries* (Leiden/Boston: Martinus Nijhoff).

Lejonqvist-Jurvanen, Nina (2004) *Betydelsen av det kvinnliga intresset i Finlands riksdag – en studie av riksdagens kvinnliga nätverk åren 1991–1999*, Master's thesis (Helsinki: University of Helsinki).

Lépinard, Eléonore (2007) 'The Contentious Subject of Feminism: Defining "Women" in France from the Second Wave to Parity', *Signs* 32, 3.

Leväsvirta (1999) *Kuntien hallinto muuttuvassa toimintaympäristössä*. Acta nro 114 (Helsinki: Suomen Kuntaliitto).

Levy, Jonah D., Alistair Cole and Patrick le Galès (2005) 'Introduction: the Shifting Politics of the Fifth Republic' in Alistair Cole, Patrick le Galès and Jonah D. Levy (eds) *Developments in French Politics* (Basingstoke: Palgrave Macmillan) pp. 1–17.

Lewis, Jane (1993) *Women and Social Policies in Europe: Work, Family and the State* (Aldershot: Ashgate).

Liebert, Ulrike (2003) 'Between Diversity and Equality: Analysing Europeanisation' in Ulrike Liebert (ed.) *Gendering Europeanisation* (Brussels: Presses Interuniversitaires Européennes) pp. 11–46.

Lindbom, Anders (2001) 'Dismantling the Social Democratic Welfare Model? Has the Swedish Welfare State Lost its Defining Characteristics?', *Scandinavian Political Studies*, 24, 3, 171–93.

Lindvert, Jessica (2002) *Feminism som Politik: Sverige och Australien 1960–1990* (Umeå: Boréa Bokförlag).

Lombardo, Emanuela (2003) 'EU Gender Policy: Trapped in the "Wollstonecraft Dilemma"?' *European Journal of Women's Studies*, 10, 2, 59–180.

Lombardo, Emanuela (2004) *La europeización de la política española de igualdad de género* (Valencia: Tirant Lo Blanch).

Lombardo, Emanuela (2005) 'Integrating or Setting the Agenda? Gender Mainstreaming in the European Constitution-Making Process', *Social Politics*, 12, 3, 412–32.

Lopez-Claros, Augusto and Saadia Zahidi (2005) 'Women's Empowerment: Measuring the Global Gender Gap' (Geneva: World Economic Forum).

Lovecy, Jill (2002) 'Gender Mainstreaming and the Framing of Women's Rights in Europe: the Contribution of the Council of Europe', *Feminist Legal Studies*, 10, 271–83.

Lovenduski, Joni, Claudie Baudino, Marila Guadagnini, Petra Meier and Diane Sainsbury (eds) (2005) *State Feminism and Political Representation* (Cambridge: Cambridge University Press).

Lovenduski, Joni and Vicky Randall (1993) *Contemporary Feminist Politics* (Oxford: Oxford University Press).

Lundin, Linnea (2006) *Är könsdiskriminering unik? En analys av argumenten för och emot en gemensam ombudsman mot diskriminering*, Thesis (Uppsala: Uppsala University).

Maddison, Sarah, Richard Denniss and Clive Hamilton (2004) *Silencing Dissent: Non-government Organisations and Australian Democracy*, Discussion Paper 65 (Canberra: Australia Institute).

Mairhuber, Ingrid (1999) 'Geschlechterpolitik im Sozialstaat Österreich seit Anfang der 80er Jahre', *Österreichische Zeitschrift für Politikwissenschaft*, 28, 1, 35–47.

Majoinen, Kaija (2001) *Mitä virkaa valtuustolla? Kuntalailla säädetyn valtuuston perustehtävän monitahoarviointi*. Acta-väitöskirjasarja 2/2001 (Helsinki: Suomen Kuntaliitto).

Martínez, Eva (1997) 'Políticas Públicas para la igualdad entre los sexos: reflexiones sobre el caso español (1975–1997)' in Edurna Uriarte and Arantxa Elizondo (eds) *Mujeres en política. Análisis y práctica* (Barcelona: Ariel) pp. 211–32.

Matland, Richard and Donley Studlar (1996) 'The Contagion of Women Candidates in Single-Member Districts and Proportional Representation Electoral Systems: Canada and Norway', *Journal of Politics*, 58, 3, 707–33.

Mayrhofer, Monika (2006) ' "Was Männer bewegt" – Neokonservative. Männlichkeitspolitik in Osterreich im Kontext der Einrichtung der Männerpolitischen Grundsatzabteilung', *Feministische Studien*, 2, 276–89.

Mazey, Sonia (2001) *Gender Mainstreaming in the EU: Principles and Practice* (London: Kogan Page).

Mazey, Sonia (2002) 'Gender Mainstreaming Strategies in the EU: Delivering an Agenda?', *Feminist Legal Studies*, 10, 227–40.

Mazur, Amy G. (1995a) 'Strong State and Symbolic Reform in France: le Ministère des Droits de la Femme', in Dorothy McBride Stetson and Amy G. Mazur (eds) *Comparative State Feminism* (Thousand Oaks, CA: Sage) pp. 76–94.

Mazur, Amy G. (1995b) *Gender Bias and the State: Symbolic Reform at Work in Fifth Republic France* (Pittsburgh, PA: University of Pittsburgh Press).

Mazur, Amy G. (ed.) (2001a) *State Feminism, Women's Movements, and Job Training: Making Democracies Work in the Global Economy* (New York: Routledge).

Mazur, Amy G. (2001b) 'Republican Universalism Resists State Feminist Approaches to Gendered Equality in France' in Amy G. Mazur (ed.) *State Feminism, Women's Movements and Job Training* (New York: Routledge) pp. 155–82.

Mazur, Amy G. (2002) *Theorizing Feminist Policy* (Oxford: Oxford University Press).

Mazur, Amy G. (2004) 'Prostitute Movements face Elite Apathy and Gender Biased Universalism in France' in Joyce Outshoorn (ed.) *The Politics of Prostitution: Women's Movements, Democratic States and the Globalisation of Sex Commerce* (Cambridge: Cambridge University Press) pp. 123–43.

Mazur, Amy G. (2005) 'Feminist Comparative Policy: Leading European Political Science into Future', *European Political Science*, 3, 2, 67–77.

Mazur, Amy G. (2007) '35 Hour Work-week Reforms in France, 1997–2000: Strong Feminist Demands, Elite Apathy, and Disappointing Outcomes', in Melissa Haussman and Birgit Sauer, *Hot Issues, State Feminism, and Reconfigured States* (Lanham, MD: Rowman and Littlefield).

McBride Stetson, Dorothy (ed.) (2001a) *Abortion Politics, Women's Movements and the Democratic State: a Comparative Study of State Feminism* (Oxford: Oxford University Press).

McBride Stetson, Dorothy (2001b) 'Federal and State Women's Policy Agencies Help to Represent Women in the United States', in Amy Mazur (ed.) *State Feminism, Women's Movements, and Job Training: Making Democracies Work in a Global Economy* (New York: Routledge) pp. 272–92.

McBride Stetson, Dorothy (2001c) 'US Abortion Debates 1959–1998: the Women's Movement Holds On' in Dorothy McBride Stetson (ed.) *Abortion Politics, Women's Movements, and the Democratic State* (Oxford: Oxford University Press) pp. 247–66.

McBride Stetson, Dorothy (2004) 'The Invisible Issue: Prostitution and the Trafficking of Women and Girls in the United States' in Joyce Outshoorn (ed.) *The Politics of Prostitution: Women's Movements, and the State* (Cambridge: Cambridge University Press) pp. 245–64.

McBride, Dorothy E. (2007) 'Welfare Reform: America's Hot Issue', in Melissa Haussman and Birgit Sauer (eds) *Gendering the State in the Age of Globalization: Comparative Study of State Feminism* (Boulder: Rowman and Littlefield).

McBride Stetson, Dorothy and Amy G. Mazur (eds) (1995) *Comparative State Feminism* (London/Thousand Oaks/New Delhi: Sage).

McBride, Dorothy E. and Amy G. Mazur (2005) 'The Comparative Study of Women's Movements: Conceptual Puzzles and RNGS Solutions', Paper presented at the Annual Conference of the American Political Science Association, Washington, DC, 1–5 September.

McBride, Dorothy E. and Amy G. Mazur (forthcoming) 'Women's Movements and Feminism', in Gary Goertz and Amy G. Mazur (eds) *Politics, Gender, and Concepts: Theory and Methodology.*

McIntosh, Mary (1978) 'The State and the Oppression of Women' in Annette Kuhn and AnnMarie Wolpe (eds) *Feminism and Materialism: Women and Modes of Production* (London: Routledge and Kegan Paul) pp. 254–89.

McLeod, Mike, David Owen and Chris Khamis (2001) *Black and Minority Ethnic Voluntary and Community Organisations: their Role And Future Development in England and Wales* (London: Policy Studies Institute).

Meehan, Elizabeth (1985) *Women's Rights at Work: Campaigns and Policy in Britain and the United States* (London: Macmillan).

Meehan, Elizabeth (2005) *The Experience of a Single Equalities Commission in Northern Ireland.* Paper presented to ESRC Seminar in Public Policy, Equality and Diversity in the Context of Devolution, Edinburgh, 10 June.

Meerjarenbeleidsplan Emancipatie 2006–2010. *Emancipatie: Vanzelfsprekend, maar het gaat niet vanzelf!* Handelingen Tweede Kamer, 2004–2005, 30420, nr. 2, December.

Meerjarennota, *Van Vrouwenstrijd naar vanzelfsprekendheid*, Handelingen Tweede Kamer, 1999–2000, 27061, nrs 1–2, March.

Meier, Petra (2004) 'The Contagion Effect of National Gender Quota on Similar Party Measures in the Belgian Electoral Process', *Party Politics* 10, 3, 583–600.

Meier, Petra (2005) 'The Belgian Paradox: Inclusion and Exclusion of Gender Issues' in Joni Lovenduski et al. (eds) *State Feminism and Political Representation* (Cambridge: Cambridge University Press) pp. 41–61.

Melkas, Tuula and Anna-Maija Lehto (2005) *Tasa-arvosuunnittelu julkisella sektorilla. Selvitys suunnitteluvelvoitteen toteutumisesta.* Tasa-arvojulkaisuja 2005:3 (Helsinki: Tasa-arvovaltuutetun toimisto, Sosiaali- ja terveysministeriö).

Meyer, David S. (2003) 'Restating the Woman Question: Women's Movements and State Restructuring', in Lee Ann Banaszak, Karen Beckwith and Dieter Rucht, *Women's Movements Facing the Reconfigured State* (Cambridge: Cambridge University Press) pp. 275–95.

MINCO (2005) Communiqué of the Commonwealth, State, Territory and New Zealand Ministers' Council on the status of Women (Sydney, MINCO) http://ofw.facs.gov.au/downloads/pdfs/MINCO_communique_sept05.pdf (Accessed 7 September 2006).

Ministerie SZW (2001) *Gender Mainstreaming. Een strategie voor kwaliteitsverbetering* The Hague: Ministerie van Sociale Zaken en Werkgelegenheid).

Ministerie van Volksgezondheid en Leefmilieu (1987) *Emancipatieraad, 1987, Jaarverslag 1986–1987* (Brussels: Ministerie van Volksgezondheid en Leefmilieu).

Ministero per le pari opportunità (2004a) *Revisione dell'attuazione della Piattaforma d'azione di Pechino e documentazione dei risultati della 23ma seduta speciale dell'assemblea generale* (Rome: Ministero per le pari opportunità).

Ministero per le pari opportunità (2004b) *Programma di lavoro della Commissione per le pari opportunità fra donna e uomo per il biennio 2004–2005* (Rome: Ministero per le pari opportunità).

Ministero per le pari opportunità (2006) *La geografia delle Pari Opportunità* (Rome: Ministero per le pari opportunità).

Molyneux, Maxine (1998) 'Analyzing Women's Movements' in Cecile Jackson and Ruth Pearson, *Feminist Visions of Development: Gender, Analysis and Policy* (London: Routledge) pp. 65–88.

Molle, Leen van and Gubin Eliane (1998) *Vrouw en Politiek in België* (Tielt: Lannoo).

Morgan, Kimberly (2002) 'Does Anyone Have a Libre Choix: Subversive Liberalism and the Politics of French Child Care Policy', in Sonya Michel and Rianne Mahon (eds) *Child Care Policy at the Crossroads: Gender and Welfare State Restructuring* (London: Routledge) pp. 140–73.

Möttönen, Sakari (1997) *Tulosjohtaminen ja valta poliittisten päätöksentekijöiden välisessä suhteessa. Kunnallisen tulosjohtamisen poliittisten päätöksentekijöiden ja viranhaltijoiden välistä tehtäväjakoa koskevat tavoitteet, niiden merkitys osapuolten väliseen valtasuhteeseen sekä tavoitteiden toteutuminen ja toteuttamismahdollisuudet valtasuhteen näkökulmasta* (Helsinki: Suomen Kuntaliitto).

Mushaben, Joyce (2005) 'Girl Power, Mainstreaming and Critical Mass: Women's Leadership and Policy Paradigm Shift in Germany's Red–Green Coalition, 1998–2002,' *Women, Politics & Policy*, 27, 1/2, 135–62.

Mustakallio, Sinikka and Milja Saari (2002) 'Tasa-arvotyö työpaikoilla tasa-arvokonsultin näkökulmasta' in Anne Maria Holli, Terhi Saarikoski, Terhi and Elina Sana (eds) *Tasa-arvopolitiikan haasteet* (Helsinki: WSOY and Tasa-arvoasiain neuvottelukunta) pp. 165–88.

Naldini, Manuela (2003) *The Family in the Mediterranean Welfare States* (London: Frank Cass).

National Council for Research on Women (2004) *Missing: Information about Women's Lives* (Washington, DC: NCRW).

Neyer, Gerda (1997) 'Frauen im österreichischen politischen System', in Herbert Dachs et al. (eds) *Handbuch des politischen Systems Österreichs. Die Zweite Republik* (Vienna: Manzsche Verlags und Universitätsbuchhandlung) pp. 185–201.

Nielsen, Ruth (1996) *Employers' Prerogatives: in a European and Nordic Perspective* (Copenhagen: Handelshøjskolens forlag).

Nieminen, Liisa (2001) 'Tasa-arvo EU:n perusoikeuskirjassa turvattuna perusoikeutena' in Liisa Nieminen (ed.) *Perusoikeudet EU:ssa* (Helsinki: Kauppakaari) pp. 179–201.

Niskanen, William A. (1971) *Bureaucracy and Representative Government* (Chicago: Aldine Atherton).

Niven, Bob (2006) 'The CEHR', *Fabian Review*, April.

Norris, Pippa (1987) *Politics and Sexual Equality: the Comparative Position of Women in Western Democracies* (Colorado: Lynne Rienner).

Nousiainen, Kevätt (2005) 'Tasa-arvon monet kasvot: Kansainvälisistä vaikutuksista Suomen tasa-arvo-oikeudessa', *Lakimies*, 7–8, 1188–1209.

Nousiainen, Kevätt, Anu Pylkkänen, Anne Maria Holli, Johanna Kantola, Eeva Raevaara, Eeva Luhtakallio and Milja Saari (2004) *Kansalaisvaikuttamisen politiikkaaobjelman valtavirtaistamisselvitys*. *Tasa.arrvon työkirja*. Available at: http://www.om.fi/28636.htm

Nyström, Birgitta (2002) *EU och Arbetsrätten* (Stockholm: Norstedts Juridik AB).

Ocampo, Luisa (2002) 'Historia do movimento das mulheres na Galiza desde 1985– 2001' in *O evidente nom existe* (Vigo: Mulheres Nacionalistas Galegas) pp. 64–98.

O'Connor, Julia S., Ann Shola Orloff and Sheila Shaver (1999) *States, Markets, Families* (Cambridge: Cambridge University Press).

Oldersma, Jantine (1999) 'Het moderne feminisme en het sociaal kapitaal van Nederland', *Tijdschrift voor Sociologie*, 20, 3/4, 415–40.

Oldersma, Jantine and Joyce Outshoorn (2007) 'The "Home Care Gap": Neoliberalism, Feminism and the State in the Netherlands', in Melissa Haussman and Birgit Sauer (eds) *Gendering the State in the Age of Globalisation. Women's Movements and State Feminism in Post-Industrial Democracies* (Lanham, MD: Rowman and Littlefield).

Olsson Blandy, Tanja (2004) *The Europeanisation of Gender Policy: New Opportunities for Domestic Equality Agencies? The Case of Sweden*, paper presented at the ECPR, Bologna 24–6 June.

Olsson Blandy, Tanja (2005) 'Equal Pay and the Impact of the EU' in Per Ola Öberg and Torsten Svensson (eds) *Power and Institutions in Industrial Relation Regimes. Political Science Perspectives on the Transition of the Swedish Model* (Stockholm: National Institute for Working Life) pp. 199–225.

Olsson Blandy, Tanja (forthcoming) *The Europeanisation of Gender Policy – New Opportunities for Domestic Equality Agencies? The Case of Sweden*, Ph.D. thesis (Uppsala: Uppsala University).

Onwen, Hanna (2004) 'Valtavirtaistaminen tasa-arvon edistämisen työväli-neenä'. Available at http://www.minna.fi/minna/artikkelit/valtvirtonwen.html Accessed 23.1.2006.

Onyango, Christine (1996) 'U.S. Women Push for Implementing UN Women's Conference Goals', *Feminist Majority Newsletter*, 8, 1, http://www.feminist.org/research/report/13.htm (Accessed 5 March 2006).

Ortbals, Candice (2004) 'Embedded Institutions, Activisms, and Discourses: Untangling the Intersections of Women's Civil Society and Women's Policy Agencies in Spain', Ph.D. thesis, (Bloomington, IN: Indiana University).

Osborne, David (1990) *Laboratories of Democracy: A New Breed of Governor Creates Models for National Growth* (Boston: Harvard Business School Press).

Oskarson, Maria (1996) 'Skeptiska kvinnor – Entusiastiska män', in Mikael Gilljam and Sören Holmberg (eds) *Ett knappt ja till EU* (Stockholm: Norstedts juridik) pp. 1–24.

Österreichischer Amtskalender 2000–2002 (Vienna: Österreichische Staatsdruckerei).

Ostner, Ilona and Jane Lewis (1995) 'Gender and the Evolution of European Social Policies' in Stefan Leibfried and Paul Pierson (eds) *European Social Policy* (Washington DC: Brookings Institute) pp. 159–93.

Outshoorn, Joyce (1995) 'Administrative Accommodation in the Netherlands. The Department for the Coordination of Equality Policy', in Dorothy McBride Stetson and Amy Mazur (eds) *Comparative State Feminism* (London/Thousand Oaks/New Delhi: Sage) pp. 168–85.

Outshoorn, Joyce (2000) 'Op zoek naar de vrouwenbeweging in de jaren negentig' in Thijl Sunier, Jan Willem Duyvendak, Sawitri Saharso and Fridus

Steijlen (eds) *Emancipatie en subcultuur; sociale bewegingen in België en Nederland* (Amsterdam: Instituut voor Publiek en Politiek) pp. 30–50.

Outshoorn, Joyce (ed.) (2004a) *The Politics of Prostitution: Women's Movements, Democratic States and the Globalisation of Sex Commerce* (Cambridge: Cambridge University Press).

Outshoorn, Joyce (2004b) 'Introduction: Prostitution, Women's Movements and Democratic Politics' in Joyce Outshoorn (ed.) *The Politics of Prostitution: Women's Movements, Democratic States and the Globalisation of Sex Commerce* (Cambridge: Cambridge University Press) pp. 1–20.

Outshoorn, Joyce and Joke Swiebel (1998) 'Feminism and the State in the Netherlands', in Geertje Lycklama à Nijeholt, Virginia Vargas and Saskia Wieringa (eds) *Women's Movements and Public Policy in Europe, Latin America and the Caribbean* (New York: Garland) pp. 143–66.

Parry, Janine Alisa (1998) *Institutionalizing Interests: Women's Commissions in the United States.* Ph.D. thesis (Pullman: Washington State University).

Partido Socialista Obrero Español (1980) *Centros Asesores de la Mujer* (Madrid: Secretaría Federal de Política Sectorial).

Parviainen, Mervi (2006) *Tasa-arvoa laskimella: Tutkimus tasa-arvolain kiintiösäännöksen vaikutuksista kunnallisten toimielinten jäsenvalinnoissa* (Helsinki: Edita).

Pels, Dick (2003) *De geest van Pim: het gedachtegoed van een politieke dandy* (Amsterdam: Anthos).

Pentikäinen, Merja (2002) 'Tasa-arvoperiaate ihmisoikeusperiaatteena. Kansainväliset ihmisoikeudet ja naiset – näkymättömästä näkyvämmäksi', in Anne Maria Holli, Terhi Saarikoski and Elina Sana (eds) *Tasa-arvopolitiikan haasteet* (Helsinki: WSOY and Tasa-arvoasiain neuvottelukunta) pp. 70–98.

Pettman, Jan Jindy (1999) 'Globalization and the Gendered Politics of Citizenship' in Nira Yuval-Davis and Pnina Werbner (eds) *Women, Citizenship and Difference* (London and New York: Zed Books) pp. 207–20.

Picq, Françoise (2002) 'Le féminisme entre passé recomposé et futur incertain', *Cités*, 100, 9, 25–58.

PICW (2000) *About the Council* (Washington DC: Department of State) http://secretary.state.gov/www/picw/about_picw.html (Accessed 3 April 2005).

Pikkala, Sari (1999) 'Sukupuolikiintiöt kunnallishallinnossa', *Kunnallistieteellinen Aikakausikirja*, 27, 4, 473–83.

Pikkarainen, Heidi (2000) *Den statliga jämställdhetspolitiken 1982–1996 – en politik om kön och makt?* Master's thesis (Stockholm: University of Stockholm).

Pincus, Ingrid and Janneke van der Ros (1999) 'A Question of Political Will? The State, Local Authorities, and Equal Status Policy' in Christina Bergqvist et al. (eds) *Equal Democracies? Gender and Politics in the Nordic Countries* (Oslo: Scandinavian University Press) pp. 208–32.

Pini, Barbara, Ruth Panelli and Marian Sawer (2007) 'Managing the Woman Issue! The Australian State and the Case of Women in Agri-Politics', *International Journal of Feminist Politics*, 9.

Plasman, Robert and Salimata Sissoko (2003) *Country Belgium: State of the Art Report* (Brussels: DULBEA).

Platero, Raquel (2005a) *Linking gender equality and sexual orientation policies. An analysis of local, regional and national equality policies,* Paper presented at ECPR, Granada (Spain), April.

Platero, Raquel (2005b) *Are lesbians considered women by Spanish femocrats? The representation of non-normative sexualities in the national and regional equality policies*, Paper presented at ECPR, Budapest, 6–10 September.

Platero, Raquel (2006) 'Entre la invisibilidad y la igualdad formal: perspectivas feministas ante la representación del lesbianismo en el matrimonio homosexual', in Félix Rodríguez and Angie Simonis (eds), *Cultura, Homosexualidad y Homofobia* (Madrid: Gedisa).

Pollack, Mark A. and Emilie Hafner-Burton (2000) 'Mainstreaming Gender in the European Union', *Journal of European Public Policy*, 7, 3, 432–56.

Post, Vincent, Jantine Oldersma and Joyce Outshoorn (2006) 'Overwinteren of geruisloze mobilisatie? Ontwikkelingen in "de" vrouwenbeweging in Nederland sinds de jaren negentig', *Tijdschrift voor Gender Studies*, 9, 2, 12–25.

Praag, Philip van (2003) 'The Winners and Losers in a Turbulent Political Year', *Acta Politica*, 38, 1, 5–22.

Presidenza del Consiglio dei Ministri (2000) *DONNE 2000 a cinque anni dalla Conferenza mondiale di Pechino. Le cose fatte, gli ostacoli incontrati, le cose da fare*, Quaderni internazionali di vita italiana (Rome: Dipartimento per l'informazione e l'editoria).

Prop. 1993/94: 147. *Jämställdhetspolitiken: Delad makt – delat ansvar.*

Prop. 2005/06 155. *Makt att forma samhället och sitt eget liv – nya mål i jämställdhetspolitiken.*

Raad van Gelijke Kansen voor Mannen en Vrouwen (1997) *Activiteitenverslag 9.93–10.97* (Brussels: Ministerie voor Arbeid en Tewerkstelling).

Radaelli, Claudio M. (2006) 'Europeanization: Solution or Problem?' in Michelle Cini and Angela K. Bourne (eds) *European Union Studies* (Basingstoke: Palgrave Macmillan) pp. 56–76.

Raevaara, Eeva (2005) *Tasa-arvo ja muutoksen rajat – sukupuolten tasa-arvo poliittisena ongelmana Ranskan ja Suomen parlamenttikeskusteluissa* (Helsinki: TANE).

Rai, Shirin (2003a) 'Introduction' in Shirin Rai (ed.) *Mainstreaming Gender, Democratizing the State? Institutional Mechanisms for the Advancement of Women* (Manchester: Manchester University Press) pp. 1–12.

Rai, Shirin (2003b) 'Institutional Mechanisms for the Advancement of Women: Mainstreaming Gender, Democratizing the State?' in Shirin Rai (ed.) *Mainstreaming Gender, Democratizing the State? Institutional Mechanisms for the Advancement of Women* (Manchester: Manchester University Press) pp. 15–39.

Ramstedt-Silén, Viveca (1999) *Riksdagsutskott eller kvinnoförening? Det kvinnliga nätverket I Finlands riksdag* SSKH Notat 4/99 (Helsingfors: Svenska social- och kommunalhögskolan vid Helsingfors universitet).

Rankin, Pauline and Jill Vickers (1998) 'Locating Women's Politics' in Manon Tremblay and Caroline Andrew (eds) *Women and Political Representation in Canada* (Ottawa: Ottawa University Press) pp. 341–67.

Räsänen, Leila (2002) 'Hallituksen tasa-arvopolitiikkaa tekemässä' in Anne Maria Holli, Terhi Saarikoski and Elina Sana (eds) *Tasa-arvopolitiikan haasteet* (Helsinki: WSOY) pp. 100–27.

Raunio, Tapio and Matti Wiberg (eds) (2000) *EU ja Suomi: Unionijäsenyyden vaikutukset suomalaiseen yhteiskuntaan* (Helsinki: Edita).

Raunio, Tapio and Matti Wiberg (2001) *The Big Leap to the West: the Impact of EU on the Finnish Political System*, Discussion Paper C 89 2001 (Zentrum für Europäische Integrationsforschung).

Red Estatal de Organizaciones Feminists contra la Violencia de Género (2003) *Caso Tey: Queja al Defensor del pueblo:* http://www.redfeminista.org/nueva/uploads/queja%20defensor%20caso%20TEY.B.pdf. (Accessed 10 February 2006).

Rees, Theresa (1998) 'Reflections on the uneven development of gender mainstreaming in Europe', *International Feminist Journal of Politics*, 7, 4, 555–74.

Revillard, Anne (2006) 'Work/Family Policy in France: from State Familialism to State Feminism', *International Journal of Law*, 20, 2, 133–50.

Robinson, Jean C. (2001) 'Gendering the Abortion Debate: the French Case' in Dorothy McBride Stetson (ed.) *Abortion Politics, Women's Movements, and the Democratic State* (New York: Oxford University Press) pp. 87–110.

Rodríguez Aparicio, José (2002) 'Al amparo del islam', *El País – Nacional*, 4 March.

Rönnblom, Malin (2002) *Ett eget rum? Kvinnors organisering möter etablerad politik*, Ph.D. thesis (Umeå: Umeå University).

Rosenberger, Sieglinde (2003) 'Gender Mainstreaming als Gleichstellungsinstrument', paper presented at the conference *Institutionenwandel und Gender Mainstreaming. Zur Notwendigkeit von vergleichenden Policy-Analysen in der politikwissenschaftlichen Geschlechterforschung*, Vienna, 28–30 April.

Rosenberger, Sieglinde (2006) 'Frauen- und Gleichstellungspolitik', in Herbert Dachs et al. (eds) *Politik in Österreich. Das Handbuch* (Vienna: Manz) pp. 743–52.

Rösslhumer, Maria and Birgit Appelt (2001) *Hauptsache Frauen. Politikerinnen in der Zweiten Republik* (Graz/Vienna/Cologne: Styria).

Roth, Roland (2005) 'Die Hartz Reformen. Ein politischer Gau' (unpublished manuscript).

RS 2002/03: 140. *Jämt och ständigt – Regeringens jämställdhetspolitik. (The Swedish Government's National Action Plan for Gender Equality.*

RSSS (1998) *Transcript of workshop for Commonwealth/State Women's Advisers on the Future of Women's Policy Structures, 12 February 1998. Political Science Program, RSSS* (Canberra: Australian National University).

Rucht, Dieter (2004) 'The Changing Role of Political Protest Movements' in Herbert Kitschelt and Wolfgang Streeck (eds) *Germany: Beyond the Stable State* (London: Frank Cass) pp. 153–76.

Rudd, Elizabeth C. (2000) 'Reconceptualizing Gender in Postsocialist Transformation', *Gender & Society*, 14, 4, 517–39.

Ruggie, Mary (1984) *The State and Working Women* (Princeton: Princeton University Press).

Ruß, Sonja (ed.) (2004) *Netzwerke.Organisationen. Institutionen von Business bis Feminismus* (Vienna: Verlag Milena).

Russell, Lani and Marian Sawer (1999) 'The Rise and Fall of the Australian Women's Bureau', *Australian Journal of Politics and History*, 45, 3, 362–75.

Russell, Meg (2005) Building New Labour: the Politics of Party Organisation (Basingstoke: Palgrave Macmillan).

Saguy, Abigail C. (2003) *What is Sexual Harassment? From Capitol Hill to the Sorbonne* (Berkeley: University of California Press).

Sainsbury, Diane (ed.) (1994) *Gendering Welfare States* (Thousand Oaks, CA: Sage).

Sainsbury, Diane (1996) *Gender, Equality, and Welfare States* (Cambridge: Cambridge University Press).

Sainsbury, Diane (ed.) (1999) *Gender and Welfare State Regimes* (Oxford: Oxford University Press).

Sainsbury, Diane (2000) 'Välfärdsutvecklingen för kvinnor och män på 1990-talet', *Välfärd och försörjning* SOU 2000:40 (Stockholm: Ministry of Social Affairs).

Sainsbury, Diane (2004). 'Women's Political Representation in Sweden: Discursive Politics and Institutional Presence', *Scandinavian Political Studies*, 27, 1, 65–87.

Sainsbury, Diane (2005) 'Party Feminism, State Feminism and Women's Representation in Sweden' in Joni Lovenduski et al. (eds) *State Feminism and Political Representation* (Cambridge: Cambridge University Press) pp. 195–215.

Santos, Nanina (1992) 'Órdago a pares ou coa demografia as voltas', *Andiana* 3, 30–5.

Saraceno, Chiara (2003) *Mutamenti delle famiglie e politiche sociali in Italia* (Bologna: Il Mulino).

Sauer, Birgit (2004) 'Taxes, Rights and Regimentation. Discourses on Prostitution in Austria' in Joyce Outshoorn (ed.) *The Politics of Prostitution. Women's Movements, Democratic States and the Globalisation of Sex Commerce* (Cambridge: Cambridge University Press) pp. 41–61.

Sauer, Birgit (2005a) 'Ein ewiges Pilotprojekt? Gender Mainstreaming in Österreich' in Michael Meuser and Claudia Neusüß (eds) *Gender Mainstreaming. Konzepte – Handlungsfelder – Instrumente* (Bonn: Bundeszentrale für politische Bildung) pp. 169–81.

Sauer, Birgit (2005b) 'Geschlechterkritischer Institutionalismus – ein Beitrag zur politikwissenschaftlichen Policy-Forschung' in Ute Behning and Birgit Sauer (eds) *Was bewirkt Gender Mainstreaming? Evaluierung durch Policy-Analysen* (Frankfurt a. M.: Campus) pp. 85–101.

Sauer, Birgit (2007) 'Re-evaluating the "Heart of Society". Family Policy in Austria', in Melissa Haussman and Birgit Sauer (eds) *Gendering the State in the Age of Globalization: Women's Movements and State Feminism in Post-Industrial Democracies* (Lanham, MD: Rowman and Littlefield).

Savola, Lotta (2000) *Naisten asema 1990-luvun työmarkkinoilla* (Helsinki: Tilastokeskus).

Sawer, Marian (1990) *Sisters in Suits: Women and Public Policy in Australia* (Sydney: Allen & Unwin).

Sawer, Marian (1999) 'The Uses of International Citizenship: Australia, The United Nations and the Status of Women' in Joy Damousi and Katherine Ellinghaus (eds) *Citizenship, Women and Social Justice: International Perspectives* (Melbourne: University of Melbourne) pp. 217–28.

Sawer, Marian (2003) 'The Life and Times of Women's Policy Machinery in Australia', in Shirin M. Rai (ed.) *Mainstreaming Gender, Democratizing the State? Institutional Mechanisms for the Advancement of Women* (Manchester: Manchester University Press) pp. 243–63.

Sawer, Marian (2007) 'Framing Feminists' in Yasmeen Abu Laban (ed.) *Gendering the Nation* (Vancouver: University of British Columbia Press).

Sawer, Marian and Jill Vickers (2001) 'Women's Constitutional Activism in Australia and Canada', *Canadian Journal of Women and the Law*, 13, 1, 1–36.

SCB (2006) *EU-sympatier 1992–2006* (Stockholm: Statistics Sweden) http://www.scb.se.

SD (1993) *De nya uppdragen – för arbete, omtanke och framtidstro. Antaget vid socialdemokraternas partikongress den 15–21 september 1993* (Stockholm: Socialdemokraterna).

SD (1994) *Kvinnor kan – och vill! Socialdemokraternas politik för ökad jämställdhet* (Stockholm: Socialdemokraterna).

Shaw, Jane S. (2002) 'Public Choice Theory', *The Concise Encyclopedia of Economics*: http://www.econlib.org/library/Enc/PublicChoiceTheory.html (Accessed 10 April 2006).

Shaw, Jo (2002) 'The European Union and Gender Mainstreaming: Constitutionally Embedded or Comprehensively Marginalised?' *Feminist Legal Studies*, 10, 213–26.

Shaw, Jo (2004) *Mainstreaming Equality in European Union Law and Policymaking* (Brussels: ENAR).

Siim, Birte (1988) 'Towards a Feminist Rethinking of the Welfare State' in Kathleen Jones and Anna Jónasdóttir (eds) *The Political Interests of Gender* (London/New Delhi: Sage) pp. 160–86.

Sineau, Mariette (2002) 'Institutionalisation de la parité: l'expérience française', in Julie Ballington, and Marie-José Protais (eds) *Les Femmes au Parlement: Au-delà du nombre* (Stockholm: International IDEA) http://www.idea.int/publications/wip/fr.cfm (Accessed 26 October 2006).

Sjegers, Sarah (2005) *Een feminisme voor alle vrouwen? De witte vrouwenbeweging in Vlaanderen in relatie tot multiculturaliteit, 'allochtone' vrouwen(organisaties) en het hoofddoekendebat*, thesis (Antwerp: University of Antwerp).

SK (2005) *En effektivare jämställdhetspolitik* (Stockholm: Swedish Agency for Public Management).

Skjeie, Hege (2006) ' "Gender equality": on Travel Metaphors and Duties to Yield' in Sirkku K. Hellsten, Anne Maria Holli and Krassimira Daskalova (eds) *Women's Citizenship and Political Rights* (Basingstoke: Palgrave MacMillan) pp. 86–104.

Smith, Andy (2005) 'The Europeanization of the French State' in Alistair Cole, Patrick le Galès and Jonah D. Levy (eds) *Developments in French Politics* (Basingstoke: Palgrave Macmillan) pp. 105–22.

Sones, Boni, Margaret Moran and Joni Lovenduski (2005) *Women in Parliament* (London: Politicos).

SOU (1998) *Ty makten är din . . . Myten om det rationella arbetslivet och det jämställda Sverige SOU 1998: 6* (Stockholm: Ministry of Labour).

SOU (2004) *Kvinnors organisering. Betänkande av utredningen statligt stöd för kvinnors organisering SOU 2004: 59* (Stockholm: Ministry of Justice).

SOU (2005) *Makt att forma samhället och sitt eget liv – jämställdhetspolitiken mot nya mål SOU 2005: 66* (Stockholm: Ministry of Industry, Employment and Communications).

SOU (2006) *En sammanhållen diskrimineringslagstiftning SOU 2006: 22* (Stockholm: Ministry of Justice).

Spencer, Sarah (2005) 'Partners Rediscovered: Human Rights and Equality in the UK' in Colin Harvey (ed.) *Human Rights in the Community* (Oxford: Hart) pp. 29–41.

Squires, Judith (2005) 'Is Mainstreaming Transformative? Theorizing Mainstreaming in the Context of Diversity and Deliberation', *Social Politics*, 12, 3, 366–88.

Squires, Judith (2006) *From Anti-Discrimination to Diversity via Gender Mainstreaming: the Evolution of Women's Policy Agencies in Britain*, paper presented at the 'Equality and Diversity' Conference, Helsinki, 12–13 January.

Squires, Judith (2007 a) *The Politics of Gender Equality* (Basingstoke: Palgrave Macmillan).

Squires, Judith (2007 b) 'Negotiating Equality and Diversity in Britain: Towards a Differentiated Citizenship?' in *Critical Review of International Social and Political Philosophy*, 10, 4.

Squires, Judith and Mark Wickham Jones (2004) 'New Labour, Gender Mainstreaming and the Women and Equality Unit', *British Journal of Politics and International Relations*, 6, 1, 81–98.

Staatsblad, 28 October 2004.

Staatshaushaltsplan (2004) *Haushalt Land Baden-Württemberg* (Stuttgart: Staatskanzlei).

Statistisches Bundesamt (2004) *Sozialreport 2004* (Berlin: Trafo Verlag).

Staudt, Kathleen (2003) 'Gender Mainstreaming: Conceptual Links to Institutional Machineries' in Shirin Rai (ed.) *Mainstreaming Gender, Democratizing the State? Institutional Mechanisms for the Advancement of Women* (Manchester: Manchester University Press) pp. 40–65.

Steininger, Barbara (2006) 'Frauen im Regierungssystem' in Herbert Dachs et al. (eds) *Politik in Österreich. Das Handbuch* (Vienna: Manz) pp. 247–64.

Stewart, Debra (1980) *The Women's Movement in Community Politics in the U.S.: the Commission on the Status of Women* (New York: Pergamon).

Stichwort Newsletter 2002, No. 14, Vienna.

STM (1997) *Pekingistä Suomeen. Suomen hallituksen tasa-arvo-ohjelma*. Julkaisuja 1997:11 (Helsinki: Sosiaali- ja terveysministeriö) http://pre20031103.stm.fi/suomi/hao/julkaisut/tasa97.htm (Accessed 25 October 2006).

Stokes, Wendy (2003) 'The Government of the United Kingdom: the Women's National Commission' in Shirin M. Rai (ed.) *Mainstreaming Gender, Democratising the State? Institutional Mechanisms for the Advancement of Women* (Manchester: Manchester University Press) pp. 184–202.

Strange, Susan (1996) *The Retreat of the State: the Diffusion of Power in the World Economy* (Cambridge: Cambridge University Press).

Stratigaki, Maria (2005) 'Gender Mainstreaming vs Positive Action: an Ongoing Conflict in EU Gender Equality Policy', *European Journal of Women's Studies*, 12, 2, 165–86.

Sullivan, Barbara (2004) 'The Women's Movement and Prostitution Politics in Australia' in Joyce Outshoorn (ed.) *The Politics of Prostitution. Women's Movements, Democratic States and the Globalisation of Sex Commerce* (Cambridge: Cambridge University Press) pp. 21–41.

Summers, Anne (2003) *The End of Equality: Work, Babies and Women's Choices in 21st Century Australia* (Milson's Point: Random House).

Sunnius, Milena (2003) 'EU Challenges to the Pioneer in Gender Equality: the Case of Sweden' in Ulrike Liebert (ed.) *Gendering Europeanisation* (Brussels: P.I.E.-Peter Lang) pp. 223–53.

Svanström, Yvonne (2004) 'Criminalising the John: a Swedish Gender Model?' in Joyce Outshoorn (ed.) *The Politics of Prostitution: Women's Movements, Democratic States, and the Globalisation of Sex Commerce* (Cambridge: Cambridge University Press) pp. 225–64.

Tálos, Emmerich (1997) 'Sozialpartnerschaft. Kooperation – Konzertierung – politische Regulierung' in Herbert Dachs et al. (eds) *Handbuch des politischen Systems Österreichs. Die Zweite Republik* (Vienna: Manz) pp. 432–51.

Tasa-arvoelinten työnjako (1995) *Selvitys sosiaali- ja terveysministeriölle* (Helsinki: Sosiaali- ja terveysministeriö).

Tavares da Silva, Maria Regina (2004) *Stocktaking Study of the Effective Functioning of the National Mechanisms for Gender Equality in Council of Europe Member States* (Strasbourg: Council of Europe).

Tecena (2000) *Emancipatie in de hoofdstroom. Tecena's rapportage van het onderzoek naar de effectiviteit van de departementale taakstellingen emancipatie voor het proces van duurzame integratie* (The Hague: Tecena).

Teghtsoonian, Kathy (2004) 'Neoliberalism and Gender Analysis Mainstreaming in Aotearoa/New Zealand', *Australian Journal of Political Science*, 39, 2, 267–84.

Temkina, Anna and Elena Zdravomyslova (2003) 'Gender Studies in Post-Soviet Society: Western Frames and Cultural Differences', *Studies in East European Thought*, 55, 51–61.

Tennessee Economic Council on Women (2005) *A Report on the Status of Job Training for Tennessee Women* (Nashville, TN: Tennessee Economic Council on Women) http://www.state.tn.us/sos/ecw/jobtraining.pdf (Accessed 26 October 2006).

Thiesen, Anne Marie, Nadine Spoden, Mieke Verloo and Sylvia Walby (2005) *Beijing + 10: Progress made within the European Union, Luxembourg*. (Brussels: Presidency of the Council of the European Union).

Toynbee, Polly and David Walker (2001) *Did Things get Better? An Audit of Labour's Successes and Failures* (London: Penguin Books).

True, Jacqui (2003) 'Mainstreaming Gender in Global Public Policy', *International Feminist Journal of Politics*, 5, 3, 368–96.

True, Jacqui and Michael Mintrom (2001) 'Transnational Networks and Policy Diffusion: the Case of Gender Mainstreaming', *International Studies Quarterly*, 45, 1, 27–57.

UNAR (2005) *Efficacia degli strumenti di tutela nel contrasto alle discriminazioni razziali e proposte di modifica alla normativa vigente* (Rome: Ministero per le pari opportunità).

United Nations (1993) *Directory of National Machinery for the Advancement of Women* (Vienna: Division for the Advancement of Women).

United Nations (2005) *The Role of National Mechanisms in Promoting Gender Equality and the Empowerment of Women. Report of the Expert Group Meeting, Rome, Italy, 29 November–2 December 2004* (New York: Division for the Advancement of Women).

US Department of Health and Human Services (2005) *The Office on Women's Health: History* (Washington DC: US Department of Health and Human Services) http://www.4woman.gov/owh/index.htm (Accessed 5 March 2005).

US Department of State (2004) The Link Between Prostitution and Sex Trafficking (Washington DC: US Department of State) http://www.state.gov/r/pa/ei/rls/38790.htm (Accessed 5 March 2005).

US House of Representatives (2005) 'Report on Accomplishments of the Congressional Caucus for Women's Issues in the 108th Congress' (Washington DC: US House of Representatives).

US White House (2002) *Trafficking in Persons National Security Presidential Directive* (Washington DC: US White House) http://www.whitehouse.gov/news/releases/2003/02/20030225.html (Accessed 5 March 2005).

US Women Connect (2000) *Report Card on U.S. Federal Government Action for Women's & Girls' Rights and Empowerment* (Washington DC: US Women Connect) http://www.uswc.org/reportcards.html (Accessed 31 January 2005).

Valanta, José et al. (2000) *Kuntajohtamisen ja demokratian käytännöt 1997–2000* (Helsinki: Suomen Kuntaliitto).

Valiente, Celia (1995) 'The Power of Persuasion: the Instituto de la Mujer in Spain' in Dorothy McBride Stetson and Amy G. Mazur (eds) *Comparative State Feminism* (Thousand Oaks, CA: Sage) pp. 221–36.

Valiente, Celia (1998) 'Feminismo de Estado en los Ayuntamientos de la Comunidad Autónoma de Madrid', *Gestión y Análisis de Políticas Públicas*, 13–14, 181–97.

Valiente, Celia (2001a) 'Movimientos sociales y Estados: la movilización feminista en España desde los años sesenta', *Sistema*, 161, 31–58.

Valiente, Celia (2001b) 'Implementing Women's Rights in Spain' in Jane H. Bayes and Nayeres Esfahlani Tohidi (eds) *Globalization, Gender, and Religion: the Politics of Implementing Women's Rights in Catholic and Muslim Contexts* (New York: Palgrave – now Palgrave Macmillan) pp. 107–26.

Valiente, Celia (2005a) 'Combating Violence against Women' in Monica Threlfall, Christine Cousins and Celia Valiente (eds) *Gendering Spanish Democracy* (New York and London: Routledge) pp. 101–24.

Valiente, Celia (2005b) 'The Women's Movement, Gender Equality Agencies and Central-state Debates on Political Representation in Spain' in Joni Lovenduski (ed.) *State Feminism and Political Representation* (Cambridge: Cambridge University Press) pp. 174–94.

VCE (2007) *Een beeje beter is niet goed genoeg. Emancipatiebeleid en gender mainstreaming bij de rijksoverheid. Eindrapportage Visitaties 2005–2006* (The Hague: Visitatiecommisie Emancipatie).

Veil, Mechthild (2005) 'Wer kriegt was? Die Zukunft der Gerechtigkeit', *Böll Magazin*, 1.

Velde, Hella van de (1994) *Vrouwen van de partij. De integratie van vrouwen in politieke partijen in Nederland, 1919–1990* (Leiden: DSWO Press).

Verloo, Mieke (2001) *Another Velvet Revolution? Gender Mainstreaming and the Politics of Implementation.* IWM Working Paper No. 5/2001 (Vienna: Institut für die Wissenschaften vom Menschen).

Verloo, Mieke (2005) 'Displacement and Empowerment: Reflections on the Concept and Practice of the Council of Europe Approach to Gender Mainstreaming and Gender Equality', *Social Politics*, 12, 3, 344–65.

Verloo, Mieke (2006) 'Multiple Inequalities, Intersectionality and the European Union', *European Journal of Women's Studies*, 13, 3, 211–28.

Verzichelli, Luca and Maurizio Cotta (2003) 'Italy: From "Constrained" Coalitions to Alternative Governments?' in Wolfgang Müller and Kaare Strøm (eds) *Coalition Governments in Western Europe* (Oxford: Oxford University Press) pp. 433–97.

Vital Voices: a Global Partnership (2006) http://www.vitalvoices.org (Accessed 2 January 2006).

Vleuten, Anna van der (2001) *Dure Vrouwen, Dwarse Staten. Een institutioneel-realistische visie op de totstandkoming en implementatie van Europees beleid* (Nijmegen: Nijmegen University Press).

Vleuten, Anna van der (2005) 'Pincers and Prestige. Explaining Implementation of EU Gender Equality Legislation', *Comparative European Politics*, 3, 4, 464–88.

Vogel-Polsky, Eliane (1982) *Historical development and descriptive analysis of national machinery set up in member States of the Council of Europe to promote equality between women and men: comparative study* (Strasbourg: Council of Europe).

Vogel-Polsky, Eliane (1985) *National institutional machinery in the Council of Europe member States to promote equality between women and men: comparative study* (Strasbourg: Council of Europe).

Vogel-Polsky, Eliane (1994) *National institutional machinery in the Council of Europe member States to promote equality between women and men: comparative study* (Strasbourg: Council of Europe).

Voorthuizen, Anna van (1996) 'Ruimte tussen de werelden. Spirifeminisme in de jaren negentig', *Lover*, 23, 1, 4–12.

Vries, Jouke de (2002) *Paars en de managementstaat: het eerste kabinet-Kok (1994–1998)* (Leuven/Apeldoorn: Garant).

Vuori, Jaana (2006) 'Tasa-arvo-opastusta maahanmuuttajille' in Ritva Nätkin and Jaana Vuori (eds) *Perhe murroksessa* (Helsinki: Gaudeamus).

Wahl, Angelika von (2005) 'Liberal, Conservative, Social Democratic, or . . . European? The European Union as Equal Employment Regime', *Social Politics*, 12, 1, 67–95.

Walby, Sylvia (2005) 'Introduction: Comparative Gender Mainstreaming in a Global Era', *International Feminist Journal of Politics*, 7, 4, 453–71.

Ward, Lucy (2004) 'Feminism: Outmoded and Unpopular', *Guardian*, 2 July, Home Pages, 3.

Weiss, Linda (ed.) (2003) *States in the Global Economy: Bringing Domestic Institutions Back In* (Cambridge: Cambridge University Press).

Weldon, Laurel (2002a) *Protest, Policy, and the Problem of Violence Against Women. A Cross–National Comparison* (Pittsburgh: University of Pittsburgh Press).

Weldon, Laurel (2002b) 'Beyond Bodies: Institutional Sources of Representation for Women in Democratic Policymaking', *Journal of Politics*, 64, 4, 1153–74.

Wendt Höjer, Maria (2002) *Rädslans politik: Våld och sexualitet i den svenska demokratin* (Stockholm: Liber).

Wersig, Maria (2005) 'Sieg der Freiheit? Zum Scheitern des deutschen Antidiskriminierungsgesetzes', *femina politica*, 14, 2, 100–4.

Whitlam, Gough (1975) 'Reply to Parliamentary Question on Women's Affairs', *Commonwealth of Australia Parliamentary Debates, House of Representatives*, 9 October.

Wiercx, Joke (2005) 'A la recherche du mouvement des femmes actuel en Flandre' in Bérengère Marques-Pereira and Petra Meier (eds) *Genre et politique en Belgique et en Francophonie* (Brussels: Academia-Bruylant) pp. 61–73.

Wiercx, Joke and Alison Woodward (2004) *Vernieuwend transnationaal gelijkekansenbeleid: de rol van sociale bewegingen en organisaties in de vernieuwing van gelijkekansenbeleid op Vlaams en Europees niveau* (Brussels: Ministerie van de Vlaamse Gemeenschap).

Wiesenthal, Helmut (2004) 'German Unification and "Model Germany": an Adventure in Institutional Conservatism' in Herbert Kitschelt and Wolfgang Streeck (eds) *Germany: Beyond the Stable State* (London: Frank Cass) pp. 37–58.

Wilson, Elizabeth (1977) *Women and the Welfare State* (London: Tavistock).

WISER (2006) *Women's pay and conditions in an era of changing workplace regulations: Towards a Women's Employment Status Key Indicators (WESKI) database* (Perth: Women in Social and Economic Research): http://www.hreoc.gov.au/pdf/sex_discrim/WESKISept2006.pdf (Accessed 17 September 2006).

Women's National Commission (2005) *Submission to the United Nations Convention on the Elimination of Discrimination Against Women Committee* (London: WNC).

Women's Rights Action Network Australia (2005) *Australian NGO Shadow Report on the Implementation of the Convention on the Elimination of All Forms of Discrimination against Women* (East Brunswick: Women's Rights Action Network Australia).

Women's Unit (1998) *Delivering for Women: Progress so Far* (London: The Cabinet Office).

Woodward, Alison (2003) 'European Gender Mainstreaming. Innovative Policy or Disappearing Act?', *Review of Policy Research*, 20, 65–88.

Woodward, Alison (2007) 'Speedy Belgians: The New Nationality Law of 2000 and the Impact of the Women's Movement' in Melissa Haussman and Birgit Sauer (eds) *Gendering the State in the Age of Globalization* (Lanham, MD: Rowman and Littlefield).

Woodward, Alison and Agnes Hubert (2006) *Reconfiguring State Feminism in the European Union: Changes from 1995–2005*. Paper presented at ECPR, Istanbul 21–3 September.

Woodward, Alison and Petra Meier (1998) 'Gender Impact Assessment: a New Approach to Changing Policies and Contents of Citizenship?' in Virginia Ferreira et al. (eds) *Shifting Bonds, Shifting Bounds: Women, Mobility and Citizenship in Europe* (Oeiras: Celta Editora) pp. 95–104.

World Bank (2005) *Women's Empowerment: Measuring the Global Gender Gap* (Geneva: World Bank).

Young, Brigitte (1999) *Triumph of the Fatherland. German Unification and the Marginalization of Women* (Ann Arbor: University of Michigan Press).

Youngs, Gillian (2000) 'Breaking Patriarchal Bonds: Demythologizing the Public–Private' in Marianne Marchand and Anne Sisson Runyan (eds) *Gender and Global Restructuring* (London and New York: Routledge) pp. 44–58.

Yuval-Davis, Nira (2006) 'Intersectionality and Feminist Politics', *European Journal of Women's Studies*, 13, 3, 193–209.

Yuval-Davis, Nira, Floya Anthias and Eleonore Kofman (2005) 'Secure Borders and Safe Haven and the Gendered Politics of Belonging: Beyond Social Cohesion', *Ethnic and Racial Studies*, 28, 3, 513–35.

Zwingel, Susanne (2005) *How do International Women's Rights Norms become Effective in National Contexts? An Analysis of the Convention on the Elimination of All Forms of Discrimination Against Women (CEDAW)*. Ph.D. thesis (Bochum: University of Bochum).

Index

313